Willem Frederik Wertheim was born of Dutch parents in
St Petersburg in 1907. Soon after the 1917 Revolution, the
family left Russia to settle in Holland. He studied law at
Leiden University, and received his doctoral degree in 1930.
He married in the same year, and in 1931 he and his wife
went to the Dutch East Indies, where he served in the
colonial judiciary service. In 1936 he was appointed
Professor of Conflict of Laws in the Law School of Batavia.
During the Second World War he was interned by the
Japanese.

Meanwhile, he had become increasingly interested in
Asian nationalism and socialist thought. After the war, he
returned with his family to Holland, and was appointed
a professor in the sociology and modern history of
Indonesia, later extended to cover the whole of South and
South-East Asia, at the University of Amsterdam, a post
he held until 1972.

His publications include *Indonesian Society in Transition*
(1964) and *East-West Parallels* (1965).

W. F. Wertheim

Evolution and Revolution

The Rising Waves of Emancipation

Penguin Books

Penguin Books Ltd, Harmondsworth
Middlesex, England
Penguin Books Inc., 7110 Ambassador Road,
Baltimore, Maryland 21207, U.S.A.
Penguin Books Australia Ltd, Ringwood,
Victoria, Australia

First published by Vitgeverij en Boekhandel van Gennep NV
Published in Penguin Books 1974

Copyright © W. F. Wertheim, 1974

Made and printed in Great Britain by
Cox & Wyman Ltd, London Reading and Fakenham
Set in Linotype Juliana

Contents

6 Contents

Foreword

In order to understand the phenomenon of revolution, we will first have to differentiate it from an allegedly normal state of affairs characterized by its absence. Since revolution by its definition implies a cataclysmic change, its absence could be defined either as a state of gradual change or as one of stability and equilibrium. Both sociologists and cultural anthropologists have mostly operated with a model in which stability and equilibrium prevail. If, however, a society is basically viewed as a structural entity, in which the various phenomena of social life are interpreted as functions of a system in equilibrium, it is difficult to imagine how revolutionary change could ever come about. In this system of analysis all social processes, even if they take the shape of conflict or disharmony, are, by definition, viewed as functions of the existing social system and the possibility of social change is reduced to minor alterations within the present social structure. Major social changes, implying a fundamental alteration of the total structure, become occurrences outside the existing social order and, consequently, cannot be understood in sociological terms exclusively adapted to a structural type of analysis.

Therefore, any attempt to approach the phenomenon of revolution in terms of structural and functional sociology amounts to an effort to square the circle.[1]

If, however, one considers evolution (gradual change) as the normal state of human societies, it then becomes easier to fit in the phenomenon of revolution (cataclysmic change). If we conceive society as an entity in constant flux, we can see that certain processes can, under certain circumstances, be accelerated in such a way as to add a quality of suddenness to the process of overall change. If the germs of revolutionary change can be detected by the sociologist within the texture of any society, then he will no longer be at a loss when encountering revolution as a recurrent, and sometimes even decisive, phenomenon within human history. Since in the past sociologists, in general, have shown little concern for evolution, a type of sociology has to be developed better adapted to an analysis of human societies in terms of evolution and overall dynamic change.

We are living in a period of human history in which revolution can no longer be ignored – even by sociologists. Though most of the advanced societies of today, if viewed in historical perspective, are the products of revolution themselves, they are generally prone to disavowing their revolutionary heritage. The establishment does not suffer reminders of a revolutionary past, except as a kind of legitimization of the present structure.

But revolution, in many parts of the world, is knocking at the door and reminding the 'old established forces' of mounting dissatisfaction and disaffection. At least two continents – Asia and America – are the scenes of perpetual unrest. The 750 millions of China, not satisfied with two major revolutions in the first half of the century, have recently enacted their proletarian cultural revolution. Asia south of China is seething with unrest. The revolutionary struggle of Vietnam may soon be matched by a much bigger one in India – of which the peasant revolt of Naxalbari (Bengal) in 1967 may have been only the beginning. And since Che Guevara's death, his spectre relentlessly haunts the subcontinent of Latin America. The slogan of 'Black Power', spreading among Negro youth in the United States, shows that revolutionary tendencies will not necessarily leave North America untouched.

My life experience has made me deeply aware of the supreme importance of revolution as a human phenomenon, and also of the fact that well-educated and intelligent people are unwilling to recognize that what they are witnessing is an occurrence of major and lasting importance for the society in which they live.

As a child, living with my Dutch parents in St Petersburg (Leningrad), I was confronted with the Russian Revolution of 1917. Everybody belonging to my parents' circle was convinced that the

Bolshevists' October revolution was only a temporary deviation. They were sure that 'the civilized world' would not tolerate the domination of a great country like Russia by a 'gang of bandits'. A period of six months' rule was the utmost that people belonging to the 'haute bourgeoisie' were prepared to grant to the group in power, before foreign intervention ended the anarchy.

Such was the blindness of those who had profited from the existing state of affairs that they could not conceive the possibility of the rise of a totally different societal structure in which the social hierarchy would be turned upside down.

When, for a second time in my life, I witnessed a revolution – the Indonesian nationalist one of 1945 – I had learned my lesson. The overwhelming majority of the Dutch, recently released from the Japanese camps where they had been interned during the Second World War, were convinced, when the Indonesian Republic was proclaimed shortly after the Japanese surrender, that 'this nonsense could not last'. The allied troops would soon put an end to this 'Japanese fabrication', and the colonial reins could be taken up where they had been put down after the Japanese invasion of the Dutch East Indies in 1942. The idea that the Dutch colonial empire was doomed and that no 'police action' would be able to stem the course of revolution did not occur even to many of the best educated and most enlightened. I remember discussing the situation in Java with the Lieutenant Governor-General H. J. van Mook, shortly after his return to Jakarta (during the period of colonial rule called Batavia). I had left the internment camp at the end of August 1945 and had been living in Jakarta for over one month. My experiences there as a Red Cross representative made me view the Indonesian revolution as an extremely serious affair. But Van Mook lightly dismissed the idea. ' Ten shiploads of food and textiles from Australia, and the whole population of Java will flow to the ports to unload the ships. That will be the end of the rebellion.'

A month later he, at least, was convinced that the revolution was in earnest – and that he had to meet Sukarno, President of the 'self-styled' Republic, who was still considered by Dutch public opinion to be a Japanese puppet.

In the same way as people around me have minimized the importance of revolutions, even though they were living in the midst of them, sociologists have up to now largely abstained from occupying themselves with this crucial social phenomenon. Their bias in favour of stability and harmony has blinded them to such an extent that they, too, have failed to appreciate the full significance of revolutions.

My aim in writing this book is to try to develop a sociological theory in which two types of phenomenon – evolution and revolution – will receive full recognition.

It is not my intention simply to add one more title to the voluminous bibliography on revolution. The viewpoint, from which I wish to approach these phenomena, is that of sociology.

The Marxist school of thought which, in a certain sense, could be called 'sociological', has incorporated revolution as an essential element of human history. Though I have certainly been influenced by Marxist thought and owe a good deal to it – as, no doubt, does any social scientist of the second half of the twentieth century, often without knowing – I still do not consider myself a Marxist in the accepted sense. My approach is not exclusively based on an analysis in terms of warring political classes. I attempt to combine certain aspects of the structural approach, characteristic of Western sociology, with a more dynamic type of analysis in which social conflicts are incorporated as essential elements of any social texture.

By dynamizing sociological theory, without rejecting its positive contributions to an understanding of human society, I hope to be able to make sociology more relevant to the most pressing issues of our present world. Sociology born in the last century and further developed in the first half of the present one, in a part of the world which by then had achieved a certain stability, was mainly adapted to analysing a society in equilibrium.

But by directing attention to societies outside the industrialized West, sociology should gain a new dimension by developing into a study of a world on the move.

A work like this owes a lot to stimulating remarks, either critical or encouraging ones. The section dealing with evolution was issued, in mimeographed draft form, as a preliminary publication by the Centre for Anthropological and Sociological Studies, University of Amsterdam (1967), and sent to several colleagues for comment.

It is not possible to recall everyone who responded. I wish, however, to mention with gratitude, along with the comments I received from several Dutch colleagues, those sent by Professor Elman Service and Dr William D. Wilder. I have seriously considered their critical remarks, although I am fully aware that they will not always agree with my new formulation.

I am also indebted to Dr Rex Mortimer for his comments on an earlier draft for the theoretical chapters four and five.

In a later stage I received generous help from Mme L. Ch. Schenk-Sandbergen, who critically read the whole manuscript, and never tired of discussing ambiguous and disputable points, for which I am most grateful. I am also indebted to Mr O. D. van den Muyzenberg, who painstakingly commented on an earlier draft of chapter eight.

Mme Hanna van Weel-Frankenhuis, Miss Hermine Kilian and Mme Cisca Wouters-Westbroek, all of them members of the administrative staff of the Department of South and South-East Asia of the Centre for Anthropological and Sociological Studies, were most helpful in getting the manuscript ready for publication.

A more comprehensive text was published in 1971 in Dutch by Van Gennep, Amsterdam. The present publication in English has provided me with the opportunity to introduce some corrections and to take account of some new developments during 1971 and 1972.

My greatest indebtedness is to Hetty who, in an article published in the summer of 1954, after we had spent a few months in Paris, foretold the forthcoming Algerian revolution; and who, in 1962, during a visit to Harlem, sensed the premonitory signs of Negro resistance in the United States, thus opening my eyes towards one of the main themes of the present work.

W. F. WERTHEIM

Part One: Evolution

1

The Vicissitudes of Evolutionary Theory

We have to get back to evolution. When we threw out evolutionism, we threw out the baby with the bathwater.

R. NAROLL

i. The Wave of Anti-Evolutionism in the West

In the second half of the nineteenth century, the prevalent general belief in progress found its expression in evolutionary theories. Darwin's definition of biological evolution in terms of random variation and natural selection was acceptable to the mind of the nineteenth-century scientist and lent authority to social scientists who attempted to conceive human history in evolutionary terms. Belief in a steady evolution of human society became common among leading social scientists.

However, after the turn of the century, evolutionary theories concerning human societies were subjected to severe attacks. These attacks went to such lengths that only a few decades ago, cultural anthropologists in the United States were agreed that 'the theory of cultural evolution ..., the most inane, sterile and pernicious theory in the whole theory of science ...',[1] had been 'effectively exploded'.[2]

But, by the time of the celebration of the centennial anniversary of the publication of Darwin's The Origin of Species, in 1959, the effects of the explosion had virtually evaporated and evolutionism flourished again. Certain evolutionist approaches – such as the multilinear brand, which, not being Marxist, was not in danger of exorcism – were more respectable than others in Western academic circles. But, at any rate, there was some common agreement by now, even among cultural anthropologists, who had never before declared themselves in favour of evolution, that social structures were involved in dynamic processes which kept them in a state of continuous change, and that this process of change was not only an intrinsic one, occurring within the structural confines of a given social order, but affected social structure as such. Though Donald T. Campbell[3] still claims that the rejection of social evolutionary theories has been overwhelming in the recent past, the fact that, in 1961, a group of scholars from Northwestern University (Illinois) came together to analyse 'the usefulness of evolutionary theory for contemporary social science',[4] is in itself a symptom of a revival of interest in evolutionary concepts among scholars studying present-day societies.

What were the causes of the strong anti-evolutionist trend in the United States, in the period after the turn of the century?

The simplest answer would be that, in a world where stability and harmony were in high regard and where theories of social evolution were tainted with Marxism, there would be a strong inducement completely to reject the idea of social evolution. No doubt this kind of motivation, perhaps unconsciously, played an important role. During the nineteenth century, there had been a general belief in human progress, which involved a steady improvement of social conditions. In this respect Marxism was no more than one specific strand within the general texture of nineteenth-century thinking. Marxism distinguished itself from other social philosophies in viewing the road towards progress as a dialectical one, fraught with conflicts and revolutions – but it shared its belief in progress, both technological and economic, with those assuming a more gradual process of evolution.

During the 'happy twenties', a completely different mood prevailed, especially in the United States. On the one hand, there was a feeling that a state of general and lasting welfare had been achieved in a society where no class differences were supposed to exist, and where even industrial labour was sharing, to a certain extent, in the general boom atmosphere, without apparently having needed any class struggle to achieve this. On the other hand, two serious traumas had frightened the Western world: the First World War, which had shaken the belief in perpetual human progress; and the Russian Revolution, that seemed to be threatening the very basis of existence in the part of the world ruled by capitalism. Since American society appeared to have attained the apex of human potential, and was more interested in conserving the achieved wealth and status than in rapid change, no belief in further human progress was needed. The First World War had shown that improved technology does not necessarily imply greater human happiness. People in the Western world were less sure about what 'progress' really meant. A more relativistic mood, together with a sceptical attitude to the idea of continuous human progress in which Western man had firmly believed throughout the nineteenth century, made many Western people doubt whether their civilization was really superior to that of people who did not enjoy the boons of industrial development. An increasing awareness of certain superior qualities of other, non-Western cultures – an awareness which was heightened by the growing acquaintance of the Western world with Eastern philosophies such as those propagated by outstanding Asian thinkers like Tagore, Gandhi and Lin Yu-tang – contributed to this relativistic mood.

Cultural anthropologists were quick to argue that there was no point in comparing the value of different cultures. According to these anthropologists evolutionist thinking amounted to applying a yardstick for which higher technology and a more developed economic organization were wrongly used as the only criteria for measuring the progress a given society had made.

Thus, we see that a general conservative mood and a distrust in the beneficence of steady technological progress was matched, as far as cultural anthropologists were concerned, with a different motivation for fighting evolutionism: a rejection of a naïve assumption of Western superiority. Nineteenth-century optimism had taken for granted that the Western industrial world had reached the summit of human progress. Other, more 'primitive' peoples had simply to follow the Western lead to progress along the same path.[5] Influential schools of Western anthropologists, however, were now repelled by the unsophisticated assumption of Western superiority, especially if the doctrine of social evolution assumed the character of Social Darwinism which had become, by the turn of the century, the reactionary branch of evolutionist thought. They had strong arguments to point out that the 'primitive' peoples, far from being really 'primitive', often showed an elaborate refinement in adapting their culture to the requirements of their own environment. Anti-racism provided a progressive tinge to their rejection of evolutionism. According to this school of thought, of which Ruth Benedict was an outstanding representative, all cultures had, in principle, an equal value. Humanity was not a drawn-out procession of people marching at different speeds and in distinct groups towards a common goal, but was divided into many discontinuous cultures, each in itself equally important as exemplifying the variability of the products of human inventiveness. If one culture – the Western one – had shown its ingenuity by greatly stressing technology and economic development, this was only a sign that the focal feature of that culture was in the realm of technology. Other cultures had shown their individuality and relative superiority in developing other cultural traits which in our Western industrial culture were held in rather low esteem.[6]

Therefore anti-evolutionism was not necessarily dictated by conservative motivations. In some respects these anti-evolutionists had a higher opinion of peoples who differed from themselves than those who, as a modern kind of missionary, longed to replace the original non-Western civilization with plain Western industrial civilization, with all its defects and inner contradictions. But their sentimental regard for the way of life of peoples not participating in modern technology often made them, willy-nilly, supporters of a colonial policy, which purposely kept these peoples and their technology 'primitive'.

Another factor contributing to a rather general rejection of 'evolutionism' after the First World War was connected with a certain one-sidedness in evolutionary views, as propagated about 1900. Social evolution was, then, viewed as a unilinear process. To quote Donald T. Campbell again:

The social evolution doctrines of Spencer, Tylor and Morgan which dominated social thought at the turn of the century were by-and-large of this [unilinear] type, even though close reading would show much more complexity and subtlety. In extreme form, such theories posit (a) that all changes in specific cultures or societies represent progress (e.g. advances in complexity of organization, division of labor, size and energy utilization), (b) that all societies, in the course of their advances, go through the same stages, and hence (c) that the less advanced societies in the contemporary world are similar to earlier stages of the more advanced peoples. It is against such a version of sociocultural evolution that the overwhelming rejection of the older theories was focused as well as most current opposition.[7]

The assumption of a unilinear advance through similar stages ran counter to modern historical research. Both the analysis of historical sources and the study of contemporary 'primitive' society had been much developed since authors such as Bachofen and Morgan had published their pioneering studies. Since it was mainly in Marxist circles that the succession of stages as conceived by Morgan and further developed by Friedrich Engels[8] was still adhered to as a matter of doctrine, it became convenient for the opponents of those evolutionist views to associate them with a theory viewed in American academic circles as unscientific and politically dangerous.

Consequently, it was not difficult at all for scholars whose ideological background was definitely non-Marxist to lay bare various weaknesses of the rigid phase concept. I will mention only a few arguments often used by them.

Firstly, they stated that, according to the nineteenth-century evolutionists, certain social institutions had arisen more than once independently, in the wake of technological improvements provoked by the challenge of the natural environment. Historical research, however, showed that in many cases it was not independent invention that had occurred, but cultural borrowing, so-called 'diffusion' which, in the view of the 'diffusionists', strongly overshadowed the impact of 'evolutionary' processes in importance. In some cases, such diffusionist arguments had certain overtones of cultural superiority: independent invention could not have occurred except in the cradle of Western civilization – Egypt.[9] Other scholars were more cautious and claimed that different cultural traits found their origin in different cultural areas.[10] In either case, however, stress was laid rather upon a search for the details of cultural borrowing than on what the critics called speculative theories as to the general course of human evolution.

The assumption that all societies go through the same stages appeared, in the light of actual research, to be unfounded. For example, the claimed universality of a phase of feudalism could be disputed with strong arguments. Of course, much depends on the way the term 'feudalism' is defined. In Marxist literature, as in many other publications influenced by nineteenth-century evolutionism, the term feudalism had such a broad connotation that it included political systems like those to be found in imperial China or Mogul India. Western scholars could, therefore, rightly point out that the political system in such Asian empires was so divergent from the type of feudal political structure known in the European Middle Ages that there was little justification for including them in the same term. Max Weber still considered those Asian empires as a sub-type of the general category of feudal societies, a sub-type which he labelled as 'patrimonial bureaucracies'.[11] Patrimonialism, in his view, implied a high degree of decentralization (Otto van der Sprenkel recently pointed out that Weber probably exaggerated the amount of decentralization present in the Chinese empires throughout the ages since the Han dynasty[12]) but it lacked the element of contractual vassalage typical of European feudalism in the Middle Ages. Other scholars preferred to define feudalism in such a strict sense as to practically limit its applicability to the Japanese and European medieval type.[13] As far as the feudal phase is concerned, scholarly arguments sometimes bordered on political ones, and a rejection of unilinearism became a badge of political orthodoxy in Western academic circles – in the same way as its acceptance became one in the world under Marxist rule.[14]

In Soviet Russia during the twenties – a period of high expectations and vigorous spiritual movement – the issue of unilinear evolution also came in for serious discussion. But the outcome of the discussion was just the opposite of that held in the West. The crucial concept was the 'Asiatic mode of production', cursorily advanced by Marx in several of his writings, some of which still remained unpublished at that time.[15] It was not made fully clear by Marx whether he considered the 'Asiatic mode of production' which, in his view, implied an absence of private ownership of land and a type of agriculture based on communal ownership and collective farming, simply as a sub-type of the 'primitive' communities supposed to have existed elsewhere, or as a more advanced type of society on a par with agricultural societies based on private ownership in the West. In some of his writings he mentioned 'oriental despotism' as a specific phenomenon, which he related to the type of communal ownership by villages known in some Asian societies.

It was logical for Russian Marxists, such as Plekhanov, to inquire whether their own Russian society showed some 'Asiatic' traits which could be related to traditional types of communal ownership and communal farming, such as the *mir* and the *artel*. Tsarist bureaucracy had shown in the past several traits in common with the Asian empires to which Marx had applied the term of oriental despotism. Was one sure that the classical sequence feudalism–bourgeois capitalism–socialism would apply to Russian society as well?

The issue had serious political implications. Stalin's attempt to build 'socialism in one country' was certainly not generally accepted, in the Soviet Union, as a viable experiment. It was Trotsky and his followers who argued that a truly socialist society could only be created in an advanced industrialized country. Russia, still being a preponderantly agrarian, backward state, was not fit for socialist experiments. If one tried to skip the bourgeois-capitalistic phase, one could not expect to achieve a socialist state; such an attempt would simply reinforce the backward bureaucratic traits of Russian society.[16]

The Stalinists, therefore, had a political stake in arguing that the Russian case was in no sense fundamentally divergent from developments elsewhere in Europe; that the 'Asiatic mode of production', if applicable to earlier stages of Russian history, could not be singled out as a link in a divergent sequence of social systems; that Russia had gone through the usual stages of feudalism and capitalism, though the latter stage had been much shorter than in other countries; that, consequently, there was at least no theoretical objection to the assumption that capitalism had progressed far enough to make a transition towards a new stage, the socialist one, possible; and that, therefore, as far as Russia was concerned, 'building socialism in one country' was in no way bound to be impracticable from the outset.

However, the actual political situation in China and the policy of the Comintern in regard to that country, also played an important role in the discussion held at that time in the Soviet Union. Stalin had deemed it expedient to label the revolutionary struggle fought in the late twenties not only as anti-imperialist, but also as being directed against the remains of feudalism.[17]

A congress held in Leningrad in 1931 established that the view of feudalism as a universal phase in human history was orthodox Marxist theory and, thus, confirmed unilinear evolution as a basic tenet. Without doubt, the decision was strengthened by a wish to stress that Oriental societies like China were not basically different from Occidental ones, and that they were to be studied in similar terms of class struggle.

However, in the past eight years the discussion on the different stages has been reopened in the Soviet Union, with a greater freedom of deviation from the orthodox view; in the context of these discussions the issue of the 'Asiatic mode of production' could again become a point of heated controversy.[18]

Meanwhile, in the Western world, evolutionary theory had become, if not proscribed, at any rate suspect. If one wanted to cling to evolution as an overall trend in human history, one had seriously to reconsider its details and to take account of the justified criticisms raised against the nineteenth-century brands of evolutionism.

ii. Multilinear Evolutionism

Among Western scholars, Leslie A. White and V. Gordon Childe[19] remained staunch supporters of evolutionism throughout the period when evolutionist thought was at a low ebb. But meanwhile a new type of evolutionist thought was being developed, in which no overall trend of social evolution was posited, but evolution was viewed as a phenomenon related to a specific culture, or at least a specific type of culture. This interpretation of evolution was, therefore, fully reconcilable with the prevailing view of cultures as distinct entities dividing humanity into different cultural areas. The main objective of this evolutionist theory was to provide an explanation of the phenomenon of cultural variation. The 'evolution' of each distinct culture or cultural type was interpreted in terms of increasing adaptation of a culture to its physical environment.

According to this theory, there was no point in looking for general trends of social development on a universal scale. All really relevant evolutionary processes were partial, and limited to the reaches of a specific culture. This did not preclude, on the basis of cross-cultural references, parallels between distinct evolutionary processes in different cultures at different times, owing to a similar physical environment. But the main attention of this group of scholars was directed towards the specific, not towards the generic.

The main representative of this multilinear evolutionism is Julian H. Steward, who succeeded in restoring a new respectability to evolutionism – but only at the cost of sacrificing its relation to a belief in human progress as an overall trend.[20]

As a matter of fact, a limitation of the concept of evolution to specific cultural processes was no solution to the problems with which we are at present concerned. Multilinear evolutionist theory did not touch upon a highly important phenomenon in human history: the continuous growth of human knowledge, and the steady improvement of human technology and of organizational devices for the management of the economic life of human beings. Evasion from any attempt at explaining this indisputable trend in world history by Western cultural anthropologists was not a sign of sophisticated wisdom, but rather playing the ostrich.

Nor was adhering to a multilinear type of evolutionism a remedy against dogmatism. The worst specimen of multilinear evolutionism, which in dogmatism far surpassed the crudest expressions of unilinear evolutionism under Stalin's rule, was the doctrine elaborated by Karl Wittfogel in his ambitious work, *Oriental Despotism*, based on the Marxist concept of the Asiatic mode of production. During the late twenties he was involved in the discussion between Marxists on the issue of whether the societies based on this mode of production should be fundamentally distinguished from those where the sequence slavery–feudalism–capitalism had been observed. Whereas the Soviet Marxists opted for a fundamental similarity, Wittfogel developed his own theory after he had broken away from communism. According to this theory, the Asiatic mode of production, which in his view was typical of societies based on large-scale irrigation, gives rise to a different line in the evolutionary perspective. The 'hydraulic' societies – in Wittfogel's theory not necessarily characterized by irrigation, but in some cases by large drainage works – are, in his view, typically oriental despotisms, exerting 'total power', ruled by an elaborate and centralized bureaucracy, and to be sharply differentiated from the feudal societies known in Western Europe and Japan.

The gist of Wittfogel's theory is that, whereas feudal societies provided opportunities for a development towards bourgeois capitalism, the Asian bureaucracies, which in his view also included Tsarist Russia, were totally unfit for any development towards more modern structures. The new political structures, created in former oriental despotic empires like Russia and China, could not be really viewed as representing a sub-type of a 'modern' society or as anything new. They were in their essential characteristics mere replicas of the traditional oriental despotisms, in which the capacity to exert absolute power and to apply terror is carried to unprecedented heights.[21] As in the Marxist view of evolution accepted under Stalin's rule, there is a strong political implication in Wittfogel's doctrine: of his former Marxist leanings nothing is left, except his attempt to fight the Marxists with their own weapon – the Asiatic mode of production – and the extreme dogmatism in his manner of arguing, adopted from Marxism as taught by its most bigoted exponents. His doctrine indicates that neither the Soviet Union nor China have anything to offer as aspirations for other peoples, and that the only road to progress is through 'modern property-based civilizations' – which, in Wittfogel's view, should not lead to socialism but 'move toward a multicentered and democratic society', 'through large bureaucratic complexes that mutually – and laterally – check each other'.[22]

Wittfogel's view of evolution should therefore be called bilinear rather than multilinear; or, strictly speaking, it could hardly be considered a true evolutionist theory. Only one of the filiation lines leads to social progress, namely the one passing through the 'property-based', 'multicentered', or, to use Popper's expression, 'open' society.[23] In the other filiation there is no true evolution – only stagnation, restoration or retrogression.

After the many intelligent and penetrating criticisms to which Wittfogel's work has been subjected, it is hardly necessary to point out all its weaknesses once more.[24]

It is undeniable that he has strongly exaggerated the amount of centralization to be found in the Asian bureaucracies, and the role played in this respect by irrigation and drainage works.[25] As a general typology, Weber's 'patrimonial bureaucracy', as a sub-type of a feudal political structure, comes much nearer to historical reality, though in the Chinese case Weber may have over-estimated the amount of decentralization within the Chinese imperial structure.[26] Ruthlessness and a pretence of absolute power on the part of emperors are not necessarily signs of strength and power – they may point towards the existence of substantial centripetal forces, and Needham has convincingly shown that throughout the ages the Chinese empires were not at all the mono-lithic structures Wittfogel mistakes them for.[27]

However, the most unconvincing part of Wittfogel's doctrine is the denial of the truly modern aspects in the social structure of the Soviet Union or the People's Republic of China. Even for one who is fully aware of the manifold traditional and even backward elements still present in those huge empires, a refusal to see the numerous accomplishments and progressive elements in those countries, not only in the field of technology[28] but in that of human organization and motivation as well, amounts to wilful blindness.

Moreover, it is probable that Wittfogel's main weapon – the pretended existence in the past of an Asiatic mode of production – is much less efficient than even his opponents have realized.

Marx's assumption of the prevalence of 'communal ownership' in India and in Java, and of an absence of private ownership of land, was based on largely erroneous interpretations, given at that time, of the actual situation in those countries.[29] As far as Java is concerned, Thomas S. Raffles had simply taken for granted the Javanese princes' pretence that they were the real owners of all the land, and that the peasant did not possess anything of his own – an interpretation greedily adopted by later colonial governments to substantiate their claims, as successors to the king, to domanial rights. Further research has also shown that the traditional collective rights and powers of the villages in Java were much less extensive than was assumed by most nineteenth-century writers and Dutch colonial officials.[30] Equally, in India, private ownership of land not only existed, but even formed the predominant basis of rural society; the same was the case in Ceylon.[31] It is a queer anomaly that at present both West and East European Marxists, in order not to leave the initiative in the use of this concept to adversaries like Wittfogel, are trying to revive the Asiatic mode of production as a truly Marxist category, in several cases without properly investigating whether it fits historical reality in large parts of Asia.[32]

Even if one admits that, against the background of dogmatic unilinear rigidity in the past, the revived discussion in the USSR and other East European countries can be welcomed as a serious attempt to provide some scope for the variability of historical processes, it can be doubted whether this reintroduction of a nearly forgotten concept from the Marxist bible may really contribute to a better understanding of the processes of evolution. I shall attempt to take account of the great variation in historical sequences along a different line of thought.

iiii. Implicit Evolutionism

There are very few scholars at present who would deny that a development towards 'modernity' is taking place in communist countries. The frequent use of this term among sociologists is, in fact, one of the best indications that evolutionist thought is far from erased from the field of social sciences – even though only a few of those using this terminology appear to be fully aware of its evolutionist implications. The overall situation is rather odd – as has been rightly pointed out by several contributors to the discussion of evolution at the Conference at Northwestern University held in 1961.[33] While cultural anthropologists were flatly denying that universal social evolution existed, in the past decades scholars from other disciplines have frequently adopted, without realizing it, evolutionist views of a rather crude and unsophisticated brand. The widely used term 'underdeveloped countries' is a case in point. Among American sociologists especially, such simplistic evolutionist concepts find ready acceptance. Daniel Lerner's commonplace model of a 'traditional' society passing through the 'transitional' stage towards 'modernity' is well known.[34] Such a modernity evidently assumes the traits of contemporary American society, or at least its image in the mind of the scholars who use this terminology. This perspective, which posits an inescapable development of all traditional societies in the direction of Western industrial society, takes us back to the very ethnocentrism which Boas and his associates attempted to overcome. But at the same time the persistence of this simplistic evolutionism proves that there are developmental trends in world history which cannot be simply ignored by positing the equal value of all cultures in the world.

Among economists, evolutionist thinking is still more widespread – Walt W. Rostow's theory of the stereotyped 'stages of economic growth' being only one example out of many which view the process of economic development as a repetitive and universally valid phenomenon. There is also no doubt in the mind of a scholar like Rostow that the Soviet Union, by achieving a high degree of industrial development, has attained the stage of modernity, defined in his theory as the stage of 'self-sustained growth'. The only point which Rostow stresses is that Russia is no exception to the general rule: that a country, to attain that final stage, has to pass through the usual take-off process. In the Russian case, says Rostow, nothing extraordinary did happen. The take-off, initiated around 1890, had been completed at the start of the First

World War.[35] Therefore, no revolution had been needed to achieve a high level of industrial growth. Again, the political implications of his doctrine, and the reasons for calling his book a 'Non-Communist Manifesto', are evident, though they may be somewhat divergent from those implicit in Wittfogel's theory, in acknowledging the Soviet Union's status not only as a highly industrialized, but as a truly modern, country.

A group of scholars prone to assume a simplistic type of development from tradition towards modernity are political scientists concerned with problems of the 'new states'.[36] Here, again, the current assumption is that the development is one from traditional through transitional or mixed towards modern political structures. Again, to quote the Introduction to the volume *Social Change in Developing Areas*, it is 'worthwhile to examine the possibility that evolutionary theory, either unconsciously or surreptitiously, may be accompanying' the inherent theory of change. Too often the Western model – formal democracy in combination with a rationalized bureaucratic government – is considered to be the summit of political development, a *non plus ultra*, which any new state should take as an example and as an aim to achieve in a distant future. If the present situation in the great majority of new states does not conform to this model, it means, according to these political scientists, that such a state is still going through the transitional stage. The evolutionist assumption – of a unilinear type – is that the transition will, in the long run, undoubtedly be in the direction of the Western type of modernity. Again, the assumption is not without political implications.

The three-stages perspective, as developed in particular by Daniel Lerner, leading, as the only possible road, towards progress (according to David Riesman, in his introduction to Lerner's book, the latter shares 'the very American belief' that there must be a way[37] from traditional through transitional towards the Valhalla of modern society), has been rightly criticized by Arnold S. Feldman in his contribution to *Social Change in Developing Areas*.[38] He characterizes the three stages – one of 'Social Lethargy', one of 'Aspirations Explosion' and finally one of 'Balance' –

and the inherent assumptions of this three-stage theory, as too static and too simplistic. At the first stage there would be a state of both low expectations and a low level of achievement; the second stage is one of high aspirations and low achievement – a situation

often associated with the political instability and violence that occurs in these areas as a consequence either of the frustrated aspirations and/or the desire for power in order to participate more fully in the new order of things. In the final stage a balance is achieved, involving a high level of both aspiration and achievement, as a source of political and social stability.

A carefully elaborated evolutionary theory is, in fact, far better than an evolutionary perspective not made explicit, and therefore exposed to all kinds of naïve and emotional prejudices and ethnocentric biases. There is enough reason to doubt the validity of a concept of modernity fully based on the model of the Western type of society. In the past few years, several sociologists and political scientists have thrown doubt on the justness of the implicit assumption that, in the 'new states', development is due to the Western model. Hoetink has called this simplistic view a 'new evolutionism' and has shown that in several Latin American countries a development occurs in a quite different direction.[39] Hoetink has, for example, attempted to show that the alleged trend away from 'particularism' cannot be demonstrated in the process of modernization in Latin American countries. The same could be argued, to a certain extent, for Japan and even for the United States.[40]

The foregoing has made sufficiently clear the urgent need to reconsider our concept of social evolution including our understanding of the world-wide processes of modernization of 'old societies'.

Social Change in Developing Areas has rightly called for 'a reinterpretation of evolutionary theory'. But the participants in the conference agreed that their contributions were still rather tentative and that the task of developing such a theory, adapted to the requirements of modern sociology, had still to be started.

Though several of the contributions provide useful insights and incisive criticisms of the currently applied models, they have done little to elucidate the most fundamental problem: the course and the direction of social evolution.

iv. *Reappraisal of the Concept of 'Progress'*

In order to elaborate a truly up-to-date evolutionary theory, we have to turn our attention to a different school of thought: the ideas developed by Leslie White and some of his students, which run parallel with a similar trend of thought developed some decades earlier in the Netherlands by the historian Jan Romein.

Leslie White had always rightly maintained that general overall evolution is an undeniable social process, to be basically distinguished from social change occurring within the confines of a given cultural area.

There are, however, some fundamental problems to be considered in relation to this general evolution.

First, there is the basic question of defining the norms or values in relation to which we have to view a definite process as 'evolutionary', that is to say, one of 'progress'. It is evident that any such assessment involves a value judgement, which was one of the principal reasons for earlier rejection of evolutionary theories by sociologists and anthropologists.[41] Is there any possibility of expressing such a judgement on a valid scientific basis?

Secondly, there is the relationship between 'general evolution' and history. If some processes are evaluated as evolutionary, then we will have to admit that not all historical processes, even though they constitute social change, can be fitted into this evolutionary pattern. We have, then, to differentiate evolutionary processes from those processes of social change that are not evolutionary.

Thirdly, we have to take into full account the time variable. Nineteenth-century writers such as Morgan and Tylor have taken for granted that differences in level can be demonstrated between simultaneously existing societies.[42] Paradoxically, they did not realize, it appears, that the differential in space–time between more or less parallel processes in the past, accounting for those in-equalities of level, might also imply time differentials in future developments. Accordingly, the problem of how precisely these time differentials would work out apparently did not worry them. The difference between two given societies might point towards a growing gap between them; but it could just as well imply that the backward society would catch up with the more advanced one. It seems that the orthodox evolutionists have too easily taken for granted that advantages once achieved would be maintained, and that future progress would be initiated by the most advanced society and others would simply have to follow suit along the path cleared by the pioneer. Tylor, starting from a mildly paternal-istic standpoint, even took for granted, on the basis of 'experience', 'that independent progress could hardly have taken place among an uncivilized in contact with a civilized race'.[43] Some new evol-utionists have even surpassed the orthodox evolutionists in the expectation that advantages once acquired are bound to be kept. The most glaring instance is Rostow, who elaborated a stage se-quence in which certain processes – the take-off towards self-sus-tained growth – would always occur in approximately the same span of time: 'a decade or two'.[44] After that more or less uniform stage, a new one of 'sustained growth' would allow the once-conquered advantage to be maintained by some intrinsic auto-matism. This assumed parallelism in terms of time spans was, for him, evidently, an additional argument for explaining away the specific significance of the Russian Revolution by claiming that the 'take-off, starting around 1890', had already been definitely accomplished twenty-five years later. We shall revert to the ques-tionable validity of Rostow's claim further on. At this point we are only concerned with the crudeness of an approach that takes a stereotyped time span over a definite process for granted.

The basic issue is, evidently, that even though a social process has been thoroughly analysed in its component elements and necessary pre-conditions, the rate at which such a process proceeds remains problematic. This variable has not yet been really studied, either by historians or by other social scientists;[45] but it is clear that if we are to develop a more dynamic approach to understand society as it is moving, we shall have to evaluate the speed at which certain processes can be expected to evolve. Since any social process consists of a combination of several, sometimes conflicting, trends, it is possible that certain tendencies which, at one given moment, are seemingly predominant, will not develop because they are overtaken by another tendency developing at a much faster rate. For example, at a given moment in a certain 'under-development' country a native rising bourgeoisie appears to aspire to a take-over of the dominant position of the former colonial rulers – yet, not long afterwards, this trend may be overtaken by a much more vigorous one in which the representatives of the rural masses take the initiative, and the bourgeoisie is put on the defensive.

It is, moreover, the relative speed which decides whether a definite process should be included within the 'normal' range of evolutionary change, or should rather be viewed as 'revolutionary'.

2

Direction and Process of Evolution

'Nothing has ever changed under the Sun,' say those without hope. But then, Man, thinking Man, how, unless you would disavow your thinking, did you manage to emerge, one day, beyond animality? – 'At least nothing has changed, nothing changes any more, since the early beginnings of History.' But then, Man of the twentieth century, how is it that you awake towards horizons, and out of fears, that your fathers have never known?

PIERRE TEILHARD DE CHARDIN

i. The Criteria of Progress

Let us first tackle the one basic problem – the issue of objective criteria, or, to quote Herbert Hochberg, 'the value mess'.[46] To state that a given situation shows 'progress' or 'evolution' – which terms I am going to use as synonyms in the context of my argument – in relation to another situation implies the use of value-loaded criteria. But if one attempts to refrain from viewing one situation as better or more desirable than an earlier state, and simply tries scientifically to assess the direction in which humanity moves, one can observe a real trend in world history. It is one thing to shun subjective value judgements, and to take a relativist standpoint which refrains from lightly assuming that one's own level of social organization, or culture, is higher than any other type. It is quite another thing to deny that levels of social organization, or of cultural achievement, can, in some ways, be compared, on the basis of criteria which are not derived from one specific culture, but are founded on a certain common scale of evaluation. As we have seen earlier, shortly after the war certain cultural anthropologists[47] argued that Western industrial culture overestimated the importance of economic and technical achievement in evaluating other cultures and thus overlooked the fact that these cultures were as advanced or more advanced, if judged by values which were focal to them. This all too objective relativism, this tendency to view each society exclusively as a cultural entity without any relationship to other cultures and without any possibility of making relevant comparisons (because value judgements are deemed to be always related to a definite cultural background) obscures an overall trend in world history. This trend, manifesting itself on a scale exceeding the reach of any single culture, simply cannot be ignored. A standpoint like Lévi-Strauss's resembles one which denies that there is such a thing as mental growth in an individual because this statement implies a value judgement or expresses an arbitrary preference for the values of the adult world over those of the child's. On the other hand, by assuming the existence of evolution one no more implies that there is moral progress than one would imply, in stating that there is mental growth, that a grown-up is morally better than a child.

The easiest criterion for measuring progress would be purely technical. Technological progress during the short time-span since what Alfred E. Emerson, with a somewhat debatable terminology, calls 'the beginnings of cultural society', that is to say 'since Magdalenian man painted herds of extinct animals on the walls of caves in France and Spain about 15,000 years ago', is not only undeniable but even 'exponential', again to use Emerson's term.[48]

It is also probable that all other developments which are being considered as parts of human, or social progress, are in some way related to technological advance. For example, Max Weber's definition of a modern bureaucracy – as opposed to a patrimonial one – implies a system in which officials are getting a salary in money, which presupposes a money economy, and a communication system which facilitates the transport of money or money valuables over large distances. One should add that a developed communication system, one of the criteria of modernity mentioned by Myron Weiner,[49] in point of fact requires an advanced technology.

Without, therefore, fully endorsing the Marxist view that cultural developments are secondary to technological change, one can assume that there is a close relationship between technological and any other cultural or social development.

Leslie White, in stressing one single criterion for evaluating general evolution, namely the total amount of energy production and transformation in a given society,[50] has chosen a factor which is indicative of all other elements of evolutionary progress. If his thesis implies that this factor, in itself, should be considered the only valid criterion of progress, I could not agree. As the authors of *Evolution and Culture* point out in a work which, in fact, has a laudatory foreword by Leslie White, general evolution is a much more complex process which involves the whole range of human activities and social organization. It could not be pinned down to one single factor, however important, except in the sense that such a factor could be used as a pointer towards a much broader range of valid factors – as a rough measure of cultural achievement.[51]

It is, therefore, understandable that several authors have proposed different criteria of evolution. Lewis Morgan stressed the accumulation of inventions in the realm of technology as the determinant of social progress.[52] Herbert Spencer, on the other hand, starting from analogous criteria in the organic world, stressed the growing complexity of organization, a more elaborate division of labour and an increase in the size of a society.[53] There is no doubt that all those factors have a certain validity, even though one no longer admits the crude parallelism with the biological world adhered to by Spencer and his followers. The criteria of complexity, of division of labour, and of size, still crop up in different forms in contemporary theories of evolution.[54]

Yet, the formula 'from-simple-to-complex' is too simplistic to be acceptable as a general criterion of evolutionary development.[55] Increasing complexity does not necessarily run parallel with technological progress and higher efficiency. 'Greater complexity may not come about with change.'[56] The complexities of an earlier stage may run counter to the requirements of a new phase in technological and social development. It is well known among linguists that development in the field of grammar is often one from complexity towards greater simplicity. Equally, the complexities of family structure, highly elaborate in an earlier phase of social development, tend to disappear as soon as the society becomes urbanized and industrialized, and hence becomes more complex in a different sense. We will return to this phenomenon, in connection with the concept of social involution as elaborated by Clifford Geertz, who found that increasing complexity may occur as a consequence of ecological, adaptive pressure and thus may become a brake on attempts at fundamental technological and social change.[57]

It would, therefore, be difficult to maintain increasing complexity as a consistent and, more significant still, as an unambiguous criterion for evolution.

The same is true as far as the rate of division of labour is concerned. Again, the parallel from the organic world had led the nineteenth-century evolutionists to undue generalizations though, as a general trend, an increasing division of labour as a concomitant of technological progress can be upheld. Campbell, in his contribution to the Northwestern University Conference,[58] mentions 'the specialization of tasks and the division of labour' as ubiquitous in complex social life and as concomitant with industry, surplus production, and other values related to technological advance. Equally, modernity in political structures is positively related to a task-oriented bureaucracy and a recruitment on the basis of skills,[59] which also presupposes an elaborate division of labour.

On the other hand, a rigid division of labour is not necessarily conducive to greater efficiency. As with complexity, much depends on the definition of the concept. For example Naroll[60] quotes some scholars who 'argued, perhaps with some merit, that from the viewpoint of individual men and women who belong to social organizations, the more highly ramified and specialized the social organizations to which they belong, the less complex are their roles'. If division of labour means extreme specialization, as would follow from the above view, it may even become a hindrance to further advance. A rapid growth of the technical level of a society sometimes requires people to have a great adaptability for new tasks for which they have not initially been trained. A learning process which enables a man to perform very different tasks, according to the situation with which he is confronted, may be a precondition for the introduction of new technical devices. Whereas in an earlier stage of industrial development a rigid specialization, as far as individual abilities are concerned, might have been inevitable, it is not at all certain that, at the stage of introduction of automation, computers and electronic machinery specialization is still a badge of progress. Making full use of the learning capacities and adaptability of man may, in the long run, prove to be a wiser policy, from the point of view of efficient organization. 'Whereas the course of biological evolution is toward a more and more rigid immutable specialization among the cells, the trend within industrial society is toward increased flexibility in the labour market.'[61]

Increase in size is an important index of technological advance. Increasing scale through time and space is a phenomenon which has been observed by many sociologists.[62] Political scientists are also paying attention to this phenomenon. Myron Weiner mentions as one of the criteria for modernity that 'the citizens of a modern society have a sense of attachment to the nation as a whole, while in traditional societies ties to kin, caste and tribe predominate'.[63] It might, however, be observed that if increase of scale results, from a point of view of political development, in the domination of the world by two warring blocks, the world situation might become anything but conducive to further evolution. Just as the huge reptiles of prehistoric times were not the most viable species in the animal world, huge states are not necessarily the most efficient ones, nor the ones most open to new developments. The same might be true of huge, monopolistic organizations in the fields of industry, trade or finance.

It might, therefore, be questioned whether in certain circumstances decrease of scale, and a breaking up of huge organizations, due to the requirement of efficiency, are not an equally valid aspect of evolution.[64]

The question arises, therefore, whether the different criteria of progress mentioned by various authors could not be reduced to some more basic principles of which these criteria are, more or less, imperfect derivatives. It appears to me that the basic principle underlying the concept of evolution could be understood as a general trend towards emancipation. At the same time, this general trend cannot be separated from an increasing human capacity to cooperate.

ii. *The Emancipation Principle*

At first, human evolution tended to emancipate mankind from the forces of nature. It is a truism to say that in the earlier stages of human development man remains largely dependent on nature. The utmost he can achieve is an adaptation of his techniques to the natural environment, in order to take advantage of the natural conditions surrounding him. Even with further progress of technical refinement, the situation does not fundamentally alter – Francis Bacon's adage *non nisi parendo vincitur* (nor is nature to be conquered but by submission) remains valid even in the most advanced stages of technological development. Yet, further technological advances increasingly free man from his natural surroundings and enable him to change his environment to suit his requirements. Gradually, it becomes less essential to him to adapt himself to his environment. It is the environment that is, to a certain extent, being adapted to his needs.

The general trend of human evolution, therefore, amounts to an increasing emancipation from the forces of nature. A mobilizing of the energy resources viewed by Leslie White in his earlier work as the basic criterion of general evolution is, therefore, no more than one of the primary aspects of emancipation in a physical sense.

However, the physical aspect of emancipation – liberating man from his dependence on the forces of nature – is not the only relevant one. If technical knowledge and skills remain restricted to a very limited number of individuals, their scientific training may achieve a good deal of technical progress. However, the limitation of knowledge and skills becomes at a certain moment a brake upon further advance. Moreover, monopoly of skills may result in an increasing domination by a restricted group over large numbers.

Since the knowledge of how to master nature can, in the long run, be equally acquired by competing groups, monopoly does not last. In an earlier phase, mastery of technical skills by a restricted group might give rise to the exploitation of large numbers of people by a few. Whereas at a low technical level it is only differences in physical strength and intelligence that matter, at a later stage the difference of abilities may be greatly increased by an oligopolistic use of knowledge and skills. A restriction of the ability to write or of the use of certain arms to limited groups may encourage the creation of specialized castes or estates. The resulting division of labour may, in the first instance, be conducive to further technological advance. However, in the long run it is the level of knowledge and training of large numbers that counts in the competitive struggle between different societies. Time and again history has proved that the higher the level of scientific knowledge and technical skills among those who form the majority of a society, the greater the chance that they will outdo, and eventually vanquish, a society dominated by those who had wanted to keep technology as a privilege of the few. To quote J. D. Bernal: 'The most important and fruitful periods of scientific advance were those in which the class barrier was at least partially broken down and the practical and the learned men mixed on equal terms.'[65] He mentions, among other examples, France at the time of the revolution, when she certainly owed her victories to the policy of 'une carrière ouverte aux talents', which included members of the Third Estate interested in science and engineering. Another example is Holland, which in the seventeenth century, when trade, industry and science flourished among a prosperous bourgeoisie, succeeded in defeating feudal Spain where many of the most talented people had been ousted. Perhaps the defeat of Hitler's Germany could also be partly attributed to a *Herrenvolk* ideology that had driven out some of the best scientists.

Emancipation from human domination, therefore, goes hand in hand with emancipation from the forces of nature. This progressive emancipation from the fetters of human domination has assumed, in the past few centuries, several forms.

First, there were different social groups within technically advanced societies which were originally excluded from education and knowledge, but gradually achieved a certain degree of emancipation. In the urban centres of Western Europe it had been, at first, the rising bourgeoisie that wrested knowledge and education from the hands of the clergy, whose more or less exclusive domain they had been for many centuries. Equally, the Western urban middle class broke through the privilege of the aristocracy as experts in warfare. In the course of these breakthroughs technology and scientific knowledge were developed to a level which could never have been achieved under conditions of a restricted class privilege.

Further emancipation extending to the broad masses of the population of advanced societies has assumed remarkable proportions only in recent times. It is, in most industrialized countries, still a far cry from a situation in which each member of the society has equal access in conformity with his talents, to the treasuries of science, knowledge, and advanced skills. Time and again those who want to restrict the scope of education, claiming that the reservoirs of real talent have been exhausted and that the actual division of labour conforms to natural endowment, are being contradicted by the facts – the societies where emancipation has progressed most are making the greatest strides, not only in technology but in motivation to proceed further. Even if there is some positive correlation between actual social stratification and natural endowment, there still remains plenty of room for impressive advances in knowledge and skills among those social groups that have been hitherto largely excluded from participation in cultural advance. The availability of large untapped reserves of intelligence and skill in the Western world is being corroborated by research experiments in the field of the sociology of education.[66]

In a similar way, emancipation has equally affected societies and peoples that, until recently, were largely excluded from modern technology and scientific training. The lead in technological progress at first achieved by a restricted group of peoples – most of them of European descent – has not been maintained as an exclusive privilege for a long period. Despite all the theories advanced at the turn of the century about a differential native ability among the various races, the development of science and technical skills among peoples not long ago deemed to be of an inferior stock has been impressive. The achievements – at that time rather imitative than creative, as those believing in Western native superiority were not slow in demonstrating – of Japanese science shortly after 1900, were only a beginning. The synthesis of insulin in China, facilitated by an environment where a high technical skill was combined with a broad participation by different research teams at different levels, is a more recent case. It might be used to illustrate the point that the greater the spread of scientific training and technical skills among broad layers of the population, the higher the yield from intellectual and educational investment. Again, it has not been a rigid division of labour which has yielded the most impressive results.

One could, therefore, argue that the struggle of the underprivileged to achieve at least parity with those possessing exclusive skills, and their resulting emancipation from the fetters of domination and ignorance, may also produce an advance in general evolution not only in the sense of levels but also of numbers.

But it is at the same time clear that those rulers or leaders, who show faith in the potential abilities of the masses of the people and are willing to enlist their support by granting them the opportunity to develop these to the full, are always at an advantage in comparison with those who, sticking to an aristocratic formula, are loath to share their prerogatives, their knowledge, and their skills with those outside the inner circle.

There are two more aspects of the emancipation movement which should be mentioned. First, there is the 50 per cent of the world population which, in the past, was largely excluded from the realm of science and technology. According to the evolutionary theory advanced in the late nineteenth century, male domination would have been a relatively late development in human history, and would have been preceded by a stage in which matriarchy was the basic social institution. Marx and especially Engels elaborated this theory to claim that male domination would have been concomitant with the emergence of private property, in both pastoral and agricultural societies, which imposed the main burden of the care of cattle, farm management, and the handling of tools, in particular the plough, on the male.[67] More recent research has shown that a state of matriarchy assumed by nineteenth-century evolutionists to have preceded in prehistoric times a patriarchal structure was probably only imaginary.[68] Here again is a field of knowledge where unilinear evolutionism has been effectively exploded by subsequent studies of early human history. On the other hand, Margaret Mead has argued, on the basis of a few local studies, that the role and specific characteristics assigned to women in the great majority of societies we have been acquainted with in historical times, are by no means universal. She notes that a distribution of roles more or less divergent from the ones prevalent in West European or American society, and in one specific case even the opposite from the stereotypes accepted in a large part of the world, occurs in some societies studied by her.[69] Although her examples and interpretations may be, in some respects, less than convincing, there remain sufficient indications that the distribution of sex roles, assumed to be based on some universal psychological traits, may be much less innate and much more associated with cultural factors than has been readily assumed by too many authors.[70]

But Engels was right inasmuch as he demonstrated a certain correlation between the subjugation of women and the social and economic structure in those agrarian and pastoral communities which were the predominant type of society in large parts of the world before the advent of modern industrial civilization. Male domination in such civilizations as the Greek and Roman empires, the Arab Islamic world, traditional India, China, and Japan could not be attributed to pure chance.[71] There were some common characteristics in the predominant type of culture in the pre-industrial world – defined by Jan Romein as the 'common human pattern'[72] – that may account for the widespread phenomenon of male domination and for the restricted participation of women in most activities outside the household.

The societies studied by Mead, though perhaps significant from a theoretical point of view, represent only a marginal phenomenon as against the full weight of the huge territories where male dominance was part and parcel of the general way of life.

However, as Engels realized, the industrial revolution has profoundly shaken the domination of the male.[73] Whereas in traditional agriculture based on the plough and in pastoral societies the greater physical strength of the male contributed to a division of labour according to which most of the farm work and the care of the cattle was performed by the male, mechanization of labour potentially all but equalized the opportunities for women, providing that no innate inferiority of the female sex in intellectual endowment and technical skills could be demonstrated. The indications to be derived from an impressive amount of evidence in recent years point, again, towards the existence of a huge reservoir of gifts and skills hardly utilized in the earlier stages of human development. It is, perhaps, too early to decide whether there is full equality of innate abilities and of learning potential in both sexes. Women having mastered advanced skills are still, in many societies, handicapped by a host of factors in their attempts fully to utilize their acquired capacities. Preconceptions inherited from an earlier phase of human evolution along with a sense of inferiority difficult to surmount and time and again reinforced by the attitudes of the surrounding society, both male and female, may still discourage women from assuming responsibilities equal to their potential capacities and on the same level as those of males with a similar educational background.

A society still largely dominated by males may prove an effective deterrent to a full realization of the potential abilities of women, even though they may be completely free to acquire the educational training needed. Social arrangements – such as the burden of household chores unshared by males, the handicap imposed by the care of small children soon after undergoing superior forms of training and education, lack of facilities (such as crèches) and discriminatory practices by employers or government agencies – may in many countries account for a defective use of the skills acquired by young women. Last but not least, the first generation of a newly emancipated group always tends to suffer from a lack of self-confidence in a society still largely ruled by representatives of the traditional dominant groups. Consequently the latter may find their preconceptions about the innate inferiority of the newcomers reinforced.

Emancipation does not necessarily run parallel with an increasing division of labour if this is understood as a differentiation of roles instead of functions. On the contrary, division of labour according to social classes, racial groups, or sexes was much more rigid in the past than it is in a rapidly industralizing society. But even a division of labour according to individual capacity or training may become less, instead of more, pronounced with further technological progress. Future training for everyone may tend towards encouraging an adaptability to several kinds of highly qualified work.

Finally, there is one more group which participates in the general emancipation of the underprivileged: youth. It may sound rather paradoxical to view youth as a special social group to be emancipated, since their emancipation will occur naturally with their coming of age. Nevertheless, even in their case a true emancipation process is under way along with other emancipation movements. In societies with a technology that is at a comparatively low level, resulting in a low *per capita* production, techniques both in agriculture and in other branches of production are largely traditional. The same holds true for political and spiritual leadership, experience and wisdom being deemed to come with age. Submission of young people to adults, and an exclusion of younger people from positions of responsibility, are characteristic of most traditional societies.[74]

Since younger people, in many societies, have a more or less marginal position and feel the stress of tradition and dead conventions more intensely than older people do, it is they who often take the lead in emancipation movements, irrespective of whether these occur on a class, a race, or a sex basis. In periods of unrest, they gain a greater share in responsibilities, and the epithet 'young' may become a badge of honour. It is no wonder that several emancipation movements after the turn of the century adorned themselves with the adjective young. The Young Turks were a model for many similar movements led by students in Asia. Movements such as those of Young Persians, Young Arabs, Young Annamites and Young Javanese followed. However, as soon as social and political consolidation takes place after an emancipation movement has won an initial victory, the gains of the youth may be more quickly erased than those of other emancipating groups. A new kind of traditionalism may arise, relegating youth again to a minor and less responsible role in society. Since those who fought in the initial emancipation movement have come of age, they may exclude those younger than themselves from sharing the responsibility. This is what happened in Indonesia after independence had been achieved through a revolutionary process, a true emancipation struggle in which both women and youngsters, and most typically young women, had participated.

It is therefore understandable that, time and again, in any social order, new or old, it is youth that has to forward its claim for a greater share in responsibilities. The ultra-revolutionary Red Guards in turbulent China, the revolutionary or reactionary students in countries like India and Indonesia, the anarchist Provos in the Netherlands, the dissatisfied students in France or the rebellious young Negroes in the United States – all of them are, in part, rebelling against the *status quo* and claiming a greater say for youth in the affairs of the state. Potentially, the emancipation of youth opens a huge reservoir of technical and other untapped skills. Moreover, emancipation of youth, more than any other form of emancipation, is a process that can never be completed and has to be newly achieved by each generation.

Emancipation from the forces of nature and emancipation from domination by privileged individuals or groups, therefore, go hand in hand to mark human progress.

I have to stress, however, that in singling out emancipation as the basic criterion of the evolutionary process, I have not returned to a position where I equate evolution with the actual course of human history. The evolutionary perspective is not a trend inherent in human history as such; it is a measure applied to evaluate the course of certain events in terms of progress, stagnation or retrogression.

On the other hand the application of the evolutionary criterion is not fully disengaged from our *perception* of the emancipation principle as an overall trend within the history of mankind, waging a continuous, and often failing, battle for ever greater freedoms.

iii. *Cooperation as a Companion of Emancipation*

However, liberation of the creative potentialities of mankind is only one aspect of the process of human evolution. Inseparable from this trend is the increasing capacity of the human race to cooperate.

Theoretically, emancipation may occur on a purely individual basis, as a process which enables a certain person to attain higher achievements, freed from previous disabilities and disadvantages. It is even possible for an individual to utilize his acquired abilities to dominate other people. In fact, the use of improved technology has, to a large extent, been dictated by individual egotism or restricted groups interests, to the detriment of the interests of the many. Therefore, such an abuse of skills is not only a theoretical possibility – it is an issue of the greatest practical significance.

If, therefore, in the following argument, cooperation is advanced as one of the main corollaries of emancipation, we must ensure that no subjective value judgement creeps in and that our criteria of progress do not become blurred by considerations outside the realm of scientific validity. Consequently, we do not have to demonstrate that emancipation without cooperation is objectionable from some normative point of view, but that, in the long run, those working on their own or on behalf of a restricted group interest only, are at a serious disadvantage compared with those seeking cooperation on a larger scale. There are sufficient indications that domination and exploitation, in the longer run, do not pay or at least contain the germs of future decay. Although parallels with the realm of biology have become somewhat outmoded since the times of Herbert Spencer, I would like to quote Alfred E. Emerson on insect societies:

But an examination of insect social evolution provides rather strong evidence that the emergence of the dominant exploiter, the aggressive predator ... is not the major nor the exclusive direction of biological evolution. The interdependencies in the intricate web of relationships within the individual organism, the intra specific population, and the inter specific community point rather clearly to the evolutionary trend toward a balanced integration, toleration, co-existence, and co-operative mutualism between the parts of all coordinated levels of organization etc.[75]

The significance of cooperation as a factor in human evolution has been implicitly recognized by the early evolutionists. The criteria of progress advanced in turn by different authors and already discussed above, such as increasing complexity, division of labour, and scale of society, are all of them formulations, however deficient or incomplete, of this concept of cooperation.

Yet, we cannot solve the issue of the course and direction of evolution by simply introducing a principle of cooperation as a second basic criterion of progress, on a par with the emancipation principle. Although cooperation may be the basic factor behind phenomena such as complexity, division of labour, and size, it is not in itself an unequivocal criterion of progress. There are types of cooperation that are conducive to increasing domination and exploitation rather than to emancipation, such as cooperation by entrepreneurs through the formation of cartels in order to keep prices high, or organized lockouts of labourers. The same applies to cooperation in the realm of international politics where big powers attempt to divide the world by treaties into spheres of influence. Therefore, I regard the principle of emancipation as the sole decisive criterion of progress, though even then the actual application and interpretation of this concept remains far from easy.

Cooperation, then, is a highly significant agent of emancipation, rather than an independent additional criterion of progress. As such, it is one of the main human inventions. Social inventions, creating new forms of cooperation, may contribute as much to human progress as inventions in the field of pure technology.

On the other hand there exist, as we have observed, forms of cooperation that are contrary to human emancipation. Moreover, despite the immense importance of cooperation as an agent of emancipation, it is not exclusive as a type of human interaction conducive to progress. In some cases, competition rather than co-operation acts as a spur for human emancipation.

Scholars have quite often opposed competition to cooperation.[76] In our Western world the concept of competition, an expression of an entrepreneurial ideology, is still so loaded with positive connotations, in the wake of a still surviving Social Darwinism claiming a survival of the fittest, that it is essential to make clear to what extent competition itself may be related to human evolution.

Social Darwinism became popular at a time when extreme individualism and profit-making were viewed as the keystones of modern society. Competition was considered indispensable in stimulating the individual to the maximum effort and thereby improving his technology and increasing the rate of productivity of his labour. In the long run the individual's effort on his own behalf would, therefore, also profit society at large – charity starts with oneself.

This view, however, was soon outmoded by actual developments. Cut-throat competition, instead of being conducive to a general improvement in the level of production and consumption among the masses, simply amounted to a system of the devil take the hindmost. And since the hindmost formed the large majority – still more so in those areas, outside the centres of technological progress, which had become the vast, colonial or semi-colonial preserves of Western imperialism – progress became very uneven, leaving the greatest part of mankind in a state of extreme poverty, ignorance and backwardness.

The great mistake made by the liberals of the Manchester school and by the advocates of free enterprise in the United States was that they were largely thinking in terms of competition among peers. But a different type of competition was developing, which was to prove much more conducive to a general improvement of the material levels of the masses: a competition between social groups. The working class in industrial societies made a great effort in terms of acquiring technical skills and education, to catch up with the prosperous bourgeoisie. This was paralleled in colonial societies by the efforts of the rising native bourgeoisie to catch up with the alien rulers. But the most interesting aspect of these emancipation movements was that the competitive struggle was not fought on an individual, but on a collective basis. The underprivileged and dispossessed of yesterday learnt the lesson that strength derives from cooperation. By creating trade unions, or nationalist organizations, an increasing proportion of the underprivileged managed to wrest part of the profits acquired through improved technology from the pockets of the captains of industry.

One might describe the process of evolution as a spreading of the sense of solidarity among ever-broadening layers of underprivileged people. Popular emancipation movements do not stress an abstract universalism as their main ideology, but rather strike a note of particularistic loyalties, the range of which is gradually extended as the movement extends its appeal. For example, the Negro emancipation movement in the United States started with a fight for equal rights which would mainly benefit the upper layers of the Negro population; next, the concept of black solidarity developed in the shape of the Black Muslim movement aiming at a collective emancipation of the blacks from white superiority in its different aspects (cultural, economic and political); later on, the trend extended its appeal, as the Black Panther movement, to other oppressed people, primarily the coloured ones, finally to achieve a still wider particularistic appeal: proletarians of all countries, unite!

Cooperation, thus, became the main source of strength for those striving for emancipation; but it was a cooperation that, at the same time, was stimulated by a sense of competition.

In this seemingly unequal competitive struggle, the former underprivileged could also turn their initial disadvantages – in training, experience and material resources – into a source of power. The underprivileged in any society – including the female sex – in order to hold their own, are forced by their situation to become, to a certain extent, acquainted with two worlds: their own, and the world of those above them, ignorance of whose ways and reactions could involve serious dangers for those who are subservient. Those above, on the other hand, generally only know their own world – of the world of the underprivileged they have, in general, a distorted picture fitting their prejudices and helping to rationalize a desire for perpetual superiority.

The underprivileged, however, were not the only ones who discovered that unity means strength. The entrepreneurs also began to realize that, by combining forces, they could much better resist competition from others and introduce all kinds of innovations which they could not have undertaken single-handed. Thus started a trend towards ever-growing commercial and industrial enterprises, and in a world where the catchword still was free enterprise the individual entrepreneur became less and less free, and more and more dominated by organizations; whereas competition was still at the basis of the prevalent ideology, practice was moving away from free competition towards oligopoly or even monopoly.[77] Competition still largely exists between huge organizations, though even here the tendency to cooperate, via cartel arrangements and a fixed distribution of markets, is becoming more and more usual.

It is clear that if the increase of scale, related to this development, should lead towards conflicts springing from competition between enormous political and ideological blocks, giant states, or huge international concerns, the resulting strife might run counter to the trend of evolution and even lead to mutual extermination.

Should, therefore, the highest form of cooperation be a world-wide political and economic organization, based solely on cooperation and excluding competition? The question immediately arises of whether such a situation would not produce full monopoly and consequently bring about a state of affairs in which there would no longer be incentives for greater effort. Would such an outcome of the evolutionary process not automatically stop further evolution, especially when there were no longer any social groups left to emancipate?

It is still a far cry from such a paradise-like situation; and, as aspirations rise, there will, in all probability, always remain room for further emancipation on a higher level. Yet, we have to consider the problem of whether, in addition to cooperation, a certain amount of competition should not be envisaged as an equally indispensable precondition for progress.

My answer to this would be that we are not yet sure whether competitive attitudes are indispensable as incentives for effort. We do not know whether education towards higher forms of technology and human organization would involve replacing competitive attitudes by a greater urge towards cooperation. There have been, in the past decades, several social experiments in which this issue was put to a test, such as the Soviet *kolkhoz*, the Israeli kibbutz, and lastly the Chinese struggle against egotism as an element in their Cultural Revolution. However, it is quite plausible that an in-built element of peaceful mutual competition would act as a spur to higher levels of cooperation. It is not improbable that, after a successful major social revolution, a conservation of elements of competition within an organizational system, as an appeal to *homo ludens*, would appear sufficient to urge him to greater efforts, even though there were no further enemies to be crushed. This issue of in-built competitive motivations 'has been crucial within the economic experiments undertaken in all the states of today aiming at a realization of socialism.

Moreover, human life will never become effortless. There will always be the challenge of ever-changing natural conditions and forces. The infirmities of old age will have to be conquered. There will be the ever-renewed emancipation struggle of youth, with its new ideas and new aspirations. And there will always remain the challenge of the human adventure into the unknown, a challenge which only recently has touched hundreds of millions who formerly were too down-trodden and too frightened to aspire to anything but a modicum of security.

Therefore, rather than advance competition as a separate element in the process of human evolution, I would prefer to view it as an element of human interaction which, alternating or intricately interwoven with all kinds of cooperation, may equally be viewed as a significant agent of human emancipation and progress – at least in certain historical periods.

iv. *Adaptation and Conflict*

Having studied the course and direction of human evolution we must now turn our attention to the second basic problem: the process of evolution. According to Emerson, progress can be measured in terms of 'increased homoeostasis'.[78] However, the concept of homoeostasis, borrowed from the science of biology, far from being unambiguous in the case of human societies, raises more questions than it solves. It takes a rather static view of human societies, assuming the existence of a certain basic equilibrium, and more or less ignoring the in-built tensions which are at the root of further evolution. But its greatest weakness is that the concept seems to include adaptation and adjustment as a basic factor in general evolution.[79] It may, however, be questioned to what extent increasing adaptation of human societies can really be viewed as concomitant with progress.[80] In the following pages I shall try to demonstrate, largely in accordance with the views advanced by Leslie White, Marshall Sahlins, and their associates, that in many respects increasing adaptation and overall progress, far from being parallel, are on the contrary mutually incompatible, even though an increase in the *capacity* to adapt might be still regarded as running parallel with emancipation and progress.[81]

We have established that the concept of evolution does not fit every historical process, even though such a process involves social change. The concept of evolution, as defined above, is selective and singles out only those processes as progressive which fit into a certain pattern. Many historical processes, however, should rather be assessed, from an evolutionary point of view, as furthering stagnation or even as regressive.

The process of evolution, far from being unilinear, is dialectical. Development does not proceed without conflicts and frictions. The Hegelian concept, endorsed by Marx, of a continuous flow from thesis via antithesis to a synthesis which again is the starting point of a new dialectical process at a higher level, at least recognized the contradictory aspect of each evolutionary process. This dialecticism is expressed in a different way by Donald Campbell: 'The wisdom of evolution is retrospective. If the environment changes, the products of past selection may be stupid.'[82] It is always wise to keep in mind the essentially dialectical character of the course of human history, and its inherent inconsistencies and inner contradictions. One aspect of this dialecticism has been explored by Sahlins and his colleagues in their study *Evolution and Culture*, where they attempt to distinguish general from specific evolution.

They try to reconcile the two major evolutionary theories of today, Leslie White's concept of general evolution, and Julian Steward's multilinear theory. Steward's concept of evolution, taking each cultural area as a separate field, attempts to explain cultural variation by demonstrating that this variation has come about by gradual adaptation of a culture to its natural environment. Inasmuch as there are parallels between developments in different cultural areas, they are to be accounted for by similarities in the natural environment.

Evolution and Culture attempts to demonstrate that this type of evolution which the authors call specific, far from running parallel with general evolution, quite often leads a society in an opposite direction. Adjustment to a given environment may result from great ingenuity – but the result is more or less passive; whereas general evolution is characterized by an increased utilization of energy resources and, instead of ending up in an adaptation to a given environment, creates an increasing independence from nature, and even submission of the natural environment to man. Therefore, the type of adaptation and of selective retention as defined by Donald Campbell, far from being consonant with the general trends of evolution as assessed above, may be in sharp contradiction with those trends.

It seems to me that Sahlins and his colleagues have made an important contribution to social science by differentiating between the two types of evolution. I would prefer not to call the type of social change involved in progressive adaptation to a natural environment, evolutionary. In many cases the term involution used by Clifford Geertz (who in turn borrowed it from Golden-weiser, though the latter used it in a different, purely cultural, sense)[83] seems more appropriate.

Taking Javanese rural society as his starting point, Geertz has described the process of increasing complexity and refinement in all kinds of social relationships in response to a growing ecological pressure. The Javanese countryside was characterized by

increasing tenacity of basic pattern, internal elaboration and ornate-ness, technical hairsplitting and unending virtuosity. And this 'late Gothic' quality of agriculture increasingly pervaded the whole econ-omy: tenure systems grew more intricate; tenancy relationships more complicated; cooperative labor arrangements more complex – all in an effort to provide everyone with some niche, however small, in the over-all system.[84]

The initial social arrangements were largely dictated by mo-tivations of social justice. In a society with a low level of *per capita* production, near the subsistence margin, there is a strong tendency to develop social arrangements and institutions intended to guarantee that nobody will need to starve, which Geertz has called a shared poverty system.

Since the growing complexity of the social system leads the society away from solutions needed to initiate true technological progress with an ensuing rise in *per capita* productivity, Geertz calls this type of development, involution – which is the reverse of evolution. 'Around 1830 the Javanese ... economy could have made the transition to modernism, never a painless experience, with more ease than it can do to-day.'[85] Essentially, as mentioned earlier, this growing complexity is a consequence of ecological pressure, a rapidly growing population in an ecological environ-ment which can absorb many more hands without substantially lowering the rate of *per capita* production. Such a situation is typical of areas where rice is being cultivated on irrigated fields. In such an ecological environment the law of diminishing returns seems to be hardly operating.

We find here an extreme case of social change motivated by adaptation to the natural environment. I would suggest that it is exactly in such cases of involution that the ecological pressure steadily reinforces the challenge to break through the existing social system. If, however, the specific evolution, the adjustment to the natural environment, has created in the past a true impasse (as is the case in Java and in many other rice-growing societies) there may be no way out through gradual evolution.

We will have to consider whether it is not a process of involution more than any other, which calls forth a revolutionary overturn of the social system in order to get the society under way on the path to true general evolution.

It seems to me that Donald Campbell's exposition of the way evolution proceeds (which, in his view, is a subject much more amenable to scholarly research and to a drawing of analogies with biological evolution than the vexed issue of the course of evolution[86]) may be valid only for the type of evolution discussed in the foregoing: the progressive adaptation to a natural environment. In these cases, Campbell's selective retention model[87] which tries to explain the wide range of variability in human culture, might be of great use in establishing the different steps in the process. It is also quite possible that he is right in stating that in these cases both variation and selective retention mostly occur in a random, unconscious, trial-and-error fashion without the intervention of any rational decision-making on the part of the leaders of a society.[88] But, even though in the case of adaptive social change Campbell might be, to a certain extent, right, one can hardly imagine that in the case of general evolution changes would occur at random and by trial and error only. C. Condit has rightly argued that even cultural systems change as a result of 'purposeful adaptation to the environment'.[89] However this may be, the type of change involved in emancipation in both its aspects, technological and social, is still far more likely to be the result of purposeful action. Equally, forms of cooperation may result, to a large extent, out of conscious efforts to surmount the weaknesses arising from single-handed activities or from traditional arrangements which no longer fit their purpose.

v. *Mental and Material Factors*

There has been heated discussion on the problem of whether the prime mover of human evolution should be looked for mainly in the material or in the mental field. For the Marxist school of thought, the basis for institutional and ideological change was a material one. This was one of the reasons why Lewis Morgan's stress on technological invention as a main factor in human evolution appealed so much to Marx and Engels.

Yet, it has been argued that one should not interpret Morgan's evolutionary theory in strictly materialistic terms: both technological invention and institutional innovation contain elements of mental growth, the germs of which are present, according to Morgan, in any branch of the human race.[90]

Marx and his followers equally attached great importance to the mental aspect of human evolution, even though they developed their theory in terms of dialectical materialism. The primary role accorded, in Marxist theory, to class consciousness shows how erroneous it would be to interpret Marxism in such a way as to deny the *mental* urge towards emancipation its preponderant role in the process of human evolution.

My own attempt to establish emancipation as the main criterion of human progress is, at the same time, an attempt to reformulate the evolutionary process in a way which implicitly acknowledges the primary significance of mental attitudes. Even though an assessment of a social process as conducive to emancipation, and thus to social evolution, may be due to a judgement *ex post facto*, it is difficult to conceive that such a process could occur without even a shade of conscious or subconscious rejection of material or institutional bonds, in an effort at liberation from forces experienced as oppressive.

There may be an enormous distance in time between the moment when the oppressive character of certain disabilities is first dimly realized and the germs of opposition are planted in the minds of the people, and the moment when the emancipation struggle assumes the concrete form of a social movement. In a subsequent chapter of the present volume the slow transformation of forms of protest from their first concealed beginning as counter-points within the prevalent social system determined by dominant values into true, ideologically based, counter-value systems will be extensively discussed.

At this point it is enough to stress that patterns of thought, which are at the root of the ongoing struggle for human emancipation, may be encountered in embryonic forms in religious concepts of equality before God, as well as in theatrical performances or popular myths criticizing the bad prince and eulogizing the simple swineherd. The tension between the urge for freedom and social reality may assume the whole range of attitudes from slight irony through other-worldly ideals to a well-organized social struggle waged by significant social groups.

It is not easy to define the different aspects of a mentality that is conducive to the ongoing process of emancipation. One could mention a certain creativity in the sense of a desire for innovation; but in so doing one should at the same time realize that innovation may also be conducive to adaptation to the physical environment, and thus lead to specific instead of general evolution. One could equally single out a desire for betterment of one's fate – but again, such a desire may lead to adaptive processes. Perhaps the most typical element in the mentality that contributes towards an emancipation process is a certain compassion with one's fellow-man, a sense of solidarity with the underprivileged, which results in an activity that is concerned with the betterment, not merely of one's individual life but of that of larger social groups, and may ultimately result in a rejection of the prevalent social and political system.

At any rate, as was to be expected, the emancipation processes cannot be reduced to a monocausal relationship.

The same is true for the adaptive processes summarized by Sahlins and Service within the concept of specific evolution. Again, no monocausal relationship can be demonstrated. But whereas, in emancipation processes, a creative urge for innovation was preponderant, adaptive processes are mostly due to a craving for safety and protection. If group emancipation generally springs from a sentiment of solidarity and compassion with the underprivileged, adjustment to a physical and social environment rather points towards a conservative mentality that wants to keep the benefits of the *status quo* for oneself and one's peers.

It is this ongoing conflict between two different mentalities which is at the root of the social conflicts that determine the dialectical course of human evolution.

vi. *The Dialectics of Diffusion*

There is, finally, one point which I would like to mention in connection with the relationship between evolution and cultural variation. Sahlins and his colleagues[91] have rightly pointed out that the scope of cultural variation diminishes with the advent of higher types of human technology and organization. Cultural borrowing was already an important phenomenon at a lower level of technology and human organization (which, of course, does not mean that cultural borrowing would be the only source of cultural parallelism; independent invention being as crucial and as significant[92]).

But at the higher stages of development, as the authors of *Evolution and Culture* have pointed out, the phenomenon of cultural domination attains an ever-growing importance. With the increase in scale, the spread of cultural traits to large populations and broad sections of a society assumes ever more significant proportions.

Certainly Jan Romein exaggerated in arguing that, before the advent of industrial civilization, there existed something like a 'common human pattern' typical of all agrarian societies. Possibly he was equally exaggerating in claiming that Western industrial civilization is already gradually spreading, in a cultural sense, to the entire world.[93] At least one should doubt whether industrial civilization, as it was developed in the West, could be equated with modern civilization. Romein himself acknowledges that the spread of this civilization to other parts of the world implies the end of European hegemony. But even though the factors making for variation, both in the past and today, may have been underrated by Romein, at any rate the trend towards *de-*

creasing variation, along with a proceeding evolution in the fields of technology and human organization, cannot be denied. This is one of the main reasons why the treatment of evolution given by those scholars who are almost exclusively concerned with variation (such as Steward and Campbell) cannot be considered truly adequate.

However it would again be a serious error to assume that the flow and diffusion of new technology and new social institutions towards other societies is a smooth, conflict-free process. To quote Kaplan:

The great complexity of highly evolved technological systems has made it possible for advanced societies to discourage and hinder its spread ... All of the European colonial powers, for instance, used their political, financial and economic power to prevent, or at least slow down as far as possible, the spread of industrialism to the less advanced countries under their political control because they were primarily interested in markets and sources of raw materials and not in creating manufacturing competitors.[94]

The attitude of these powers, therefore, is rather one that is related to a quest for stability and resistance to change, than with an urge for true social innovation.

Whenever the dominant culture actually spread to other societies, it was mainly because the latter could wrest political and, in certain cases, economic control from the hands of the former colonial or imperialist power-holders. Again, the phenomenon of diffusion of dominant cultures or of specific techniques, institutions or capacities may, under certain conditions, be viewed as contributing to the general emancipation process.

David Kaplan is well aware that mental factors may account for the ultimate success of retarded societies in grasping the new technology through 'actively resisting the political and economic domination of a more advanced form'.[95] He points towards the 'nationalistic movements sweeping across the so-called underdeveloped countries of the world'. But he wrongly interprets these movements in terms of a simple cultural borrowing, as a kind of cultural lag, produced by the fact 'that in the spread of more advanced culture types very often the ideological component will

tend to spread farther and faster than its technological component'.[96] Kaplan evidently starts from the assumption that, generally
speaking, technology is the prime mover in the evolutionary
process. He wants to 'distinguish between the origin of the cultural phenomenon and its spread to some particular society. From
a general evolutionary perspective, an industrial technology gives
rise to an appropriate social system and ideology'.[97]

In my own view, there is nothing unusual in the phenomenon
that the mental urge towards a wholesale innovation of technology and social institutions precedes their actual spread. The
mental aspect of emancipation either precedes, or is a concomitant
of, technical and institutional innovation, including the process of
technological invention as such. It may be true that the ideological content of this urge for emancipation is often formulated
in terms derived from the dominant culture, as is for example the
case with the nationalist ideology or with Marxism. Nevertheless
the urge as such is genuine, and identical with the spiritual prime
mover in the general evolutionary process.

In the preceding discussion of Romein's view on the spread of
Western industrial civilization to other parts of the world I have
already touched upon the question as to what extent non-Western
countries could be expected simply to follow the Western evolutionary road. Paradoxically enough, it is Romein's own 'law of
the retarding lead', a basic element of the concept of 'the dialectics
of progress as developed by him in the thirties, which blurs
the simplified unilinear picture that one could wrongly draw from
his subsequent studies on dominance and diffusion published
during the fifties. But here we already touch upon the third aspect
of general evolution to be discussed: the time differential.

The foregoing exposition of the way dominant cultures spread
may partly serve to explain the dialectical course the evolutionary
process takes in terms of time differentials. It is largely through
the eternal tension between the urge for emancipation and a tendency towards consolidation and stability, that the time factor
comes in, as a significant variable in the evolutionary process.

3

The Time Differential

We have to learn from rapidly changing systems: Ordinarily we learn from stable systems.

KENNETH E. BOULDING

i. Romein's 'Dialectics of Progress'

The nineteenth-century evolutionists seem to have been relatively little worried by the theoretical problem posed by the unevenness of development levels among human societies. Morgan suggested that the main cause was the extreme difficulty and rarity of new inventions and the consequent arrest of progress in cases where isolation prevented physical contact with cultural areas from which technological change could have been borrowed.[98] Yet, if one assumes the unity of mankind and one single locality as a cradle of human species, the uneven development of different societies should have presented something of a problem to those who conceived human history in terms of perpetual, gradual change. How could the enormous gap between civilized and primitive societies be explained?

Social Darwinism could provide an explanation – although not a very satisfactory one. The paradox remained that the unfit not only survived, but even flourished in large parts of the world. If the primitives, who were more or less equated with the ancestors of the civilized peoples, were not excluded from the universal process of evolution, and in this respect the leading nineteenth-century evolutionists agreed, the latter had to account for the anomaly that in the past some peoples had moved faster than others. Would, in the further evolutionary process, the gap tend to widen? If, through a selective process or as a consequence of a differential climate, one human group had achieved a certain advantage over others – the distance could only increase, never decrease, if the same factors that had produced the initial advantage remained operative. The only possible way of preventing the gap from widening would be by consciously spreading higher forms of civilization to the primitives, and this was exactly the position of those who, like Tylor, combined an evolutionist outlook with a belief in a colonial *mission sacrée*: the 'white man's burden'.

The consequence of this view would be that, once achieved, the advantage would last, and that the centres of political power, technological superiority, and cultural excellence would remain constant. Unfortunately for the unilinear gradualists, historical evidence, far from confirming this supposition, points in an opposite direction.

It was Jan Romein who was the first to deal with the 'skipping' phenomenon in human history as a general trend. Naturally, there had been many thinkers before him who had noticed the phenomenon of shifting centres of human civilization or political power. But the historical sequences were mostly analysed, at that time, in terms of the rise and fall of empires, of flowering and decay of civilizations. Oswald Spengler, in his *Der Untergang des Abendlandes*, elaborated the rise-and-fall concept as a world-wide cyclical movement from which no human civilization could escape, comparable with the flowering and decay of living organisms. For Romein, on the other hand, the shift in power centres and technological achievements was not identical with a continuous process of flowering and decay. The different civilizations in his view are not disconnected entities, each with its own, more or less analogous, life-cycle. In Romein's view, though he opposed the unilinear evolutionary concepts current before the First World War, a general world-wide trend towards progress was undeniable. Similarly, in his treatise, two main criteria are applied for establishing progress: technological proficiency and organizational expediency. But he adds, to this universal process, one more dimension: evolution, in his view, is a discontinuous process. Therefore, the skipping of phases and the shifting of power centres from one locality to another does not contradict the evolutionary principle as was argued by those who were reasoning in terms of flowering and decay. On the contrary, it is an adequate description of the way human evolution generally proceeds.

On the basis of the recognition of this fundamental truth, Romein developed his hypothesis of the 'dialectics of progress'.[99]

He demonstrates, with a wealth of examples drawn from human history, that far from developing in a gradual way, human history progresses with leaps and bounds, comparable to the mutations known from the world of living nature. A new step in human evolution is not at all likely to occur within the society which has achieved a high degree of perfection in a given direction. On the contrary, the progress once achieved in the past is liable to act as a brake upon further progress. Both an atmosphere of complacency and vested interests tend to oppose further steps which might involve a complete overhaul of established institutions or equipment.

Again, we may recall the discussion in chapter two of the mental aspect of evolutionary processes. If specific evolution, finally resulting in adjustment and stabilization, creates a mood hostile to fundamental change, a new spurt on the evolutionary ladder is more likely in a society where a sense of being underprivileged creates a potent urge for emancipation.

Therefore, further progress in human evolution is much more likely to occur in a more backward society where resistances to social change are weaker. Romein shows that leadership in human evolution perpetually shifts from one society to another, after over-specialization has led yesterday's leader into a blind alley. He draws his examples from both the realm of technology (including armaments and warfare) and social institutions. The following are a few striking illustrations from his thesis: the introduction of electric lighting in London was retarded as this was the first city to develop illumination with gas and to carry it out to a remarkable perfection; the lagging behind of the productivity of collieries in Britain, France, and Belgium, the countries which were the first to develop large-scale coal mining; the advantage of late-comer Japan over Britain as far as modernization and rationalization of textile industries is concerned; and finally the occurrence of the proletarian revolution in backward Russia contrary to the prophecies of those Marxists who had expected this revolution to take place in Germany, at that time industrially the most developed

T—C

country. The general design of his argument is to show that back-wardness may, under certain circumstances, act as an advantage and a spur to further effort whereas rapid advance in the past may act as a brake. This is what he calls the 'dialectics of progress' or the 'hypothesis of the retarding lead'.

To what extent was Romein's contribution to evolutionary theory an original one? He mentions in his article several authors who occasionally had expressed similar views on some definite historical issue, though none of them had ventured to elaborate this view, like Romein, into a full-fledged theory.[100] Most of those scholars quoted by Romein are Marxists, which is not surprising if we consider the extent to which dialectical thinking had per-meated Marxian philosophy. The Dutch Marxist astronomer Pannekoek even suggested the paradox: 'Survival of the Un-fittest'.[101]

Romein might have mentioned Engels who argued that Ger-many had been able to initiate a higher stage of civilization (namely feudalism) than Rome had ever been able to attain, be-cause in Germany elements of an earlier, 'barbarian', phase were still operative whereas the Roman empire had got stuck in the first phase of civilization, slavery. 'And in conclusion, if they could develop and universally introduce the mild form of servitude which they had been practising at home . . . to whom was it due, unless it was again their barbarism thanks to which they had not yet arrived at complete slavery . . .?'[102]

It is interesting however that Romein, himself a Marxist, in his argument clearly deviated from the conventional Marxist view of social evolution. It is, in particular, most curious that neither Stalinists nor Trotskyists could endorse the dialectical perspective in which Romein viewed the Soviet experiment.

The crucial issue is whether it is ever possible to skip a phase in human evolution, in particular the bourgeois–capitalist one, and whether the Russian case could be considered a deviation from the classical sequence feudalism–capitalism–socialism. In the evolution-ary view, as accepted among leading Marxists, each previous phase had to be completed before a new phase could begin.[103] Their dialectical way of thinking deviated from other evolutionary views in so far as they regarded each new phase as being born in antithesis to the prior phase, each stage producing, at its peak, the very counter-forces that would eventually bring about its doom. There was a difference of opinion among Marxists regarding the way the qualitative change would be brought about: gradually, or by revolutionary means, thus channelling the accumulated quantitative elements towards a sudden, cataclysmic, qualitative transformation. But neither of the schools of thought seemed to doubt that in principle each single phase should pass through the usual processes of birth, flowering, and decay.

In accordance with this view, Marxist thinkers, around the period of the First World War, agreed that a socialist phase could not be born except in the society where bourgeois capitalism had achieved its *fullest* growth, i.e. Germany, the most highly developed industrial country in that period.[104] The first socialist revolution, however, occurred in Russia, which at the time could be considered a rather backward country. From a theoretical point of view this looked like a paradox, the more so since the enactment of a socialist revolution in Russia was a deliberate choice made by a group of leading Marxists. We are therefore interested in how the Marxist political leaders interpreted the apparent deviation from the Marxian pattern of evolution.

Lenin's attempt to kindle the proletarian revolution in backward Russia was a well-considered one. One of his original contributions to Marxist theory was the insight that, in order to defeat capitalism, the chain of imperialist fortresses should be attacked in their weakest link: not in the central seat of power but in the soft underbelly of capitalism, the colonial or semi-colonial backyards which capitalism, in its imperialist shape, was exploiting in such a way as to provoke strong popular counter-forces.[105] It was the peasantry of Eastern Europe, Asia, Africa, and Latin America who had been turned by capitalist exploitation into an impoverished and restive international proletariat.

In this connection Lenin even used an image which shows a certain similarity with Romein's 'hypothesis of the retarding lead'; he spoke of 'backward Europe and progressive Asia'. As a matter of fact, according to Lenin, Europe was backward inasmuch as its leaders supported anything in Asia that was agonizing and medieval, whereas Asia was progressive since its mass of the people got support from the rising Western labour class.[106]

However, there is a fundamental difference from Romein's idea: in Lenin's view it was still the European proletariat who would be the decisive factor in bringing about a proletarian revolution and calling into being a socialist society. The decisive struggle for power would be fought in Germany. The general expectation among communist leaders was that the Russian revolution would spread to other parts of the world and that the German bourgeoisie, weakened by the loss of the Russian hinterland, would suffer a defeat from the most developed and most progressive labour class. The proletarian revolution, started in Russia, would spread to Germany and hence conquer the world.

When neither a world revolution nor a socialist revolution in Germany materialized, the communist leaders in what had become the Soviet Union had to reconsider the new situation. The well-known dispute between Stalin and Trotsky focused around the problem of whether it would be possible to build socialism within one country. Lenin died in 1924 before the dispute had really started.

In his *History of the Russian Revolution* Trotsky expounded his views on this crucial issue. At the same time, he tried to demonstrate that his views were largely in agreement with those of Lenin. There are, in his work, expressions that anticipate Romein's 'hypothesis of the retarding lead'. He uses the term: 'the privilege of historic backwardness' and mentions the possibility of 'skipping a whole series of intermediate stages'. For example, in its economic evolution Russia had 'skipped over the epoch of craft-guilds and manufacture'. Romein himself drew attention, in his essay, to Trotsky's following comment on the rapid development of Russian industry: 'Actually the possibility of such a rapid growth was precisely determined by the backwardness ...'[107] Sahlins and Service, who have recently rediscovered the 'law of the retarding lead' without being aware of Romein's study, which was never published in English, even mention Trotsky as the only scholar who had anticipated the significance of this phenomenon 'as a scientific law'.[108]

Notwithstanding the notable attempt in Trotsky's argument to cope with the dialectical element in history, I could not agree with either Romein or with the editors of *Evolution and Culture* that he should be viewed as a precursor in the true sense. Trotsky's basic argument amounts to a denial that Russia, as a backward country, could skip over the capitalist phase. The 'law of combined development', formulated by him,[109] rightly posits that, in a revolution like the Russian one, highly progressive and traditional elements work in combination. In his conception, however, the remnants of tradition play a decisive role. The essence of his argument is that although the Russian environment, because of its backwardness, was propitious for starting the socialist revolution, its consummation could never occur in a backward country. The numerous backward aspects of Russian society were, in Trotsky's view, an insurmountable obstacle to a truly socialist development. An attempt to build socialism within one country would inevitably defeat itself and produce a restoration of state capitalism, a bureaucracy with many backward, partly feudal, traits. Taken as a whole, Russia's backwardness, in Trotsky's view, could not be considered an advantage for a truly socialist experiment.[110]

It is difficult to decide whether Trotsky is right in his claim that Lenin, too, had never thought of the possibility of building socialism within one country.[111] It is more important to us to assess to what extent Stalin's actual attempt to do so was based on a theoretical concept comparable with Romein's idea of dialectics of progress.

There exists an apocryphal anecdote on a dispute allegedly held between Stalin and his opponents, among them Trotsky, in the Executive Committee of the Communist Party at a time when Stalin had still to argue, not being able yet to impose his views. Stalin is reported to have said, in reply to those who argued that according to Marxist theory socialism within one country was impossible: 'You are duller than chickens. If one draws with chalk a circle around a chicken, it dares not overstep the circle. But you have drawn the circle you dare not overstep yourselves.'

Stalin was in the first place a pragmatist. His attempt to build socialism within one country was dictated by practical necessity rather than by theoretical considerations. He did not claim any original theoretical basis for his bold experiment. He always argued that what he tried to achieve was in full accordance with classical Marxism. He was not consciously deviating from the theoretical sequence feudalism–bourgeois capitalism–socialism. In the Russian case the capitalist phase had been pretty short. But he would not allow such trivialities to deter him from trying to achieve things that would have been easier had the Soviet Union found partners all over the world. If Germany did not join the effort, if the world revolution had not yet materialized, the Soviet Union would go it alone.

In Stalinist Marxism, however, there was no sign whatever that the Russian way was considered to be a deviation from the usual succession of phases. On the contrary, the Stalinists seemed rather to assume that if it proved feasible to build socialism within one country, this also demonstrated that the previous phase, bourgeois capitalism, had matured to such an extent that the next phase, that of socialism, was able to take place.

It was this view which was contested by Romein. Agreeing that Russia was building socialism within one country, he argued that the experiment was successful not because capitalist society had been maturing but on the contrary *because it had never matured*. The same factor, Russia's backwardness, which had turned the country into propitious soil for a proletarian revolution, made it equally fit for a building up of socialism. Not only could certain elements of the capitalist phase be skipped over. Capitalism as such was a phase which, in the Russian case, proved to be an unnecessary circuit. Russian backwardness could, thus, be turned into an advantage over more developed societies.

The Soviet slogan *dognat' i peregnat'* (to chase and overtake, i.e. the capitalist countries), far from being a vain phrase, in Romein's view was a clear expression of what actually would happen and was already happening during the successive Five Year Plans.

It is often claimed that evolution only proceeds in minimal steps. Several contributors to *Social Change in Developing Areas* still take a similar view: 'Change occurs in small steps. It is continuous and not linked, autonomous and not imposed.'[112] Similarly Edward B. Tylor had assumed 'that the changes were minute rather than large and that their effect was cumulative rather than abrupt'.[113]

Romein has demonstrated that this view of evolution is unrealistic. He attacks the ancient saying *nil natura per saltum* and proposes to replace it by the following ones: *nil natura nisi per saltum*, and *nil humanum nisi per saltum*.[114]

ii. Service's 'Law of the Evolutionary Potential'

Elman R. Service in his contribution to *Evolution and Culture*, evidently unaware of his Dutch precursor, developed his theory which resembles Romein's thesis even in details.[115] The independence of his discovery is expressed in a nomenclature different from the terminology used by Romein. The skipping of phases is called by Service 'the leapfrog effect'. What Romein calls 'the dialectics of progress' is termed by Service 'the phylogenetic discontinuity of progress'. The reason why the term 'dialectics' is shunned by Service is because, in his view, it was Hegel's dialectical conception which prevented Marx and Engels, and their followers, from considering the possibility of a discontinuous evolutionary process.[116]

The continuous shifting of centres of cultural and technological advance, implied by Romein in his overall concept of *verspringing* which includes both the skipping and the shifting phenomenon, recurs in Service's analysis as the 'local discontinuity of progress'.

Finally, Romein's 'law of the retarding lead' recurs, in Sahlins's study, as 'the law of evolutionary potential'. Both laws implicitly contain what the two authors have independently termed 'the privilege of backwardness'. Service, like Romein, related the phenomenon to the often discussed, but never understood, phenomenon of the rise and fall of civilizations.

The most important original contribution by Service and his associates is that they relate this law to the distinction between two types of evolution discussed earlier. Service expresses this relationship as follows: 'The more specialized and adapted a form in a given evolutionary stage, the smaller is its potential for passing to the next stage' or, putting it more succinctly: 'specific evolutionary progress is inversely related to general evolutionary potential.'[117]

Service's examples partly coincide with Romein's. In the same way as H. G. Wells attributed the Chinese backwardness to a script which initially could be viewed as the most advanced in its time, Service explains that phonetic spelling could not be realized in Egypt precisely because of the over-elaboration of the cumbersome hieroglyphic system, whereas the East Mediterranean peoples 'had *no writing at all* and ... could, therefore, make a fresh start'.[118] Further illustrations of the 'law', in Service's study, concern the shifting of cultural centres in Meso-American early history and in the Mediterranean ancient past. Like Romein, Service also comments on the unequal rate of modern industrial development in different countries. The most interesting illustrations in Service's study, however, refer to China, which country was hardly touched upon in Romein's study.

Earlier in the volume, Sahlins had ventured a new approach to the issue of transition from feudalism towards capitalism, thus shedding an illuminating light on the problem with which both Marxist unilinear evolutionists, and multilinear evolutionists such as Wittfogel, have been grappling.[119] In Sahlins's view, feudalism had preceded capitalism, not because it was the highest developed societal type of its period, but because feudalism is only a specific, backward form of this order of civilization, an underdeveloped form that happened to have greater evolutionary potential than the others and historically gave rise to a new level of achievement: '... it represents a lower level of general development than the civilizations of China, Ancient Egypt or Mesopotamia, although it arose later than these civilizations and happened to lead to a form still higher than any of them'.

Sahlins, therefore, disagrees both with the Marxists who extended the concept of feudalism to the Chinese case, and with Wittfogel who practically restricts the term 'feudalism' to the cases of Western Europe and Japan but considers it a higher form of development than the 'oriental despotisms'. Sahlins and his associates only agree with Wittfogel inasmuch as they point out the specific difficulties for a country like China in achieving modern development, and the impossibility of her attaining it along the capitalist road.

At the end of his study[120] Service returns to this problem, making a specific comparison between the Japanese and the Chinese case:

Japan, once a poor cultural relative of China, moved into the modern industrial stage of coal and oil energy and became dominant in the Far East. Partly, this could occur because of its backwardness and 'newness' as opposed to the great inertia of the ancient, highly adapted and specialized agricultural civilization of China.

Service does not repeat that Japan owed both its backwardness and its evolutionary potential to its feudalism, but this is evidently what he had in mind.

But at present the situation is reversed:

... now, perhaps paradoxically from the point of view of Japan, China has greater potential for moving into the new and radically different industrial stage to be based on the electronic storage and transmission of such new sources of power as atomic and direct solar energy. China is not nearly so adapted as Japan to the present and soon-to-be-outmoded industrial complex of coal and oil energy.

He adds:

It is Marxian justice, perhaps even poetic justice, that because of her 'premature revolution' Russia is already so committed to the present form of industry that she might be eclipsed by a still newer industrial region.

In this connection Service also quotes an interesting comment by Mao Tse-tung on China being like 'a sheet of blank paper'. Mao has succinctly expressed the advantages of backwardness in the following words:

This may seem to be a bad thing, whereas in reality it is a good one ... Nothing is written on a sheet of paper which is still blank, but it lends itself admirably to receive the latest and most beautiful words and the latest and most beautiful pictures.

Even in matters of minor importance, says Service, China can profit from her initial backwardness. Whereas China was outdone, in the field of script, by newcomers introducing phonetic spelling, at present China could lead the way in introducing 'phonemic spelling' – to fill Mao's 'blank sheet of paper'!

Are these forecasts of a true Chinese 'great leap forward' only expressions of wishful thinking? Or are they based on some concrete indications in the present situation? Service and his associates were, at the time of their writing, not yet able to measure China's achievements in the field of nuclear explosions, the launching of satellites, and the synthesis of insulin. But Service was able to demonstrate that at the present epoch

the new areas cannot industrialize with small beginnings, as did the West, and then proceed through the original stages of growth, creating capital in the process. They will begin with the latest and most advanced of the known technologies and attempt to create the complete industrial complex at once, skipping whole epochs of our development. This requires a huge capital investment. The economy, therefore, must be socialistic; the government rather than private persons provides most of the capital by necessity.

Moreover, the new industrial beginnings had to be developed 'in the face of challenge and opposition from outside powers'.

Thus far the argument in favour of a revolutionary overturn, a socialist building up, and a despotic government, was valid for Russia as well as for China and contained no more than Romein's analysis of the Soviet experiment. But China may be able to outdo the earlier industrial giants not only because of her huge reservoir of man-power able to provide the required investment capital by excessively hard work, but still more because of her apparent determination to transform her economic system at all costs, as she indeed must.[121]

Service's argument, therefore, confirms Romein's view that higher evolutionary stages are bound 'to appear in new areas in the form of revolution'.[122] He could also have used the term 'law of revolutionary potential'.[123]

iii. *Reappraisal of Romein's and Service's Theories*

It is now possible to reconsider once more the time differential in social evolution. Although it is not yet feasible, with our present knowledge, to forecast the speed at which an evolutionary process will proceed, we are now able to account, to a certain extent, for the manifold retardations and accelerations in social evolution. The key to understanding the retardations is the issue of specific adaptive evolution as elaborated by Sahlins and his associates. In due course, this type of evolution may produce stagnation, termed involution by Clifford Geertz.

Where involution has taken place, there will be a moment when a breaking-point is reached. The relative stagnation and backwardness associated with involutional processes will eventually result in a crisis expressing itself in serious dissatisfaction and restiveness among significant sections of the population. As soon as the dead end produced by over-specialization is reached, only a forceful and cataclysmic breakthrough can produce a reversal of the involutionary trends. Previous retardation thus produces acceleration in the further course of evolution. We could deduce from this that revolution is most likely to become the obvious way out. There remain, however, a few basic questions.

How far does the law, developed by Romein and Service with a different nomenclature, extend? If it is a real law, any retardation would result in an ulterior acceleration or, to use the common term, revolution. Does this hypothesis conform with historical reality as we know it?

It is hard to give a definite reply, precisely because the time factor is so difficult to handle in a scientific way. It is always possible to argue that, if in a given society where involutional trends are operative a revolutionary breakthrough has not yet occurred, this is due to the fact that the situation is not yet ripe and that consequently the revolution will follow in due course. But such an argument would be tautologous. Our criterion of whether a situation can be identified as involutionary in such a way as to produce the privilege of backwardness, would only be answered by the real occurrence of a subsequent revolution! There were in the past many backward societies, and there are still quite a number of them where no revolutionary change giving expression to the privilege of backwardness has occurred. It would be rash to assume that all of them are going to profit from this privilege – although the proceeding emancipation of mankind may, in the long run, refute the sceptics of today.

Moreover, the case of the Russian revolution makes clear that, even if a phase in the evolutionary sequence can be skipped over, certain important elements of the traditional structure remain operative for a lengthy period and affect the further course of social development. What Trotsky called 'the law of combined development' no doubt did function, though Trotsky probably seriously overrated its importance. However, this problem of persistent elements borrowed from an earlier phase has to be thoroughly studied along with the phenomenon of skipping phases.

On the other hand, the numerous illustrations produced by Romein and Sahlins to demonstrate 'the law of the retarding lead', and the many more examples with which they could be supplemented, do not prove that a society that initiated the earlier progress could *never* make the next step. In the following section we shall revert to the manifold cases where an initial advantage was kept for a considerable time. Since it is not yet possible to measure exactly the rate of change and to predict exactly the future course, I would prefer not to speak of a law of evolutionary potential but rather of a trend, the strength and the universal validity of which has still to be thoroughly investigated. What Romein and Service did prove is that quite often it is easier for a less advanced social structure to respond to the challenge of entering new avenues. Making a law out of this trend is to deny the possibility that, to a certain extent, the actual response to such a challenge depends upon more or less voluntary, rational, human decisions. Not only nineteenth-century unilinear evolutionism but also nineteenth-century rigid determinism is a thing of the past. Many of Marx's followers still viewed evolution, as they conceived it, as fully determined by inescapable laws. They had, in some way, to solve the paradox that revolutionary change was essentially predetermined, yet had to be brought about by human beings. In the epilogue of the present book I hope to substantiate my view that the issue of determinism is no more than an imaginary one, and that the power of man, within certain bounds to determine his destiny, cannot be denied on rational, scientific grounds. Perhaps Romein realized this. He used the term *law* only twice in his article and both times he put the word between quotation marks. Elsewhere he used the term hypothesis.

Instead of formulating quasi-scientific laws suggesting, by the use of the term evolutionary potential (which recalls the distinction between potential and kinetic energy in physics), a greater precision than is justified by the available evidence, I would prefer to elaborate and test a series of more or less concrete hypotheses, in order to find out under *what* conditions the trend of the retarding lead and the privilege of backwardness is operative. This is one of the tasks I have set myself in the present study.

Moreover, Romein did not give full weight to the fact that it is never the most backward society which makes the leap forward, and therefore it is not enough merely to stress 'backwardness'. The specific characteristics of a society earmarked for the next evolutionary step should be indicated.[124] Service was more cautious in his formulation by restricting the operation of his law to those societies which had already attained a definite evolutionary stage: 'The more specialized and adapted a form *in a given evolutionary stage*, the smaller is its potential for passing to the next stage.'[125] However, he does not define the concept of 'stage' and hence leaves in the dark the query as to what extent societies, having attained different levels (like imperial China and feudal Japan), could be considered as belonging to the same 'evolutionary stage'.

Geertz's concept of involution may give a clue towards defining the conditions for an operation of the law, but it still lacks the precision needed to enable us to make a valid forecast. The illustrations mentioned by Romein and Service mostly concern cases in which the leapfrog belongs to the past. A true criterion for a scientific law remains, however, the forecast that is confirmed by actual developments. Without forecasts, corroborated by facts, it seems impossible to establish a valid interpretation of the world and of human society – or to attempt to change the world.

As things stand, the precision of 'the law of evolutionary potential' or, to use Romein's term, 'the law of the retarding lead', is hardly greater than that of the biblical saying: *And the last shall be the first.*

iv. Modernization and the Dialectics of Progress

Eisenstadt's analysis of the modernization process, which should be reckoned as one of the most elaborate, shows, at least superficially, a certain congruency with Romein's hypothesis of the retarding lead.[126] However, there are also some glaring discrepancies between the two approaches. It seems useful to compare these two, in order to test the appropriateness of the dialectical perspective, expounded in the foregoing, for a deeper understanding of how the world actually moves towards modernity.

Eisenstadt's approach is certainly not unilinear in the normal sense. He fully realizes that the modernization process tends to develop more rapidly among the newcomer nations than among the nations which started to industrialize as early as the nineteenth century. The author has adopted from Gerschenkron his series of propositions regarding the correlation between a given country's degree of economic backwardness on the eve of its industrialization and the course of the latter. I have selected the following ones: the more backward a country's economy, the more likely was its industrialization to start as a sudden great spurt proceeding at a relatively high rate of growth of manufacturing output; the more pronounced the stress in its industrialization on bigness of both plant and enterprise, the more pronounced the coerciveness, and the heavier the pressure upon the levels of consumption of the population.[127]

Eisenstadt extends these propositions, which in Gerschenkron's thesis applied to the economic field only, to all major institutional spheres, including political structure, thus adopting a differential rate of growth as a matter of principle.

Nevertheless, there remains a basic difference between his view and Romein's 'dialectics of progress'. Eisenstadt does not mention

the possibility of the backward society overtaking the industrialized states by adopting drastic measures which the latter are
unwilling to introduce. He views the race between old-timers and
newcomers in terms of catching up only – the 'sudden great spurt'
being necessary to make up for the initial disadvantage. Moreover,
in Eisenstadt's theory, the chances that the sudden spurt will be
successful are rather slight. The initial backwardness remains in
his analysis a serious disadvantage throughout the modernization
process. The odds are that the development will be hampered by
serious tensions or eruptions, and even breakdowns are far from
unlikely.

In my view, Eisenstadt's analysis shows several fundamental
weaknesses. In pointing them out, I hope at the same time to provide a modest contribution to the modernization theory on the
basis of the evolutionary perspective outlined above.

It strikes one as an omission that, in his discussion of the situation among the newcomers, Eisenstadt only deals with the intrinsic factors within each society as being accountable for the
specific course modernization has taken in each separate case. It
apparently did not occur to him that since these non-Western
countries started, all of them, their modernization process in a
definite period of world history, the main factor responsible for a
deviating course might be looked for in the overall world situation. Consequently I should like to suggest that, whereas a gradual industrialization process through the efforts of private
entrepreneurs still remained within the realm of possibilities
throughout the nineteenth century, this possibility may have been
effectively blocked from the onset of this century by the dominant
position of huge world concerns.[128] Eisenstadt, in his otherwise
judicious study, did not touch upon the impact of these external
factors.

It was this overall historical situation which, in my view, called
for new, unorthodox measures to promote modernization. Gerschenkron's correlations between the rate of backwardness and the
rate and type of industrial development are, to some extent, correct.[129] The specific role played by the state in the more backward
society, and the priorities defined by the state are not, however,

simply functions of the initial backwardness; more often than not they are necessitated by external factors operating at the time when the backward society attempts to join the race.

The required extra effort, however, puts an additional strain upon the existing social structure and political system. I agree with Eisenstadt that in the earlier industrializing societies the politically more articulate claims of the broad masses only made themselves felt at a later development stage. An analysis of the different emancipation movements shows that the spread of the boons of progress to broader layers of the population is one of the main aspects of emancipation. Eisenstadt is, however, right when he maintains that, whereas in the earlier industrial nations far-reaching political and social demands were generally not put forward by broader layers of the population until the society had achieved a certain maturity in the economic and educational field, in the new states the broad masses, having become acquainted with the cheap products of Western industry and with foreign ideas spread through mass communication channels, are forwarding claims on the central political institutions at an earlier moment in the modernization process. Again, it is the general world situation which affects the modernization sequence in the non-Western world (excluding Japan that had an earlier start). The mass communication systems may have acquainted people in the farthest outposts of the world with the Russian, Chinese and Cuban revolutions, and with all the turmoil that these events produced in other places of the world, and thus account for a stronger political consciousness among industrial workers and among the peasantry. Whereas in the Western world the native bourgeoisie had plenty of time to consolidate its position after having wrested power from the *ancien régime* aristocrats, the Westernizing and modernizing elites of the new states feel much less secure because they are confronted, soon after their accession to power or even earlier, not only with the competition and power of foreign capitalism, but with an upsurge of the proletarianized mass. Accordingly, the bourgeoisie reacts differently, as Wagley says about Brazil:

The middle class is, in a sense, the most conservative social segment of their society. Because they are insecure in their position, they make a point of preserving most of the old Latin American values and traditional patterns of behavior.[130]

The difference between Eisenstadt's and my appreciation of this situation appears to be that his evaluation of the impact of the factor of growing popular demands, 'the revolution of demands' as it is sometimes called, is largely negative, whereas in my more dialectical perspective this seething mass unrest may be the source of a more successful type of modernization.

In the old-timer societies the proletarian emancipation movements were also operative and functioned as a challenge to the existing political system and social institutions. Though Eisenstadt views the resulting conflicts and disturbances as forms of social disorganization, one still gathers the impression from his analysis that he admits the possibility that higher forms of integration may have been forthcoming from these expressions of protest.

In the case of the newcomers, however, he does not appear to expect a positive contribution to the modernization process from the mass unrest prevalent in those areas. Eisenstadt places too much stress on adaptation and integration as the main goals of social progress. He evidently did not realize that the mass protest movements and the eruptions provoked by these may be a reaction to a situation in which adaptation to and integration with the existing physical environment have assumed such forms that the ensuing situation is one of stagnation or even involution, to use Geertz's terminology again. In such cases, the broad protest movements may bring about precisely the type of modernization which is suitable for a given geographical region in a specific historical period.

Eisenstadt does not believe that serious social conflicts or bad economic conditions in certain cases necessitate a revolutionary solution. 'Conflicts or economic problems of what initially seemed alarming magnitudes probably did exist, and have been resolved, even if only partially, in other modern or modernizing countries.'[131] But the author does not show that these solutions or part-solutions were still found during the historical period with which we are concerned here: in the twentieth century, at the height of capitalist and imperialist power, and in the face of fierce competition from huge international, commercial and industrial concerns.

Gerschenkron, therefore, errs in attributing the phenomenon of an accelerated rate of development to some intrinsic automatism. Professor Witold Kula has demonstrated that in Poland a spurt towards a 'take-off' has broken down three times throughout its economic history.[132] In so doing, he has basically refuted Rostow's all too rigid development scheme with its facile attempt at quantification of different stages of growth. Backwardness tends to present a challenge, which may evoke the right response. But this response cannot be disconnected from drastic changes within the political system.

As I pointed out earlier, the dialectics of progress do not constitute something like a law, as Service seems to claim when he formulates 'the law of evolutionary potential'. Eisenstadt also rightly insists that there is no automatism in the modernization process and that every historical choice is not preordained and may to no small extent be influenced by accident and vicissitudes.[133] My quarrel with him is only where he underestimates the significance of mass-based political upsurges in bringing about the right response. A revolutionary upsurge, more in particular of the impoverished peasantry, may be needed in order to bring to power a type of government that will be able to tackle the huge task of resisting these strong foreign powers, and of initiating a process of rapid economic growth.

Whereas he, in this respect, underrates the importance of the political factor, he seems to overrate the significance of the political element when discussing the phenomenon of the breakdown of modernization in countries such as Indonesia or Burma. Kula's discussion of the Polish case raises the question of whether breakdowns in the economic field are not much more frequent, even in the history of the Western world, than one could deduce from Eisenstadt's study. Retrospectively, most countries of Western Europe seem to have undergone a process of continuous economic growth. But several of them may have experienced periods of stagnation and even of relapse, which sometimes even exceeded in duration the periods of breakdown in the present-day new states. Not all the early new nations were, from the beginning, as successful as Lipset claims that the United States was in overcoming initial difficulties like those with which the new nations of today are grappling.[134] Viewed in this long-run perspective, the manifold breakdowns in the present-day transitional societies of Asia, Africa and Latin America may possibly be viewed with less alarm than Eisenstadt's analysis would seem to justify.

No more than with his claim of an historical continuity of the Western modernization process, could I agree with Eisenstadt's picture of the present trend as one of sustained growth. I do not deny that the theory of discontinuous evolution, as elaborated by Romein and Service, should be supplemented with an elaboration of those cases in which an initial advantage could be kept for a comparatively lengthy period. It is quite possible that the myth of continuous, gradual progress in England could be substantiated to a large extent by critical historical analysis. The relative flexibility of British political institutions may serve as a partial explanation of this protracted receptivity to innovation.

Yet I doubt whether Eisenstadt has not grossly overstated the case for sustained growth. The concept seems to indicate a certain automatism attained after the take-off has occurred – and I tend seriously to question whether such a guaranteed, automatic progression has ever been achieved in human history. It sounds, for example, slightly ethnocentric and self-contented to view our own West European societies as still representing the summit of modernity in a situation where our relative technological backwardness, in comparison with the USA and the USSR, becomes more and more palpable.

Many European politicians have recently warned that Western Europe is no longer able, if only for financial reasons, to keep up with technological advance in the United States and that its arrears increase with time. The same point has been pungently made by Servan-Schreiber.[135] The dependence of Western Europe on American patents and know-how, especially in the fields of advanced electronics and nuclear technology, is developing into a new kind of colonial relationship. It is not essential whether growth is, for the time being, sustained or not; it is the comparative rate of growth that matters in the long run.

A better insight into the 'dialectics of progress' might teach us a greater modesty – and prevent us from stepping in the pitfall of the Manchu emperor Chi'en Lung, who, in 1793, claimed in self-satisfaction that China could expect nothing from foreign barbarians. Eisenstadt's ideal type of self-sustained growth gives the impression, despite his attempt to include the Soviet Union among the countries to which he applies the concept, that he is arguing from a preponderantly Western societal model. The Western type of modernization is, to him, the normal and regular, homogeneous one. His terminology reveals a distinct bias in favour of the Western type of development, which he views as a more harmonious one than other patterns which he equally includes within the modernization concept. His stress upon adaptation and integration as basic requirements for sustained growth,[136] his view of political eruptions as symptoms of unsuccessful adaptation, as external manifestations that the more normal, smooth road towards modernity has been blocked,[137] betray a preference for the type of gradualism evidenced in the Western model of growth.

Apparently, he does not realize that violent eruptions represent a different, but equally elementary, and under certain circumstances, inevitable, type of modernization – necessitated by a too high degree of adaptation, amounting to stagnation or even involution, and of integration which is nothing more than an underdevelopment equilibrium.[138] Eisenstadt's model should be supplemented with the discontinuous type of development made necessary by a different world situation and a different array of social and political forces.

v. Modernity and After

Is there any possibility of predicting the future course modernization will take?

First of all, it seems prudent not to count upon an automatically continuing sustained growth in the future – lest growth should recede in the absence of sustained effort. On the other hand, we should not consider the retarding lead as an inescapable fatality, foreboding a future recession as compared with a group of rapidly spurting newcomers. We should simply take into account the possibility that breakdowns, perhaps in the shape of fierce political reaction, will occur in societies which, up to that point, were apparently showing sustained growth. If the leaders of such societies should lack the amount of empathy (which, according to Lerner and Eisenstadt, is a characteristic of modernity!) required to understand why other societies had to follow a different route to modernity, their type of modernism might be turned into a new kind of traditionalism! In that case, the retarding lead might exert its full impact. But challenges are there to be answered, and backsliding may be countered by a new, more or less revolutionary upsurge.

To predict the shape of new types of modernity would seem too rash an undertaking. Kenneth Boulding[139] suggests that the period of civilization, which in his definition implies a moderate level of technology, urban dominance over the countryside, great differences in wealth and power, and the prevalence of war, is nearing its end and is bound to be superseded by a period of post-civilization on a much higher level of technology. The contours of such a society are already discernible in an embryonic form in some of the most industrially developed societies. But, in his opinion, this transition into a new period of post-civilization will require in many respects a complete reversal of existing trends in production and political attitudes, if we want to escape from great dangers, including the complete annihilation of man.

Again, Boulding rightly does not view the transition from civilization to post-civilization as a matter of sustained growth, but as 'nothing short of a major revolution in the human condition'.

Revolution appears to be a basic element in the process of human evolution. For the present world it is even truer than for earlier times that basically 'development does not proceed along an evolutionary, but along a revolutionary road'.[140]

4
Towards a Dynamic Model of Society

Admittedly conflict is without doubt aimed at upsetting the existing order, but in our opinion, it is directed just as much towards the establishment of a new order, however temporary that may be ... The commonest cause of conflict seems to be the necessity of finding a new form of society. When the existing order is attacked in the conflict, that is not because it is an order but because it is no longer regarded as legitimate by the protesting party.

J. M. G. THURLINGS

i. Wanted: A Sociology of a World on the Move

In the earlier chapters, I have attempted to restore the concept of evolution to its old glory. However, this is not nearly enough if we want to elaborate a new concept of society sufficiently dynamic to encompass both evolution and revolution as phenomena inherent in the social process. What I shall attempt to do in the present chapter is to sketch a short outline for such a conceptual model, as a kind of interlude before we finally shift our attention to the problems of revolutionary change. The reason for inserting this interlude is that, in order to understand revolutions as cataclysmic eruptions of the social and political order, we will have to view them in the right perspective, as logical sequels to the phenomenon of periodic acceleration, typical of most evolutionary processes. That is to say, we will have to develop a conceptual framework in which the process of emancipation, as a decisive force both in evolution and revolution, has to be incorporated from the outset as a basic element, instead of being viewed as a force alien to the social reality with which sociologists are concerned. This should lead us to a basic reappraisal of sociological theory as it stands.

Implicit in most branches of sociological theory is an assumption of a state of equilibrium as typical of any society. Though many sociologists and cultural anthropologists are certainly aware that, in fact, the assumption is only partially valid, they hold the opinion that a sociological theory could only be built on a state of equilibrium as a hypothetical basis.

In this chapter an attempt will be made to demonstrate that there is an alternative possibility, and that it is by no means impossible, in the field of social sciences, to start from a much more dynamic conceptual model.

In the earlier chapters, I attempted to elaborate a more dynamic view of social change than would correspond with an approach to society in strictly structural and functional terms. A purely structural societal model does not leave room for structural change as an integral part of the anticipated flow of events; and if a process of social change is being viewed only as a 'function' of the prevalent structure, one automatically excludes from one's perspective processes directed at change of the system as such – or discards them as disfunctional or anomic. If human evolution, as we have tried to establish, is a general, though not unambiguous, trend in human history, our societal model, first of all, should be constructed in such a manner as to allow for structural shifts. But at the same time, our model should take account of the irregular and dialectical course which social evolution actually follows.

If social, as opposed to biological, evolution generally implies a permanent trend towards emancipation, this means that established status systems are likely, as a reaction, to provoke in the long run a contrary trend either towards increasing equality, or even towards a reversal of the existing hierarchial order. In this emancipation process, revolution generally occurs as a last resort. It mostly erupts when other avenues are blocked, either through lack of receptivity among those in power to the urge for emancipation among certain segments of society, or because of the prevalence, within society, of a kind of immobility of dominant traditions or institutions, which may assume, in more extreme cases, the character of involution.

But although revolution, as such, mostly has the character of an action of despair only, it does not occur without premonitions which sometimes have a long history. It is a purpose of the present chapter to attempt to develop a societal model in which the elements which may become the harbingers of future revolution are built in from the outset.

It is gradually being recognized that sociology as it stands is not capable of predicting outbursts which may threaten the existing structure of society. The structural and functional approach is too static to be able to take account of the more dynamic aspects of social life. Yet, forecasting future developments appears to be a keystone for an achievement of acknowledged status for sociology as a science. If sociology could not be used, at least within certain limits, in predicting future events, sociology as a science would make a poor showing. Naturally, the predictions need not be long-term ones, encompassing the future trends of society as a whole; short-term or middle-range predictions can be at least as useful. But however this may be, somehow the sociologist is rightly expected to foresee more than plain common sense, without specialized training, would allow. Otherwise, sociology would soon be unmasked as a jargon concealing ignorance.

The lack of predicting power has been abundantly proved during the serious student riots and concomitant labour strikes in France, in May 1968. Raymond Aron has argued in Le Figaro (4 June 1968) that nobody – and he himself no more than the authorities – had been able to foresee what would happen. His assertion would seem to imply that sociology as it stood had proved itself fully incapable of predicting such a course of events. His incrimination is not completely justified. At least one French sociologist, Alain Touraine, foretold in early March the coming social unrest among students, though he had not predicted the spread of the unrest to other layers of French society, including industrial labour.[141] But this does not absolve sociology as such. At most it proves that there may be some schools of sociological thinking that are more aware of what moves society than others. But even in the case of Alain Touraine, it may be doubted whether his relative foresight was due to his training as a sociologist or to his individual intellectual qualities. The failure of sociology as a discipline cannot be exculpated by the presence of one or two individual scholars who have developed a sufficiently keen sensitivity to underground stirrings to be able to forecast a near-revolutionary development more or less accurately.

If sociology as a science is to prove itself a viable tool for assessing what moves human beings in a society, it has to develop techniques to gauge future events that can be used by any qualified and sufficiently sensitive expert.

ii. *Shortcomings of Structuralism: Reification of Society*

In the following discussion I shall attempt to demonstrate that the structural approach prevalent in sociology could never fully account for the rifts and fissures which are present in any society, though they remain in many cases hidden beneath the surface. Harmony and acceptance of the prevalent social and political order is only one side of the story.

I shall try to elaborate the concept of counterpoint as a basic complement to any hierarchical social order, and at the same time a source of social dynamics that give rise to the process of evolutionary and, in more extreme cases, revolutionary emancipation.

First of all, I would like to point out that such a departure from the usual societal model prevalent in contemporary sociology originates from a different view of norms and values as determinants of social reality.

Social structure is generally viewed, in modern sociology, as a construct basically corresponding to social reality. It is deemed to be objectively present in the social body, though not necessarily experienced as such in the mind of those who make up part of a given society. To quote Stoodley: 'Social structure is as objective as a church, a bank, or a school.'[142] Discovery of the basic structural elements of a society is considered to be the task pre-eminently incumbent upon the sociologist.

Constructs such as the status system, the opposition between centre and periphery, the division of society into primary and secondary contact groups, and the composition of social networks that facilitate the flow of decisions and information, are generally regarded as objectively valid elements of the social texture. They are taken for social realities objectively present even if the participants in social life are not fully aware of them. It is not sufficiently realized that any assumed order of a society, hierarchical or not, is dependent upon conscious or unconscious acceptance by those who form part of a society. Such an acceptance can never be given *a priori*. It is determined by psychological factors expressing themselves in norms and values.

In contemporary sociology norms and values certainly occupy a significant place. They are viewed as the determinants of culture. But structure and culture are considered, by most modern sociologists, as more or less distinct entities. No doubt they recognize a certain interrelationship between the two sub-systems, the social and the cultural one. For example, Talcott Parsons holds that 'to survive and develop, the social community must maintain the integrity of a common cultural orientation, broadly (though not necessarily uniformly or unanimously) shared by its membership, as the basis of its social identity'.[143] He also admits that 'cultural value patterns provide the most direct link between the social and cultural systems in legitimizing the normative order of society'.[144]

This insight does not prevent Parsons, however, from viewing the social system, once the legitimization has been demonstrated, as an integrated, hierarchical structure, characterized by a consistent distribution of positions and roles. Thus, in his view, it is the social system that provides the basic structural skeleton to any collectivity. The description of the primitive society of aboriginal Australia by Parsons is wholly conceived in structural terms.[145]

There are other authors who are even more explicit than Parsons in positing the social system as an independent entity that exists and functions. Though they view the social system as more or less related to a specific culture, to a distinct set of values and norms, they still hypothesize it as something real and present in the world.

Reification of social structure started with Durkheim. Being a true positivist,[146] he claimed as early as 1895 that social phenomena were things and should be treated as such.[147] He viewed social structures, such as clans, as realities, and developed the view that the more complicated social structures were due to a more elaborate division of labour.[148]

This type of reification is also clearly demonstrable among British social anthropologists who have continued Durkheim's legacy. In his posthumously published chapter on social structure Radcliffe-Brown does not show any awareness of the limitations of the structural approach. He writes:

Thus in looking for the structural features of social life we look first for the existence of social groups of all kinds, and examine also the internal structure of those groups that we find. But besides the arrangement of persons into groups and within those groups we find also an arrangment into social classes and categories.[149]

And Nadel, too, though treating the subject of social structure and of its relationship to subjective images present in the mind of those who live within that structure in a much more sophisticated manner, insists that institutions really exist.[150]

In the United States reification of social structure is also rife among both sociologists and anthropologists. Linton's discussion of status and role does not evidence any doubt about the reality of the structural phenomena described.[151]

iii. Max Weber's Criticism of Reification: The Concept of Kollektivgebilde*

It is important to note that Max Weber, who is still revered as one of the founding fathers of modern sociology, has never taken any part in this reification. On the contrary, he has always seriously warned against *falschen Begriffsrealismus* (false conceptual realism).[152] He never used the term structure, but preferred to speak of *Gebilde*. Therefore it is surprising that in the new *Encyclopaedia of the Social Sciences* Weber's views are more than once mentioned as having paved the way for structural analysis.[153]

In Weber's view, all kinds of social institutions – including the family, the church, the state – do not exist except inasmuch as those concerned subjectively accept their uniting function.[154] The

* *Kollektivgebilde*: collective constructs.

crucial concept is a type of social action: *Vergesellschaftung* (socialization). This process makes possible a creation of continuous (*perennierende*) *Gebilde*. Again, however, authority within these units is ultimately dependent upon acceptance by those subjected to it.[155]

According to Weber these collectivities (*Kollektivgebilde*), derived from everyday speech or legal terminology, are nothing but *images* in the minds of real people. As such, however, they may have an immense influence as orientation concepts for human action.[156]

In Weber's view, the only thing that is real about these *soziale Gebilde* can be expressed in terms of the chance that certain kinds of social action will or will not take place. 'This one has always to keep in mind, in order to avoid a "substantial" interpretation of these concepts.'[157]

This warning has not been sufficiently heeded by modern sociology. Why was Weber so averse to viewing collectivities as real?

First of all, we have to take into account Weber's affiliations with philosophers from the neo-Kantian Heidelberg school. Heinrich Rickert, who was a personal friend of Weber's,[158] considered history to be an individualizing science, in contrast with the natural sciences. In his view any attempt at formulating general laws would be out of place in the social sciences: they were ideographic, not nomothetic.

Weber was ambivalent towards this philosophical view. On the one hand, Rickert's standpoint, in which he differentiated between cultural and natural sciences, appealed to Weber.[159] On the other hand, he felt compelled, throughout his sociological studies, to utilize general categories which, besides their individualizing historical aspect, also inexorably pointed towards the prevalence of all kinds of regularities in the social processes. The German philosopher, Helmuth Plessner, who had known both of them personally, in his address to the Nederlandse Sociologische Vereniging, on the occasion of Weber's centenary (1964), recalled how Weber was continuously under fire from Rickert's annoyed criticism: '*Da fängt der Kerl schon wieder an zu generalisieren!*' ('The fellow is starting to generalize all over again!')

In his article for the *Encyclopaedia*, Bendix seems to overstress the distance between Weber's views and those of the historicist school.[160] A recognition of the essentially historical element in all social processes ('*der ewig fortschreitende Fluss der Kultur*' ['the eternally advancing stream of culture']) was certainly instrumental in his adoption of general categories as 'ideal-types' serving the conceptualization by the scholar rather than a description of reality.[161] And it is again the individualizing character of sociology, as understood by Weber, that accounts for his negation of '*soziale Kollektivgebilde*' as realities. At the same time, this negation amounted to a kind of 'debunking' (*Entzauberung historischer Gebilde*).[162] According to Marianne Weber, in his quest for truth, Max had consistently '*Magie van seinem Pfad entfernt*' (swept myth from his intellectual path).

On the other hand, Bendix and others[163] attribute Weber's rejection of a structural interpretation of collectivities to his 'nominalist position in social science'. Here they are right only to a certain extent. Surely, Weber was still under the impact of the 'nominalist view of individual action as the basic datum of sociological inquiry', which was essentially a typical *Weltanschauung* from the nineteenth century. What is being overlooked is that Weber's rejection of social structure may have had deeper roots than an individualistic philosophy. Even though the neo-Kantian view of history as a purely individualizing science will hardly find supporters any more, and although Weber's nominalist reduction of social phenomena to purely individual actions, with the concomitant introduction of the concept of chance, would equally appear highly debatable to a scholar living in the second half of the twentieth century – yet, there may still have been a profound wisdom behind Weber's criticism of a reification of social structures.

His macro-sociological approach, combined with his immense knowledge of human history, made him more sensitive to the relativity and transience of social institutions than many of those sociologists who are mainly concerned with the problems of their own present-day society. He was aware that *Kollektivgebilde* pretending to be perennial could easily vanish into nothingness once the people concerned withdrew the legitimization from the prevailing power structure.

Reification of social phenomena may serve the interests of those in power; it adds a quality of endurance to the present distribution of positions and roles. Weber was too truthful to take the appearance of abstract validity for the *Kollektivgebilde* at face value. Through his more relativistic and subjectivistic interpretation he contributed to the *Entzauberung* (demystification) of authority, whether based on a rational legal system of or charisma.[164]

It is understandable that in times of relative stability, sociologists, confronted with the limited pragmatic problems of their society, could do their work in a satisfactory way, starting from a purely structural approach. Weber's relativism and subjectivism would have been felt as a hindrance in making a sociologist's concepts operational in the social field at hand.

However, at a time when we are experiencing the impact of macro-sociological and historical processes as a challenge to the prevalent static view of society, Weber's psychic relativism with regard to social structures may become highly relevant again. It is very possible that the existing, still rather meagre, amount of precision in sociological research has been obtained at the expense of sacrificing an access to the most significant aspects of social life, and more particularly of social change. We should inquire whether our tools of field research could be appreciably refined, not by throwing away the gains acquired by steady structural analysis, but by adding a diachronic factor that may open our eyes to rifts and fissures even in the apparently calm waters of a stable society.

iv. The Integrationist Model of Society

It is not to be denied that an analysis in structural terms is an indispensable tool for our understanding of societies. On the other hand, the acknowledgement of this fact should not obscure our insight into the relative and subjective quality of each interpretation of social life in structural categories. Social structure can be no more permanent than the social consciousness deriving from a more or less explicit system of values that is at the base of a given structural principle.

Let us take social stratification as an example.

The Yankee City study by Lloyd Warner and his associates was the first attempt to analyse a modern society in its totality in terms of social class structure.[165] As we know Warner was inspired, in his structural approach, by his own study of primitive societies that were, at the time, also analysed in largely structural terms by leading British anthropologists such as Radcliffe-Brown and Bronislaw Malinowski. His theoretical and methodological inspiration was mainly drawn from Émile Durkheim.[166]

The aspect that concerns us here is that social anthropologists and sociologists, in their structural approach, both assumed without further questioning that the structural elements which they discovered corresponded with definite segments of social reality. In Warner's view a social class, or a clique, is not a construct of the human mind, useful as a tool to make highly intricate social relationships approximately understandable, but part of the social fabric, equally real as a molecule or an atom and ready to be discovered by an experienced and perceptive social scientist. In his detection of the concealed structural elements the social scientist has to amass a huge amount of factual information, through interviews or participant observations, of the way people behave or speak among themselves. All these pieces of factual information are, in his view, mere symbols of structural principles discernible underneath the surface. In the same way, social anthropologists are accustomed to considering the basic structural elements of a primitive society, such as clans, phratries or moieties, as social realities, and not as more or less adequate constructs of a rather fluid and intricate composite of social relationships, partly derived from the image of social reality in the mind of those participating in it.

I shall revert to the problem of the validity of the structural approach to primitive societies further on. First, I will have to show the inadequacy of this approach in doing justice to social reality in modern society.

Some of the critics of Lloyd Warner's basic approach have taken

issue with his functionalist interpretation of social reality, which
led him to construct a rather too integrated image of the communities he studied.[167] The selection of Yankee City as a study
object was based on the assumption that this community 'was a
"working whole" in which each part had definite functions which
had to be performed, or substitutes acquired, if the whole society
were to maintain itself.'[168] This type of functionalism, which pic-
tured societies as smoothly running and well-integrated entities,
was again derived from Durkheim, via Malinowski and Radcliffe-
Brown. In Durkheim's theory, as we have seen, modern societies
were much more complex than primitive ones, owing to a far-
reaching division of labour. Though there had been a transformation of the prevalent solidarity from a mechanical into an organic
one, integration as such had been preserved – except in cases
where phenomena such as anomie and the occurrence of suicide
were indications of a pathological state of affairs.

One could not deny that Durkheim's functionalism fulfilled a
much appreciated function in the United States during the
thirties. Since the middle of the nineteenth century the spectre of
communism had been haunting European industrial society as a
well-integrated whole. Was it not the conservative British politician Disraeli who maintained that each country was divided into
two nations: the rich and the poor? In Marxist theory, the division had been still more accentuated by the concept of basic class
antagonism. The Marxist image of society had crystallized into a
model in which not integration but conflict prevailed. There is,
according to this view, no hierarchy except one imposed by force,
and no integration except that brought about on a class basis, by
fostering class consciousness.

In the United States this Marxist view had never been widespread. For the white immigrants and their descendants there had
always been ample opportunities to make good in society – at least
if one compared their prospects with the country of origin in
Europe. According to a current stereotype American society was,
unlike Europe, not torn by class distinctions. 'Everyone was
middle class,'[169] or could aspire to enter it.

This prevalent sphere of optimism was badly shaken during the economic crisis. It was no wonder that precisely in that period there arose among leading circles of American society a need for a model of society that could counteract the nascent trend towards class antagonism and labour unrest. It was Radcliffe-Brown's functionalist school of social anthropology which at that time fulfilled a very much appreciated and manifest function in American society: to provide a model of an integrated, well-structured whole in which any conflict could be smoothed down to strains and stresses of a psychological nature.

I would suggest that Warner's borrowing of his societal model from the Blackfellows of Australia could be explained, to a certain extent, by the longing of modern industrial society for a Paradise Lost – just as civilized and unharmonious eighteenth-century France, as a reaction to the *homo homini lupus* philosophy of Hobbes and his followers, had to rediscover its *bon sauvage*.

Warner's integrationist approach has been under fire from different quarters. An important element in the criticisms of Warner's image was his theoretical neglect of conflict as a highly significant factor in social life. It should be admitted that Warner knew very well that there were many American urban communities where his harmonious picture would not hold. He purposely selected towns where integrationist models could be more easily applied. He wrote:

It seems wise, however, to say here that one of the reasons we abandoned any idea of investigating Cicero and Hawthorne [where the Western Electric factory which he had been studying was located] and other industrial subcommunities in the area of Chicago was that these districts seemed to be disorganized; they had a social organization which was highly disfunctional, if not in partial disintegration. If we were to compare easily the other societies of the world with one of our own civilization, and if we were readily to accommodate our techniques, it seemed wise to choose a community with a social organization which had developed over a long period of time under the domination of a single group with a coherent tradition. In the United States only two large sections, New England and the Deep South, we believed, were likely to possess such a community.[170]

T–D

It is only fair to mention that, later on, Warner's associates have been studying, under his sponsorship, part of a city that, in the first instance, had been rejected on account of its disfunctional aspects.[171]

Even so, Warner's approach showed a definite bias towards integration. He even hoped that his publications might contribute to social stability. In the Preface to one of his works he wrote:

It is the hope of the authors that this book will provide a corrective instrument which will permit men and women better to evaluate their social situations and thereby better adapt themselves to social reality and fit their dreams and aspirations to what is possible.[172]

A growing awareness of the full significance of conflict for understanding society was not forthcoming until the fifties, when field workers began to realize that even primitive societies were far from conflict-free. It was within social anthropology dealing with non-Western countries that, during the fifties, new concepts began to develop. The Gluckman school of Manchester, for example, was struck by the prevalence of conflict in African societies. Part of it was due to the colonial or post-colonial situation, with the concomitant stress and growing unrest; but another part of it appeared to be embedded within the warp and woof of African tribal society.

Yet, in my view, the manifold attempts to cope with social conflict as a basic element within any society have not been radical enough. The way social conflict is being generally interpreted does not yet signify a departure from the integrationist model. There remains a tendency to view social conflict, and the continuous process of fission and fusion, as factors that do not produce a lasting cleavage within society. According to this picture of society all members of society fundamentally accept the same social values. Coser has stated this integrationist position in clear language: 'Conflict, rather than being disruptive and dissociating, may indeed be a means of balancing and hence maintaining a society as a going concern.'[173]

However, the unrest prevalent throughout Asia, Africa and Latin America calls for an entirely different approach.

v. *Subjective Values as Determinants of Hierarchy*

The only way to dynamize our image of social reality, and to incorporate conflict of values and cultural pluralism within our theoretical model from the outset, would be to return to Weber's view of social institutions as nothing but projections of our image of society into real life. Structural interpretations do not take sufficient account of the time-factor as a fundamental ingredient of any section of social life. It is not possible to present an adequate synchronic image of society or of separate societies as things and to introduce diachronics as a purely external factor.[174]

A reduction of *Sozialgebilde* to images subjectively perceived alternately by different individuals, 'layers', or 'groups' within a society, to which the one drawn by the investigator himself could be added, may return a truly dynamic quality to social reality.

It seems to me, therefore, that the most fundamental criticism of the Warnerian approach is embodied in O. C. Cox's remark:

There is, in fact, no such thing as an objective social class amenable to physical circumscription; neither is there a recognizable social-class hierarchy in class systems of advanced western society ... Stratification is an idea only.

And further on:

The researcher who goes into the field looking for a social class is hunting for something that is not there; he will find it only in his own mind as figments of the intellect.[175]

In my opinion, Cox is right in so far as he has revealed, in the foregoing quotation, the basically subjective character of any assessment of a person's position in social class terms. Social class is not an objectively demonstrable entity, but a projection of society in terms of superiority and inferiority in the minds of some people; and, as we saw earlier, we cannot be at all sure that the evaluation among all those who could be said to constitute the society would tend to coincide.

One could ask whether the subjective character of any status rating is not exclusively inherent in judgements regarding more or less vague phenomena such as social class. One could argue that economic criteria are much easier to handle in a quantitative and, hence, objective manner.

However, acceptance of wealth or economic power as a status criterion is, again, a subjective value judgement. Rejection of wealth as a valid status criterion is inherent, not only in most religious philosophies, but in several secular ideologies as well, as for example Marxism.

Now it is clear that viewing people in terms of superiority and inferiority presupposes a hierarchical principle applied by those who determine one's status. Evidently, it is always norms and values that are at the root of any structuring in terms of hierarchy and stratification. Social status is, by definition, an acknowledged status. Does it make any difference whether a hierarchical order is being viewed as an objectively valid structural element of a society or as a subjective projection of social relationships in the mind of the people? This depends, primarily, on the amount of convergence of social ratings in the mind of the people who together form a society. Several investigations have shown that convergence of status ratings is far from universal. Elizabeth Bott, who studied concepts of class as current among her interviewees in Greater London, found far-reaching differences in the assessment of the class structure of their neighbourhood. A division into two strata ('two-valued power models') was used 'by people who identified themselves strongly with the working class and felt no desire or compulsion to be socially mobile'. 'Three-valued prestige models were used by people who placed themselves in the middle class.'[176] Her conclusion is as follows:

Distortion is inevitable. People must make use of their personal experience to reach a working definition of the class structure, and their personal needs and wishes enter into it too. Concepts of class are used for general orientation in the society at large, for placing strangers, and for evaluating one's own position and that of others. But the definitions are flexible. They are often internally inconsistent, but since they are used differently in different contexts and for different purposes, individuals need not be made aware that their concepts are not completely logical and consistent.[177]

It is not sufficient, however, to demonstrate the amount of subjective divergence. One should realize that findings such as these throw doubt upon the validity of the concept of social stratification as something that objectively exists.

Now, it is certainly true that a high degree of convergence and a transmission of cultural values within a society, in many cases contributes towards a significant amount of uniformity among individual ratings. The point is, however, that the convergence is never absolute. And it is precisely the scope, necessarily left in any actual society for divergent values or norms held either individually or by distinct social groups, that is basically at the root of fundamental social change and of the dynamics of social evolution.

A general convergence of social ratings, moreover, does not preclude great variations in awareness of status differentials from individual to individual, and from social group to social group – by which term, again, I do not mean anything objectively demonstrable within society, but a cluster of individuals viewing themselves and viewed by outsiders as such. Social perception is always much more sharply focused upon the group one knows and upon differentials within that group than upon those with whom one has but few personal contacts.

For example, in his prewar study of the society of southern Celebes (Sulawesi), Indonesia, the Dutch colonial civil servant, H. J. Friedericy, paid a great deal of attention to all shades of differences among the numerically very limited native aristocracy. On the other hand, the great majority of the people constituting over 90 per cent of the total population were lumped together as free commoners which were, in Friedericy's study, enumerated according to occupations but not classed according to social status – though, in his enumeration, an attempt to apply some ranking order is discernible. It is evident that Friedericy derived his image of social structure from the social group with whom he, as a civil service official, had the closest contact: the local aristocracy.[178]

When, about fifteen years later, the *adat* law expert and social anthropologist H. Th. Chabot investigated the same area, he purposely directed his attention not to the aristocracy, but to the commoners.[179] In his study the commoners who, in Friedericy's work, had been lumped together, appeared to be engaged in a continuous effort to improve the status of their family *vis-à-vis* other families. Within this group of commoners, Chabot demonstrated an intricate system of status differentials of which the aristocracy, evidently, was completely unaware, in the same way as the commoners had little interest in the intricate shades of status distinction within the restricted group of aristocrats.[180]

Similarly, in prewar Jogjakarta (a self-ruling Sultanate in Java which at that time was incorporated in the Netherlands-Indies), the nobility was aware of an intricate system of social rankings among their own group. Selosoemardjan, who in his description of the prewar society of Jogjakarta apparently identifies himself with this group, presents a picture of the commoners that clearly reflects the stereotypes of the ruling nobility:

The rest of the Jogjanese society which did not belong to the above two classes [the true nobility, and the officials who were called *priyayis* or *abdi dalem*. W.] was lumped together as the class of the commoners or *kawuladalems*, literally, 'subjects'. It was also referred to as the class of the *wong tjilik*, or the 'little men', which included peasants, merchants, and laborers in private enterprises and in free trade ... The commoners, though belonging to Jogjanese culture along with the nobility and the *priyayis*, constituted a class which was by and large socially set apart from the others. In keeping with their name, this class felt that it was endowed only with duties and possessed few rights. Nonetheless, they looked up to their Sultan with a feeling of deep respect and unlimited faith, believing that he was the link between this world and the world beyond human life.[181]

Compare with this a description, of the same community, by the outsider H. J. van Mook who was a civil officer at that time and apparently less influenced by aristocratic outlooks than his colleague Friedericy. He also starts with the ruling *abdi dalem*. However, Van Mook views their position as decidedly less superior to that of other classes than does Selosoemardjan:

The administrative officials have much less influence there [in the small town of Kuta Gede in the Jogjakarta Sultanate. W.] than elsewhere, especially when they are not well-to-do. It is often difficult, and financially disastrous, for them to keep up with the wealthier inhabitants of Kuta Gede.

Those wealthier inhabitants make up the second category ... Though they are usually of the lesser nobility if they are noble at all, they occupy a very special place in the community. In them nothing is to be detected of the obsequiousness usual in the principalities, for many of them are, on a lesser scale, what Rothschild was on a grand scale: the creditors of princes.[182]

This conveys a somewhat different impression of the attitudes of at least some among those whom Selosoemardjan identified as *wong tjilik.*

The differences in class perception are also clearly brought out in the *Deep South* study of Warner's associates. The picture of society as a whole and the terminology used to denote separate groups is strongly dependent upon one's own position within society.[183]

Another indication that observers may sometimes have been unduly influenced by views prevalent among the top layers and by subtle differentiations made within these layers, can be found in the way attention is distributed, in the Yankee City study, among the different classes. The majority of the fourteen profiles deal with the upper classes, who represent only a small percentage of the total population.

It seems to me that this phenomenon of difference in focus has some deeper implications. The structuralists would, perhaps, tend to intepret it simply as a difference in knowledge and awareness of shades of status distinction which, as a matter of fact, exist but are not perceived as such by those socially far removed from the social class concerned. In my view, however, the phenomenon is note-worthy in bringing to light the subjective character of any status evaluation.

Moreover, it is not simply a question of smaller or greater awareness of status distinctions. Lumping together over 90 per cent of the population as commoners without any distinction, is not simply a symptom of lack of concrete knowledge. It gives expression to a clear-cut ideology, which basically asserts that the common people do not really matter. In the same way the lower classes are labelled, by the upper ones in Old City of the *Deep South* study, as 'nobodies' or 'no 'count lot'. In the eyes of the common people of south Sulawesi, on the other hand, there are several status differentials among them, that bring those with the highest status much nearer to the aristocracy.[184] Again, this image gives expression to an ideology, a system of values.

The structuralists, however, would retort that apparently the commoners still acknowledge the higher status of the aristocracy, even though they are not concerned with the manifold status distinctions which the members of the aristocracy themselves relish. They claim that only one value system can be sociologically valid.

According to the study by Warner and Lunt, only one of the value systems can be considered to be sociologically relevant. In the profile chapter 'All Men are Born Free and Equal' in *The Social Life of a Modern Community* they show that in a gathering of a veteran association which includes all social classes and has adopted egalitarianism as a guiding principle, class distinctions still remain visible. One of the members of the upper upper class plays the egalitarian role quite well: when the president of the Veteran Club, belonging to the lower middle class, gets up and goes over to him (indicative of the president's inferior class status), he invites the latter to sit down beside him; he accepts the cigarette offered him by the president and both light their cigarettes from the same match. But the president calls him Mr Marshall, and he calls the president by his Christian name.[185] The upper class have pre-arranged the election of a new president and have been able to make sure that their candidate, himself a member of the lower upper class, would win. After the egalitarian gathering, when people return home, the class distinctions become visible as ever in the companies that gather to chat and have a drink.

The implication of this chapter is clear: sociologically, only the class structure matters. The egalitarian principle has no real sociological significance, except as an expression of the American Dream.

One could, however, read the same chapter with a quite different implication. The egalitarian ritual reinforces the claim to equality among those who feel themselves to be underprivileged.

Their sense of dignity was enhanced by the ritual. Hence, when they dimly understood that the vote had been pre-arranged and slyly handled by the upper class, they resented the status hierarchy still more. This resentment – which, as a matter of fact, is nothing but an expression of protest against the class hierarchy – is clearly indicated in the part of the chapter 'All Men are Born Free and Equal' that describes the talks in a club of mostly lower-class people after the veteran gathering. A trade-union organizer manages to profit from the resentment that has grown out of the gathering and to win over some of his lower-class companions as members.[186]

There are also enough other indications, in the Yankee City study, of the hidden protest against the class hierarchy. A middle-class member, according to the lower-class workman, 'does not work'. 'Hell, no, he sells insurance.'[187] Lower-class people deeply resent the intrusion of the truant officer and the upper middle-class social worker in their family life. 'Mrs Jones smelled cigarette smoke on her, and any woman who would smoke would do anything.'[188] Their protest, open or concealed, gives expression to a competing value system.

vi. Counterpoints and Conflicting Value Systems

All this does not imply that the competing value systems have an equal sociological relevance. There is, in any society, generally one more or less coherent value system that is dominant. But it would be a serious mistake to view this dominant value system as one consistently held in common by all the members of a society.

The inherent assumption of the integrationist model is that within a society the value system which is at the root of the social structure is universally accepted. On the other hand, the conflict model starts from the premise that the basic values are divergent and even conflicting for different layers of society. According to the latter model, part of those forming the society reject the basic values imposed by those in power. Therefore, they will accept their status only as long as it is being enforced by strong social sanctions.

I would suggest that both views are lacking in depth. A primary characteristic of values is that scarcely any individual or group of individuals either completely accepts or completely rejects certain values or sets of values. Simultaneous acceptance and rejection is a phenomenon that is much more common than is often realized. Only by taking account of the complexities due to this subjective instability of value orientation (a phenomenon of which Weber appears to have been more aware than many sociologists of today) that is, to a smaller or larger extent, operative in any human society, can dynamic social processes be understood in such a way as to trace the early seeds of radical social change.

The structuralists claim that the dominant value system of any society is, in essence, accepted by its members and that it is this basic acceptance that holds society together. To a certain extent they are right. The claim of an aristocracy to a superior status is indeed, being accepted *but* ... It is this 'but' that is crucial for understanding the relative and subjective character of any rating of the status of individuals. It is equally crucial for a basic modification of our concept of society in order to make it understandable as a dynamic entity.

Ralf Dahrendorf has attempted to resolve the contradiction between the two models in an ingenious way. He writes:

In sociology (as opposed to philosophy) a decision which accepts one of these theories and rejects the other is neither necessary nor desirable. There are sociological problems for the explanation of which the integration theory of society provides adequate assumptions; there are other problems which can be explained only in terms of the coercion theory of society; there are, finally, problems for which both theories appear adequate. For sociological analysis, society is Janus-headed, and its two faces are equivalent aspects of the same reality.[189]

This view could be compared with the well-known complementary theory as formulated by Niels Bohr: some natural phenomena are better understood by applying the wave model, other ones by applying the particle model. In a similar way, Dahrendorf appears to acquiesce in this duality: some aspects of society are better approached by an integrationist, other ones by a conflict, model.

I would like to suggest a different line of reasoning.

Sociological theory generally starts from the assumption that, among the members of a given society, a value is either accepted or rejected. The conflict model qualifies this assumption by positing that if one class fully endorses the dominant value system, another class basically rejects it – although, in its dialectical form, the model allows for a certain inconsistency of values, the *Klasse an sich* growing gradually towards greater awareness as a *Klasse für sich*. Even so, however, both assumptions are, in my view, excessively rigid. The important point is that not only may value orientations among the members of one society diverge, but that even within one and the same individual, different value orientations may be observable – even simultaneously.

The value attitudes of many people are ambivalent. It is not at all a rare phenomenon that one and the same person endorses and, at the same time, rejects a distinct value orientation and the criteria for rating an individual's status. Conflicting value systems may operate within one and the same person. On the one hand, he may accept the higher social status of those born from a certain parentage. But at the same time he may adhere to a religious value system declaring that all men are equal, or to an ethical one that declares that individual merit not birth should determine one's status.

One cannot reduce this ambivalence to a difference in roles performed by the same individual on different occasions. It is true that most individuals adjust to divergent social situations and play a role in accordance with their positions in the given surrounding. Warner and Lunt observe, in connection with the ability of the upper-class member Mr Marshall to play different roles in different situations, that

it is not necessary to impute insecurity or hypocrisy to him or to others like him. The behaviour of an individual changes as he shifts his position in the social structure. Individuals incapable of such shifts are improperly adjusted.[190]

Evidently, the authors do not believe that the different value systems, attached to different roles, may bring about a true inner conflict within an individual; still less do they realize that, in more extreme cases, such an inner conflict may forebode an ultimate defection from a dominant value system. Only by assuming that one may come to realize the inner contradiction between two roles and ultimately refuse to play one of them, can we grasp the real dynamics of social change.

This concept of ambivalence, then, could serve as a starting point for transcending the dualistic position taken by Dahrendorf, and for combining his two complementary models into a coherent whole. I would suggest that, in any society, more than one value system is to be found as a determinant of human behaviour and judgement. These systems meet with different intensities of acceptance, varying from group to group and from individual to individual. Generally, however, as we saw earlier there will be one more or less consistent and more or less explicit set of values which is dominant and is cherished and protected by those in power.

The protection and enforcement of the dominant value system is being brought about by different means of social control. Any authority attempts to maintain its ultimate power through creating a general atmosphere of acceptance to its claim to authority. Both moral and legal systems may serve as means of social control, in addition to a sanction which those in power may try to obtain from religious norms and institutions. But ultimately any authority is supported by a physical force, of which the members of a society may remain unconscious most of the time, but which comes into action as soon as the dominant values are really threatened from without or from within.

The contrary sets of values may function as a kind of counterpoint to the dominant set. This counterpoint concept, which I have already suggested in several earlier publications,[191] may provide a conceptual frame for incorporating both structural consistency and dynamic change within one more embracing diachronic perspective. It incorporates the disruptive elements within the total picture from the outset, and in theory provides a possibility of assessing, at any moment, their relative intensity and strength.

Society is transformed, by this attempt to add a temporal dimension to the total picture, into a system of more or less opposing and interrelated structures, each of them derived from subjectively accepted, mostly collective, images of social reality, as present among those who take part in social life. The incessant interplay and mutual competition of the different structural models in which, generally, only one is dominant, could be viewed by the observing sociologist as the 'true' social system which is being kept, in periods of relative stability, in a somewhat precarious equilibrium.

In their most embryonic shape, those counterpoints only manifest themselves under disguise. In more primitive societies they mostly appear as tales, jokes and myths, which give expression to the deviant sets of values. In an urbanized society, one could think of examples such as graffiti, badges and soap-box oratory. From the fact that in such cases the contrary set of values expresses itself in an institutionalized form, it can be deduced that it is not merely an individual expression of protest against an over-rigid cultural pattern, but a group protest which has a certain sociological meaning. At the same time the institutionalized form points towards a grudgingly permissive attitude on the part of those in authority. In many cases, the countervalues remain hidden behind an appearance of acceptance of the dominant value set. They cannot be simply viewed as latent values. Often, certain expressions of the counterpoint value system are intentionally permitted as a kind of outlet, a *Ventilsitte*. For instance, a measure of dissatisfaction with the prevalent status hierarchy has been allowed to express itself in specific ways. The medieval institution of the royal buffoon served to mitigate the strict observance of princely authority and etiquette. Similarly, theatrical performances, in which the poor but virtuous swineherd married the princess, might alleviate the inequalities of actual life. In other cases, as I shall point out further on, the countervalue system seeks expression in religious ideology. But in none of these cases is it allowed to express itself in such a manifest form that the dominant value system is threatened. Those in authority generally keep tight control over potential expressions of social protest.

In diverting the contrary elements into an institutionalized form, the society at the same time canalizes these forces and prevents them from becoming disruptive factors in the overall social structure. To that extent the institutionalizing process may, sometimes, perform an integrative function within society.

A temporary truce may also be arrived at by the institutionalization of the counterpoint within one restricted field. For example, the principle of egalitarianism embodied in Christianity was, for many centuries, rendered innocuous by those in power through relegating it to the realm of the church and to the After Life.

But, essentially, leaving a religious outlet for social protest tended to reaffirm the dominant social order. Most religious establishments endorsed the official hierarchy. Yet the seed of egalitarianism had been sown, and would tend, in the course of history, to reassert itself. Institutionalization as a device for diverting the protest from the dominant social order would become increasingly difficult. The contrapuntal value systems remain virulent, though they are dormant – and abide their time. Under circumstances favourable to them, they may produce a basic change within the dominant structure. Therefore, any description of a given society has to take account of the deviant value systems as basic elements in the total fabric of social life.

vii. *Social Structure and Plurality of Value Systems*

The weakness in the structuralists' approach is, therefore, that they start from the assumption that only one set of values is sociologically relevant, within one society. If they encounter conflicting value systems within a society, they are prone to assume that only one of them is sociologically valid. Before the war, E. S. Bogardus and others administered social distance tests which, at the same time, claimed to establish a rank order of ethnic groups in the United States. When, in replying to social distance tests, Negroes and members of other minority groups essentially adopted the same ranking order of ethnic groups as the whites, with the one exception that they put their own group on top of the whole scheme, this was interpreted as a kind of psychological defence mechanism, without any sociological significance. The 'real' status system was, according to this interpretation, the one with the whites on top.[192] This interpretation overlooks the sociological implications of the tendency to put one's own group on top: potentially, it is this self-assertion that, in later years, has given rise to such explicit protest expressions as the Black Muslim, Black Power and Black Panther movements. A more sociologically sensitive evaluation of the outcome of the ranking order tests would have revealed its counterpoint character from the outset.

In a similar way, sociologists have tended to misinterpret the dualism of formal organization versus informal organization.[193] In the Hawthorne investigations of industrial relations it was discovered that, in addition to the formal organization claimed to be valid by the management, there also existed an informal one that was set up spontaneously by the workers themselves and that, in fact, determined to what extent the aims of the management could be realized. Again, the assumption of some sociologists is that, since only one structure could be sociologically valid, this should be the informal one. The other one remains, to a certain extent, no more than 'a dead letter'.[194] It is not realized that, again, two competing value systems were in action, both of them sociologically relevant. The formal organization is the dominant structure, viewed as valid by those who are heading the organization. The informal organization forms, to a certain extent, a protest structure which, for example, serves to attain aims rather different from the management's. If, for example, the management strives for a maximization of production, the informal leaders strive for a moderate working tempo, as a defence mechanism against too strict requirements on the part of the managers.

Again, one cannot truly understand the workings of society except as an interplay of different value systems, each of them embodying a different image of the social order. As far as one can speak of a 'real' social order, it is this interplay of different value systems, with the inherent dynamic struggle for ascendancy, that provides the main structural principle. The different hierarchical orders, more or less explicitly present in the mind of individuals, or smaller or larger groups of them, are certainly real enough as elements of the overall social structure. However, the basic societal model is not a logical, harmonious, static structure, but at best an uneasy co-existence of several divergent and competing value systems, some of them more explicit, others hidden beneath the surface, and generally one of them dominant, as an expression of the existing power structure – for the time being!

Our last question in connection with the structural approach concerns the so-called primitive societies where there appears to be a much stronger consensus regarding the social structure and the underlying value system, and where social groups such as clans and moieties seem to be real enough.

It might be true that, in many of these societies, the convergence of structural concepts as present in the mind of the people is, at first sight, definitely greater than in modern society. But, even there, the counterpoints are rarely completely absent. For example, the principle of the rule by elders is never as absolutely accepted as would appear to follow from the officially held value system; nor are the values of the adults, as distinct from those adhered to by youngsters, as unchallenged as anthropologists assumed in earlier years.

This point is well illustrated by Margaret Mead's successive experiences in her research into Manus society. During her first visit in 1928–9, she was struck by the discrepancy between childhood and adulthood, by the seemingly unbridgeable distance between the social roles expected from the children and from adults. She was well aware that the child's world formed a kind of counterpoint to the acquisitive adult world, a more or less separate subculture in the total fabric of Manus culture. But the existence of this set of contrary values did not impair the integrative quality of society. In her opinion the acceptance of the specific values of the child's world did not last beyond the individual's entrance into the adult one. She took 'the triumph of the adults' for granted, and only wondered 'how these children, permitted a life so at variance with the life of their elders, developed into men like those same elders'.[195]

Her main experience of 1953 was that, as a matter of fact, they had not. She discovered that the discrepancy between the values accepted in childhood and in adulthood had been one of the potent factors bringing about social change, though 'the contrapuntal experiences of childhood were not sufficient in themselves to enable Manus adults to throw over the institutions of their culture'.[196] But it was the vigorous impact of the West which released the dynamic forces dormant within Manus society and turned a universal polarity between generations into a true conflict of generations.

It is also important to point out that, even apart from status systems, structuralization of society is always a largely psychological phenomenon. We should not look for an objective division of a society into clans, phratries, or moieties but rather find out the way these divisions and the delimitations between the 'ins' and the 'outs' are perceived by the people themselves or by different segments of the society. A good deal of subjective convergence may lead to results rather similar to those that would proceed from a purely objective structural view. Again, however, it is the subjective perception of structuralization, and interpretation, divergent from the official one, that may become the source of social dynamics and of disputing the dominant social order.

viii. Counterpoints and Collective Action

It is now clear that a sociologist or social anthropologist has to develop a capacity to discover the potentially disruptive elements within a society with the same sense of empathy as he has used, in the past, to lay bare the structural, more or less fixed, characteristics of a social body.

It is not enough to realize, like Talcott Parsons, that the social system as a whole is dependent upon legitimization by acceptance of the underlying values and norms by the people at large. All the shades of subjective acceptance or rejection, or both, have from the outset to be introduced in the total picture that a sociologist draws of society as it moves. It is a highly important phenomenon that cultural norms and values are generally not restricted to one or two individuals; that on the contrary most of them are shared in common, even if they are only counterpoints to a dominant value system, by large numbers of the society who recognize these values with different shades of intensity. Transmission of cultural values remains, in our view, a highly significant process, even though we try to avoid any reification of society as distinct from the individual.

But even values exclusively adhered to by one or two individuals may, in the long run, become sociologically relevant if these individuals, for some reason, enjoy a high prestige within society.

It is, in primitive society, quite often the shaman or witch-doctor who, by his recognized authority as an interpreter of the will of the gods, may initiate or sanction social change.

No society is culturally and structurally completely homogeneous. The seeds for dissension and growth are omnipresent. So is, in my view, the counterpart phenomenon, as a source of all emancipation movements and of social evolution.

In order to substitute a new societal model for that of Dahrendorf, which, somehow, got stuck halfway in an attempt to dynamize sociological theory, we will have to elaborate how a counterpoint, from its tiny and apparently futile beginnings, may evolve into a powerful stream leading humanity, or part of it, towards evolution and, in more extreme cases, revolution. How can a counterpoint, at first perceptible in a more or less veiled form, develop into a decisive factor in the process of human emancipation?

The problem is extremely complex and its phenomenological appearance highly variable. The competition for supremacy between different sets of values develops on different levels of social life. A countervalue usually derives its strength from the fact that it is collectively adhered to, in different shades of intensity and openness, by many members of a society. It starts to threaten the established authority when it has grown into a more or less consistent set of countervalues, openly professed by a social category, for example one trying to achieve solidarity on a class basis. In such a case, it should not be called a counterpoint any more, but a social protest movement.

On the other hand, as we have seen, those in authority will unceasingly try to isolate or neutralize the expressions of social protest in some institutionalized form. The canalization of social protest forms into more innocuous avenues and suppression under the guise of a certain recognition, are well-known devices of social control. Whenever the threat of physical force, hidden behind the more indirect means of social control, becomes apparent, the professed leaders of the social protest may choose the easier way of adjusting themselves, through institutionalization, to the prevalent power structure, thus becoming, to a certain extent, part of the establishment.

True emancipation movements are incessant, often silent, struggles. On the one hand, we find large numbers led, on the basis of an ideology, by some leaders into action against certain elements of the established order. On the other hand, there are always the efforts of the latter to wean some influential popular leaders away from their radical course through granting them a more or less secure position in a niche opened and left in peace by the establishment. After the movement has been insulated – which may have been accompanied with physical force applied against those followers who continued to protest – what remains is sometimes no more than a counterpoint. The history of religious sects is full of instances of this continuous process of mass movements that finally get stuck through treason and compromise. The same is true for labour movements, the leaders of which accept a secure position within the establishment, at the expense of their freedom openly to oppose the prevalent power structure.

Under what circumstances may an institutionalized counterpoint become active again, or may a protest movement develop outside the institutionalized sphere where it had been insulated in an earlier phase?

Again, a great variety of possible factors may be operative. First, there may be some external factor, introduced from without, which may awaken the dormant forces that had allowed themselves to be neutralized and isolated within an institutionalized framework. For example, an occupation by a foreign power may undermine the idea of the acceptance of authority. But the influence of foreign ideas or foreign economic forces should not be underrated either. However, more often than not, factors from within will have a decisive influence upon the ultimate course of events. Economic or ecological factors may play an important role as causes of growing dissatisfaction expressing itself in values divergent from those upheld by the authorities. But the behaviour of those in authority may equally change the prevalent atmosphere. A frequent recourse to brutal oppression, a growing discrepancy between the way of life of those allied to the establishment and those who belong to the 'outs', a growing awareness among large numbers of people that those in power are behaving in a way that is far removed from the dominant values they profess to believe in, may make people aware of the deeper meaning of countervalues that had remained dormant within an institutional frame. The manner in which collective discontent expresses itself may vary from claims made quietly through legal channels, through the whole range of movements for social emancipation, to revolutionary outbursts directly threatening the prevalent power structure. But even in the last-mentioned case the movement is nothing but a highly invigorated form of the same contrapuntal elements which a sociologist with a keen sense for symptoms of dissent may discover within any society, however stable it might seem at first sight.

Thus far, we have only considered countervalues of a more progressive nature than those adhered to by the official authorities. In such cases the counterpoint concept could function as a germ of both evolutionary and revolutionary developments, that is to say of developments conducive to a process of emancipation. It goes without saying that countervalues may just as easily express positions more conservative than those adhered to by the authorities, particularly in such situations where some room is left for emancipation along an evolutionary path. In such cases, countervalues may well represent a disruptive element within society, as relics of a period of the past, even if they are again made seemingly innocuous by institutionalization. A church, an army, or a foreign service may function as a depository of values opposing the process of emancipation and potentially endangering its further course. And in the same way as counterpoints may contain the germs of revolution, they may equally forebode future counter-revolutions.

ix. Conflicts and Conflicting Values

In the foregoing sections I have tried to demonstrate the prevalence of conflicting value systems within any society as the basic source of social dynamics – both in an evolutionary and a revolutionary form. The stress laid, in the following parts of my study, upon revolutionary change, could easily convey the impression that the existence of conflicting values within a society should automatically imply a prevalence of social conflict. However, the relationship between these two factors is a more complicated one.

First, there are those scholars – such as Lewis Coser and Max Gluckman – who consider social conflict as fulfilling, in many cases, an integrative function within a society. In such a case the conflicting parties have no quarrel about the norms to which their life is subjected – they only interpret them differently in connection with the matter in dispute. It is evident that where conflict amounts to no more than this, its rise as well as its solution in accordance with the accepted norms may be considered as only strengthening the prevalent social order. In such cases 'conflict . . . does not necessarily lead to change'.[197]

On the other hand, conflicting values within a society need not necessarily lead to actual conflict. Gluckman argues that value inconsistency may be contained within one social system,[198] and my analysis of the counterpoint opposing the dominant value system, as a universal phenomenon within society, is essentially in accordance with Gluckman's view. However, the existence of contradictory values within one single social unit may engender the seeds of future conflict. I am not even sure that Gluckman's attempt to reduce most social conflicts to differences in interpretation of commonly accepted values could be upheld. This view is based on an overestimation of the significance of *formally* accepted norms, often of a legal character. Differences in interpretation of such legal norms may, basically, spring from a different position in the official social hierarchy and, thus, fundamentally point towards a potential difference in value orientation.

However this may be, conflicting values may become apparent in many different shapes. In the context of our present study they are mainly of interest whenever they have a certain bearing on a tendency towards emancipation. In that case, their link with the process of evolution becomes apparent. It is this relationship with the emancipation process which lends the societal model designed in the present chapter its dynamic quality. It is the persistent, mostly silent, struggle for the recognition of values neglected under the dominant social order that becomes one of the principal agents of fundamental social change.

The ensuing social or political conflicts are mostly being fought in a slow struggle of attrition, through negotiations and other legally admitted methods of pressure. For example, female emancipation has, up till now, been achieved nearly exclusively by this type of silent struggle, supported by a basic change within the prevalent economic structure which made this emancipation, in the long run, attractive to significant sections of the dominant male society. During periods of sharp political conflict – revolution or wartime – the process of female emancipation was much accelerated, because the warring parties needed the actual support of women and were short of all types of indispensable labour. Of course, the actual use they made of this additional source of moral strength and labour force was to a certain extent dependent upon the prevalent ideology. But this gain in times of stress was always in danger of going to waste after the return to normalcy, unless the silent emancipation struggle was sustained, and, if possible, intensified.

What matters in connection with our main problem is that even this type of peaceful emancipation and evolution is basically connected with both social conflict and conflicting values. The most fundamental advantage of the dynamic societal model, expounded in this chapter, is that it provides a framework in which the universal process of emancipation and human evolution becomes understandable.

At the same time, however, the conflicting value systems engendered in any existing social order contain the germs for a much more explosive type of social and political conflict: revolution.

x. *Legal Order and Social Structure*

Revolution is, by definition, always directed against the prevalent legal order, whereas evolution may proceed within legal boundaries. This generally accepted distinction raises the query of the relationship between the concept of legal order and the dynamic view of society as developed in the present chapter.

The legal order, and social structure as conceived in current sociological studies, have in common that both of them provide an image of society as conceived by the leading circles of a society. This does not mean that they fully coincide, as apparently claimed by two Dutch students of the sociology of law, who argue that it is law that determines the structural framework of society.[199] Actually, sociology has abundantly shown that social structure implies much more than the totality of legal norms. Sometimes the structural principles as upheld by those in power are even at variance with legal norms. The latter may embody a good deal of social hypocrisy. There are, for example, few legal systems in the present-day world that will openly acknowledge inequality between social classes. Modern legal systems generally uphold the fiction of equality of all before the law. Yet, social stratification is an undeniable social reality if a society is being looked at from the point of view of those upholding the established order.

One could, therefore, argue that the legal system provides the formal structural frame of society, over against the sociological structure, including the social stratification system, as the informal one upheld by the prevalent social forces. But, as with the general distinction between formal and informal organization, neither of them could claim the exclusive right of being considered the real social structure. Both present partially coinciding, partially divergent, value systems attached to the dominant established order. Both value systems, however, are challenged by others, less prominent for the time being but potentially embodying the dominant social order of the future.

This protest against the established order can, in certain cases, be reinforced by the discrepancies between legal order and prevalent social structure. The legal order is, as we have seen, not necessarily more conservative than the prevalent informal structure. In the following chapter it will be shown that a revolutionary ideology often claims to be harking back to a previous, maybe illusory, legal order that is assumed to have been corrupted by those in power. It is also possible that a revolutionary movement appeals to certain principles, for example egalitarian ones, contained in the formal legal body which are waived by those in actual power. Similarly, a counter-revolutionary movement may, in some cases, embody a reaction, on the basis of the actual power structure, against distinct legal prescriptions that are too egalitarian for the taste of a powerful upper stratum. Therefore, it would be erroneous to view a legal order in its totality as the inevitable target of any revolutonary movement.

On the other hand, it is true that evolutionary, as distinct from revolutionary, change is easier to achieve through a scarcely noticeable process of structural transformation within a society than through a constant revision of legal rules. In cases where the way towards gradual fundamental change is not blocked, a certain rigidity of the formal legal order need not provoke its equally formal, that is to say revolutionary, rejection.

As is the case with informal social structures, legal orders are essentially based on a certain amount of subjective acceptance by those who constitute a society. Owing to the universality of conflicting values, the recognition will often be less absolute and all-embracing than is claimed by the lawgivers and by those in power. A certain rejection of parts of the law is fully compatible with a general acceptance of the legal order as such.

The official legal norms provide the warp of society. The woof consists of the extended body of social life that is proceeding and progressively changing beyond the framework of the legal order and, in many cases, contrary to it, and sometimes even far beyond the borders of the predominant social structure.

It is this inherent protest against legality as a sociological phenomenon that, again, could be considered the main agent of social change, in more extreme cases amounting to revolutionary action.

Part Two: Revolution: General Aspects

Introduction

One of the striking features of the rather voluminous literature on revolution is that systematic attempts to study this social phenomenon in its most general aspects hardly exist. In the second part of this study, an attempt is made to fill at least some of the existing gaps.

It appeared necessary to devote a whole chapter, the fifth one, to the concept of revolution and to an attempt to distinguish different types of revolutions, against the background of social dynamics as developed in part one. The closing sections of this chapter, mainly dealing with the historical setting of revolutions, are not at all ambitious. They do not pretend to sketch a world history of revolutionary change, couched in terms of the progressive emancipation of mankind. This task would appear, for the moment, a Sisyphean one. They have no further objective than to determine which of the historical events, currently called revolutions, are being rightly termed so, in order to make sure that, in grappling with our next task (a discussion of the origin and course of revolutions, chapter six), there will be no ambiguity as to the identification of certain occurrences as revolutions.

In the main, however, the second part may be viewed as a general prelude to a more detailed discussion in the third part, of revolution as a phenomenon in the world of today – and, in particular, in the Third World of today.

Only with reference to the actual situation in the world today will a certain operationalization and concretization of my analysis of revolution as a sociological phenomenon prove possible.

5

Concept and Types of Revolution

Any definition that would call both the victory of George Washington and the victory of Francisco Franco by the same name is bound to confuse more than define.

HERBERT APTHEKER

i. Revolution and Rebellion: Some Preliminary Remarks

Louis XVI, on learning of the attack on the Bastille, is supposed to have suggested that this was a *révolte,* and the Duc de la Roche-foucauld-Liancourt to have retorted: '*Sire, ce n'est pas une révolte, c'est une révolution.*'

Whatever the truth of the story – which may be as apocryphal as most anecdotes about royalty are – it proves at least one thing: that in common linguistic usage a distinction is being made between 'revolts' and 'revolutions'. Consequently, in defining the concept of revolution as it will be used throughout this book, we should contrast it not only with the concept of evolution as defined in the first part of it, or with the concept of counter-revolution as defined in the next section, but also with a host of occurrences denoted by such terms as 'revolt', 'rebellion', 'mutiny', 'uprising', 'insurrection', etc.

Evidently, what Liancourt meant was that what was going on was more serious and would have a greater and more lasting impact upon the prevalent state of affairs than a simple revolt. But is the difference simply one of magnitude? – as Hannah Arendt seemed to imply when she wrote that, behind these words of Liancourt's,

we still can see and hear the multitude on their march, how they burst into the streets of Paris, which then still was the capital not merely of France but of the entire civilized world – the upheaval of the populace of the great cities inextricably mixed with the uprising of the people for freedom, both together irresistible in the sheer force of their number.[1]

Hannah Arendt herself, however, amplifies the quantitative criterion with a qualitative one:

The king, when he declared that the storming of the Bastille was a revolt, asserted his power and the various means at his disposal to deal with conspiracy and defiance of authority; Liancourt replied that what had happened there was irrevocable and beyond the power of a king.[2]

According to her, it was evidently the multitude which made the movement 'irresistible and irrevocable'. To use Hegelian terminology: quantity was being transformed into quality.

The criterion applied by Arendt seems, however, debatable. If 'irresistibility' and 'irrevocability' are used to distinguish revolution from simple revolt, there could be a question neither of abortive revolutions nor of successful revolts. Yet, one would have radically to twist common linguistic usage if one were to assert that what failed in 1848 in France or in 1905 in Russia were not revolutions; or if one were to call the successful overthrow of one military junta by another one, in some Latin American country, a revolution. Evidently, there is an additional quality inherent in the concept of revolution, which revolt lacks and which basically distinguishes revolutions from any other disturbance, insurrection, or coup d'état. I would suggest that the basic criterion is that a revolution always aims at an overthrow of the existing social order and of the prevalent power structure; whereas all other types of disorder, however they may be called, lack this aspiration to fundamental change and simply aim to deal a blow at those in authority, or even to depose or physically eliminate them.

So far the distinction seems clear. It is more difficult, however, to decide to what extent the aspiration to fundamental change should be present, as a conscious aim, in the minds of those participating in the upheaval, or at least among some of its leaders. Or should the decisive factor be whether an historian can afterwards establish that such a basic change has actually been brought about or, at least, has been a significant potentiality?

If we consider the subjective purpose to be conclusive, we would view each abortive movement, however small and insignificant, as revolutionary if its leader himself, possibly a local mystic or a madman, tries to gather a following with the explicit purpose of overthrowing the existing social order and establishing some kind of ideal society. It does not seem very useful to extend the term revolution to any short-lived messianic or millenary movement of this type. On the other hand, if the subjective intention does not matter and everything depends upon the objective danger to the established order inherent in a movement, a disturbance starting as a simple revolt with a restricted objective could easily be labelled a revolution because of the inherent danger that the disturbance could spill over its original borders and erupt into something much more consequential than the leaders and participants themselves had in mind.

But as an indication that a revolution is afoot the objective criterion may suffice. It is not at all uncommon that movements starting as occasional outbursts develop, through the logic of actual conditions, into something much more fundamental and significant than the initiators had in view; but it is unlikely that a movement, starting as a pure rebellion, would develop into something much more consequential unless there are some personalities who are aware of its potential and succeed in taking over its leadership in a later phase. Generally, in a revolution which could be assessed objectively as such, the sense of significance of what is occurring will be present at least among some of its leaders and participants; consequently, a patent discrepancy between the outcome of applying an objective as contrasted with a subjective criterion, is hardly likely to occur in actual practice.

Therefore, I would suggest that what distinguishes revolution from any other type of disturbance is the actual tendency towards a fundamental change of the prevalent social order inherent in a movement. Although subjective aspirations remain highly relevant, the actual danger for the established order may provide the indication that a revolutionary movement is afoot.

Several characteristics could be mentioned which distinguish other types of disturbances from each other. Although it would not be at all easy to differentiate between 'rebellion', 'revolt', and 'uprising', it is clear that the term 'mutiny' mostly refers to an insurrection within a military or quasi-military apparatus, that a '*jacquerie*' is always a peasant uprising, that a 'riot' is a local affair only, and that the term '*coup d'état*' refers to a sudden attempt to grasp the state power at the top level, without a prior mobilization of popular movements from below (the same applies to what is called a 'palace revolution'). None of these terms, however, refers to movements aiming at a lasting overthrow of the social order – and this is precisely the quality by which we discern a revolution, whether it is successful or abortive.

At this point I can also clarify my position as regards Hannah Arendt's quantitative criterion. In order to be called a revolution, a movement should present a substantive danger to the prevalent social order. This implies a certain magnitude of the movement. But numbers are not enough. *Jacqueries* may involve broad peasant masses, but they mostly lack the motive force to overthrow the prevalent social order.

I may refer to Barrington Moore who applies exactly the same criterion. Discussing the peasant revolts in ancient China, he observes: 'We may nevertheless take judicial notice of the fact that these were rebellions, not revolutions; that is, they did not alter the basic structure of the society.'[3]

ii. *Revolution and Counter-Revolution*

There is, however, a still more basic difficulty in determining a chain of events as revolutionary. Is any sudden overthrow of the prevalent power structure to be viewed as revolutionary or should we reserve this term for changes taking place in one given direction? More concretely: is the term counter-revolution meaningful and, if so, how should we distinguish it from 'true' revolution? Again, the issue of objectivity versus subjectivity is involved; this time, however, it is not the subjective state of mind of the leaders or participants in a movement which is at stake, but our own objectivity or subjectivity in assessing the main direction of a movement as progressive or reactionary.

Essentially, the issue does not differ from the one we tackled in discussing the possibility of determining the course of evolution or human progress in an objective way. What distinguishes revolution from evolution is, as I put it earlier, the cataclysmic character of the social change brought about. The criteria determining to what extent progress is involved remain basically the same, regardless of whether the change occurs in a gradual way or suddenly. I would like to recall the criteria established in the previous discussion of the concept of evolution. Progress can be expressed as the process of human emancipation – either from the forces of nature, or from the fetters of social hierarchy and domination by man; it generally implies an increase in the rate of human cooperation. The same criterion can be used to distinguish revolution from counter-revolution. The emancipation aspect was already perceived by Condorcet: 'The word "revolutionary" can be applied only to revolutions whose aim is freedom.'[4] The consequence of this standpoint is that revolution-like risings aiming at a restoration or reinforcement of the traditional social order should be termed counter-revolutionary. In so far as the terms progress and evolution can be defined in an objective way, the same is true of the term revolution as distinct from counter-revolution.

Unfortunately, it is not at all easy to draw a clear-cut line. Most revolutionary movements try to legitimize themselves by professing to aim at a restoration of an earlier, more righteous, state of affairs. Hannah Arendt, basing herself on the *Oxford English Dictionary*, claims that the term 'revolution' was used for the first time as a political term precisely to denote a true 'restoration': the overthrow of the Rump Parliament in 1660, on the occasion of the restoration of the monarchy in England.

In precisely the same sense, the word was used in 1688, when the Stuarts were expelled and the kingly power was transferred to William and Mary. The 'Glorious Revolution', the event through which very paradoxically the term found its definite place in political and in historical language, was not thought of as a revolution at all, but as a restoration of monarchical power to its former righteousness and glory.[5]

It is irrelevant to my argument that at least the second 'restoration' in seventeenth-century England could not be viewed, in my terminology, as a counter-revolution, since it contributed to the strengthening of civil rights. It rather had the traits of a 'palace revolution' with a strong backing among several strata of British society. What matters is that, even when towards the end of the eighteenth century the term revolution became popular in its present sense of an overthrow in the direction of greater freedom and social progress, true revolutionaries in France and America, according to Arendt, claimed that they were restoring an earlier legitimate state of affairs which,

had been disturbed and violated by the despotism of absolute monarchy or the abuses of colonial government. They pleaded in all sincerity that they wanted to revolve back to old times when things had been as they ought to be.[6]

Apparently, for a long time it remained difficult for a politician to envisage the possibility of establishing a completely novel social and political order. At that time novelty was not yet in vogue as it became in the course of the nineteenth century, when evolutionary views gradually gained general acceptance. To present one's ideas and ideals as something yet unknown and untested in practice would be too rash an undertaking, hardly likely to attract the following prospective revolutionary leaders so badly needed. It was much safer to profess a wish to restore an earlier – though according to the historical evidence available to us imaginary – idyllic state of affairs which had been corrupted by those in authority who had allegedly usurped illegitimate powers.

A complicating factor is that the claim for a restoration of earlier civic rights and freedoms was not necessarily imaginary. The actual process of modernization implied, in many instances, an abolition of traditional freedoms, an increasing inequality within the urban community, and a growing rate of economic exploitation. For example, in the Netherlands during the 1780s, prior to the French Revolution but under the inspiration of the American one, a revolutionary movement developed under the banner of the Patriotic Party, led by the democratic nobleman Joan Derk van der Capellen (1741–84). This movement, which was directed against the attempt of the Stadtholder, Prince William V of Orange, to assume sovereign powers, harked back to a previous more democratic political order, which had allowed the urban citizens to run their own affairs autonomously. In 1787, the Patriotic revolution was crushed by the prince who, with the assistance of the Prussian army, effected a *true* 'restoration'.[7] But, despite its ultimate failure, the Patriotic revolution was typical in combining an urge for thorough innovation in the political and social field and for emancipation of significant groups of the population from aristocratic rule with a pretence of restoring old freedoms upon which those in authority had made serious infractions.

In the same way as modernization, owing to an increase in size of bureaucratic structures, could imply a trend away from democratic rights – thus, dialectically, in its turn eliciting an emancipation movement on a broader basis which could assume a revolutionary character – it was also liable, during the rise of capitalist society, to increase economic and social inequality.

In the course of the nineteenth century, the modernization process characterized by technological growth, a more elaborate division of labour and, once more, increase in size, led to a mounting discontent erupting in revolutionary emancipation movements. Though the claim for greater economic equality was, to some extent, present in the French Revolution, it achieved its clear expression only in the second half of the nineteenth century. But even the outspoken innovators and revolutionaries, Karl Marx and Friedrich Engels, did not manage completely to dispense with an appeal to an imaginary past. They found their societal model in tribal primitive communism which, though being superseded according to their evolutionist view by later, more advanced stages in which private property and private exploitation had taken the place of early forms of cooperation, still held out the promise of a return to a communist society based on cooperation at a higher level of human development. Similarly, the state, which had been a product of civilization mainly serving the interests of the owners as a tool for repression but had been absent from more primitive social structures, would wither away with the advent of higher forms of communism.

It is interesting to note that, even within their dialectical method of reasoning, which accepted modernization with all its corrupting aspects as an inevitable process, they clung to an idealized past, a kind of Golden Age, as a Paradise Lost to be restored by revolution.

If therefore revolutionary movements often present revivalistic aspects, counter-revolutions on the other hand may contain elements which, despite their generally reactionary character, could be assessed as progressive. The path of progress and modernization is often tortuous, even paradoxical. Though a counter-revolution, by definition, aims at a restoration and reinforcement of traditional authority and entails a repression of forces that are striving for emancipation, its outcome may be much less unequivocal. Not only will increased repression, by the dissatisfaction it engenders, in its turn increase the urge for emancipation – just as, on the contrary, revolutionary movements tend to reinforce the Thermidorian popular desire for stabilization; the counter-revolutionary movement itself, by its internal logic, may produce certain organizational effects which could be assessed as conducive to further modernization. For example, if a counter-revolutionary regime tries to win the allegiance, or at least a tacit submission of broad layers of the population, it will have to perfect its communication system and thus willy-nilly expose the populace to all kinds of external information. Such a regime is, moreover, frequently forced to further its technology, if only for the sake of warfare, which in turn necessitates a thorough technical training of broad layers of the population.

The ambiguous character of many revolutionary or counter-revolutionary movements sometimes makes it difficult to put the right label on a movement. Since the term revolution is, in many circles, less tainted than counter-revolution, few movements will openly present themselves as counter-revolutionary. The so-called *Gestapu*, the *coup d'état* of 30 September 1965 in Indonesia, in which dissatisfied officers opposing the army leadership were the main participants, though the Communist Party was incriminated in masterminding it, was labelled by its opponents as a 'counter-revolutionary' movement after its failure, in order to tarnish it in the eyes of the Indonesian public. The surviving army leaders (six of them had been murdered on the night of 30 September) thus reserved the true revolutionary fervour for their own regime. Only towards the end of 1967 did the acting President, General Suharto, openly admit the counter-revolutionary character of the military regime which had deposed President Sukarno, by ordering that the independence struggle against the Dutch of the years 1945–9 should no longer be called a revolution – evidently in order to erase any idea that revolution could be a thing to be applauded!

The counter-revolutionary leaders in Brazil, in power since the *coup d'état* of April 1964, are more astute; they continue to call themselves revolutionaries.

The events in Hungary in 1956 were still more ambiguous. Whereas the Western press claimed that the movement headed by Nagy was a revolution against the dictatorial aspects of Stalinist rule, the communists themselves tended to view the revolt as a reaction against a progressive government. Both views are, to a certain extent, justified. If stress is being laid on a rapid socialization of the means of production as a criterion for progress, the movement, which aimed *inter alia* at a reversal of the collectivization of agriculture, should be viewed as counter-revolutionary; on the other hand, in so far as the amount of democratic rights is being used as a yardstick, the movement should be assessed as revolutionary and to a certain extent progressive.

There are certainly many more cases in human history where progressive and reactionary elements within a movement of a revolutionary character were kept more or less in balance. But this does not mean that the label used is arbitrary; if we keep our main criteria as defined in our discussion of the concept of evolution in mind, we will usually be able to assess the general tendency of a movement, despite its sometimes confusing or paradoxical secondary traits or tendencies.

Thus far we have only considered the direction of sudden change as a criterion to distinguish revolution from counter-revolution. Are both phenomena in other respects similar in character; that is to say, do both of them fit the definition of revolution as attempted in the first section of this chapter?

There are a few elements in our definition of revolution which seem less compelling as characteristics of counter-revolution than they would be as characteristics of a true revolution.

First, one could ask oneself to what extent the aspiration to overthrow the existing social order should be viewed as inherent in counter-revolutions. As I have pointed out, the basic aim of a counter-revolution is to restore or reinforce the traditional social order, which seems, at first sight, exactly the opposite of what a revolution is supposed to do.

However if we look at social change in evolutionary terms, we may arrive at a different conclusion. We speak of counter-revolution whenever a prevalent tendency towards emancipation is being stopped or even reversed by a sudden attempt to overthrow a prevalent power structure that was more sympathetic towards the emancipation trends. In the previous chapter I pointed out how, in a situation where the prevalent power structure is sympathetic towards an evolutionary process of emancipation, more reactionary countervalues may remain active within the prevalent structure. Equally, we speak of counter-revolution when a true revolution had already started but is being countered by a movement basically aiming at a restoration of the pre-revolutionary structure.

In both cases, more than a simple *coup d'état* or palace revolution is intended, inasmuch as the insurrection does not content itself with a change of personnel at the top level, but actually aims at a reversal of the prevalent trends of basic social change.

Secondly, one might doubt to what extent the leaders of a counter-revolution are moved by an ideology, a definite cultural ideal, in the same sense as revolutionaries are, who consciously aim at the creation of a new society.

Here we may observe that counter-revolutionaries quite often profess to aim at a complete renewal of their society. They often use a terminology borrowed from the armoury of true revolutionaries, as was the case with the followers of Hitler, who called themselves national 'socialists'. It is exactly this revolutionary vocabulary which makes it difficult to distinguish counter-revolutions from revolutions. However, one could maintain that in the case of counter-revolutions the professed ideology serves more or less as a cloak to disguise the conservative trend of the movement, in order to enlist wider popular support.

Thirdly, one may ask to what extent counter-revolutions, like revolutions, require a significant mass support. Here, again, a certain difference can be demonstrated. Counter-revolutions mostly do not rely on popular mass support, but rather on segments of the regular military forces. To that extent, it is sometimes difficult to distinguish a counter-revolution from a *coup d'état*. But the basic element of any revolutionary movement, the aspiration to overthrow the established power structure and not only a group of individuals in power, remains inherent in counter-revolutions as well as in revolutions.

Consequently, what happened in Indonesia on the night of 30 September 1965 was really a *coup d'état*, whereas the counter-movement unleashed by the army leaders and culminating in the dethronement of President Sukarno had an outspoken counter-revolutionary character in that it aimed at restoring the ownership rights of the rural propertied class and at curbing the peasant and labour emancipation movements.

There is another point which has to be investigated in order to clarify the concept of revolution as contrasted with counter-revolution. In the previous section revolution was defined as a sudden overthrow of established authority, aimed at a fundamental change of the existing social order.

First, I would like to explain why I used the term fundamental social change, and tried to avoid the more common term structural change. Structural change would more or less imply an acceptance of a structuralist view of society, which was rejected in chapter four. The term would seem to reflect an interpretation of a revolutionary process in such a way that one social structure is being substituted for another. We have seen that any attempt at describing a society in structural terms, more specifically in terms of a rigid hierarchical system, ignores the contradictory trends and dynamic tendencies to be observed in any social unit. A structural view of society can never be accepted as an objectively valid description of how people behave. At best it expresses a subjective interpretation of society peculiar to a particular segment of it. And even this term, segment, suffers from a too strong reification, since the division of a society into social layers or social classes cannot be disconnected from preconceived value judgements which are at the root of an interpretation of society in hierarchical terms.

Therefore, I could not endure a definition of revolution in strict terms implying that one definite social order, with a distinct social class on top, is supposed to be replaced by another one, with the former ruling class being thrown out of power and a new one occupying the top layer of society.[8] Of course such a complete overturn of a previous hierarchical order would provide an exemplary illustration of what the term revolution could mean. However, such an ideal constellation could hardly be expected ever to occur and a restriction of the term to such extreme events would exclude some of the most typical cases of historical revolutions from our definition. What is relevant is that in any social constellation, but most evidently so in pre-revolutionary ones, there is no unambiguously valid social hierarchy. Different hierarchical systems are claiming preponderance, but mostly only one of these systems is dominant and decisive for the temporary power structure. It is the temporary *balance of power* between different hierarchical systems, expressing itself in a given *political* order with its justifying ideology and its attached 'establishment', that is being overthrown by a revolutionary course of events. The result of a revolution, again, is not a complete reversal of the social 'structure', but rather a clear-cut reversal in the balance of power between two or more contending hierarchical systems.

It is the reversal in balance of power, affecting the relative strength of the contending value systems and related hierarchical orders subjectively adhered to by different segments of society, which could be defined as a fundamental change to be interpreted as a truly revolutionary overturn.

Such a fundamental change, therefore, does not necessarily imply a decisive ascendancy to power of a social class which, in the previous situations, had a subordinate role. It is sufficient, in order to be able to speak of a revolution, that the balance of power between different hierarchical systems, potentially present side by side within one single political unit, has been overturned and consequently a door, formerly closed, has been reopened for further strides on the way towards emancipation.

Therefore, there is certainly some relationship between revolutionary change and class struggles. But the relationship is much less direct than would follow from a definition of revolution as structural social change. A revolution is, basically, not a social but a political phenomenon affecting the *status quo* in terms of power.

On the other hand, there are sudden overthrows of an established political order which we label as counter-revolutionary. Could we, in such cases, equally speak of a sudden change in the balance of power between competing systems of social hierarchy? Certainly yes, but there is still a basic difference from the case of a true revolution. A counter-revolution does not generally open a perspective to large social groups, that were hitherto excluded from power, of being able to realize their aspirations for a greater scope of action and greater political influence. Counter-revolutions are basically aimed at fortifying the political power of social groups that were already very influential within the established political order. They are generally intended, as we have seen, to stem the tide of emancipation which was proceeding through legal, evolutionary means for which some scope was left within the prevalent political structure. Only in this respect is a prevalent balance of power being reversed through a counter-revolution – not in the sense that social groups hitherto excluded from the establishment are winning a greater share of political recognition and responsibility. Therefore, the term structural change would be highly inappropriate for a counter-revolution; and even the term fundamental change should be taken, in this case, in a less specific sense than in the case of true revolutions.

iii. *Violence and Non-Violence*

Another important issue in defining the concept of revolution is to what extent violence belongs to its basic characteristics. Earlier we have stated that what distinguishes revolution from evolution is its cataclysmic quality, the acceleration of the evolutionary process and the upheaval of the social order which accompanies such a chain of events. But does this necessarily imply that violence is a basic element in a revolutionary process as Hannah Arendt appears to assume? She writes 'that revolutions and wars are not even conceivable outside the domain of violence'.[9]

Naturally, it would not do to try to refute this view by pointing to expressions such as 'industrial revolution', 'demographic revolution', or 'electronic revolution'. It is clear that in these cases the term 'revolution' is being used in a metaphorical way and refers to the element of rapid development and thorough renewal in the fields where 'revolutionary' change occurs.

But even in the case of political revolutions there is enough reason seriously to consider to what extent violence is an elementary criterion for appraising a chain of events as a revolution.

There have been in history several instances where rapid structural change took place with remarkably little bloodshed. The events in Czechoslovakia in February 1948 could certainly be called revolutionary, considering the popular masses which had come into action to effect a thorough overthrow of the existing social order – yet there was hardly any actual violence.

Perhaps one could argue that the vicinity of Russian army units, though they remained inactive and in the background throughout the revolutionary period, embodied a potential use of violence which was a decisive factor in the actual power structure. The nomination of Klement Gottwald as a prime minister in 1945 had been made possible by the military presence of the Soviets.

Therefore, to a certain extent, the Czechoslovakian example raises this question: can a mass movement against a government be called revolutionary if it has been handled by part of that same government? If so, could there be any relationship between the relative lack of violence and the participation of part of the establishment in a revolution?

The same semantic problem is manifest in the case of Japan. The Meiji restoration of 1868 (sometimes called the Meiji revolution) was partly inspired from above by circles that pushed forward the young emperor as a symbol, partly supported from below by a class of *samurais*, especially the lower ones, who had become outsiders during the Tokugawa period of rule by a *shogun* assisted by his *daimyos*. However, in this case the amount of violence involved in the overthrow was quite considerable.

One could also mention the Chinese case, in connection with the recent cultural revolution. Here is a case in which popular masses – most prominently youth – have come into action, but throughout the process had a firm support from a significant section of both the Communist Party leadership and the army. Despite numerous contrary reports in the Western and East European press, the amount of true physical violence has remained limited throughout the process; it was a marginal phenomenon in a development which was largely characterized by mass demonstrations, group discussions on a huge scale, and mass propaganda. The amount of leadership from above becomes evident, for example, from the general support the cultural revolution in the form advocated by Mao Tse-tung himself received from the publicity media, after a short period of hesitation in early 1966 when there appeared to be some dissent, or at least discrepancies in interpretation, between the army press and the party press. Apparently, from the first of June 1966 onwards, those in authority backing the Red Guards and the revolutionary rebels, in the course of the process, kept the decisive mass propaganda media firmly in their hands.[10]

Here we encounter the phenomenon of a revolution from below led from above, at least by a sector within the power structure. It can be questioned, again, whether the Chinese case fits our definition of revolution. I would suggest that, since the movement aimed at profound changes in the prevailing social order, and in the process was largely directed against the ruling institutional apparatus, both centrally and locally (the party and the bureaucracy), it should still be comprehended within our concept of revolution. To quote Joan Robinson: 'It was a popular rising instigated and guided by the leader of the very régime which was established before it and which remains in being.'[11] On the other hand, the support from above makes it understandable why the revolution could occur with a minimum of actual physical violence, though again it could be argued that the strength of the military apparatus supporting the movement was in the background.

We have, however, still to deal with the problem of whether revolutionary change – in the sense of highly accelerated fundamental change – can ever be brought about without violence, by a true movement from below, that is to say without any substantial, real or potential, support from a sector within the existing power structure. Here the issue of non-violent struggle is at stake.

In the past decades there have been several movements in different countries advocating a struggle for a better world and ultimately aiming at an overturn of the existing power structure by non-violent means. The names of Mahatma Gandhi, Albert Luthuli, and Martin Luther King stand for an ideology rejecting violence as a matter of principle. Their preachings, however, raise the question as to what extent radical structural change in the realm of politics can be brought about by civil disobedience on a mass basis, without any resort to violence or the threat of it.

First of all, we have to decide whether those movements really aimed at rapid social change; that is to say, whether the plea for non-violence is not at the same time, consciously or unconsciously, a plea for gradualism and patience. If this is the case it would imply that non-violent struggle could never be comprehended under the heading of revolution, but should simply be viewed as one of the roads along which evolution – in the sense of gradual emancipation for certain social groups – could be achieved.

It is certainly true that the ideology of non-violence starts from a distinct preference for non-violent means even if the use of these would mean a slowing-down of the envisaged political and social process. The philosophy of the advocates of non-violence is based on the assumption that, even though the method of achieving one's aim is slower and requires more patience on the part of those oppressed by the present power structure, the ultimate results will be more stable and more lasting. The argument runs that the use of violence always creates much opposition and dissatisfaction which will provoke all kinds of reactions in a later stage of development; moreover, violence as a method for achieving their ends infects those involved in an emancipation movement and, by its own logic, produces an atmosphere in which the use of violence may be considered normal. The most incisive formulation of this way of reasoning is Gandhi's, who argued that one cannot separate ends from means, since the means used necessarily affect the end one intends to achieve.

However, though one may readily agree that non-violent action is much to be preferred to violent action even if it amounts to a certain slowing-down of the process, one basic problem is whether non-violent action can ever be successful in a situation characterized by involution in the social and economic field, or in a situation where for some other reason, for example the rigidity of the prevalent power structure, there are strong forces operative which inhibit the urge for emancipation as expressed by significant groups. We have seen that it is exactly in cases where the process of gradual evolution has been blocked that a radical acceleration of certain processes is needed to stop the involutionary trends and to reverse the general direction of social and economic development. Can such a revolutionary acceleration be brought about by non-violent means, or is the belief in non-violence, in such a situation, an illusion only? In other words, can the advocates of non-violent action be considered as true revolutionaries, only distinguishable by the methods they are willing to allow, or is their belief in non-violence a symptom of either self-deception or a lesser commitment to radical structural change?

There is no doubt that at least Gandhi thought of himself as a true revolutionary. The leadership he gave in massive civil disobedience and non-cooperation and his readiness to accept imprisonment as a consequence of such actions were certainly intended as a new form of revolutionary activity. And there is, definitely, some reason to argue that the achievement of political independence for India was accelerated by Gandhi's non-violent civil disobedience, compared with what would have happened if the nationalists had adhered to strictly legal action – though it remains difficult to decide whether violent action would not have produced the same result and maybe at an even earlier date.

Even if non-violent action may, in certain circumstances, be subsumed under the general heading of revolutionary actions, it must still be asked whether the conditions in which such a non-violent action may produce the intended result – an overthrow of the existing social and political order – should not be specified with greater precision.

Gandhi always considered his appeal for moral restraint and justice as directed not only at his followers, but equally at his adversaries. Although, in his view, colonial rule was necessarily demonic, and though he was fully aware of its inhumanities, yet those in authority were, in his opinion, reasonable human beings susceptible to a moral appeal.

His partial success throughout the colonial period could be attributed to the fact that the British democratic tradition, though seriously impaired in the colonial situation, still allowed him a certain room for manoeuvring and for expressing his views in public. There were also elements within the British government that were prepared to listen to him, as evidenced by the invitation extended to him to attend the second Round Table conference in London, in 1931. As Nehru writes in his *Autobiography*: 'For some reason or other the British Government was very keen on having Gandhiji in London, and avoided, as far as possible, doing anything to prevent this.'[12]

The same modicum of British liberality, which allowed Gandhi to go on with his political activities during certain periods when he was not in prison and even made him acceptable as a partner in negotiations, may also account for the ultimate success of the movement led by him. The decision of the British postwar government to grant India independence without having been forced to do so by a large-scale armed insurrection, as occurred in colonial countries such as Indonesia and Vietnam, can be attributed partly to the fact that the country was ruled by a government that was, to a certain extent, responsive to the non-violent type of mass action unleashed by Gandhi.

The complete failure of Luthuli's action in South Africa testifies to the restrictions inherent in the character of the authority opposed by a mass movement. If those in power turn a deaf ear to all the claims of those striving for emancipation and radical change, non-violent action, even though its leaders deny being revolutionaries, will be met by brutal oppression. The appeal to reason, as advocated by followers of Gandhi, will remain unheeded, and its moral strength will be wasted on those who possess the power to suppress.

We could, then, presume that the only cases in which a non-violent revolution may be successful are such in which those in command show, to a certain extent, some understanding for the emancipation movement and are, consequently, either amenable to reasonable argument or, at least, prepared to let economic or other interests prevail over emotional and legalistic considerations connected with chauvinism and prestige. These cases can be considered as an extension of the previously mentioned situation in which the movement from below gets real support from part of the actual power structure.

At the same time, the Indian example may indicate that non-violent action can only be successful in some types of revolution. The Indian revolution was a national one and did not aim at a complete overhaul of the social order. Gandhi did not preach social revolution. The large landowners and businessmen had not much to fear from his ascension to power. This may, on the one hand, account for his feeling for compromise which was one of the aspects of his choice in favour of a peaceful road. On the other hand, it may make us understand why the British in the specific postwar conditions were willing to make a deal before armed insurrection became inevitable. It appeared possible to safeguard the main British economic and political interests without clinging to paramount political powers.

There are, however, movements which are not content with a

transfer of formal power and with legal equality. A true social revolution aims at radical social change, seriously affecting the propertied classes and, in particular, large landowners. It is not to be expected that those in power will easily yield to a mass action which appeals to reason but lacks arms. It is difficult to imagine that such a propertied class, and a state power representing their interests, will ever be willing to give them up without a fight. Gandhi and his follower, Vinoba Bhave, hoped that the large landowners would renounce their excess of land. But Leo Tolstoy, so much revered by Gandhi, was himself a member of the landed aristocracy and consequently less naïve than the latter. To quote Edward A. Ross:

Tolstoi, who knew his class, describes the manifestations of a newborn social conscience in the Russian landowner. The nobleman came to feel sorry for the *moujik* under him. He would change his position to make himself a little easier to carry. He would speak kindly to the *moujik*, would even bend down and wipe the sweat from his brow. His conscience had become so sensitive that he was willing to do *anything* for the poor fellow – anything, that is, except get off his back![13]

The foregoing analysis may provide a reply to our previous query whether, in a situation where involution prevails or the way towards progress appears to be blocked through the rigidity of the prevalent power structure, a decisive acceleration of emancipation processes can be brought about by non-violent means. There are, unfortunately, strong vested interests resisting any serious claim for emancipation and protected by a powerful state apparatus. In such cases a non-violent *social* revolution seems out of the question.

Maybe this also accounts for the difficulties non-violent action encounters in the United States. Martin Luther King and the organizations adhering to his principle of non-violence might be moderately successful provided that their activities were mainly directed at integration at a level where the basic economic and political power of the whites was not threatened. But as soon as the issue of segregated living quarters was at stake, with the concomitant irritant of the decreasing value of real estate, the attitude of those in actual power hardened. In order to be able to pursue its more radical aims, a strong section within SNCC (Student Non-violent Coordinating Committee) felt compelled to reverse its stand and to relinquish non-violence as a principle, while at the same time writing the revolutionary slogan of Black Power on its banner.[14]

If we could, therefore, agree that violence is not an indispensable attribute of revolution, we should at the same time be aware that in all probability, non-violence as a method for achieving fundamental change is applicable only under rather narrowly circumscribed conditions. If the movement has no substantial support from a significant sector of the actual power structure, non-violent action is likely to be promising only in cases where the envisaged overthrow of the prevalent political order is not too radical and does not threaten the basic interests of those in actual command.

iv. Internal and External Causes

A further problem connected with our attempt at delineating the concept of revolution is to what extent revolutionary movements, and more particularly those which do not find any support among those in power and which aim at an overthrow of the existing authority structure, can be viewed as true outbursts of popular discontent brought about by a culmination of frustrations within the existing power structure. We are not concerned, here, with the genesis of revolutionary movements. This issue will be dealt with in the next chapter. The only point that concerns us at present is whether revolutions are, by definition, movements that can be accounted for primarily in terms of internal stirrings within a society.

This is often denied. To quote Lyford P. Edwards: 'It is a matter of common knowledge that in every social upheaval the party attacked claims that the trouble has been stirred up by outside agents and agitators.'[15] It is true that revolutionary movements often get inspiration and even, in some cases, leadership from outside. We shall discuss later the phenomenon of how these elements provide an international aspect to internal wars. Modelski rightly points to 'the revolutionaries of the type of Lafayette or Che Guevara who join up with an insurgent movement irrespective of their original political affiliation',[16] that is to say, irrespective of their national status. However, revolutionary movements generally get some help, and even ideological guidance in formulating their political ideas and organizational structure, from elements outside the sphere of mass support. A peasant revolution, for example, generally draws a certain amount of leadership from a different, more urbanized and sophisticated sphere, or at least from people who are more or less marginal to the main force.

The real problem, however, is not whether elements from outside develop certain activities. The issue at stake is whether one is ever justified in attributing the movement to those outside agents and agitators. Those in power usually claim that there is a contented, but not too intelligent, population that has no fundamental reasons for dissatisfaction. Outside agitators, however, incite this population to make all kinds of unrealistic claims and demands and *create* a dissatisfaction without any real foundation, and thus stir up trouble in an otherwise harmonious community.

We know from historical evidence that revolutions, in several thoroughly studied cases, had deeper roots within society and were the logical outcome of a prolonged process of dissatisfaction and frustrated expectations. We also know that those in authority are quite often unaware of the reality or keeping up a pretence, as in the case of Louis XVI who viewed the storming of the Bastille as a rebellion and wrote in his diary under that date: *rien*; or Lieutenant-Governor General H. J. van Mook, who, as I have already mentioned in the foreword, still held the opinion, as late as October 1945, that a few shiploads of food and textiles from Australia could stem the tide of revolution in Indonesia.

The real problem is whether it is ever possible to incite a movement of a certain scale without there being a real basis for such stirrings within the prevalent social and political order.

No serious politician will pretend that, in the field where agitators operate, there is nothing wrong at all. In order to do them justice, we have to put the problem in a different way. Is it possible for outside agents to provoke a movement of a truly revolutionary character and amplitude without serious and profound tensions within the society where they are operating?

It should be possible to put this hypothesis to a test, for example by experiments within smaller hierarchical units. As far as historical evidence is available, however, it seems a highly improbable one. Potential agitators and instigators of unrest can be found in any society. Their effectiveness and eventual success, however, depend upon the amount of support they get, for quite a long period, from the people among whom they are operating. In societies where dissatisfaction and frustration have not crystallized to any considerable extent, their chances of ultimate success, or even of commanding considerable support, seem very slight indeed.

v. Some Types of Revolution

Another important issue is the distinction between types of revolution. In the foregoing discussion we already encountered the distinction between national and social revolutions, the former one presenting an ambiguous character: for those in authority it is a civil war – if not a simple rebellion – whereas for the insurgents the movement is from the outset a war of independence, directed against foreign occupation.

Social revolutions, on the other hand, are essentially uprisings of one class against another. The basic distinction in most classic Marxist literature is the bourgeois revolution, directed against a ruling aristocracy, as differentiated from the proletarian revolution, upheld by industrial workers and directed against the ruling bourgeoisie.

The question arises to what extent an uprising, starting as a bourgeois revolution, can be transformed in its course into a proletarian one. The two Russian revolutions of 1917 showed that, in practice, it was possible, as both Lenin and Trotsky had already foreseen, though in different formulations, at the time of the 1905 revolution.[17] The issue, however, also presented some theoretical implications in connection with the much disputed concept of permanent revolution, to which we shall revert further on.

According to Marxist analysis, national liberation movements generally amount to bourgeois revolutions. In many cases they produce a number of democratic political institutions; however, even if the national liberation struggle involves large sections of the population, in itself it cannot be equated with the second phase, the proletarian revolution, implying a transfer of power from the bourgeoisie to the working class.

Most national revolutions were, according to the Marxist evaluation, only halfway revolutions. And if the nationalist struggle was waged by reactionaries, they could not even be viewed as bourgeois revolutions. For this reason, in the 1840s Marx supported the national movements of the Poles and the Hungarians, but opposed those of the Czechs and the Yugoslavs, as Stalin pointed out in his *Foundations of Leninism* in 1924. On the other hand, in other recent cases, as a consequence of the support given by the peasant masses or agricultural labourers, a national revolution can transcend its bourgeois origins and develop into a proletarian or socialist one – as seems to have been the case in Vietnam and in Cuba (inasmuch as the Cuban revolution can be considered to have been directed against American economic domination).

Mao Tse-tung and Lin Piao in his wake, even defined a specific type of revolution directed against imperialism, feudalism, and bureaucratic capitalism and therefore clearly distinct from the bourgeois type of national revolution: the 'new-democratic revolution', characterized by proletarian leadership.[18]

The revolutions of Vietnam and Cuba would certainly fit this concept which Mao and Lin distinguish from a socialist revolution occurring in a later phase.

This takes us to the highly important issue of agrarian revolutions as a specific sub-type of social ones. In earlier Marxist literature these were not distinguished as a special type. Most Western Marxist theorists did not consider that peasants were fit to unleash a true revolution. Peasant uprisings were classed rather as *jacqueries*, as outbursts which had no prospect of making a fundamental change within society. Peasants were acknowledged as potential participants and allies in either a bourgeois or a proletarian revolution. But they were not viewed as suitable to play an independent role, their status as small landowners without any specialized training relegating them to a position of members of the *petite bourgeoisie*.

The Marxists were not the only ones to underrate the potential significance of the rural element for revolutionary movements.

Even in the late thirties Crane Brinton, in his *The Anatomy of Revolution*, treated the peasantry as a negligible factor, devoting only one page to them and even in that single page dealing with them in a casual, somewhat cavalier way.[19] In this respect, Brinton simply conformed to the stereotype of the peasantry which had been held by a great majority of Western historians in the past. This stereotype amounted to an assessment of the peasantry as a basically conservative class keeping aloof from the mainstream of human history.

Marx himself had not fully disengaged himself from this stereotype. The *Communist Manifesto* characterized the peasantry as part of the lower-middle class, struggling against the bourgeoisie in order

to save from extinction their existence as fractions of the middle class. They are therefore not revolutionary, but conservative. Nay, more, they are reactionary, for they try to roll back the wheel of history.

And England was, according to Marx's view in 1870, the country where a serious economic revolution was primarily to be expected: 'It is a country that has no more peasants.'[20]

However, there are also a few statements in Marx's work that point towards a more positive assessment of the revolutionary potentialities of the peasant class. For example, in 1856 he wrote to Engels that the only chance of a proletarian revolution in Germany succeeding would be to get a backing from 'some second edition of the Peasants' War'. And during the seventies, after he had become somewhat disillusioned as to the revolutionary potential of West European industrial workers, he started to view the backward Russian peasantry with more sympathy, and even began to consider them as potential allies in a struggle for a socialist society.[21]

It has been rightly suggested by G. J. Harmsen that whenever Karl Marx mentioned the peasants' conservatism and bourgeois attitude, he probably had in mind the West European agriculturalist-landowners, who were rather farmers than peasants. Writing about the German and Russian agriculturalists as a potentially revolutionary group, on the other hand, Marx probably had in view the small peasants of part of Central and most of Eastern Europe, who had never achieved the status of fully independent landowners.[22] For most Asian peasants the gap separating them from a Western farmer is much wider still. Nobody would ever think of present-day French or Dutch peasants as a revolutionary force. On the contrary, Poujadism in France and the Farmers' Party in the Netherlands have, from the very beginning, been openly conservative or even reactionary. The reason is clear: as the prewar British conservative prime minister, Stanley Baldwin, is once said to have put it: 'If you want the people to be conservative, then give them something to conserve.' The West European farmer is a bourgeois because, despite his manifold complaints, some of them quite justified, he has a stake in maintaining the present state of affairs. An Asian peasant, on the other hand, is a near-proletarian, and he has nothing to lose by revolution but the chains binding him to his landlord or his moneylender – which, incidentally, are sometimes spiritual chains: peasants are frequently tied to powerful local lords by patronage relationships.

Gradually, Marxist theorists have become more aware of the revolutionary potential among the peasantry. Marxist theory gradually adapted to the new realities of revolutionary practice especially when, after 1900, revolutionary movements arose in predominantly agrarian Russia. In particular, Lenin increasingly stressed, from 1905 onwards, the importance of the poor peasantry as a revolutionary factor, as contrasted with the larger landowners who aligned themselves with the conservative forces. He criticized Trotsky, in 1915, for underrating the significance of this class that

he put on a par, as a potential revolutionary force, with the industrial workers, whereas Trotsky not only kept stressing the necessity for urban proletarian leadership but denied that the peasantry,
whom he considered backward, could play an independent role.

During and after the Russian proletarian revolution that materialized in November 1917, as a sequel to the bourgeois revolution, the significance of the peasantry as a revolutionary force
and an important ally of the urban workers was clearly demonstrated. Since the expected socialist revolutions in other European
countries were not forthcoming, the Soviet leaders increasingly
directed their attention to Asia, where an impoverished peasantry
could play a similar revolutionary role.

However, the idea that the industrial workers had to be the
main core and proletarian vanguard of the revolutionary movement was never relinquished in Soviet Marxist theory.

It was left to the Chinese brand of Marxism as elaborated by
Mao Tse-tung to demonstrate the immense revolutionary potential
in an impoverished Asian peasantry, in a country where an industrial working class is only rudimentary. But even Mao has never
ventured to label a revolution of the type realized in China as an
agrarian one. Though stressing the importance of the rural component much more than Soviet Marxists have up till now, he has
always kept to the Marxian principle that a socialist revolution
has to be effected under the leadership of an industrial proletariat.
In the practice of Chinese strategy this meant that, throughout
the revolutionary movement of the thirties and the forties, the
primacy and initiative were to reside with the Communist Party
leadership that was assumed to represent the industrial proletarian element.[23] Although, throughout the cultural revolution, leadership by the Communist Party appeared to be
seriously shaken, in the course of 1968 the pre-eminent role of the
industrial workers, as the main core of the purified Communist
Party, seemed to be gradually restored.

In this respect, Castro's interpretation of the Cuban revolution
is not very different from the Maoist one, the most striking
difference being that leadership by revolutionary intellectuals is
explicitly mentioned in addition to proletarian leadership – which

may be explained by the minor role played by the Communist Party as such in the Cuban revolution.[24]

In more recent Marxist literature, however, there is a growing tendency to recognize the successful revolutions of the recent decades as essentially agrarian ones. According to the Austrian Marxist Franz Marek, agrarian revolutions have been the only ones that have succeeded in establishing Marxism as an officially accepted ideology.[25]

Soviet Marxist theory, on the other hand, considers the agrarian component in a social revolution as being basically *petit bourgeois* in character, which in many cases deflects it from its socialist course. According to Soviet Marxist ideology, it is exactly this component which constitutes the basic weakness of the Chinese experiment and accounts for its 'deviations' from the Soviet model which is still considered the most successful example of a proletarian revolution.[26]

In Western non-Marxist political science, the importance of the rural element in revolution is also being increasingly realized.

A few years ago, an American political scientist, Barrington Moore, published a comparative study of revolutions.[27] Like Crane Brinton, he included the British and French revolutions among those to which he paid special attention. But he added three important Asian countries to the Western model. This can be explained by the fact that his assessment of the significance of the peasant element widely diverges from Brinton's. In Moore's view rural conditions play a crucial role in determining the course of social and economic development in a given country. A numerous, impoverished peasantry may be at the root of a special type of modernization, namely economic and, in particular, industrial development along dictatorial lines as was, for example, the case in Germany and Japan.[28] In France, the peasantry played an equally significant role. Though the French Revolution was far from being a peasant revolution, yet, according to Moore, 'the peasantry was the arbiter of the revolution'.[29] As long as the peasants marched along with the Parisan *Lumpenproletariat*, the *sans-culottes*, the revolution could continue. When, however, the regime had become, under Robespierre, too radical to satisfy the property-owning peasants any longer, they deserted the revolutionaries – and time was ripe for Thermidor and 'white terror'.

As far as the Russian and Chinese revolutions are concerned, Moore views both of them as being basically 'peasant revolutions'. In his analysis, 'in China, even more than in Russia, the peasants provided the dynamite that finally exploded the old order.[30]

Yet, though acknowledging the peasantry as an important revolutionary force, Moore considers them a class that has spent its force as soon as the aim of revolution – modernization through industrial development – is achieved. The result of the modernization process is, in his opinion, the annihilation of the peasantry as a class.[31]

In the course of this study, I shall revert to this thesis. For the moment it is important to note that Moore's work is a symptom of a much greater comprehension among present-day non-Marxist authors of the significance of the peasant element in revolutions.

We thus arrive at the following distinctions. The primary distinction is the one between national and social revolutions.

In the classical national revolution it is the bourgeoisie, in itself a far from unambiguous category, that assumes the leadership, although the peasantry may participate in the liberation struggle. In the present world situation, however, the bourgeoisie is, in most cases, too closely allied to foreign interests to be able to provide effective leadership for a protracted struggle. Therefore, national liberation movements may assume new-democratic characteristics, which means that both the urban proletariat and the peasantry are assuming much more prominent roles. A new-democratic revolution, either from the outset or in its later course, transcends the borderline between national and social revolutions.

Social revolutions, on the other hand, are present whenever one social stratum, cooperating on a solidarity basis – or, to use Marxian terminology, functioning as a political class – attempts to wrest political power and social ascendancy from the ruling stratum. The older type of social revolution, known from Western history, was characterized by a struggle of the bourgeoisie against a ruling aristocracy.

In the present world, it is the 'fourth estate' that challenges the power of the ruling bourgeoisie. But, contrary to classical Marxist theory, in the Third World of today it is no longer the urban proletariat that plays a decisive role in these social revolutions. The peasantry is increasingly acknowledged as a strong revolutionary force, although Marxists still claim that a certain leadership from other social categories, either the urban proletariat or the intelligentsia, remains indispensable.

vi. World Revolution

Another concept, which has to be discussed, is that of world revolution. Marx and Engels were fully aware that a communist revolution, in order to succeed, should transcend national borders. In *Grundsätze des Kommunismus*, a preparatory study for the *Communist Manifesto*, they argued that such a revolution should at least break out simultaneously in England, America, France, and Germany, the countries where the class conflict between bourgeoisie and proletariat had sufficiently matured.

In 1905, Lenin expanded the concept beyond the confines of the Western world and beyond the limitations of simultaneity, and redefined it in terms of an 'uninterrupted revolution'.[33] He developed the idea of a possible growth of a movement starting as a bourgeois-democratic revolution, such as the one that at the time of his writing raged in Russia, into a socialist one, which simultaneously could signal the eruption of socialist revolutions in Western Europe. About the same time, Trotsky propagated similar views. From then on, the concept of world revolution was foremost in the mind of the Russian revolutionaries, until the events of 1917 put to the test the theory that a Russian proletarian revolution would spark off one in other industrialized countries of Europe.

The expected chain effect did not come about, although proletarian solidarity, in the shape of strikes by dock workers and a mutiny of the French fleet in the Black Sea, was effective enough in hampering the War of Intervention waged against the new Soviet state by Allied Forces.

If, therefore, the Soviet leaders hoped for a chain effect, they had to direct their attention to a different type of country: the predominantly agrarian ones in Asia and other parts of the world, many of them still under colonial rule. This shift in theoretical and tactical approach was in accordance with the discovery of the impoverished peasantry as a powerful ally. At the same time, it was in harmony with Lenin's and other Marxists' analysis of imperialism as the highest stage in the development of capitalism. If capitalist exploitation has grown into a world system founded upon a chain of military and political bases all over the world, revolution has to attack it at its weakest link – which is more likely to be discovered in a country like India than in the industrialized part of the world.[34]

However, in 1924, at the time of Lenin's death, the world revolution had not materialized and the Soviet Union stood isolated in a hostile world.

The Soviet leaders were confronted with a dilemma: had they to give first priority to internal security and economic development of their own country, or should continued action prevail in order to provoke revolutionary outbursts in other countries? The controversy between Stalin and Trotsky was mainly focused on this issue, the latter developing the concept of 'uninterrupted' revolution advanced in earlier writings by Marx, Lenin, and himself[35] into a theory of a 'permanent' revolution. Trotsky's distrust of the peasantry as a revolutionary force made him look towards the industrial proletariat of Europe as the only factor that could rescue socialism in Russia.

But it was Stalin who got the upper hand with a strategy that was dictated by pragmatic rather than theoretical considerations. It amounted to advancing the thesis of the possibility of establishing gradual detachment of Comintern activities from Soviet foreign policy that was mainly directed towards an achievement of external security for the Soviet state. World revolution was not relinquished as a theoretical principle and the seditious activities of the Comintern for a long time haunted the established powers all over the world as a terrifying spectre, which prevented a genuine acceptance of the Soviet Union as a partner in international relations. Gradually, however, the dominance of the Soviet Union within the Comintern and the rise of Hitler to power in Germany led to attempts to tone down activities aiming for a world revolution. The security of the Soviet Union as a state was viewed, by Stalin and his followers, as the main guarantee for an eventual victory of a world revolution. In the process, however, the Soviet leadership lost some of its attraction as a world centre of revolution for the true proletariat outside the Western world who have nothing to lose but their chains. This process has been considerably accelerated since the end of the Second World War.[36]

Since it became clear, in the course of the Chinese revolution, that it was not the industrial proletariat of the developed countries but the rural proletariat of the under-developed ones that would play a major role in future revolutionary developments, the term world revolution has acquired a different meaning: one coined by Lin Piao in his previously quoted famous speech of 3 September 1965, 'Long Live the Victory of the People's War!' In it, Mao's strategy of a spread of the internal revolution from the countryside, where there is enough room for manoeuvring, towards the cities, effected by an encirclement of the latter, was extended to encompass the world: the poor nations, with an impoverished peasantry, should be viewed as one huge countryside whereas the industrialized countries represent the cities of the world. The present phase of the world revolution, in this view, started in the countryside of China and is bound to spread to other parts of the world. It should result in a serious weakening of the economic, political and military power of the strongest industrial capitalist power of today, the United States.[37]

vii. Internal and External War

Another issue to be discussed in this chapter dealing with terminology is the intertwining of national and international aspects of revolutions, to which the discussion of the concept of world revolution was more or less a prelude. The term civil war refers to the internal aspect of a revolution which is normally considered to occur within a state as a political unit. The term national revolution however implies, as we have observed earlier, that at least one segment of the political unit does not recognize it as representative of its popular aspirations. A national revolution, therefore, necessarily entails that the same movement which, seen from the angle of those representing the existing political structure, has the character of a civil war, from the standpoint of the revolutionaries shows an international aspect aspiring at the liberation of one nation from the domination by another.

However, even social revolutions generally present an aspect that spills over national borders. 'Every war has two faces; it is a conflict both between and within political systems: a conflict that is both external and internal.' 'Every internal war has wide international ramifications and ... may lead to and include external war.' In these two concise statements, George Modelski summarizes the interrelationship between internal and external wars.[38]

The former statement concerning the civil war aspect of every war – I would prefer to say of nearly every war – has been elaborated by a number of Dutch historians. Jan Romein has expressed the opinion that even in early history nearly every war showed certain aspects of a civil war. In some way or other a war was generally at the same time a contest between mutually competing social groups, who had potential allies within the country of the 'enemy'.[39] The American Revolution was not only a struggle of a rising bourgeoisie against the British aristocracy at home; it was also directed against the latter's allies, the royal functionaries and large landowners in the New World. 'Are we sure that more Americans fought under the American flag than under British colours?' asks Jacques Presser of Amsterdam University.[40] It seems to me that Karl Deutsch gives a reply. He starts with the estimate from which Presser evidently derived his query, 'that roughly one-third of the colonial population supported the Patriots in that conflict; another one-third was neutral.' Deutsch adds, however, a most significant rider:

Although the two main factions were thus evenly matched, the Patriots produced 400,000 enlistments in the course of the conflict, while the Loyalists produced only 50,000 or one-eighth the rate of their opponents.

He considers this as an indicator 'of the morale and the intensity of motivation of each side'.[41]

Even so, the civil war character of the American national revolution is clearly demonstrated in the foregoing figures.

Perhaps another historian and political scientist from Amsterdam, Jef Suys, was to a certain extent right when he wrote about the First World War: 'This war was one between states, without or nearly without civil war aspects'.[42] Yet we should not forget that the Germans provided facilities for Lenin, who had advocated a transformation of the imperialist war into a civil war, to return to his homeland. And if we look beyond the European borders, we notice that the Germans incited Muslim Indians to rise against the British, in the same way as the British used Arab nationalism against the Turks.

On the other hand, nobody would take exception to Suys's contention that 'in the Second World War the civil war element was unmistakable'.[43] A considerable number of Chinese large landowners aligned themselves with the Japanese whereas Pétain was a potential ally of Hitler's from the outbreak of the Second World War. Suys states that the amount of French collaboration with the Germans could not be explained without this civil war aspect. High treason, fifth column, defeatism – they are all concepts that are related to internal social tensions rather than due to personal depravity or lack of character.

It is the world-wide conflict, rooted in the Cold War, between ideologically diametrically opposed powers that makes the interrelatedness between external and internal war such an acute problem in the present world. It is impossible to define the boundary between civil and external war. What is a police action for one party becomes a colonial war for the counterpart. What started as a domestic affair develops, as soon as the insurgents achieve certain successes and acquire a measure of international recognition, into an international conflict. Still more confusing is the situation where one nation has been divided into two, mostly through the intervention of a foreign occupation army. When the division has lasted for some time (Korea, Vietnam) the social and political systems have taken highly divergent directions. A revolutionary development within one of the parts – expropriation of large land-owners, forced industrialization – is artificially blocked in the other one. Each of the regimes finds allies among the population of the other section. An armed conflict can hardly be avoided – and intervention by more powerful allies is what one would expect.

Throughout world history, all types of intervention, open or disguised, have been attempted in the form of aid to the opponents in a civil war. Those who support the legal authorities, and thus defend the *status quo*, are generally in a safer position and can be less easily charged with aggression and meddling in domestic affairs than those who support the insurgents. The support to insurgents may be given in different forms, including expressions of sympathy, the provision of asylum for political fugitives, mat-erial support in the shape of equipment, the supply of infiltrating individual agents or technical specialists to make guerrilla troops more effective, the provision of training facilities on its territory for insurgents and, finally, as the highest form of support short of military intervention, a dispatch of volunteers.[44]

Whether a charge of aggression will be levelled against these types of intervention depends upon several factors, most of all the mutual balance of power. As we have seen, the authorities against whom the revolution is directed will tend to overstress the influence of outside agents.

viii. Export of Revolution or of Counter-Revolution

It is the Marxist ideology of world revolution that has attracted so much attention to communist subversion since the Russian Re-volution of November 1917. Interestingly, soon after the revo-lution, the Soviet leaders developed the theory that revolution was not an object for export. How can this theory be reconciled with the patently seditious activities of Comintern, reflecting the ideo-logy of world revolution?

The 'no export' theory, however, has little to do with indirect types of support. It is only directed against the Bonapartist tendency of carrying a revolution abroad through the armed forces. What the Soviet Marxists mean by this thesis – which is also, in essence, endorsed by the Chinese communists – is that a revolutionary movement should mature from within and that military intervention by a socialist state should be avoided lest the popular masses be estranged from the socialist ideology.

In practice, however, the Soviet state was more than once caught in an insoluble dilemma and could not avoid a certain amount of 'export of revolution'. The first theoretical controversy arose about 1920, after a young officer, Tukhachevsky, had invaded Poland with a measure of support from Lenin but against fierce opposition from Trotsky. The latter, though the staunchest advocate of world revolution, felt that military intervention would hamper the spread of a genuine revolutionary atmosphere. After the failure of the Polish expedition, Tukhachevsky attempted publicly to defend his actions, but in vain. The 'no export' theory was adopted as a matter of principle.

This does not mean, however, that from that time onwards no export of revolution has occurred. There were several instances of intervention by the Red Army, all of them within the territory that was claimed to belong to the Soviet orbit, and every time with the argument that the army was supporting a communist insurrection that had already arisen. It was, in particular, the intervention of the Red Army in Georgia in the early twenties, on Stalin's orders, that came in for serious criticism not only from Trotsky but eventually also from Lenin. Again, the conflict between the pragmatist Stalin and the theorist Trotsky became manifest.

But Stalin's very pragmatism also induced him, after he had come to power, to the greatest caution as far as the use of the Red Army was concerned. No Bonapartism carried the revolution across the borders established in the early twenties. And even when, after the Second World War had been successfully concluded, the Red Army had penetrated deep into the territory of the enemy, Stalin remained cautious in his external policy. The external security of the Soviet Union was his primary concern. This implied that in East European countries bordering on the Soviet

Union, he actually practised 'export of revolution', relying upon the Red Army that had chased the retreating Germans, a method that Deutscher has called 'revolution from above'.[45] In countries farther removed from the centre of Soviet power where he feared American intervention, however, Stalin, in accordance with the division into spheres of influence agreed at the Yalta Conference and elsewhere, practised a policy of abstention and even withdrawal, notwithstanding the fact that in some cases there was a strong revolutionary movement and that the upheaval occurred near the Soviet borders. Greece, North Iran, and China are typical cases in point.[46] The invasion of Czechoslovakia by armed forces of the Soviet Union and other signatories to the Warsaw Pact in August 1968, is a recent instance of this type of export of revolution – but at the same time it raises, more urgently than in earlier cases, such as the Hungarian one, the query whether it is still revolution that is being exported and not its opposite.

China, equally, has abstained, thus far, from direct military intervention, except in the case of Tibet which she considered to be a part of Chinese territory. In Korea, the intervention was officially restricted to a dispatch of volunteers, at a moment when General McArthur was nearing China's borders and threatening to bomb Chinese industrial installations. For the rest, Chinese strategy sometimes appears to amount to extreme aggression in words, and extreme cautiousness in action. This attitude may be explained by the dilemma in which they are now caught, just as the Soviet Union was in the period between the two world wars. On the one hand, they want to retain their reputation as revolutionaries keeping up solidarity with the progressive forces all over the world, since the Soviets have been losing their position as a centre of world revolution,[47] while on the other hand they wish to avoid unnecessary war risks in cases where their vital interests as a state are not threatened.

There remains, however, a highly significant difference between the Soviet and the Chinese attitude with respect to the danger of war. The Soviets try to prevent or discourage the outbreak of revolutions in many parts of the world, lest they would be forced to intervene, which would increase the danger of a nuclear war. The

Chinese stand, on the other hand, seems to imply that the more the Americans are disturbed by revolutionary movements all over their economic and political orbit, the less will they be able to wage a major war, including the use of nuclear arms.[48] According to this view, a consistent application of the concept of world revolution as upheld by the Chinese is the best guarantee against the eruption of a major world war.

The preoccupation, in many parts of the world since the Russian revolution with the danger of communist subversion, has been reinforced since the end of the Second World War by the possibility that an internal war could be transformed into a major external, and at worst, even a nuclear war. After 1945, war prevention, which had already been on the programme of the League of Nations between the two world wars, became a major concern of the United Nations. But attempts to deal effectively with the issue of revolution conspicuously failed. One of the main reasons is that the United Nations is, to a large extent, based on the legal *status quo* and the defenders of legality have always been in the majority, at least in the Security Council. Revolutionary action, on the other hand, is always in some way opposed to the legal *status quo*, even if the revolutionaries can provide some legal basis for their actions.

Some attempts were made to extend the concept of aggression in order to include more indirect methods of subversion. The term 'indirect aggression' was sometimes used to denote all kinds of moral or material support short of military intervention as aggression which should provoke a justified reaction on the part of the United Nations.

However, it proved impossible to reach any agreement on this point. Several member-states, among them outright defenders of the *status quo*, wanted to keep their hands free to provide all kinds of moral and material support short of direct military interference, in case the insurgents abroad were ideologically on their side and opposed a government that was either belonging to the opposite bloc or, at least, was not considered a reliable ally. Halpern writes about a period when the United States government considered taking steps in this direction:

T–F

After our Lebanese intervention, our Secretary of State, forgetful of the origins of our travail, thought of asking for a U.N. resolution against 'indirect aggression' but relented when he remembered how vulnerable we would be both in the debate and through the intended law.[49]

It is, moreover, to be doubted whether any inclusion of 'indirect aggression' among types of aggression condemned by international law would really contribute to diminution of the danger of a major war. On the contrary, it might provide an excuse for branding normal expressions of sympathy, in the press or speeches, with internal opponents of any power that be. If 'indirect aggression' were to be made an infraction of international law, the resulting risk of war would, maybe, strongly increase rather than diminish.

This draws our attention to the fact that, contrary to the myth of world-wide revolutionary subversion, the world of today is at least as much disturbed by counter-revolutionary subversion. It is not revolution, but counter-revolution that is mostly being exported, even through open military intervention.

Export of counter-revolution is not just a recent phenomenon. In earlier times the defenders of the *status quo* could largely confine themselves to supporting the legal powers. The Unholy Alliance was established at the time of the Vienna Congress of 1815, creating the concert of Europe against a possible resurrection of revolution. The British-Russian Treaty of 1907 was not only intended to contain Germany; at the same time it effected a division of Asia into spheres of influence. This was to ensure that neither lent support to nationalist revolutionaries within the other's sphere of influence. The British government's, and especially Lord Curzon's, alarm about the nationalist riots led by Tilak in India, and Russian uneasiness about the Young Persian's Movement were, most probably, important considerations for concluding the treaty. Without any doubt Lenin was right in asserting that, in concluding such treaties and agreements, the big powers of Europe were helping Russia to play the role of 'Gendarme of Asia'.[50] Earlier in China, foreign military support had been used by the Manchu dynasty to smash the large-scale Tai-ping rebellion, which was without any doubt a true revolution.

In the Spanish Civil War, however, the normal sequence was reversed. Here, a more or less progressive government had been established by legal means – though the legality was, as usual, contested by its opponents. German and Italian auxiliary troops, however, helped the insurgent troops of the officer Franco to power. This amounted to patent export of counter-revolution.

Since the end of the war, assistance to counter-revolutionary movements has become a normal course of action for the Americans, whenever the ruling class, allied with American interests, is threatened by popular forces. A system based on capitalism accounts for a world-wide range of economic interests, supported by a net of military bases spread over the world. These investments are threatened by official steps to restrict foreign economic power. Hence military intervention is used as a means to defend American interests against 'legal' powers. American interventions in Guatemala, and the Dominican Republic are the best-known examples, in addition to the Vietnamese war which, however, seems to have been intended rather to serve the defence of American interests outside Vietnam proper.

However this may be, export of counter-revolution is rife today and was even for some time formally advocated as 'containment plus'. It constitutes a much greater menace to world peace than export of revolution. Looking at the world map, it is clear that it is decidedly not the Chinese who are blurring, with their everyday actions and interventions in other countries' internal affairs, the borderline between internal and external war; and the Soviet Union, even though guilty of such intervention as late as August 1968, has practised a remarkable amount of restraint both in the Czechoslovakian and in earlier comparable cases.

Revolution has shown itself, up till now, much more aware of national borders and of the basic interests of mankind in the world of tomorrow than counter-revolution.

ix. The Historical Setting of Revolutions

In the previous sections I have attempted to define the concept of revolution, taking as my starting point the preceding theoretical analysis of social realities. We are now able to study further the revolutionary phenomenon against the general background of world history.

Although the definitions and distinctions developed in this chapter were, as far as possible, illustrated with actual historical events, it should be possible to elaborate our analysis of the revolutionary phenomenon as it manifests itself throughout the history of mankind.

The aim of this study is to deal with revolutions as social processes. In part one I attempted to analyse the process and course of social evolution; in the following chapter I shall concentrate on the genesis, process and ultimate outcome of revolutions. In order to tackle such an analysis in sociological terms, I shall have to refer back to the societal model outlined in chapter four, where an attempt was made to expose the deeper roots of the revolutionary phenomenon, as well as of the general process of human evolution.

Any analysis of the revolutionary process should be preceded by a discussion of the extent to which revolution, as defined in the earlier sections of this chapter, has been a permanent feature throughout the history of mankind, and of how its character has been affected by the process of human evolution as mirrored in the ever-changing pattern of social and political reality. This is the task I have set myself in the remaining sections. Accordingly, I shall have to clarify what type of historical events commonly termed revolutions should actually be viewed as such and hence be included in the discussion, and distinguish them from those occurrences that are, in current literature, wrongly defined as revolutions.

As a criterion I shall use my previous definition of revolution as an overthrow of those in power, aiming at fundamental change in the direction of emancipation. We shall see, however, that the application of this criterion in an actual historical context may sometimes present nearly insurmountable difficulties.

x. Revolutions in Modern Times

We will look first at the more recent cases of overthrow of power in human history, referred to in some publications as the 'Great Revolutions'.[51] There can be little doubt about the revolutionary character of at least some of these occurrences. The French Revolution was a typical case of a social revolution. Even though the current popular view that a truly fundamental social change was being effected in the sense that the aristocracy as a ruling class had been replaced by the bourgeoisie would appear too simplistic, yet it is true that the overthrow of the *ancien régime* had created a situation in which different layers of the French Third Estate witnessed a considerable increase in their potential participation in national affairs. Despite several subsequent reverses – the Thermidor of 1794, the ascension of Napoleon to absolute power, the Restoration after Napoleon's defeat – some of the achievements and fundamental changes wrought by the French Revolution could never be completely undone.

Similarly, the two 'Great Revolutions' in Russia in 1917 certainly stand the test of our previous definition. The February revolution could again be considered, to a certain extent, a bourgeois revolution, whereas the October revolution was under much stronger influence of the urban working class as represented in the local Soviets. Again, an interpretation in terms of a simple overthrow first of the aristocratic class by the bourgeoisie and, later on, of the latter by the working class, would too much simplify, if not actually distort, the picture. The only thing one could say is that the October revolution created a situation in which the chances for emancipation of the urban working class were much improved, although subsequent developments were far from taking a rectilinear course.

Equally, it is proper to label the two Chinese revolutions (the bourgeois one of 1911–12 and the socialist one ending with the establishment of the People's Republic of China in 1949) this way.

Another 'Great Revolution' – the American one of 1775 and the following years – combined elements of a social revolution with traits of a national one, directed against British ascendancy. This type of war of independence, implying the elimination of a foreign ruling class, has been more common during the past few centuries than purely social revolutions. Throughout the nineteenth century nationalism was a strong motivating force for popular movements in Europe and Latin America, and it has become so in Asia and Africa in the twentieth century. There is no point in attempting to enumerate the frequent wars of independence characteristic of the past 150 years, several of them successful.

As far as purely social revolutions are concerned, the harvest would appear to be much less substantial. Several of them could be said to have been abortive as, for example, the Paris Commune of 1871, or the Russian revolution of 1905. Though both of these could, with some justification, be called revolutions, they certainly were not successful ones. One could even express some doubt as to whether the upheaval in Germany in 1918, resulting in an overthrow of the Hohenzollern dynasty and the establishment of the Weimar Republic, completely fits our definition of revolution. 'The Kaiser went, the generals stayed,' as it was pungently put, and in the early twenties it became clear that no major social transformations were to be expected.

It is outside Europe that one has to look for fairly successful social revolutions, apart from the French and Russian ones already mentioned. An exception should be made for those in Eastern Europe that occurred at the end of the Second World War in the wake of the victorious advance of the Red Army. Of this series of overthrows the Yugoslav example probably comes nearest to a true social revolution, mainly due to internal factors.

Other successful social revolutions which were not primarily wars of independence were the one in Turkey in 1919 and the following years led by Mustapha Kemal against the Sultanate; the Mexican revolution of 1911; and the Cuban revolution in 1958.

During the nineteenth century there were also, outside Europe, two major civil wars which have sometimes been counted as revolutions.

One of them is the abolition of the Shogunate in Japan in 1868, which is generally called the Meiji restoration or Meiji revolution.[52] Sansom states his position with regard to this term in the following way:

In the foregoing pages the word revolution has been used to describe the process by which the remnants of feudalism were destroyed. But in its origins it was not a revolution comparable to the English revolution of 1688[53] or the French revolution of 1789. It was a civil war fought with both political and military weapons by one section of a dominant military class against another. Its purpose was to replace an administration giving scope to new men. The leaders of the victorious party stood for no new political theory, as is clear from the divisions that soon split them; but having achieved their purpose of securing power they found by trial and error that they must discard certain institutions. In other words, the abolition of feudalism was an afterthought.[54]

I would like to endorse Sansom's view that the Meiji restoration and its aftermath was no revolution in its proper sense, but for somewhat different reasons.

On the one hand, one could admit that the outcome of the Civil War offered a broader scope for action and political influence to a social group that had, hitherto, been excluded from actual power: the impoverished class of minor *samurais* who increased their influence at the expense of the larger feudal lords, the *daimyos*. One could also concede that the Civil War produced a situation in which the door was thrown wide open for different types of emancipation: there were experiments with parliamentary institutions, rather radical agrarian reforms were introduced, a basis was laid for rapid industrial development, and educational facilities were increased.

One could not even deny that the abolition of the Shogunate had a revolutionary quality because it amounted to a restoration of the emperor to a position of actual power: the loyalty to the emperor was used as a political expedient, by the engineers of the overthrow of the existing feudal system, to attain a maximum allegiance among the common people as well as among different groups of aristocrats. The use of the young emperor as a unifying symbol could serve to bring the revolution or whatever it should be called 'to a successful and relatively bloodless issue', to quote

Sansom.[55] The situation, therefore, could to some extent be compared with the Chinese Cultural Revolution where part of the establishment, led by Chairman Mao, gave actual guidance to the revolution against the Communist Party and the bureaucracy as exponents of the established order, and thus secured a relatively non-violent process.

On the other hand, it is precisely this comparison with the Chinese Cultural Revolution which brings to light the features of the Meiji restoration that prevent us from calling it a revolution in a true sense. The *samurais* who were the engineers of the restoration did not operate as an organized group. No popular mass movements were involved throughout the whole process. The forces which brought about the overturn were not popular armies but regular military forces summoned by feudal lords. Moreover, as Sansom rightly observes, the rebellious *samurais* lacked a distinct revolutionary ideology.

It is for these reasons that the term 'revolution' seems inappropriate for the Meiji restoration. At its inception, the restoration was a *coup d'état* rather than a revolution, although in its further course the movement began to show some revolutionary aspects.

As far as the American Civil War is concerned, we could make the following observations. Generally, the American Civil War is viewed as a revolution. Barrington Moore[56] calls the Civil War 'the last revolutionary offensive on the part of what one may legitimately call urban or bourgeois capitalist democracy', and refers to the term 'Second American Revolution' used by Charles and Mary Beard. Yet, further on in his study[57] Moore asks himself: 'Was it a revolution?' For the Northern radicals

the Radical version of reconstruction came down to using the North's military power to destroy the plantation aristocracy and create a facsimile of capitalist democracy by ensuring property and voting rights for the Negroes. In the light of Southern conditions at the time, it was indeed revolutionary.[58]

But if the aims were revolutionary, could the methods used be called so? Can the use by the established authorities of their regular military forces against an antiquated social and political structure in one particular part of the country be called, with any justification, a revolution? Technically, in my view, the Civil War decidedly had some aspects of a counter-revolution (at the time of its occurrence it was generally called a rebellion in the North): an attempt by the ruling elites of the slave-holding Southern states to secede from the Union at the moment when Lincoln had been legally elected as President and, in such a manner, frustrate the plans of the official authorities to abolish a social and economic system by legal means. It was the insubordinate action by the ruling elites of the Southern states in order to block a true emancipation movement favoured from above, that provoked *military* intervention from the North and, thus, made a Civil War inevitable.[59] The counter-revolutionary elements present in the American Civil War make one aware that in recent history counter-revolutions have been more frequent than social revolutions: the ascension to power of Benito Mussolini, Admiral Horthy, Chiang Kai-shek, Adolf Hitler and Franco are unmistakable specimens of counter-revolutionary takeovers.

xi. *Revolutions in Earlier Centuries*

All the revolutions dealt with in the last section occurred in the course of the past two centuries. In some way or other they were all related to the process of rapid transformation in the economic and social fields characteristic of the modern world. As far as true social revolutions were concerned, they mostly occurred on the eve of a period of fast industrial development and were preceded by the growth of classes claiming a greater share in economic benefits and political power. A rising native bourgeoisie was challenging the prerogatives of a gentry that occupied most of the positions of power within the traditional political structure. In some cases an incipient process of industrial development had already created a class-conscious and vociferous urban working class which could play a decisive role in the revolutionary process (this was particularly true for the Russian revolutions of 1917 and the second Chinese revolution).

Now one could ask oneself whether the phenomenon of revolution is in some way inextricably connected with the class struggle accompanying modern economic growth. Is it possible, in any scientifically valid sense, to speak of revolutions for premodern times when economic growth was comparatively slow and class consciousness was generally not too well developed?

We could at least agree that the revolutions of the eighteenth century were not the first ones to occur. Both the Dutch uprising against Spanish domination in the second half of the sixteenth century and the 'Great Rebellion' of the English Puritans in midseventeenth century were, to all intents and purposes, true revolutions. The former one was at the same time a national and a social revolution, the second one exclusively social. In both, a rising native bourgeoisie challenged the prerogatives of an aristocracy which, up till then, had occupied most positions of power.

It is sometimes claimed, with a certain justification, that the Dutch uprising against the Spanish rule of King Philip II had some retrogressive trends. For example, the uprising ran counter to the trend of centralized bureaucratic rule under the Burgundian and Hapsburg princes and resulted in a restoration of special privileges for certain aristocratic groups or urban autonomous bodies abolished by the former rulers. Yet the general trend of the rebellion was an attempt at a wholesale renovation of Netherlands society. Therefore, its general tendency was truly revolutionary, not merely in its national but in its social and economic aspects. It inaugurated a true emancipation movement in the newly created United Republic of the Seven Provinces.

Our conclusion might be that revolutions could have occurred in any type of society. But it is clear that the chances for very fundamental changes are greatly increased in a situation where a rapidly progressing technology has created an environment that is very stimulating for the emancipation struggle of social groups that hitherto had lacked a sufficient outlet for their discontent with a prevalent order, as well as a viable solution for their problems.

xii. *Religion and Revolution in History*

In the discussion thus far I have implicitly rejected the idea that true social revolutions could only successfully occur in a period when the ideology of revolutionaries is no longer predominantly based on religious concepts but is put on a more rational footing. Both the Dutch uprising against Spanish rule and the 'Great Rebellion' in Britain were defined as revolutions, although the ideology behind the revolutionary struggle was expressed in religious terms: Protestantism as against Catholic rulers or rulers sympathizing with Catholicism. It appears from these examples that religion used as a driving force to smash the existing social order is not necessarily of an escapist nature, as is the case with most millenarian movements.

For nineteenth-century Asia both the Tai-ping rebellion and the Indian Mutiny could be mentioned as true revolutions, with a motivation partly couched in religious terms.

In the past, any social value found a ready expression in religious terms. Religious values could represent the interests of those upholding the established order; they could equally contain a hidden protest against this order; they could erupt into escapist rebellions attempting a magic short cut towards an ideal social order; and, finally, they could vitalize a true revolutionary movement consciously aiming at wholesale social change along more or less rational lines.

Therefore, we could relate the operation of religious factors both to the type of social control exerted by those who represent the established order and to protest phenomena, connected with the concept of counterpoints and countervalues elaborated in chapter four. Several religious systems subservient to the established order have functioned, or still function, as a mechanism to avert latent discontent, and concomitant aspirations for a better life towards a realm outside reality. The promise of Heaven after death or of a reincarnation as a higher being could provide, for many of the underprivileged, an escape clause from the bitterness of real life.

Concealed protest, however, could also assume religious forms.

Countervalues mitigating or opposing the established order also find expression in the realm of religious beliefs. The hierarchy of the accepted social order is counterbalanced, in several religious systems, by the concept of intrinsic equality of all human beings before God. This hierarchy may even be reversed by the concept of superiority of the underprivileged as embodied in several places in the Gospel according to Luke, as for example in the Benedictions, in the parable of Lazarus (Luke xvi, 20–25), or in the near impossibility 'for a rich man to enter the kingdom of God'.

Thus, Sunday church could provide, as a counterpoint to the harshness, drudgery and recurrent humiliation of daily life, a strong emotional outlet for those who had the satisfaction of listening to sermons in which the high and the mighty, to whom they had to bow outside the church, and who had preferential seats within, were to bear the brunt of the castigations dispensed from the pulpit.

In many cases, however, the hidden protest inherent in religion could burst into forms of open protest. Nearly all of these movements were, however, doomed to remain abortive. The escape from reality inherent in many religious manifestations certainly affects the character of religious forms of open protest. The countervalues embedded in religious ideas could express themselves in millenarian movements in which a religious leader with his followers challenged the powers that be and attempted to establish a new lasting social order in which these countervalues could prevail. Unfortunately the new social order was not viewed as a result of a protracted and systematic struggle based on social, economic, and political realities, but as a completely new world born all of a sudden from God's will, expressing itself through the intermediary of the religious leader claiming to be his mouthpiece. Though the millenarian movement showed some characteristics of a revolution inasmuch as it aimed at fundamental social change, the inefficacy of the means used to achieve the millennium relegated the movement to the level of a local rebellion. Soon the leaders were either eliminated, despite their faith in God, reinforced by magic practices, or had to submit to established authority by dropping the truly revolutionary aspects of their teachings and practices. In the end, no real fundamental change had occurred and the protest movement had only provided some temporary and emotional relief. For a short period there had been a semblance of escape from the realities of life; but soon these realities reimposed themselves upon the ruins of a short-lived dream. The short cut towards a new lasting social order must, necessarily, fail.[60]

What all these movements have in common is the limited scope of real social change they can achieve. They are not completely ineffective. Though they present consistent features of a certain escapism, their after-effects can be gauged in terms of social realities. Though unsuccessful as far as their attempt at fully-fledged social change is concerned, they may be operative, at a more limited level, in fostering an ideologically based group solidarity transcending prior bonds based on the membership of genealogical or territorial units. Consequently, they may prepare the ground for future evolutionary developments or revolutionary transformations of a more embracing character. But as such they cannot count as revolutions; at the most they may be reckoned as religious rebellions.

However, true social revolutions in earlier times showed a religious component as well. This is understandable. In a world where ideas are generally couched in religious forms, one could hardly imagine that a non-religious ideology could inspire broad masses into action. One could even maintain that in the modern world the religious element is not altogether absent from revolutionary movements.

It is well known that in the French Revolution religion was conspicuously absent from the prevalent ideology. A-religious rationalism was the prevalent trend of thinking in the Age of Enlightenment. Yet the revolution produced at the time of supremacy of the radical wing, the Jacobins, a movement which, both in its psychological and ritualistic aspects, presented a kind of substitute for religion: the Worship of Reason. Robespierre, who had opposed the movement, now elicited a decree of the Convention calling into life a similar movement, the Worship of the Supreme Being, culminating in the Mammoth Festival in Paris on 8 June 1794. Robespierre himself 'officiated as a kind of priest of the Republic as tens or hundreds of thousands watched'.[61] Evidently, in order to attract broad masses, a revolution needed elements of popular cultism that had hitherto been associated with religion.

In later revolutions there were similar experiences. One could quote in this connection the Lenin cult in the Mausoleum on the Red Square in Moscow, or certain facets of the Mao cult in China today.

Evidently, the kind of fervour earlier associated with religious movements seeks expression in familiar forms even though the prevalent revolutionary ideology is a-religious or anti-religious, as, for example, the branding of religion by classical Marxism as 'Opiate of the People'. Each revolutionary movement, though rational in its means and immediate political aims, represents, at the same time, the dream of a fully renewed social order, and this dream may find expression in quasi-religious forms.

On the other hand recent developments, especially in Latin America, have shown that, even in the contemporary world, a traditional religion like Christianity, under certain circumstances, may regain the original revolutionary qualities inherent in the teachings of Christ, and add fervour and inspiration to a revolutionary movement. Religion is not necessarily an 'Opiate of the People'. Sometimes it is a pep-drug of the people. Whereas the large majority of the clergy remain more or less associated with the establishment, a significant number of clergy join the revolutionary movement without rejecting their relationship with the church. We shall revert to the phenomenon in the third part of this book.

In the foregoing sections I have provided a historical background for the task I have set myself in the following chapter: to make some general observations on the conditions under which revolutions arise and on the course they take. It is against this historical background that we may now attempt to discover general patterns of the origin and course of revolutions, without limiting ourselves from the outset to the few cases registered as the 'Great Revolutions' in the annals of European modern history.

6

The Genesis and Course of Revolutions

The costs of moderation have been at least as atrocious as those of revolution, perhaps a great deal more.

BARRINGTON MOORE JR

Class conflict is the mother of revolution, misery its progenitor; the role of midwife, however, is fulfilled by the spiritual idea which grows from material conditions but at the same time transcends them.

ERICH KUTTNER

Revolutions are the festivals of the oppressed and the exploited. At no other times are the masses of the people in a position to come forward so actively as creators of a new social order as at a time of revolution.

V.I. LENIN

i. Theories on the Revolutionary Cycle

Is it possible to discover a regular sequence in the way revolutionary movements develop from their first beginnings, and pursue their course through an eruption to an ultimate stage? The best-known attempt to elaborate such a stereotyped sequence of events is Crane Brinton's *The Anatomy of Revolution*.[62]

Brinton has attempted to construct a kind of general model of revolutions by analysing four case studies: the English, the American, the French, and the Russian. In all these cases revolutions have run, according to Brinton's analysis, more or less through a uniform sequence of stages: preliminary signs, manifesting themselves in a defection of intellectuals from the old regimes, and culminating in the 'Eternal Figaro' who openly gives expression to the omnipresent dissatisfaction; the first stages of revolution in which constituted authority is challenged by illegal acts of revolutionists; after a certain amount of bloodshed the old regime crumbles, and a short 'honeymoon' occurs in which 'the people' who have defeated the 'oppressors' appear united. The following stages show that unity was only temporary and superficial: after 'the rule of the moderates' follows an 'accession of the extremists', accompanied by a 'reign of terror and virtue'. Finally, a universal reaction occurs, a return to 'normalcy', introduced by a 'Thermidor'.

Brinton's study, though remarkable for its pioneering character, is marred by many weaknesses. The most manifest one is the limitation of his analysis to four case studies. For example, the restriction of his survey to Europe and North America has led him seriously to underestimate the peasant element in revolutionary movements, although the inclusion of the Russian Revolution should have made him realize its significance.

The greatest defect, however, is the rigidity in an approach which aims at establishing a fixed and more or less stereotyped sequence of phases, instead of allowing for a great variety of potentialities dependent, for example, upon the historical period and the sociological constellation in which a revolution occurs. His rigid scheme more than once induces him to do violence to reality in order to make it fit his model.

Furthermore, a basic weakness is his treatment of revolutions as a kind of illness with the accompanying imagery borrowed from the vocabulary of pathology. Brinton regards 'revolutions as a kind of fever'.[63] After a few '*prodromal* signs, indications to the very perceptive diagnostician that a disease is on its way' there 'comes a time when the full symptoms' of the fever disclose themselves. 'This works up, not regularly but with advances and retreats, to a crisis, frequently accompanied by delirium.'

After the crisis comes a period of convalescense, usually marked by a relapse or two. Finally the fever is over, and the patient is himself again, perhaps in some respects actually strengthened by the experience, immunized at least for a while from a similar attack, but certainly not wholly made over into a new man.

He tries to explain, that, in using this metaphor, he does not mean to express a moral judgement nor to imply that revolution is necessarily an evil to be cured.[64] Yet the use of this metaphor in itself induces him to think of revolution as a state of instability eventually leading to a reimposition of stability. Brinton recognizes that, after the 'recovery' of the sick social body, the patient will never be quite the same as he was before the 'illness'. Yet, implicit is the assumption that, as a matter of fact, a revolution did not produce any basic structural change. Revolution is, according to this view, a kind of disequilibrium to be restored in the long run by a recovery 'back to normalcy'.[65]

From the natural sciences Brinton also borrowed the term 'equilibrium' as a characteristic of a social system not torn by revolutions, although he is fully aware that 'any human society can be in but an imperfect equilibrium'.[66]

Brinton's unsuccessful attempt to introduce a quasi-universal, cyclical model of revolution in terms of a stereotyped sequence of revolutionary phases is symptomatic of the danger inherent in any attempt to deal with the genesis and process of revolutions in general. There is also an enormous situational difference between most revolutions in the past, occurring in pre-industrial agrarian societies, and similar occurrences in the contemporary world where rapid industrial development has strongly affected social, economic, and political conditions, even in pre-industrial societies outside the centres of rapid industrial growth.

Moreover, really to understand revolution as a social phenomenon and as a process, we must disengage ourselves from the implicit assumption that revolution has to be contrasted with stability and equilibrium.[67]

ii. Revolution as an Integral Element of Social Change

The cyclical model discussed in section one starts from the assumption that revolutions are deviations throwing a social body out of gear. In order to be able to analyse the process of revolution, however, we must first put it in its proper perspective: as a specific form of the universal phenomenon of human evolution. Even if one rejects Brinton's static view of revolution as a fever, as opposed to a normal state of health, one may still cling to a position in which revolution remains an out-of-the-way phenomenon, deviating from a healthy, that is to say evolutionary, type of social change. Barrington Moore, however, takes issue even with such a view. He starts from the assumption that social change is the general rule and not an exception. He disagrees with the 'widespread assumption in modern social science that social continuity requires no explanation' whereas change does.[68] Moore argues that 'normal' society with its 'day-to-day repression' is wrongly taken for granted and hovers only dimly in the background of most history books. 'Even those radical historians who emphasize the injustices of pre-revolutionary epochs generally concentrate on a short span preceding the immediate outbreak.'[69]

There is a strong bias in our Western world in favour of gradual evolution as opposed to revolution. Barrington Moore disagrees with this type of reasoning:

For a Western scholar to say a good word on behalf of revolutionary radicalism is not easy because it runs counter to deeply grooved mental reflexes. The assumption that gradual and piecemeal reform has demonstrated its superiority over violent revolution as a way to advance human freedom is so pervasive that even to question such an assumption seems strange.

He confronts 'the comforting myth of gradualism' with 'the costs of going without a revolution'. 'In the backward countries today, there continues the suffering of those who have not revolted.'[70]

Evidently, in Barrington Moore's view, the general preference for gradual evolution as contrasted with revolution is based on a *moral* bias, which amounts to a deprecation of revolution as inhuman.

The idea embodied in Moore's argument has been expressed with still greater eloquence by Mark Twain:

There were two 'Reigns of Terror', if we would but remember it and consider it; the one wrought murder in hot passion, the other in heartless cold blood; the one lasted mere months, the other had lasted a thousand years; the one inflicted death upon ten thousand persons, the other upon a hundred millions; but our shudders are all for the 'horrors' of the minor Terror, the momentary Terror, so to speak;

whereas, what is the horror of swift death by the axe, compared with lifelong death from hunger, cold insult, cruelty, and heartbreak? What is swift death by lightning compared with slow death by fire at the stake? A city cemetery could contain the coffins filled by that brief Terror which we have all been so diligently taught to shiver at and mourn over; but all France could hardly contain the coffins filled by that older and real Terror – that unspeakably bitter and awful Terror which none of us has been taught to see in its vastness or pity as it deserves.[71]

It is against the background of evolution as a normal process not necessarily assuming gradualist forms but rather appearing as a process in which periods of slowing-down alternate with periods of acceleration that we will have to view the latter type of change, called revolution, as a recurrent phenomenon in the history of mankind, and to analyse its genesis and course.

iii. *The Genesis of Revolutions: Some General Observations*

Harry Eckstein has rightly and, to quote Lawrence Stone, 'cruelly' exposed the subjectivity, ambiguity, and partial self-contradiction of most theories that have attempted to explain the genesis of revolutions. To quote Stone's paraphrase of Eckstein's arguments:

He has pointed out that commonly adduced hypotheses run the spectrum of particular conditions, moving from the intellectual (inadequate political socialization, conflicting social myths, a corrosive social philosophy, alienation of the intellectuals) to the economic (increasing poverty, rapid growth, imbalance between production and distribution, long-term growth plus short-term recession) to the social (resentment due to restricted elite circulation, confusion due to excessive elite recruitment, anomie due to excessive social mobility, conflict due to the rise of new social classes) to the political (bad government, divided government, weak government, oppressive government). Finally there are explanations on the level of general process, such as rapid social change, erratic social change, or a lack of harmony between the state structure and society, the rulers and the ruled. None of these explanations are invalid in themselves, but they are often difficult or impossible to reconcile one with the other, and are so diverse in their range and variety as to be virtually impossible to fit into an ordered analytical framework.[72]

Stone then asks: 'What, then, is to be done?' I shall try to answer the question by formulating the problem in more specific terms.

First of all, we should try to study a broader range of revolutionary events than do those authors who restrict themselves to the 'Great Revolutions' best known to Westerners. So far as we deal with objective factors characteristic of a pre-revolutionary situation, we should try to take account of several types of revolution, distinguished in chapter five. However, it seems to me that the most promising way of extending our understanding of the genesis of revolutions, is to try to link up the treatment of pre-revolutionary situations with the analysis of conflicting values developed in chapter four, in an attempt to connect a pre-revolutionary situation with the early germs of fission and conflict discernible in any society. In so doing, we will have to attempt to distinguish tendencies pointing in the direction of revolution from those pointing in the direction of general unrest which may take on a counter-revolutionary character as well. Therefore, our discussion will have to give full scope to the emancipation issue which is generally decisive in determining a trend as either progressive or retrogressive.

In this respect, my analysis will basically diverge from analyses like those by Chalmers Johnson[73] who distinguishes between revolutions, military coups, and rebellions, but treats them as similar kinds of insurrection, or Harry Eckstein[74] who refers indiscriminately to 'internal wars'.

In attempting to locate the genesis of revolutions, we will have to distinguish two aspects of the pre-revolutionary situation: the more or less objective, situational aspects, and the subjective psychological ones.

iv. *Situational Aspects*

Is there any uniformity to be discovered in the manifold situations throughout world history which we can assess, by hindsight, as pre-revolutionary? Do revolutions occur in situations of extreme misery or, on the contrary, under conditions of economic growth? Are clear-cut class divisions more propitious for revolutions than a situation where class borders are more or less blurred and where a certain amount of social mobility prevails? Do revolutions appear under political conditions of extreme harshness or, on the contrary, under regimes where political control has been somewhat relaxed and, consequently, the dissatisfied groups enjoy some latitude for manoeuvring?

It should be clear from the outset that, on the basis of the relatively rare historical instances of actual revolutions, an unambiguous and generally valid reply to such questions is hardly to be expected. We come across a great variety of revolutions that could be subdivided into several types. Both the kind of society and the historical period in which a revolution occurs may widely differ and, consequently, influence the impact of separate factors.

A cursory survey of the different revolutions may elucidate our point. There have certainly been historical cases where a revolution broke out under conditions of extreme misery for the large mass of the peasantry and the urban population. This is true of the Russian revolutions (both in 1905 and 1917) and of the Chinese communist revolution.[75]

However, in the case of the British Puritan revolution of about 1640 the situation is much less clear, and nobody has ever asserted that general impoverishment was typical of the situation before the American Revolution of 1775. But if we try to relate this to the fact that the American Revolution was basically a national one, we should at the same time admit that in some other cases of national revolutions against a foreign power impoverishment has been a potent factor. We could think of the Indonesian revolution of 1945 and following years against Dutch colonial rule, which was certainly precipitated by the misery caused by the Second

World War and the Japanese occupation; we could also mention the Dutch revolution against Spanish rule, which started with the widespread acts of iconoclasm that came in the wake of what Erich Kuttner, in his brilliant study of the causes of the revolution in the Netherlands, has called The Hunger Year.[76]

It would be equally difficult to assert, as a universal truth, either that revolutions start in situations of extreme harshness or that they are provoked by a weak, indulgent policy by those in power. One could mention instances of both. Cuba under Batista, China under Chiang Kai-shek and even, despite his inefficiency, Russia under Tsar Nicholas II were instances of ruthless suppression and an absence of liberal institutions as an effective check upon arbitrary power. On the other hand, the English and French revolutions were precipitated precisely through the creation of parliamentary checks upon absolute power.

Again, it appears difficult to develop a theory in generalizing terms on pre-revolutionary situations. This may be due, to a large extent, to the restrictions inherent in the predictability of developments in the social and political field. If one attempts to identify a social and political situation as pre-revolutionary, one can easily convey the impression that in such a situation a revolution is inevitable. Lawrence Stone criticizes, on similar grounds, Chalmers Johnson's attempt to identify the causes of revolution:

Johnson leaves too little play for the operation of the unique and the personal. He seems to regard his accelerators as automatic triggers, ignoring the area of unpredictable personal choice that is always left to the ruling elite and to the revolutionary leaders, even in a situation of multiple dysfunction exacerbated by an accelerator. Revolution is never inevitable – or rather the only evidence of its inevitability is that it actually happens.[77]

The only way to deal, more or less effectively, with the situational aspects of pre-revolutionary situations, is to relate them, tentatively, to the different types of revolutions and, even then, to treat them as potential factors rather than as actual and inexorable determinants of forthcoming revolutions.

v. Economic Conditions

There are basically two conflicting theories on the economic causes of revolutions; they are, to quote Lawrence Stone, 'the contradictory models of Marx and de Tocqueville, the one claiming that popular revolution is a product of increasing misery, the other that it is a product of increasing prosperity'.[78] De Tocqueville claimed that the latter was the case in France, which Hobsbawm and other authors deny.[79]

In recent literature it is the latter model which has gained much support. Crane Brinton, although admitting that, to use George Pettee's expression, certain groups were *cramped* in their economic activities, yet maintains that the societies where revolutions occurred have been, in the years preceding revolution, 'on the whole prosperous'.[80] This theory has been, on the one hand, elaborated in greater detail, but, on the other hand, qualified by James C. Davies.[81] He argues that revolutions do not occur in cases of utter distress, but rather in situations where a period of improvement and rising hopes has been followed by a short-term recession during which serious frustrations manifest themselves. As a graphic expression for such a development Davies uses the 'J-curve',* which is meant to demonstrate a discrepancy between steadily soaring expectations created by a period of growth and the actual level of satisfaction of needs lagging far behind these expectations.† To quote Lawrence Stone's attempt to paraphrase Davies's thesis: 'Successful revolution is the work neither of the destitute nor of the well-satisfied, but of those whose actual situation is improving less rapidly than they expect?[82]

Although admitting that 'the Davies model fits the history of Western Europe quite well', Stone cautions the reader that a purely economic explanation will not do. He points towards the psychological factors related to changes in wealth and power, and towards the relative nature of the standards used to measure one's economic position within society.[83] Similarly, according to Davies, all depends upon 'a state of mind, a mood in a society'.

* Graph 1.
† Graph 2, as presented and explained by Davies.

However, one could even question the general validity of the de Tocqueville element within the Davies model. There have been, certainly, revolutions which did not arise under conditions of extreme misery. The American one of 1775 is the most convincing example of a revolution that was certainly not due to extreme poverty. Crane Brinton even maintains that 'the early years of the 1770's were distinctly years of prosperity. There were economic stresses and strains in colonial America ... but no class ground down with poverty'.[84]

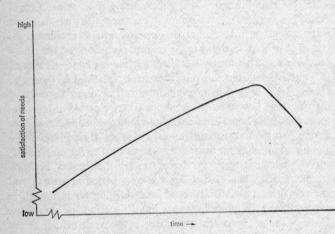

Graph 1. J-curve according to James C. Davies.

And although the rural mass of the population in England, throughout the reign of Charles I, would have been miserably poor according to any standard derived from present-day conditions in Western Europe, there seems to be unanimity among historians that it was not this poverty that was the driving force behind the Puritan revolution. Those who were dissatisfied and revolted were members of a vigorous rising merchant and yeomanry class.[85]

But then, both revolutions were typically bourgeois ones. In such a case, it seems only plausible that the pre-revolutionary period should have been one of general, though definitely uneven, economic growth. But even in the case of some bourgeois revolutions the situation may have been more complicated. The bourgeois revolution in the Netherlands was preceded by long-lasting economic troubles, culminating in the 'hunger year' of 1566. A

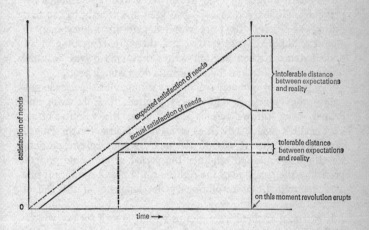

Graph 2. J-curve; relationship between satisfaction of needs and revolution (according to James C. Davies).

true revolutionary movement started in the southern Netherlands, which was suppressed, but then spread to the northern Netherlands where it was more successful. In this case, James Davies's J-curve would appear to apply: a long-term period of industrial growth followed by a recession. But, according to Kuttner's analysis, in this case the recession had lasted for many years.

An interpretation in terms of the J-curve model has been presented for the French Revolution. For example, Brinton, who maintains as de Tocqueville did that the pre-revolutionary period in France was one of increasing prosperity, admits 'that in some respects 1788–9 was a bad year'.[86] Eric Hobsbawm conveys a much more gloomy picture. In his view, the late eighties were a period of 'a profound economic and social crisis'.[87]

Similarly, Palmer writes: 'Prices of agricultural products had been declining for more than a decade, so that the burden of rents, dues, tithes, and taxes was heavier on the peasants.' He holds that 'all Western Europe in 1789 was in the grip of an economic depression'. 'The harvest of 1788 had been disastrously bad so that bread was scarce.' 'Its price was momentarily higher than in almost a hundred years.'[88] It seems, therefore, something of an understatement when Brinton writes that 1788–9 was 'in some respects' a bad year, and 'by no means a deep trough year'.

The picture of economic conditions throughout the decade preceding the French Revolution, as painted by Hobsbawm and Palmer, even throws serious doubt upon the validity of de Tocqueville's model, as well as of Davies's J-curve for the French case. Granted that it was, in the main, a bourgeois revolution, we still may question whether the period of economic growth preceding the recession of the eighties could play a significant role as a determinant of revolutionary developments at the end of the decade.

It is true that there were groups within French society which, while enjoying a certain prosperity as members of a rising middle class, were a driving force behind the revolution. But it seems somewhat far-fetched to link their role with a period of increasing prosperity in a rather distant past which may have been effectively erased from their memory by subsequent setbacks, as Davies asserts when he writes: 'The crucial factor is the vague or specific fear that ground gained over a long period of time will be quickly lost.'

De Tocqueville's model, however, definitely crumbles if we shift our attention from bourgeois towards proletarian, and more specifically peasant, revolutions. Nobody could maintain that the Chinese communist revolution occurred in a period of increasing prosperity. During the thirties it was said 'that a large proportion of Chinese peasants are constantly on the brink of actual destitution',[89] and that 'the rural population suffers horribly through the insecurity of life and property'.[90] The Japanese war made the already precarious situation much worse. Brinton claims, on the basis of his study of four 'great revolutions', that these 'revolutions are not started by down-and-outers, by starving, miserable people'.[91] Similarly, Davies writes: 'Far from making people into revolutionaries enduring poverty makes for concern with one's solitary self or solitary family at best and resignation or mute despair at worst'.[92] If anything could disprove the general validity of this thesis, at least as far as peasant revolutions are concerned, it is the Chinese case.[93]

But even for the Russian case one could claim that the events of 1917 were due to utter distress rather than to previous 'economic growth'. Brinton's argument to the contrary, based on the contention that, at the time of the First World War, Russia 'was progressing rapidly toward economic maturity',[94] neglects the much more significant factor that the war years had been a period of great sufferings for the mass of the population. The immediate precipitant of the February revolution was bread shortage in the capital of Petrograd, provoking a massive women's demonstration.

Still less convincing is Davies's interpretation of the Russian case in terms of a J-curve if one adheres to Davies's own picture of Russian economic history. He posits that the recession had essentially started as early as 1904. According to Davies 'the years from 1905 to 1917 formed an almost relentless procession of increasing misery and despair'.[95]*

As in the case of the French Revolution, one could argue that, in so far as the February revolution was a bourgeois one, a rising middle class played a significant role which could, to a certain extent, be explained by their economic advance in an earlier

* Graph 3.

period. But actual developments throughout 1917 proved that this bourgeois current was overtaken by a much more powerful wave of revolutionary activity rooted in broad popular masses, both urban and rural, for whom prewar economic growth could hardly have any meaning at all. The only economic reality they were aware of was the unbearable situation of the present.

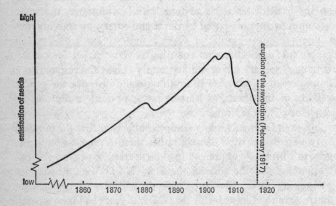

Graph 3. J-curve in Russia according to James C. Davies.

If, therefore, we wish to relate economic conditions to various types of revolutions, we might be justified in connecting de Tocqueville's model, as modified by Davies, with more or less restricted bourgeois revolutions, and the Marxist model with popular ones.

Unfortunately, the historical material available is very restricted, and this should restrain us from rushing into broad generalizations. Moreover, it appears difficult to single out economic conditions, as described above, as pre-revolutionary. To quote Barrington Moore: 'Massive poverty and exploitation in and by themselves are not enough to provide a revolutionary situation.'[96]

Moreover, in the cases where economic distress was followed by serious disturbances, there are several instances of movements that should be assessed as counter-revolutionary rather than revolutionary. What happened in China in 1927, in Brazil in 1964, or in Indonesia in 1965, is indicative of the counter-revolutionary potential inherent in serious impoverishment among the peasantry. As far as economic conditions are concerned, there seems to be little that distinguishes a pre-revolutionary situation from one where either nothing dramatic, or just the reverse of a revolution, occurs.

It is even easier to mention historical cases where long-term economic growth, followed by short-term recession, did not produce anything like a revolution. If the J-curve was really indicative of a pre-revolutionary situation, revolutions should have occurred all over the world in the early thirties of this century.[97] Evidently, more is needed than merely bad or worsening economic conditions, in order to create a pre-revolutionary situation. We will have to find out what additional factors are relevant in creating a truly revolutionary atmosphere.

De Tocqueville's model, on the other hand, presupposes economic conditions conforming to a pattern of economic growth and hence conducive to a bourgeois revolution. In such a case one could easily assume that the link with the emancipation issue is self-evident: if a rising bourgeoisie forwards claims for a larger say in decision-making at the level of central authority, the evolutionary perspective seems undeniable. However, even then the prevalent economic conditions as such may provoke the reverse of a revolutionary development. Counter-revolutions are mostly intended to stop a prevalent tendency towards emancipation, and may precisely occur in situations where the powers that be want to entrench themselves behind traditional insitutions in order to ward off the onslaught of newly emerging forces. The counter-revolution of 1787 in the Netherlands was a clear instance of such an anti-bourgeois reaction.

Again, there seems to be nothing compelling about economic conditions which could induce a drastic urge for emancipation.

vi. *Social Conditions*

The emancipation issue has a sociological, in addition to an economic, aspect. Social groups led by an economic motivation to improve their welfare are, at the same time, trying to improve their status within the social hierarchy. One could ask whether a prerevolutionary situation is characterized by a serious cleavage between the different social strata, or rather by a tendency for borderlines to become blurred through increasing social mobility. An emancipation movement presupposes that a significant segment of a given social group seriously considers the prospects for an improved position for the group as a whole within society and, consequently, no longer views its place within society as ordained by supernatural powers or unalterable institutions. This can only occur in a situation where there is a widespread discrepancy between actual status and potential ambitions, which is hardly imaginable under a system where status roles are permanently and rigidly fixed. One may, therefore, readily assume that a prerevolutionary situation will be characterized by a considerable amount of social mobility, both vertical and horizontal.

Yet the true relationship might be more complicated. We should, again, attempt to distinguish between different types of revolutions. Unfortunately, we do not possess the necessary quantitative data, as in the case of economic preconditions, to measure the amount of social mobility prevalent, for example, in prerevolutionary France, in the same way as economic historians have been able to measure the rate of economic growth during the *ancien régime*. Under such conditions we cannot do much more than advance some guesses as to the probable relationship between the rate of social mobility and the occurrence of several types of revolutions on the basis of the scanty and fragmentary knowledge available to us.

I would like to start with the anti-colonial Indonesian revolution in 1945 as I am fairly well acquainted with its sociological background. As I have pointed out earlier, it was essentially a bourgeois-nationalist revolution. We could, first of all, consider the groups that belonged to the traditional higher strata of Indonesian society which, during the closing decades of colonial rule, had been able to enjoy modern Western education. To a certain extent, their social mobility had been furthered through these educational facilities which provided many of them with a chance to achieve a position and a status unattainable before. On the other hand, it was precisely the colonial 'caste' system which precluded them from achieving positions within the government bureaucracy commensurate with their educational qualifications. Under colonial rule, most positions of real responsibility remained closed to those who belonged to the subjected race, and it was precisely their educational achievements which made these Indonesians aware of their underprivileged position. During the economic crisis of the early thirties the prospects for this group became even worse. Even the traditional aristocrats, who had been used by the Dutch from the nineteenth century onwards to bolster up the colonial structure, were accorded, within the Civil Service system, positions lower than those of the corresponding European section of the administrative corps.

Therefore, it was at the same time increased social mobility and lack of social mobility that gave rise to the general discontent during the closing decades of colonial rule.

Nor should developments during the Japanese occupation be disregarded. Although the Japanese also reserved the key positions for themselves, they were nevertheless forced, through lack of personnel and experience, to admit Indonesians to positions of higher authority and greater responsibility than they had ever been able to attain under colonial rule. The European caste, including most Eurasians, had been removed from the bureaucratic structure and nearly all of them were interned within the camps.

To a certain extent, therefore, the situation at the start of the Indonesian revolution could be represented in terms of a kind of reversed J-curve, the opposite phenomenon of the one assumed by Davies to be typical of pre-revolutionary economic trends.* A long period of frustrated aspirations towards increased social mobility

* Graph 4.

was followed by a short period during which, for the members of the new bourgeoisie, a sudden rise on the ladder of social stratification had been made possible through the occupation of a foreign power. The promise of future independence for Indonesia, made by the Japanese in 1944, strongly enhanced such aspirations. Return of the former colonial rulers would certainly mean, for this

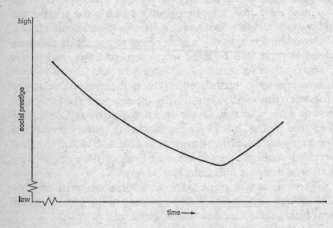

Graph 4. Reversed J-curve; vertical mobility; some increase after steady decline.

group, a serious reduction of positions of authority and prestige open to them, even though the Dutch would have been forced significantly to modify the prewar colonial set-up.*

These personal ambitions of the rising bourgeoisie certainly must have played a role in stimulating the nationalist revolution, even if they only reinforced the genuine idealistic motivations rooted in love of liberty and concern for the plight of the mass of the population.

For other layers of Indonesian society the situation, as far as

* Graph 5.

social mobility was concerned, was different. There was the urban group of so-called semi-intellectuals who had also enjoyed a certain measure of modern education but who could not aspire, on the basis of their educational qualifications, to positions of authority. For this group there certainly were, during colonial rule, all kinds of openings within an expanding colonial economy, both in

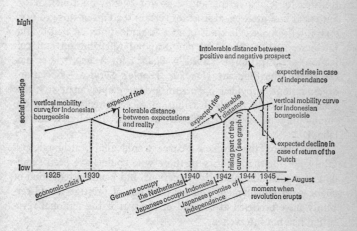

Graph 5. Reversed J-curve; relationship between vertical social mobility and a bourgeois revolution (Indonesia).

government administration and in the service of large Dutch or foreign companies, especially since they were cheaper to employ than the Eurasians, who had formerly monopolized lower administrative functions. But it became increasingly clear that the economy was not expanding fast enough to accommodate the ever-growing group of semi-intellectuals appearing on the labour market. The authorities largely attributed the communist risings of 1926 and 1927 to the growth of an intellectual proletariat. The

T-G

retrenchment of educational facilities during the world crisis was no doubt due, to a certain measure, to this fear of potential leaders of sedition and subversion.

As with the higher bourgeoisie, the economic crisis of the early thirties also seriously reduced the occupational facilities for the group of semi-intellectuals. The thirties could therefore rightly be termed a period of decreased vertical mobility. During the Japanese occupation, on the other hand, there were increased opportunities for employment and even for occupying functions of authority and prestige, at least for certain sections of this group of semi-intellectuals. All kinds of new organizations created by the Japanese, such as the *Bagi dan Kumpul* (distribution and collection) organization described by Piekaar for Acheh,[98] later succeeded by the different *Hokokai* (People's Service Association) organizations, provided opportunities for employment in fields such as food and textile distribution, rice requisitioning, or the summoning of *romushas* (forced labourers, literally: heroes of labour).

Here, again, the reversed J-curve would apply, although certainly not for the majority of those who could have been candidates for such administrative functions. But again, a reduction of chances for employment and for positions of prestige would certainly have occurred at the end of the war if the national revolution had not intervened.

Another group that should be considered is an embryonic class of Indonesian small traders, especially in the island of Java. Their rise was not due to new educational facilities, but rather to the introduction of a money economy and to increasing shortage of land which drove many into trade. Trade had previously been scorned by most people who lived in the rural aristocratic tradition of Java and had been largely left to foreigners – mostly Chinese. It was the near-monopoly of trade by the latter group which prevented significant social mobility for those Javanese who turned to trade, and the rise of the Sarekat Islam in 1912 and the following years reflected the urge for emancipation on the part of the rapidly expanding class of Islamic traders and small industrialists.

The economic crisis seriously affected the opportunities for trade, in the fields both of distribution of commodities and of collection of agricultural products for export. On the one hand, a large number of landless peasants turned towards commerce as a profession, thus swamping the urban markets with increasing numbers of petty traders and contributing to the 'shared poverty' pattern described by Clifford Geertz.[99] Consequently, the opportunity for individual urban traders to make good as established merchants and shopkeepers appreciably diminished. On the other hand, the Chinese competitors were equally seriously hit by the crisis. At any rate, for traders, the colonial period could hardly be counted, in general, as one of increased vertical mobility, although some Japanese import houses started to employ Indonesian middlemen in increasing numbers. The expanding native weaving industry in the mountainous interior of West Java could be counted among the few areas of increasing social mobility.[100] During the Japanese occupation, on the other hand, there was a distinct policy in favour of Indonesian traders against their Chinese competitors. In the consumer cooperatives created as servicing and distribution centres, Indonesians were given executive positions. Again, a reversed J-curve could be observed, although, as far as economic conditions were concerned, the occupation period remained one of hardships also for the professional trader class.

There is another class of independent entrepreneurs that should be separately considered: the native growers of rubber in the so-called Outer Islands of Indonesia. For them, the boom period of the 'happy twenties' was one of rapidly rising hopes and, for some of them, of easily earned wealth. In some parts of Sumatra a class of newly rich rubber growers and traders arose, who ostentatiously showed their capacity to emulate the status symbols of the families of native chiefs. Schrieke attributed some of the agrarian unrest in West Sumatra during the twenties, which culminated in the communist risings of early 1927, to the disequilibrium brought about in the social hierarchy by these new opportunities for upward mobility.

If there was considerable upward mobility in the twenties, during the crisis of the early thirties the opportunities for social

advancement seriously declined. The rubber export and quota
policy of the Dutch distinctly favoured the Western-owned plantations, and consequently the opportunities for native entrepreneurs were severely curtailed. A prominent Dutch civil
servant even indicted the colonial government for having caused
misery and famine among the population of a large area of Sumatra by its highly oppressive and unjust export duties on native
rubber.[101] It was the preferential position of Western-owned
plantations that evidently thwarted the upsurge of the new entrepreneurial class. Only after a new quota system was introduced
in 1937 could the Indonesian entrepreneurs regain some of their
former prosperity.

In the period of Japanese occupation, no reversed J-curve can
really be demonstrated. As far as I am aware, Japanese policy
laid such a stress upon food production to the detriment of
export products such as rubber, that it is likely that native
rubber growing as a source of increasing social mobility all but
vanished.

Yet similar considerations to those operative for other sections
of the Indonesian bourgeoisie were, no doubt, operative among
this entrepreneurial class in its overall support for the nationalist
struggle. National revolution could seriously impair the position
of the Western companies owning the large rubber estates in East
Sumatra which were serious competitors for the native rubber
growers in other parts of the island and in Kalimantan. Again,
chances for upward social mobility may have played a considerable role in creating a revolutionary atmosphere.

If we turn our attention, however, to the broad masses of the
peasant population, especially in Java, the picture becomes basically different. For them, throughout the time of the so-called 'Ethical Period', starting in 1900, there was hardly any prospect of
vertical social mobility. The failure of the ethical policy and its
fundamental causes have been extensively commented upon.[102]
If there was, during that period, an increased mobility, it was in a
geographical sense as a horizontal mobility rather than in a sociological sense. There was, certainly, more movement to the towns,
and at the same time growing numbers of poor peasants were

employed as plantation workers, either in Java or as bonded labourers on Sumatra's east coast.

During the economic crisis of the early thirties opportunities for social mobility, if anything, declined. Horizontal mobility may have increased, although many unemployed people returned from the towns or plantations to the countryside of Java.

Under the Japanese occupation hardly any increased opportunity for social mobility occurred for the Javanese peasantry. It was they who had to provide the main body of *romushas* shipped overseas or used as forced labour for work on such projects as fortifications, or mines. No reversed J-curve was in evidence for this category.

Yet one could venture the suggestion that the increased horizontal mobility of the peasant population contributed to the support they gave to the anti-colonial revolution in many areas of Java. It has been claimed, sometimes, that returned *romushas* (very few of those shipped overseas, incidentally, returned alive) played a prominent role in the unrest in different areas of Indonesia; the Indonesian revolution has been called a revolution of displaced persons.

It seems rather rash to draw generalizations from the experiences of one single country, to illustrate the relationship between social mobility and the rise of a pre-revolutionary situation, the more so since the previous argument demonstrates the extreme intricacy of the problems of social mobility. Yet, on the basis of this brief analysis, certain suggestions could be made, and some avenues indicated for further research.

It appears possible that, as with economic aspects, we should distinguish between bourgeois and peasant revolutions. As far as bourgeois revolutions are concerned, it is likely that a pre-revolutionary situation can be generally characterized as one of increased vertical social mobility. We do not know whether a temporary decline in the amount of social mobility for the new bourgeoisie, as evidenced during the economic crisis, is more crucial than a temporary increase, a reversed J-curve, as evidenced during the Japanese occupation which was, otherwise, a period of serious economic decline, harsh suppression, and utter misery for the mass of the people. But it is clear that blocked avenues for social mobility, caused by a rather rigid colonial 'caste' system, played an important role in producing a pre-revolutionary situation. To use Chalmers Johnson's expression: an 'intransigent elite', blocking avenues for gradual, evolutionary emancipation, is as essential for a pre-revolutionary situation as the existence of a group aspiring at social advance and determined to achieve its objectives.

At any rate, the short experience of the Japanese occupation, providing increased opportunities for different groups of the bourgeoisie, may have contributed towards a growing impatience on its part with the colonial caste system.

On the other hand, the active participation of the Javanese peasantry in the revolutionary struggle might indicate that, for a peasant revolution, increased vertical social mobility is not essential. Increased horizontal mobility, on the other hand, especially if indicative of increasing hardships, might be highly important, and even essential, in promoting a pre-revolutionary situation. It is this increased horizontal mobility which brings people from different areas into a rural society, thus facilitating the creation of all kinds of nation-wide organizations. Intensified rural–urban relationships might equally increase the revolutionary potential while, at the same time, facilitating communication lines for revolutionaries.

In the case of China, the Japanese occupation of large territories and the ensuing horizontal mobility combined with utter misery, may have played a decisive role in the same way as in the Indonesian revolution. For Russia, the First World War was also of the greatest importance in increasing geographic mobility and thus seriously weakening the traditional social institutions.

However, if increased vertical mobility is characteristic of a bourgeois revolution, and increased horizontal mobility of a peasant one, those are not characteristics that present, with any cogency, distinctive traits useful to differentiate a situation preceding a revolution from one where nothing at all or even the reverse occurs. It is, for example, easy enough to enumerate historical situations where increasing vertical social mobility did not give rise to anything like a revolutionary development. It would be equally easy to mention instances where a situation with increased social mobility was followed by a counter-revolution. Since counter-revolutions are intended to stop a process towards emancipation which is legally under way, such a correlation between increased social mobility and counter-revolutionary activities is what one should expect.

Another possible approach would be to try to define a pre-revolutionary situation in terms of a diminishing cohesion, and a decreasing significance for broad layers of the population, of a number of social institutions, which in an earlier period functioned as pillars of the social order. For example, a pre-revolutionary situation may be marked by a crumbling of royalty as a symbol of national cohesion; by a weakening of the grip of the official church, as a supporter of the established order, on the mass of the population; by a loss of power of a ruling aristocracy to fulfil its function as patrons for a significant segment of the mass of the peasantry; by a refusal of the elite to accommodate 'fresh blood' and to grant newcomers equal status on the basis of achievement.

To a certain extent, such inconsistencies within the social order coincide with what Chalmers Johnson defines as 'multiple dysfunctions' within a society characteristic of a pre-revolutionary situation.[103] It seems to me, however, that the explanation of the rise of a revolution as a consequence of 'dysfunctions' is basically tautological. What is really changing is not the functioning of social institutions as such, but rather the significance of these institutions in the light of the values to which people adhere. It is mainly in the realm of values as a driving force that a pre-revolutionary situation may be distinguished from one where a counter-revolution is more probable. A revolutionary development will be characterized by the prevalence of an ideology directed towards the future and criticizing institutions from the point of view of a struggle for emancipation. Counter-revolutionary movements, on the other hand, basically attempt to bolster up, and even to strengthen, existing institutions.

It follows that in the case of social institutions and their changed relevance for society as a whole, it is not so much the situational aspects that matter, but rather the related mental attitudes. Still more than in the case of economic conditions, actual social conditions are closely connected with the state of mind, the mood within a society.

Of course, the same is true, to a large extent, for the issue of social mobility discussed before. It is not so much the objective status and position of an individual that matters, but rather the reference system against which he measures his own position and that of other persons. Frustrations and a sense that avenues for social advance are blocked are largely determined by the values to which an individual adheres. The emancipation issue is at least as much one of values and subjectively held aspirations as one of objective class conditions.

In the case of increased horizontal mobility for the rural masses, as a precondition for a peasant revolution, it is clear that what causes the situation to become tense to the point where a revolution may occur is not so much a change in actual class conditions as a growing awareness of their debased class position among growing numbers of poor peasants set adrift through the operation of external economic forces.

vii. Political Conditions

Since revolutions, as we have seen, essentially embody a fundamental change within a *political* structure, it is obvious that we should try to define a pre-revolutionary situation primarily in political terms. The most significant variable seems to be the extent to which a political system can be considered repressive.

In this respect, the different historical instances of revolutionary movements show a considerable uniformity: the political systems against which they arise may be generally defined as authoritarian and oppressive.

The only case where the structure against which a revolutionary movement was directed was not bluntly authoritarian, was the American revolution. However, even in this case the democratic aspects of the British regime were basically irrelevant, since it was a colonial situation, and consequently a national revolution. The revolution was essentially directed against taxation without representation.

In some of the historical cases a revolution did not occur at the height of repression, but when the amount of repression had been somewhat relaxed. One could mention, in this connection, the British revolution which occurred shortly *after* King Charles I had put an end to the period of personal rule which had lasted eleven years, and had called a Parliament. Similarly, the French Revolution occurred *after* King Louis XVI had summoned a meeting of the Estates-General, which had not met since 1614! This phenomenon has also been observed by Harry Eckstein: 'The worst situation of all seems to arise when a regime, having driven its opponents underground, inflamed their enmity, heightened their contempt, and cemented their organization, suddenly relaxes its repression and attempts a liberal policy.'[104] One could try to interpret the phenomenon again in a graphic way, as a reversed J-curve.

However, I would suggest that this coincidence has little to do with the basic aspects of the pre-revolutionary situation, and should rather be treated under the heading of accelerators, as in the next section.

It seems to me that as far as political conditions are concerned, a neat distinction could be drawn between situations propitious for revolutions and conditions conducive to counter-revolutions. If revolution mostly occurs in situations of harsh repression, counter-revolution is likely to occur in a situation where a certain scope is being given for peaceful transformation and emancipation along evolutionary lines. A counter-revolution is, mostly, intended to replace a government considered to be 'weak' and 'soft' by a more authoritarian one that will withstand pressures for further emancipation.

From the foregoing it follows that, as far as the political aspects are concerned, we may define a pre-revolutionary situation in a way which is clearly to be distinguished from a situation that may give rise to a counter-revolution.

We could try to define the situational aspects of a pre-revolutionary situation in the following way.

A peasant revolution is most likely to occur in a situation where extreme poverty and a lack of opportunities for vertical social mobility for the mass of the population are combined with an increasing horizontal mobility and a harsh and oppressive political system. However, a specific 'accelerator' may be needed to call a true revolutionary movement into life.

On the other hand, the requirements for a bourgeois revolution, and specifically for a nationalist one, may be less strict. Economic growth and increasing vertical social mobility may produce a revolutionary movement if there is an intransigent elite that clings to its traditional privileges and if the political system is preponderantly authoritarian. In this case, again, an 'accelerator' may be needed to trigger a revolutionary development.

viii. Accelerators

If it is possible to distinguish a pre-revolutionary situation from one which presages counter-revolution, it is less easy to tell at what moment harsh oppression will lead to a revolutionary outburst. The difficulty in defining a pre-revolutionary situation is that even in cases of extremely harsh oppression it is hard to maintain that revolution is inevitable. There have been long periods of harsh oppression in human history without true revolutionary outbursts occurring. As Lawrence Stone correctly remarks: 'Revolution is never inevitable.'[105]

Johnson maintains that, in order to understand the way revolutions arise, we have to introduce another type of intervening factor: the accelerators. If only we do not attribute to these accelerators the character of 'automatic triggers ignoring the area of unpredictable personal choice that is always left to the ruling elite and to the revolutionary leaders', we may find this concept a very useful one to explain the actual occurrence of revolutions. Eckstein uses, in this connection, the term 'precipitants'.[106]

Looking at our historical materials, there are two factors that appear to play a preponderant role as accelerators.

The first one is, of course, a lost or losing war. The first, abortive, Russian revolution of 1905 was certainly largely due to the defeat in the Russo-Japanese war. If the situation in Russia before 1914 was again pre-revolutionary, owing to the repressive and authoritarian political system combined with widespread poverty and crumbling social institutions, a number of serious defeats during the First World War were needed to bring general dissatisfaction into the open. Germany, Hungary and Turkey, the losers of the First World War, experienced serious disorders of a revolutionary character at the end of the war. After the Second World War a number of revolutions again occurred, precipitated by defeat, as for example the Indonesian revolution against the Dutch or the Vietnamese revolution against the French who, to all intents and purposes, could be held to have been the losers in the Pacific War.

The reason why a lost war functions as an accelerator is evident. An oppressive regime is mainly dependent on the reliability of the armed forces and the police. But in a losing war the cohesion and reliability of this apparatus may be seriously impaired. Dissatisfaction among part of the officers' corps and among the rank and file of the military forces transform the latter into an apparatus that is not only seriously weakened as a tool of the *status quo*, but may even shift its allegiance to the competing elite of revolutionaries. But here we already touch on the psychological factors operative in a pre-revolutionary situation.[107]

As we have observed, a war does not need to be lost in a technical sense to function as an accelerator. The Second World War was, according to any formal criterion, won by the Allied Powers including China under Chiang Kai-shek. Yet, this is not exactly how it must have looked, for example, to the large majority of the Chinese people. The Japanese had conquered extensive Chinese territories, and if there were Chinese troops that offered effective resistance to the invaders, they were units of the Red Army rather than Chiang Kai-shek's troops. In occupied territories there were many Kuomintang officials and army officers who collaborated with the Japanese.[108] In the final victory over Japan the Chiang Kai-shek regime had hardly any active part to play.

Hence, throughout the protracted war, Chiang Kai-shek's military force had lost its inner cohesion and its reliability as a prop for Chiang's authority. Consequently, in the course of the postwar revolution, defection of army units to the revolutionaries occurred on a large scale.

There are other factors inherent in a situation of war, apart from the weakening of the army, that may also help to explain its functions as an accelerator. For example, economic dislocation, increased vertical mobility for certain categories, and increased horizontal mobility for the masses, may contribute to the same effect.

Another type of accelerator can be observed in several earlier revolutions: a critical situation in the state finances. This factor played an important role both in the English Puritan revolution and the French Revolution. The American Revolution was equally hastened by an attempt from the English colonial power to introduce a Stamp Act.

Brinton shows that the deplorable state of government finances induced both King Charles I of England and King Louis XVI of France to call a Parliament, after a long period of authoritarian rule, in order to obtain some support among the citizenry for their financial projects. And, as we have seen earlier, it was precisely this sudden relaxation of authoritarian rule which triggered the subsequent revolutionary development.

Brinton includes the bad financial state of the public administration among the deeper causes of a revolution.[109] It is only in this sense that he is prepared to admit that something like an economic crisis or breakdown may have been at the root of the revolutions dealt with in his study. We could add that a bad state of government finances may result in a failure to pay the regular troops which, in its turn, may affect the reliability of the armed forces.

It seems plausible that serious financial difficulties for a government administration cannot be considered as an isolated phenomenon. In many cases, especially in predominantly non-industrial societies, these difficulties are nothing but a reflection of a general state of impoverishment among the rural mass of the population. The deeper roots of a revolution, and more specifically of a peasant revolution, are not the bad finances of the state but the tensions created by this impoverishment of the peasantry. The financial weakness of the state may function, in such cases, as an accelerator only.

However, Brinton rightly argues that a bad state of government finances does not necessarily reflect a situation of general poverty. The American Revolution and the English Puritan one are instances of bourgeois revolutions where bad state finances were not due to general impoverishment. If, however, other factors are operative, as for example a general dissatisfaction among a rising urban bourgeoisie, the difficult financial situation of a state may, again, have functioned as an accelerator.

That a financial state crisis is not a cause in itself becomes evident if one considers the fact that world history is characterized more by governments suffering from shortage of financial means than by abundancy of such resources. However, the fact remains that most states suffering from financial shortages are *not* shaken by revolutions. If they were, revolution would be a more common phenomenon than it is.

Other accelerators suggested by Johnson are ideological beliefs powerful enough to convey to those opposing the reigning powers a sense of ability in overcoming the armed forces.[110] Elsewhere, he mentions 'the effects of organizational activities by a revolutionary party that is attempting to create a rebel infrastructure in order to launch a militarized mass insurrection'.[111] However, these could hardly be viewed as independent accelerators. They are rather part and parcel of revolutionary strategy and, in certain cases, preconditions for a successful revolutionary struggle. They are not conditions leading towards a mature pre-revolutionary situation and, thus, preparing the ground for revolutionary strategy. I would prefer to reserve the term accelerator for factors operating within society or even external factors – such as a weakening of foreign powers upholding the *status quo* – independent from revolutionary strategy as such. What the accelerators, acknowledged as such in my argument, have in common, is the weakening of the state apparatus as an instrument of suppression. If not only intellectuals but also military people and other parts of the state apparatus are prone to transfer their allegiance, revolution is near at hand.

ix. *Psychological Aspects*

The foregoing treatment of situational aspects of pre-revolutionary situations has to be supplemented with a discussion of psychological aspects which may lend our treatment of the genesis of revolutions a certain perspective in terms of dynamic sociological processes.

In chapter four I dealt with conflicting values as an important source of both evolutionary and revolutionary change. I developed there the counterpoint concept as a useful tool to define the total fabric of society in terms of ever-present protest elements against the predominant hierarchical order. It proved possible to reduce overall views of society in terms of stratification to subjective interpretations of the human environment mostly, but not necessarily, shared by large groups of individuals. A mental rejection of hierarchy as upheld by those in actual power, which is at the root of any emancipation movement, appeared to be embryonically embedded in the warp and woof of any human society.

Our task in this section will be to link up this overall view of social change with the problem of the genesis of revolutions. Is it possible to relate a pre-revolutionary situation, especially in its psychological aspects, to conflicting values and to the counterpoint phenomenon as defined in the earlier chapter?

I must first remind the reader that social change in terms of emancipation proceeds, to a large extent, in evolutionary forms. Wherever conflicting values are allowed to express themselves in a legal way and to realize a gradual transformation of the social order, the cataclysmic type of social change termed revolutionary may be avoided for long periods.

As I have already pointed out, counterpoints may even be used by those in power to ward off embryonic symptoms of social protest through allowing them some scope for expression in the institutionalized form. Therefore, a permissive attitude as regards disguised protest elements may even function as a tool whereby those in power can avert the danger of real concessions. Consequently, it is quite possible that institutionalized counterpoints will be largely prevalent in societies where not much scope is left for real emancipation. In this sense, one might suspect that a society where protest elements are isolated within institutionalized patterns of disguise is nearer to revolutionary change than one where social protest may be expressed overtly and consequently avenues for gradual social and political change are left open.

One may ask, therefore, in what way a society can develop from one where social protest has to be disguised and institutionalized, since open expressions of protest are suppressed, into one where a pre-revolutionary situation prevails.

Firstly, do dynamic developments arise within the same social group that was adhering to a distinct value system which had to be concealed in a contrapuntal form? Or do these developments occur among a social group aspiring to emancipation, different from the one that had allowed itself, in an earlier phase, to be weaned away from the emancipation course through permissive concessions in the more or less innocuous realm of religion or fiction? Secondly, are dynamic developments leading towards a pre-revolutionary situation to be viewed mainly as a maturing of age-old protest elements, gradually strengthened and no longer prepared to let themselves be shut away in an innocuous institutional frame? Or are they largely due to external developments, for example in the realm of human ecology (scarcity of land, migration, new techniques, the intrusion of foreign enterprise) which may set old protest elements, dormant under an institutional cover, into motion again?

I would tend to advance, in both cases, the second alternative as the more likely answer to our query. But I am aware that much more historical and psychological research will be needed before such questions as these could be answered with any amount of confidence. A general theory of the genesis of revolutions is still far away.

What we can try to do is to define a pre-revolutionary situation in terms of an uneasy and shifting balance between different value systems, and then to point out to what extent it may be distinguished from one that is either conducive to the evolutionary type of emancipation, or characterized by a partial acceptance of concealed and institutionalized protest forms.

We could, then, start by referring to Crane Brinton's attempt to define a pre-revolutionary situation in terms of mental attitudes. Firstly, then, he refers to the 'Eternal Figaro' as a 'preliminary sign' of a brewing revolution.[112] Secondly, he points to the rise of competing ideologies challenging the established order, and the ensuing 'transfer of allegiance of the intellectuals' towards one of the centres of these dangerous ideas.[113]

What strikes us immediately is that in these cases the protest elements can no longer be manipulated at will by those in power. Whereas the theatre screen in any society may be a shield behind which countervalues are, to a certain extent, allowed to be expressed, even if objectively they represent 'dangerous thoughts', the 'Eternal Figaro' is much more than a fictitious dream reality allowing the audience to let off steam. In Beaumarchais's *Figaro* revolution itself found a highly effective tool for expression. The repetition, evening after evening, of seditious sentences which the audience revels in, may become a strong motivating force; even though many among the spectators would have reason to be seriously worried if they had really understood what they were listening to: the impending doom of their class as a privileged layer of society. In theatrical performances or novels of the 'Eternal Figaro' type the 'counter-elite' consciously inspires protest and rebellion among those who have, until recently, only passively experienced a certain uneasiness about the prevalent state of affairs. Theatrical performances are well-devised challenges to those in authority, who have to choose between keeping up a pretence of permissiveness over contrapuntal phenomena and the odium attached to overt repression.

Similarly, ideological countervalues are, in a pre-revolutionary situation, more or less openly expressing themselves in opposition to the official value hierarchy. As we have seen in the previous chapter, revolutionary ideologies have, in a more distant past, repeatedly assumed religious forms. The Calvinist ideology could be mentioned, both in the Netherlands in the sixteenth and in England in the seventeenth century. In such cases, however, the social protest which assumes religious forms is basically different from religious protest which functions as a counterpoint in the less dynamic type of society. In the latter case, the religious protest may have started as a true rebellion against the established order of things. But what had started as a rebellious, mostly millenary, sect could be isolated, by those in power, into some institutionalized form where egalitarian ideas could be accommodated and relegated to a mere symbolic existence or to the realm of *the Great Beyond*.

What, therefore, characterizes a pre-revolutionary situation, in psychological terms, is that the conflict of values has come into the open, and that those rallying around a set of conflicting values have been building up one or more power centres opposing the official hierarchy.

It is typical of the pre-revolutionary situation for broad sections of the population no longer to consider the prevalent social order to be self-evident. A rising bourgeoisie aspires to positions of economic power commensurate with its newly acquired wealth, but is barred from some of these positions by institutional privileges accruing to a traditional aristocratic elite. But it is not only the objective lack of privilege that matters. Still more important is the psychological factor of how it is subjectively experienced by the dissatisfied group. Its claims may be expressed in the shape of new values, such as freedom, or a career open to talent. Figaro's soliloquy gave a clear and witty expression to these new values.

In the case of the dissatisfaction of the broad rural masses with their miserable economic plight, foreboding a peasant revolution, psychological factors may, again, be at least as important as the objective state of affairs. We have seen, in one of the preceding sections, that increased horizontal mobility (urban migration, plantation labour, enlistment for military works) may be typical of a pre-revolutionary situation. This becomes understandable if we take account of the fact that physical mobility may loosen many people from their natural environment and produce a greater awareness of the fact that society as it exists, with its injustices, inequalities and misery, is not unchangeable. Propagandists of a communist ideology, promising land for all and a new and better society, may gain access to remote rural areas as a consequence of increased horizontal mobility.

In the social field, again, psychological factors seeking expression in new values may be at least as important as the class situation. As I have pointed out in chapter four, social stratification always rests on a set of accepted values expressing themselves in hierarchical terms. Dissatisfaction with the status of one's group always comes down to a more or less explicit acceptance of a different set of values. For example, as we have seen in Indonesian pre-war colonial society, a rising bourgeoisie claimed equality with Europeans on the basis of educational qualifications interpreted in terms of achievement. The existing status structure, on the other hand, was based on elements of ascription, the highest positions being reserved for those who by birth belonged to the colonial upper caste. Any revolutionary ideology explicitly challenges the official status hierarchy, mainly in terms of a class struggle. In order to challenge the privileges of the few, the many will first have mentally to reject their sense of inferiority.

Equally, the crumbling of existing social institutions, as for instance a church, or slavery, may be interpreted in terms of changing values. As we have seen in chapter four social institutions have no real existence. They only exist because people believe in their reality. Therefore, changing values may shake the foundations of an institution which was dominating a society in an earlier phase.

Erosion of values predominant in a former phase is, therefore, a natural concomitant of a crumbling of institutions once impressive and seemingly omnipotent.

We now come to the political field. Here, again, the psychological aspect is at least as important as the situational one. Again, it is not merely the oppressive character as such of a political system that matters. A pre-revolutionary situation is characterized by a mounting impatience with the prevalent political order.

Rejection of a political order will not occur unless the people concerned are subjectively convinced that the way towards realization of what they assume to be their lawful aspirations is blocked. A precondition for such a feeling is, again, a recognition of values in the realm of political ideas, such as liberty, equality, brotherhood, human dignity for the downtrodden, that cannot be realized to any significant extent within the prevalent political order.

Among the psychological preconditions for a revolution, therefore, one should include a feeling among relatively large groups that avenues towards emancipation are consistently blocked. This blockage may be experienced as lack of opportunities in the economic field, as obstacles to social mobility, or as restriction of civilian rights and political liberties. Although the issue of revolution basically centres around the political order, yet it seems to me rather simplistic to reduce a pre-revolutionary situation, as Lawrence Stone does, to an incongruency between the social and the political system.[114] It is rather a combination of three types of frustration that accounts for the rise of a revolutionary mood. Johnson is right in claiming that it takes two to make a revolution – a dissatisfied mass and an intransigent elite. But it is not only the political behaviour of the elite that matters, but equally its economic behaviour and its attitudes in terms of class and social status.

x. Some General Conclusions as to the Genesis of a Pre-revolutionary Situation

In the foregoing discussion, pre-revolutionary society, both in its situational and in its psychological aspects, was mainly dealt with in terms of a prevalent state of affairs, even though this state of affairs was defined as an uneasy balance between conflicting trends. It is still much more difficult to generalize about how such a pre-revolutionary situation has come about.

Evidently, there is not one single model explaining how pre-revolutionary situations do arise. We might deduce that bourgeois revolutions *may* occur after a period of economic growth, although this is far from universally valid. There *may* have been a short-term recession, in conformity with Davies's J-curve model.

As far as peasant revolutions are concerned, they arise in a situation of extreme poverty. Probably they are preceded by a long period of gradual impoverishment, but it would be difficult to demonstrate this as a general phenomenon. It is true that a serious short-term dislocation and growing misery through war has, more than once, preceded a peasant revolution.

From the Indonesian case one may deduce that it is still more difficult to generalize concerning previous trends in social mobility. For different social groups there were, in Indonesia from 1900 onwards, divergent trends as to rise or decline in status. The only generalization that seems justified is an unmistakable rise in status for certain groups who could be considered a new rising bourgeoisie, and who find their aspirations blocked by an elite monopolizing all positions of power and prestige.

Another general trend might be a growing horizontal mobility for the rural masses.

A gradual crumbling of several social institutions could also be considered a process leading to a pre-revolutionary situation. As for political developments it is hard to decide whether, during the period preceding a pre-revolutionary situation, there has generally been a hardening of political repression, or simply a situation of permanent oppressive government meeting with increasing resistance on the part of an awakening population. Again, I would prefer not to generalize.

It appears less risky to discuss some general aspects of the ripening of a revolutionary atmosphere in the realm of values and psychology.

I have already touched upon the somewhat doubtful question as to what extent the rise of a revolutionary ideology should be viewed as a bursting into the open of certain psychic forces that had already been latent for a long time, as counterpoints basically in opposition to the prevalent social hierarchy.

We are ignorant of the true character of the transformation of a hidden protest into an open one in which such countervalues no longer remain isolated within a restricted institutional frame, accorded by those in power as a kind of emotional safety valve. We could try, however, to view this problem against the background of the general societal model developed in chapter four, in which plurality of values and of value systems was established as typical of any society.

We have, first and foremost, to find out how dominant values and the social institutions based upon them are gradually eroded and give way to new mental attitudes critical of the established order. What concerns us in particular is how a counterpoint may grow, either through its own impetus or through the operation of external forces, into a defection from the establishment and into a revolutionary process leading to a reversal of the established order. Usually there is a measure of general acceptance of the hierarchical order as claimed by those in authority. Even if divergent value systems are simultaneously acknowledged by part of the people, either explicitly or in more latent forms, the idea that the established order could be made a matter of dispute, is not easily admitted. For a long time countervalues may remain concealed, and influence the course of events by provoking passive opposition to those in authority or by restraining the latter by giving them a bad conscience. Those in power may attempt to neutralize and isolate the protest through granting the countervalues an institutional outlet: theatre and other art forms, or religion. But situations may develop where such strategies do not work. A true theory of revolution should attempt to establish in what kind of situations this is likely to occur, and what types of factor are operative in transforming a concealed protest into an open one. It is still too early to advance such a theory in general terms.

In the end, if a value system deviating from the dominant one acquires a strong emotional significance for an individual or group of individuals – for example this may be the case if the system is incorporated within a religious movement with a strong ethical appeal – it may assume ascendancy in the mind of these people. The acceptance of the hierarchical order becomes psychologically conditional upon the adherence, by those in power, to the 'higher' moral principles. This is already, to a certain extent, a form of erosion of the established order. There may be, for a very long time, numerous deviations by those representing the official order from the specific norms held in such a restricted group, before one becomes aware of the basic incompatibility between the two value systems. For a long time, there will remain a tendency to consider the deviations from the stricter norms as individual cases of human frailty: 'The police act arbitrarily, but if those in authority knew . . .', or: 'The king is all right, but his advisers are evil. We should try to rescue him from his bad environment.' Crane Brinton calls this the 'good man' fallacy. But after the illusion that abuse could be attributed to 'evil men' has been destroyed, people start to realize that they suffer because of 'evil institutions'.[115]

xi. *The Process of Revolution*

We have seen how difficult it is to make any valid general propositions about the genesis of revolutions. Yet, since we could analyse a pre-revolutionary situation in terms of overall economic, social and political conditions, and of common psychological moods and reactions, it was possible, on the basis of the historical evidence available, to make some observations of a general nature.

This is hardly the case once a revolutionary movement has really started. Therefore, the rare attempts made to develop a universal model dividing a revolutionary process into several distinct phases, are very unlikely to provide more than a rather fortuitous sequence of events in a few better-known single cases. Some of the sequences presented as part of a 'natural history', as for example the succession of 'the rule of the moderates' by an 'accession of the extremists', accompanied by 'a reign of terror and virtue', are evidently based on one single case: the French one.[116] One could even call this preoccupation with the revolution of 1789 'a French bias', common among many historians, and political scientists.

Brinton himself acknowledges that in the American revolution there has never been anything like 'an accession of the extremists' in a true sense, following upon 'a rule of moderates'.[117]

But the model is fitting only in a restricted sense for the Russian Revolution as well. Whereas in France the extremists, the Jacobins around Robespierre, were radical in their attempts to carry a bourgeois revolution to an end, in Russia the extremists, represented by the Bolsheviks, aimed at something completely different: they started a new revolution which got its main support from the urban and rural masses and was directed against both the *ancien régime* and the bourgeoisie. This explains why Brinton's sketch of the general course of revolutions does not apply to the Russian case. He writes that as power moves from right to centre to left, 'it gets more and more concentrated, more and more narrows its base in the country and among the people, since at each important crisis the defeated group has to drop out of politics'.[118] In Russia, exactly the opposite happened: with the victory of the proletarian revolution, the popular basis of the revolutionary regime was widened since it could now count upon the support of the urban and rural masses. The decisive importance of this support was well illustrated during the Wars of Intervention, where the Red Army, fighting against well-trained regular troops, was able to gain a final victory thanks to this support from the people.

Therefore, even if the division into moderates and radicals could be endorsed as a fairly universal phenomenon, the sequence of events escapes any attempt at stereotyping. This is logical if one takes into account the great variety of historical events gathered, even starting from my rather restrictive definition, under the general heading of revolution; it becomes even more understandable if one includes revolutions that miscarry among those to be considered. It would be surprising if it were otherwise. The actual course of revolutions is so dependent upon chance events, personal factors and specific historical circumstances that it needs a true Procrustes to believe that all these unique processes could be forced into one single and universal pattern. Even less than with the long-term processes of *evolution* is a fixed sequence of historical stages to be expected here.

Therefore, it seems to me that our approach to the course of revolutions should be different. It seems much more promising to analyse the process of revolution in terms of revolutionary strategy and its chances and potential consequences under different circumstances. Certainly, in this connection, the distinction between moderates and radicals remains an important factor. What Brinton calls the reign of terror and virtue may also have significant aspects: revolutionary leaders may gain an enormous influence if they seriously try to live up to the new revolutionary values which ordinarily include a much more sober way of life than that followed by the ruling elite under the *ancien régime*. A forceful pursuit of this new style of life may also prove of the utmost importance in increasing the rate of saving and investment, in order to speed up economic reconstruction along new revolutionary lines. A sober and Spartan mentality may equally increase the efficacy of a revolutionary army in defeating internal and external enemies that are lacking the revolutionary spirit and the motivation for self-sacrifice.

If, however, a prevalence of new virtues does much to increase the chances of success for the revolutionary strategists, an application of terror to enforce conformity with the new revolutionary values may have an opposite effect. The use of sheer terror to achieve conformity with a prescribed pattern of behaviour – not to speak of thought – in the short run only produces reticence and disaffection, and in the longer run counter-conspiracies, sabotage and resistance. It is quite understandable that a 'reign of terror and virtue' as practised under Robespierre produced a Thermidorlike reaction. It is *not* proved, by this unique coincidence, that either of these phases is inevitable in the 'natural history' of revolutions.

If new virtues are introduced through massive persuasion and education rather than through terror, as has been largely the case in China during the fifties, it may be possible even for radicals or extremists of the Mao Tse-tung type to establish a much more permanent regime based on definite revolutionary principles.

Although the selection of specific problems for discussion is rather arbitrary, I would like to restrict my argument to three distinct aspects of the course of revolutions. They are:

1. The effect of surprise at the collapse of authority which now seems in retrospect to have been a 'paper tiger';
2. certain aspects of revolutionary strategy;
3. the effects of revolutions in terms of emancipation.

xii. *The Crumbling of Political Authority*

In an earlier section I observed that it may take a long time for an individual to relinquish his loyalty towards the political authorities. Although a long process of maturing must precede such a shift in allegiance, during which time he must become gradually aware of the incompatibility between the value system he adheres to, and a loyalty towards authorities that repeatedly trespass against it, the final recognition of this truth must come with a traumatic shock.

Similarly, broader sections of a population may suddenly appear to lose their traditional awe in face of the established authority. A revolution may expose the fundamental weakness of a long-respected political regime in such a decisive way that the whole authority structure tumbles down within a short span of time.

Since political institutions, like social ones, have no real existence of their own but are fully dependent upon being accepted as authoritative among large sections of the population, the efficacy of the state apparatus crumbles as soon as the authority of those in power is challenged, not only by the people but by some of those who form part of the state apparatus, including the army and police corps.

Brinton has also observed this frequent phenomenon of sudden collapse: 'the hated old regime has been conquered so easily!'[119] The much-feared lion appears as a 'paper tiger', granting all kinds of concessions and no longer able to withstand all kinds of popular pressures. Those who yesterday still shouted 'Hosanna', now are yelling: 'Crucify him!'

Yet, we should not generalize about the rapid collapse of the prevalent political order. Such a collapse occurred in the cases we have specifically studied as successful revolutions. But there are revolutions that fail, and in such cases the ruling authorities are evidently able to withstand the onslaught of new thoughts and revolutionary fervour, and to rally sufficient support to suppress popular movements.

Neither the occurrence nor the success of a revolution is ever inevitable in the strict sense of a predetermined chain of events. Even an accelerator does not function as an automatic trigger. Personal decisions and human frailties may play such a decisive role in a course of events, that trends of a sociological, economic, or psychological nature do not materialize. Even where the ground for a revolution has been fully prepared both by the revolutionaries and their conservative and intransigent opponents there is still a need for men who will be capable of grasping their chance to make a revolution and bring it to a successful conclusion.

Therefore, we cannot disconnect the issue of the vulnerability of a political structure from the problem of revolutionary strategy.

xiii. Revolutionary Strategy

Although much more than organization alone is needed to get a revolution going, even in a situation where there exists widespread discontent and enough fuel to start a revolution, organization in itself is essential both in the preparation and in the execution of a revolution in its different stages. In order to be able to face the strong official state apparatus, the revolutionaries need much more than mere revolutionary fervour and popular support. Many organizational forms are possible, depending on the type of revolution envisaged (for example national versus social, or bourgeois versus peasant revolutions), ranging from revolutionary clubs operating mostly in the capital of the country, nation-wide political parties of the communist type with international ramifications, which are often forced to operate partly as underground organizations, or a semi-military guerrilla organization occupying relatively inaccessible mountainous areas in the interior and thus creating a rallying place for insurrectionary forces. In any of these cases, organization has to be supplemented with an ideological content, embodying new values that might make the competing power centre attractive to many followers and win the allegiance of a large proportion of the intelligentsia. The latter achievement is the more important since a transfer of allegiance of many well-trained people to the revolutionary power centre may seriously affect the chances of the legal authorities keeping the government apparatus going.

For example, during the Indonesian national revolution, after the second Dutch military action (December 1948) which started with the conquest of the Republican capital Jogjakarta (Central

Java), the refusal of the Sultan of Jogjakarta, who had been a minister in the Republican government, and of many of his functionaries, to work for the Dutch, seriously undermined the position of the latter and essentially sealed the fate of the previous colonial power.

In the course of a revolution, the strategy of different groups of revolutionaries may widely differ. Brinton shows how, in a power struggle between 'moderates' and 'extremists' after the first successes in revolution, the more extreme revolutionists' organizations (Jacobins in France, Soviets in Russia) may take over a large part of governmental powers.[120] Although these few historical cases should not be extended, in my view, to anything like a universal model, yet as examples of how revolutionary organizations may operate and attempt to gain ascendancy, they are highly significant.

Relationships with foreign powers are equally significant aspects of revolutionary strategy. Both withdrawal from war, like Lenin's decision to conclude the peace treaty of Brest Litovsk, and expansion of the revolutionary movement through war as carried on by French revolutionary forces, may embody certain aspects of revolutionary strategy.

Again, our only general conclusion could be that the course of revolution is highly dependent on individual decisions as embodied in the functioning of revolutionary organizations which attempt to combine effectiveness as a fighting force with a certain ideological content aiming at a new society, giving room for emancipation of social groups that were suppressed under the old regime.

xiv. *The Effects of Revolutions in Terms of Emancipation*

Revolutions may produce effects in very different areas of social life. They generally result in fundamental changes within the political structure, mostly leading to an increased participation of the people in decision-making. No doubt dictatorial phases in a revolutionary process may seriously restrict the newly acquired freedoms. In chapter ten we will revert to this phenomenon. Brinton does not consider the ultimate fruits of revolutions, in terms of greater freedom, to be very impressive,[121] which is understandable in the light of his view of revolutions as pathological occurrences which ultimately result, after a Thermidor and restoration, in a convalescence of the sick society. Yet it is certain that in any successful revolution some groups, that were formerly excluded from the political power structure, acquire chances which were formerly denied to them.

In the field of social mobility emancipation for all kinds of groups is most likely to occur. An increased access to positions of status and prestige for people who were formerly denied vertical mobility, to the detriment of members of former ruling classes, typically belongs to the first revolutionary achievements.

In the economic field, certain significant changes occur, mainly as a result of a serious dislocation brought about by revolution as such. These changes generally embody a certain amount of emancipation for groups that were formerly relegated to positions lacking economic power.

However, it is not at all self-evident that a revolution will effect a true economic transformation of society. Important changes in the political power structure do not necessarily forebode a fundamental change in the economic system. Generally, basic economic change is much harder to achieve than a shift within the political system. For example, a revolution resulting in agrarian reforms does not automatically produce a fundamental change in the forms and techniques of agricultural production, and does not necessarily solve the basic problems of rural poverty. The Mexican revolution of 1911 and following years is a case in point.

Another significant aspect of revolutionary emancipation is a sudden extension of educational facilities.

But the most significant emancipation generally occurs in the psychological sector. The heightened sense of human dignity and a fresh belief in new social values may produce such a transformation of mentality that this, in itself, may forebode a fundamental transformation of society. The mental forces released through a revolution may embody its most important effect on a society.

xv. *The Ultimate Effect of Revolutions*

The weakness of Brinton's quasi-medical approach becomes especially visible in his treatment of the Thermidor issue. His view of revolution as a process of illness induces him to look, in any single case, for a kind of restoration which is foreboded by a period of moderation, a Thermidor. It is certainly true that in every revolutionary development there arise strong forces aiming at a kind of stabilization; these forces are easily understandable if one takes into account the strength of the urge for safety and stability, present in every human mind, and conducive to a process of adaptation rather than to an ongoing innovation; these forces may find support in the interests of a new elite which wants to be safeguarded against new intrusions and claims on the part of those who, throughout the revolutionary struggle, had helped them to power, and now demand their share in the drive for emancipation. Yet, the real outcome of revolutionary processes is much less simple than that.

In order to make the facts fit his model, Brinton sometimes has to force his concept far beyond its proper scope. For example, in order to substantiate his general scheme, he claims that what occurred in the Soviet Union during Stalin's rule was a kind of 'complicated and prolonged' Thermidor.[122] This view is not completely without justification. Stalin's rule certainly contained distinct elements of stabilization and of a return to a hierarchical and bureaucratic order, in which many original elements of the Russian Revolution got lost. But at the same time, the period of Stalin's rule witnessed so many fundamental innovations (such as the collectivization of agriculture and the forced industrialization engendered in the successive Five Year plans), that one cannot fail to characterize this period as a continuing revolutionary burgeoning forth of the original impetus that had given rise to the upheaval of 1917.

Interestingly enough Barrington Moore, though basically in disagreement with the pathological metaphor, also has strong reservations as regards the eventual outcome of revolutions. After having shown that absence of revolution may produce a good deal of suffering, he continues to argue that 'revolutionary violence has been part of the break with a repressive past and of the effort to construct a less repressive future'. But it was only in the Western democratic countries that revolutionary violence 'made possible subsequent peaceful change'. For the communist revolutions of the present century, however, the outlook, in his opinion, would seem to be much more gloomy. At the same point where 'the gradualist argument seems shattered', 'the revolutionary argument also collapses', says Moore.[123] The communist revolutions do not produce 'a higher form of freedom' as they had claimed. Pessimistically, Barrington Moore adds 'that there is no evidence that the mass of the population anywhere has wanted an industrial society, and plenty of evidence that they did not'. This accounts, in his view, for the abortiveness of revolutions in so far as they embody an aspiration for a greater amount of freedom. They may only succeed in the extent to which they further material welfare, by making industrial development possible.

This dismal perspective is not identical with Brinton's view that every revolution is bound to get stuck in a Thermidor, as a first step towards some kind of restoration. But at the same time it runs decidedly counter to the leading theme of the first part of this work where emancipation of ever larger groups was posited as a central theme of human evolution; although it was admitted that the process, far from being a unilinear, unambiguous, and irreversible one is rather essentially discontinuous.

Different from Brinton's diagnosis, however, Barrington Moore's analysis does not claim universal validity. It is concerned with a specific situation in the world of today. A more profound discussion of the issue of freedom in connection with the revolutions of the present century, and of the never-ending struggle between the impulse for innovation and emancipation on the one hand, and the urge for stability and safety on the other, should therefore be reserved for the third part of this book.

I found it far from easy to establish any universal regularities in the genesis of revolutions, except for some general observations on the situational and psychological preconditions for such revolutionary outbursts; I found it almost impossible to find such regularities in the process of revolutions once they had erupted. I also found the way other authors attempted either to define pre-revolutionary situations or to establish a stereotyped sequence of revolutionary phases, lacking in depth and in many respects too crude and too simplistic. Although I have attempted to make some general observations, in particular with regard to the situational and psychological aspects of a pre-revolutionary society, I do not find it very fruitful to try to replace the more or less elaborate speculative conjectures, developed by those authors, by my own, no less speculative, constructs.

In order to be able to cope with revolutionary phenomena in truly sociological terms we should restrict our field to a much narrower range of phenomena, where we can try to develop, not a grand, universal theory of revolution, but a more modest middle-range theory.

Therefore, part three will deal with the actual problems of revolutions in the world of today.

Part Three: Revolutions in the World of Today

Introduction

There is no doubt that, since the Second World War, the problems of revolution or evolution have been largely centred on the non-industrial countries of the Third World. It is these countries that are experiencing the misery of backwardness, in the face of the technical progress and material wealth achieved by the industrialized part of the world. They are not only underprivileged in comparison with the latter countries – there is reason enough to maintain that it is partly their misery and distress that has made the continuous accumulation of wealth in the industrialized part of the world possible. The low wages paid to workers in non-industrial countries, employed in the plantation or mining sector, mean that the raw materials produced can be bought very cheaply and shipped to industrialized countries for processing into expensive, finished goods, some of which are then sold back to the poorer nations.

The almost complete failure of the three UNCTAD conferences has shown that there is little inclination in the industrialized world to sacrifice this most profitable aspect of its economic relationship with the Third World.

It is the permanent state of poverty and, in the worst cases, the involutionary trends in many non-industrial countries, in contrast to the euphemistic whitewash about developing countries, which seem to transform them into suitable breeding grounds for revolutions. Where the way towards evolutionary development is blocked, revolution appears to become the only viable alternative.

Yet, the fact remains that, since the Second World War, only a few underdeveloped countries have definitely embarked upon the social-revolutionary road. Most of them have gone through a national bourgeois revolution which, however, did not basically change the prevalent social system and power relationships, at least as far as internal forces were concerned. China, North Korea, Vietnam and Cuba remain isolated instances of more or less successful social revolutions, although they are significant enough from the viewpoint of numerical strength and political impact upon other countries.

We should, therefore, attempt to assess both the factors that foster social-revolutionary movements in non-industrial countries, and those that oppose them. Chapter seven will stress the constant or slowly changing factors related to the social and economic structure of these countries, and the prevalent trends as far as the situational and psychological aspects are concerned. In chapter eight, 'Prevention of Revolutions', we will look at the operational devices intended to stem a threatening tide of revolution. Together, the two chapters may provide some insights into the intensity of the revolutionary potential present in the Third World. Chapter nine, 'Dissensions on Revolutionary Prospects and Strategy', will touch upon the evaluation of the revolutionary potential by forces that claim to be positively interested in promoting such developments. A final chapter, entitled 'Social Revolution and After', will deal with perspectives for the future in countries where revolution has, in the first instance, succeeded. The Thermidor issue will be discussed in detail here.

7

Conditions and Trends in the Third World

Day by day the peasants make the economists sigh, the politicians sweat and the strategists swear, defeating their plans and prophecies all over the world.

TEODOR SHANIN

i. General Survey

The countries we are dealing with in the present chapter are preponderantly agrarian. This does not mean that agriculture has been developed at the expense of other branches of production, including industry. Underdevelopment, first and foremost, affects agricultural production. Even though traditional agricultural techniques may be very elaborate and, especially in areas where rice cultivation is being practised on irrigated fields, productivity per surface area may be fairly high, *per capita* production, owing to a lack of mechanical tools, remains miserably low. Consequently, rural poverty remains the most conspicuous feature in all non-industrial countries.

If the countries concerned are called agrarian it is not because of any specific quality of agrarian production, but rather because of a one-sidedness of the overall economic and occupational structure, evidenced by a deficient or seriously underdeveloped industrial sector.

Other economic activities such as trade, mining, lumbering, commercial crop-growing, and the running of factories oriented towards a processing of commercial crops are, in many countries of the Third World, well developed. But these activities do not change the overall picture of a lop-sided economy. The management of many of the larger units – mining companies, commercial enterprises, plantations – is directed by foreigners. Consequently, especially in areas where agricultural production is largely oriented towards the cultivation of food crops, the native business class is mostly rather weak. In contrast with the situation in Europe at the time of industrial revolution, it does not form a strong 'Third Estate' aspiring to emancipation from aristocratic rule and an assumption of political power. As a potential 'revolutionary class' it is rather insignificant.

If one wants to distinguish a kind of 'bourgeoisie' in the countries of the Third World, one should look for it rather among the extended body of salaried officials or employees and clerks, serving either in the government bureaucracy or in large private enterprises. It is they who may claim a greater say in the body politic; the revolution they were aspiring at under conditions of colonial rule, before and shortly after the Second World War, was a national rather than a social one. At present their political aspirations, as far as they are directed against an oligarchic ruling elite, may partly merge with those of the urban and rural masses, in which case the revolution they are aiming at could be regarded as a 'new-democratic' one, in the Maoist sense.

In most of the countries concerned an industrial labour class is only weakly developed. Their restricted numbers generally prevent them from becoming the assertive leaders of a revolutionary class struggle as prophesied by Marx and Engels. Moreover, in certain types of factory, their wages may be far enough above the general level of living both in urban and in rural environments to prevent them from becoming the most obvious proponents of social discontent. The revolutionary leadership claimed by orthodox Marxists for the industrial labour class in any country is not necessarily forthcoming as a major revolutionary factor in countries where the overall structure is as sketched above.

Consequently, in most of the countries under review, it is the impoverished peasantry that can be expected to provide the main driving force for a revolutionary transformation of society. It is the peasant class that forms the large majority in most of the countries concerned – less so in the countries of Latin America than in those of Asia and Africa – and it is they whose labour is indispensible in creating the bulk of the national product.

ii. *Economic Conditions*

The economic situation may fundamentally differ according to the type of agriculture practised and the density of the rural population. In sparsely populated areas there may still be a reserve of waste lands that can provide an outlet for a substantial proportion of the impoverished peasantry. Even so, dearth of agricultural lands already under cultivation or cultivable without great effort, combined with a rapid population growth, may make life difficult enough for subsistence farmers, small tenants or land labourers eking a meagre living out of a tiny plot of land. But in sparsely populated tropical areas – of course I exclude arid countries – there may always be a way out for a substantial proportion of the rural population, through reclaiming waste lands, through developing commercial crop cultivation (tree crops in particular), or through moving to the cities, even though the migrants would have to content themselves for a long period with bad living conditions in shanty towns or slum areas.

In such sparsely populated tropical areas – typical of large territories in Latin America and Africa, and of some parts of South-East Asia, such as Sumatra (Indonesia), Malaysia, Laos – the peasantry will not necessarily experience their situation as unbearable. Not all the roads towards improving their lot are blocked; consequently, the situational conditions for a peasant revolution are not optimally fulfilled, except in areas where the dominance of big landowners is such that reclamation of waste land or attempts at a shift from subsistence agriculture towards commercial crop growing are practically out of the question for the large majority of small agriculturists.

As a rule the situation is much more stringent in densely populated areas, in particular those where rice cultivation on irrigated fields is prevalent. In such areas there is generally no land available to provide an outlet for the steady population increase; a systematic shift from food production towards commercial crop growing would seriously endanger the food situation, and urban employment opportunities fall miserably short of the necessary requirements.

The countryside in these countries increasingly suffers from symptoms of overpopulation. Fragmentation of land use, as a consequence of a substantial, natural increase and scarcity of cultivable lands, result in hidden unemployment of serious proportions. Land ownership may be highly fragmented, whereas in other areas landlordism and a high tenancy rate may accompany the fragmentation process. Sharecropping, which is a very common form of tenancy in these countries, generally accounts for a subsistence type of farming which, in case of crop failure, entails severe risks for the sharecropper and aggravates his state of indebtedness. Moreover, the sharecropping system has an inhibiting influence on production, since neither the landowner nor the tenant fully profits from higher yields obtained through increased inputs. Consequently, neither of them is motivated to make significant investments.

The only way population increase can be met in a country where industry is largely lacking is through steady intensification of land use. This may be feasible, in the case of irrigated rice cultivation, as a consequence of the ecological characteristics of this type of agriculture. In this specific case such an intensification does not necessarily result in diminishing returns of *per capita* production. A regulation of the distribution of water, especially if it contains fertile volcanic sediments which fulfil the function of a fertilizer, may keep the fertility of the soil constant despite a higher input of labour. Even so, progressive intensification of the rice cultivation can hardly achieve more than a keeping pace with the steady population increase – or, to use Clifford Geertz's term, 'treading water'.[1]

In this connection we may recall the concept of involution, coined by Clifford Geertz and discussed in the first part of this book. The involutionary trends imply that the processes taking place in such a society cannot be assessed as contributing towards what we should call 'progress'. They do not lead to emancipation of the poor peasantry from the fetters of natural conditions as well as from economic exploitation by larger landowners (whose plots in such densely populated areas are generally 'large' only in a comparative sense and may not exceed some five hectares), money-lenders, or local officials.

In densely populated rice-producing areas such as Java, central Luzon (Philippines), central Vietnam, Bangladesh, the Ganges valley of India, and the wet zone of Ceylon, the involution pheno-menon has assumed such proportions that it has become a serious obstacle to any attempt at finding a way out for the rural surplus population. In such cases, the peasantry may grow into a truly revolutionary force, as far as economic conditions are concerned.

Such a situation also prevailed, at the end of the Second World War, in large parts of central and southern China, as well as in the Tonkin Delta of North Vietnam. This may, to a large extent, account for the revolutionary potential manifested by the peasantry of those two countries – a most convincing instance of 'Dialectics of Progress'.

From a purely economic angle, therefore, the actual situation in the countries under review may be largely assessed as a pre-revolutionary one. Especially in densely populated rice-growing areas there is a tendency towards a steady impoverishment, which seems conducive to the eruption of a peasant revolution.

However, economic conditions are by no means the only rele-vant factor in assessing the revolutionary potential in a country. The social structure and political system are no less significant, sometimes as a motivating, but more often as a retarding, or even prohibitive, force.

iii. Social Hierarchy

According to any standard derived from Western social con-ditions, peasants in Asia, Africa and Latin America are poor. Ac-cording to Sun Yat-sen, there were two classes only in the Chinese countryside: those who were miserably poor, and those who were less miserably so.

Nevertheless, Gunnar Myrdal has rightly pointed out that class distinctions play a pre-eminent role in Asian rural societies. In the discussion I shall largely restrict myself to the countries of

South and South-East Asia dealt with by Myrdal. Despite the numerous attempts, like those by Gandhi and Sukarno, to idealize traditional Asian societies as examples of rustic simplicity, where everyone lives in harmony with his neighbour and shares whatever little he has with those still poorer than himself, social reality is different from this idyllic picture. Asian peasants are generally status conscious and, contrary to the stereotype of an ideal community embracing all villagers, the more prosperous ones often recognize mutual social obligations only towards those whom they consider to be their peers. In village society, it is not so much absolute wealth that matters, but rather the relative position vis-à-vis other villagers.

Myrdal demonstrates how status differentials, as experienced within village society, affect the behaviour of those who regard themselves as a village elite.

Thus it may well be the case that the upper strata in a poor village in India do not have a significantly higher income than sharecropping tenants or landless peasants. Yet there is an important difference between these groups: the former often receive incomes without working while the latter do not.[2]

The general attitude of those who view themselves as an elite is to a large extent determined by their wish to keep up prestige as members of a local upper class. They mostly stress patterns of behaviour that symbolize their capacity to enjoy some leisure and to dispense with physical labour which they prefer to leave to less privileged social groups. If members of the older generation of the village gentry still retain some interest in agriculture and keep the supervision of work on their farms in their own hands, the younger generation is likely to look for employment in the administrative sector outside the village. They lose interest in agriculture and content themselves with gathering the rents paid by sharecroppers.

This quite common development is of great influence upon agricultural conditions. It strengthens the tendency, already prevalent in traditional peasant society, to discourage productive investment. To quote Myrdal again:

Economic prospects are curtailed by status restrictions. The fact, therefore, that everyone in a village may be almost equally poor does not imply that everyone is equal; on the contrary, they are all so poor because they are so unequal.[3]

Profits or surpluses are generally not channelled into technical improvements, such as terracing of land or purchase of more efficient tools, but are earmarked for purposes viewed as enhancing the landowner's prestige. Much of it is spent on expensive marriages or other ritual ceremonies and festivities. Whatever saving occurs may be invested in the purchase of gold or jewelry which is either ostentatiously worn by the landowner's wife or shut away in a trunk under his bench. But the most attractive investment is purchase of land, which again cannot be regarded as conducive to increased production. The plots of land spread over different villages belonging to a larger landowner are generally not brought together into a single productive unit, comparable with a Western manor or plantation, but are parcelled out to sharecroppers on a profitable basis, without any attempt to introduce modern farming techniques. Therefore, this type of investment in land purchase only amounts to accentuating the social inequality in village society.

If social stratification, largely viewed in terms of a distinction between peasantry and gentry, is fairly well pronounced in the Asian countryside, it is still more obvious in urban society. Those possessing a modest wealth or having enjoyed more advanced forms of education, especially the younger members of the family, tend to move to the towns where they will not have to suffer from what they consider to be 'the idiocy of rural life'. There they may join one of the sectors of the rising native bourgeoisie. On the other hand, many of the poor peasants, landless or forced by debt to sell or mortgage their land, are driven to the towns in search of a meagre living. Although for certain individuals in an urban environment there may always be some windfalls or opportunities to get ahead, and some of the youngsters may make headway through higher education, the large majority of the new migrants from the villages will be doomed to stay in the squalid quarters of the urban poor and to eke a miserable living out of whatever work is at hand – not to speak of begging or prostitution. Lack of industrial development in these Asian towns seriously restricts employment opportunities and throws the fortune seekers from the villages back upon insecure and seriously overstaffed minor service trades such as hawking, tricycle driving, boot shining, street cleaning or water carrying, whereas the more fortunate ones are able to secure a less unstable position as messenger or 'peon' in an office, house servant, docker, or labourer in the building business.

The total picture of these societies shows a general lack of opportunity for vertical mobility for the large majority of the peasantry as well as the urban poor. On the other hand, horizontal mobility is on the increase. Consequently, from a sociological point of view, certain characteristics are shown which we assessed, in the last chapter, as tending to a pre-revolutionary situation.

Why, then, in most of the cases do the people not revolt?

iv. Patronage and Other Protective Institutions

The structure of traditional agrarian societies has been generally conceived by sociologists and cultural anthropologists in terms either of genealogical units (such as clans, moieties, phratries) or of social stratification. The latter approach predominated in looking at societies with an aristocratic orientation, where a landed gentry was keeping itself well above the mass of the rural population.

This approach, however, neglected another principle which may be at least as important in understanding the functioning of this type of society. This principle is related to the frequent occurrence of a certain type of personal bond, between individuals or families, running across the dividing line between common people and gentry. It is this supplementary principle, called patronage, that is often overlooked by those who want to assess the revolutionary potential among a rural population. Its significance can be illustrated by the thesis that the patronage institution may function as one of the potent counterforces opposing the emergence of social revolutionary movements in the Third World.

It is only in the last few years that the issue of patron–client relationships has become fashionable. In all kinds of societies dependency relationships are being discovered; these vertical lines cut across the social class divisions and provide an additional starting point for an analysis of all types of social relationships.

However, the literature on patronage often conveys the impression that it is simply a phenomenon typical of certain cultural areas but absent in others. It would appear to be confined mainly to the Catholic Mediterranean and to Latin America, where the institution of spiritual kinship, called into life by the custom of wedding sponsorship leading to a network of godparent relations (compadrazgo), served as an instrument for establishing patron-client relationships.[4] Such patronage institutions are also acknowledged in different African societies.

As a matter of fact patron–client relationships are by no means peculiar to specific cultural units, but on the contrary are a basic element discernible in any traditional society with a more or less pronounced social stratification. India is a case in point. Only fairly recently, however, have studies of Indian society paid more attention to inter-caste relationships.[5] In the earlier literature, these relationships were largely neglected, since according to official ideology social relationships could only exist between members of one caste. In the thirties, however, William Wiser[6] described the pattern of reciprocal services exchanged by members of different castes within a village as constituting what he called the jajmani-system. Wiser has been criticized for drawing too harmonious and functional a picture of this exchange pattern and for claiming that everyone in his turn could enjoy the services of members of other castes and, in so doing, become jajman, master, in relationship to a member of a different caste. Beidelman[7] demonstrated, about ten years ago, that the system was not at all as harmonious and functional as Wiser conceived it, but rather asymmetrical and characterized by exploitation, the members of the dominant caste in any village invariably fulfilling the role of jajman whereas the others had to render their services as kamin.

Beidelman is right in pointing out the exploitation factor that

certainly exists and has always existed in these inter-caste relationships. However, he appears not to have paid enough attention to the fact that what characterizes relationships between
large landowners and the members of castes performing all kinds
of services, either ritual or secular ones (as for example agricultural work), is the specific bond between two individuals and their
families. This bond consists, apart from the material reward for
the services rendered and other favours bestowed upon the client,
in a measure of security provided by members of the dominant
caste for the clients and their families, for example through inter-
cession on their behalf with the local authorities in cases of
emergency.[8]

One could still maintain that the dominant castes, in their turn,
provide certain services to the clients. These are, however, services
in the realm of government and administration, in accordance
with their specific status and political influence. In providing
these services the members of the dominant caste do not depart
from their role as gentry. Equally, the specific favours which they
have to provide in exchange for the labour furnished by their
clients do not transform the relationship into a symmetrical one.
They never become 'servants', as Wiser puts it, but always remain
patrons. The prestige they enjoy as such may, however, increase if
they show themselves good patrons, not too greedy, and capable of
providing a certain amount of protection to their clients.

Another important aspect of these vertical inter-caste relationships is the division of village society into factions. The influential
families of the dominant caste attempt to build up a following
among members of the other castes in order to strengthen their
social prestige and political influence. But generally the power of
one group of families is challenged by others who also function as
patrons for a number of clients. As a consequence, a situation
arises where a village society is generally divided into two or more
factions, each of them vertically cross-cutting the caste divisions.[9]

These factions provide the members of the lower castes with some
room for manoeuvring, since the clients may, under certain circumstances, shift their allegiance from one patron to another. But

whenever the power position of the dominant caste is really challenged, its members are ready to forget their factional strife and combine forces to keep the lower castes in their traditional place.

The Indian case shows certain characteristics which may elucidate the functioning of patronage relationships in general. Social relationships of the patron–client type have generally not been much publicized. The belief is still strongly held that social relationships only exist among peers, either caste members as in India, or people of equal status elsewhere. Relationships of the asymmetrical type, consequently, have been more or less kept in the background, which may account for the general neglect of the patronage phenomenon in earlier literature. Horizontal stratification is in accordance with official aristocratic ideology, whereas personal patron–client relationships, though essential for the functioning of any aristocratic society, are to a certain extent felt as deviations from the official code.

We may conclude that in a society where the government administration fails to provide a minimal standard of living and security for the rural masses, patron–client relationships dependent on the goodwill of a member of the gentry may function as the only available protection for a significant section of the poor peasantry, against natural or social forces experienced as inimical. On the other hand, the patron who manages to extend his protection over a relatively broad category of clients, thereby often making use of intermediaries or 'brokers', may gain social prestige and political influence, in addition to manpower used as sharecroppers or labourers for his lands.

In a rural society where traditional patron–client relationships are still a living reality it is hardly to be expected that poor peasants will unite on a class solidarity basis. Even if they are aware of being exploited by the patron they will still tend to rely upon his protection, which is the only security, doubtful though it is, in which they have learned, throughout a life of hardships, to put some faith.[10]

Therefore, if we regard general economic conditions, lack of vertical social mobility, and increased horizontal mobility which may at the same time provide an escape for some of the poor peasantry from their rural bondage, as conducive to a pre-revolutionary situation for the mass of the peasantry, the tradition of patron–client relationships, on the other hand, may be viewed as a delaying factor.

Patron–client relationships are generally characterized not only by social inequality and consequently by a cluster of asymmetrical obligations, but by their informal nature, although a certain institutionalization, for example through marriage sponsorship and an ensuing spiritual kinship tie, may take place. These relationships, however, undergo a certain change under conditions of modernization.

A discussion of the political aspects and consequences of this process of social change and its impact upon the genesis of a peasant revolution, however, will have to be postponed till after we have dealt, in the next section, with the general erosion of traditional institutions and social values, as a corollary of recent economic developments.

Naturally, patronage is by no means the only social institution lending a certain cohesive quality to rural societies. There are more institutions transcending status borders and fostering a sense of solidarity among members of different status groups. Kinship relationships may be a case in point, especially in societies characterized by clan organization. Poorer relatives may count upon a certain measure of support and protection on the part of more prosperous members of the same lineage, who have achieved gentry status.

This integrative function of the 'joint family' system may be of less importance in Indian society, where, apart from the cases of 'ritual kinship' studied by L. K. Mahapatra,[11] genealogical ties do not transcend caste borders and, consequently, class differentials within a joint family are restricted owing to the requirement of a common caste membership. Even if a sub-group within a caste, having achieved a certain measure of prosperity and aiming at a higher status through 'sanskritization', has constituted itself as a separate sub-caste, such a collective step will generally imply a disruption of recognized family ties with the poorer relatives belonging to the original caste and an attempt to achieve endogamy within the newly created caste.

On the other hand, Chinese society before the communist revolution probably provided an exemplary model of a society where clan affiliation offered a certain protection for poorer relatives belonging to the same lineage. However, it is likely that even within one lineage patronage relationships could flourish, for the more prosperous clan members were to a certain extent free to recognize or ignore family ties according to personal acquaintance or preference. Patron–client relationships were also possible within the frame of a clan organization.[12]

Equally, religious or ethnic bonds could provide for a certain amount of group solidarity transcending the general class division between gentry and peasantry. This was particularly true in societies where differences of religion or ethnic identity were to be found within a local community.

In traditional rural societies, forms of concealed protest against the hierarchical order may occur. Generally they will have a counterpoint character. Open protest may assume religious forms and be embodied in messianic movements. Peasant rebellions may also occur, but they will hardly grow into true revolutions.

v. The Erosion of Institutions or Social Values

Traditional institutions are mostly weakened by the impact of external and internal economic forces. The introduction of a money economy brings about the rise of a restricted class of rural capitalists, and consequently a certain commercialization of tenancy and agricultural labour relationships. A rapid natural increase of the rural population, due to slightly improved medical care, may diminish the readiness of more prosperous people to play their role as patrons for the weaker members of their lineage or local community. Businesslike management of large plantations or *haciendas* does not allow labour relationships to retain a more or less personal, paternalistic character. Increase in the scale of economic activities and improved communications creates a need for a number of provisions and social institutions transcending face-to-face relationships as well as the borders of village society. Extended educational facilities and economic dislocation diminish the readiness of the economically weak to accept a near-complete dependence upon individual masters. Minimal provisions by a government administration may offer alternatives for those who are economically weak. Increased horizontal mobility may create alternative employment opportunities, for example in nearby towns or in plantations.

All such changes which have, to a greater or lesser extent, occurred in most of the societies under review, are likely to affect traditional institutions. According to a simplified image of Western social history, the growth of modern capitalism and the ensuing urbanization process would have been accompanied by a breaking up of all kinds of traditional institutions, such as the large family as a basic economic unit, serfdom or peonage, religious homogeneity centred around the village church, mutual aid among neighbours as an arrangement for the exchange of agricultural labour, all kinds of folklore, etc.

But, even for the purposes of characterizing the modernization process in the Western world this picture may be too simplistic, since traditional institutions often regained a new vitality in an urban environment. For example, the extended family could serve as a quite suitable organizational form for establishing modern business firms. New forms of human bondage replaced the traditional ones. Religious parochialism was transferred from the village to the modern city.

For the Third World it is even more true that traditional institutions do not necessarily vanish as a consequence of external and internal economic forces, but are often transformed. This is understandable if we take into account that social change in that part of the world may be called a modernization process only in a restricted sense. If we disengage ourselves from Lerner's assumption that societies touched by the impact of Western capitalism should be viewed as 'transitional', that is to say, as developing from tradition towards modernity, we may as well accept the attempt of the Geertzes to characterize societies like the Javanese one as 'post-traditional'.[13] This term allows for two alternative potentialities:

the society may be moving towards a type of modernity basically different from ours, or it may move away from tradition without heading for a new type of integration.

It is beyond doubt that many of the traditional institutions are losing their original function. However, in many cases a transformation occurs which provides the age-old institutions with a new function more in accordance with contemporary economic developments.

For example, it was assumed in India that institutions such as caste, or the joint family, would crumble in the wake of urban development and the introduction of a money economy. But sociologists concerned with India are now discovering that these institutions, far from crumbling, are acquiring a new lease of life under the changed social, economic, and political conditions.[14]

This kind of transformation also occurs with patronage relationships which may undergo an increase in scale and become more or less adapted to the requirements of modern nationhood. However, such changes cannot be disengaged from developments in the political field. The same is true for the transformation of caste in India into a new type of collective organization. The revitalization of traditional institutions, at least, shows that disappearing traditional values are being replaced by new integrative ones which may lend a society a new type of cohesiveness.

However, even if traditional institutions are being preserved and transformed in such a way that they acquire a new integrative function, it cannot be denied that the original values on which they rested have been seriously eroded. There is a wealth of literature on the extent to which a caste which is being transformed into a tool for collective political action can still be called a caste.[15] Similarly, one may doubt whether a joint family working together on a purely utilitarian basis can still be equated with the traditional joint family as a true local *Gemeinschaft*.

It is undeniable that, in a post-traditional society, many of the traditional values have undergone erosion. This erosion becomes evident from several recent studies of social change in village India. Masters, belonging to the dominant caste, no longer feel responsibility for the sustenance of their servants. The latter no longer feel obliged to stay with their traditional masters.[16] Artisans no longer feel the responsibility for serving the other villagers.[17] Many young people no longer respect caste restrictions about food; they only formally adhere to them if people from their village, especially older ones, are present.

Mounting corruption may also be considered as a symptom of erosion of traditional values, although there are certainly forms of corruption which can be conceived in terms of conflicting loyalties, in which case the culprit, through his behaviour, may give expression precisely to a tendency to let traditional familial values prevail over modern national ones.[18] But there are, indeed, many cases of corruption which may simply be viewed as signs of a decreasing regard for communal interests and an increasing craving for personal gain, fostered by habits of conspicuous consumption introduced by foreigners or by a rising native bourgeoisie. Finally, there is generally a serious erosion of religious values which hold sway over the masses within traditional society. A measure of school education and improved means of communication contribute to a weakening of popular acceptance of these religious values as directives for behaviour.

This analysis may convince us that within the societies of the Third World there are many factors that may be considered as favouring a peasant revolution, although there are certainly traditional institutions and factors which have not yet been eroded and which tend to delay such a development.

The most disturbing part of the argument, however, is that we did not find any indication of whether the situation of general imbalance as I have sketched it is likely to develop in the direction of revolution or of counter-revolution. In order to be able to find a reply to this basic question, we have to shift our attention from economic and social conditions to the political structure. Therefore, we have now to concern ourselves with the political situation in the new states of the Third World.

vi. *Political Situations under Populism*

The institution of patronage has been discussed, largely in its sociological aspects, as an interpretation of asymmetrical personal relationships between members of the gentry and members of the peasantry in traditional rural societies. However, the factionalism related to the patronage institution also carried a political aspect within the village sphere. It is even possible to maintain that the most suitable way of analysing the political system of many recently established states is to view it from the angle of patronage-like relationships dominating political life within those societies.

What kinds of developments are bound to happen in these societies as soon as they have achieved political independence, mostly through a national–bourgeois revolution, requiring the creation of a more modern political structure? In the new situation the vertical relationships crosscutting the social layers, as far as they survived colonial rule, are being more or less preserved. At the same time they are being transformed into more formal relationships that extend their networks beyond their region of origin. It is, first of all, the introduction of elections depending partly upon a rural vote that forces those who aspire to political power to establish a true clientele at the village level. It is, as yet, the traditional factions pervading village society that are decisive for the outcome of the rural vote. The landless are still, in great majority, dependent upon their master who may employ them as sharecroppers or land labourers. This is the only security, meagre as it is, that they enjoy in a society where labour is abundant, and where an administration based on objective and impersonal norms is still a distant dream.

Other important factors favouring the creation of supra-village organizations are a progressive monetization of the economy, improved communications, mounting horizontal mobility, growing urbanization, and extended educational facilities.

What distinguishes the patron–client relationship in a new state from its counterpart in a feudal one, either colonial or pre-colonial, is the integration of these factors within formal organizations at a supra-local or national level, such as political parties or all kinds of unions. A faction joins a political party whose ideology is less important than the fact that the rival faction is likely to join the other party.

It is mainly during the 'populist' stage of development in the new states that vertical formations corresponding to a quasi-patronage pattern dominate political life. The ideology of populism pretends to weld the unity of the people. The latter are not viewed as building a stratified society divided into classes, but as representing an ideal community regulated by traditional values such as the principle of mutual aid and a smooth give-and-take.

Peter Worsley[19] has shown that this revivalist political ideology is generally connected with the stage in which the large majority of the people are still living in the countryside. It is an ideology typical of a nation consisting predominantly of small landowners. This ideology, accentuating the unity of the people rather than a horizontal division into classes, can be maintained as long as class conflict between large landowners and poor land labourers or sharecroppers has not yet crystallized. In Asia, the ideology found its most prominent advocate in Sukarno, the late ex-President of the Indonesian Republic. He called his ideology 'Marhaenism', after a peasant named Marhaen who had told him about his extremely sober, but not truly proletarian, life as owner of a small plot of land, with a hut and a few tools of his own. This ideology is very remote indeed from a Marxist type of analysis stressing class conflict. In Sukarno's view, the great majority of the Indonesian people was composed of 'Marhaens', either rural or urban small owners, experiencing a community of interests in which class conflict was absent. Consequently, 'Indonesian socialism' as propagated by Sukarno had nothing in common either with Western socialism or with Asian rural communism. It was, essentially, a populist ideology mainly based upon a more or less independent small peasantry.

Equally, one could view Sun Yat-sen with his three People's Principles, and Gandhi with his nostalgia for an idealized past and a rustic simplicity and his negation of class conflict, as typical representatives of populism. The people are always unified – the enemy is outside. A radicalism in foreign policy serves to cover up the internal rifts that could endanger the unity of the people.

None the less, the fissures are undeniable. But they do not immediately develop into class conflict, but rather into factions dividing society along vertical lines. Here, again, the phenomenon of increase in scale is manifest. Modern organizations, such as political parties or peasant unions, are striving for total domination, the former of society as a whole, the latter of the peasant element in it, both at the national and at the local level. In populist style they pretend to represent either the people as a whole or the total peasant population. But social and political reality is characterized more by division that transforms each faction into a more or less stable following of certain political leaders at the national level. At the local level the people have never learnt how to approach the government or its agents in order to invoke objective justice. They would not commit themselves to such an experiment, and generally for good reasons! It is the patron, transformed into the leader of an organization, who will have to intercede every time a member of his clientele needs his sponsorship.

At the national level the leaders are engaged in a struggle for power and here the unity postulated by populism as an ideology is mostly absent as well. However, the charismatic leader of the populist state is entrusted with the task of bridging the rifts and realizing a semblance of unity. He either introduces a single-party system or attempts to attain a compromise between the major parties, as Sun Yat-sen and Sukarno tried to enforce. In either case, the national leader has to perform acrobatics, if only temporarily, in order to achieve such a compromise.

One might ask whether the situation is not essentially different in cases where political parties and organizations are not constituting themselves as factions with a more or less similar ideology, as is the case in the Philippines where the American model was followed, but represent an ideology expressing a clearly defined class position. The erstwhile powerful PKI (Communist Party of Indonesia) could be mentioned as an evident case in point.

However, even in this case our previous analysis holds partly true. In a series of studies Geertz describes Javanese society at the local level as one dominated by so-called *alirans*, that is to say, ideological orientations. In each locality the principal orientations (Muslim, nationalist, and communist) compete among each other and produce a split within traditional society, either urban or rural. The specialized organizations (women's unions, youth organizations, sports clubs, peasant unions) are all associated with a specific ideological orientation and in some way or other affiliated to the political party embodying that particular *aliran*.[20]

Geertz and his colleagues who studied Javanese society during the fifties, have made it clear that the ideological divisions do not necessarily coincide with class distinctions.[21] Although on the average the economic status of those adhering to the Muslim or nationalist *alirans* was undoubtedly superior to that of the communists, the division was decidedly less sharp than one would have expected according to Marxist theory. In several villages one could find rich peasants, sometimes even village chiefs, who were heading the local PKI branch or that of the affiliated peasant union, the BTI (Barisan Tani Indonesia). This situation could be manipulated in order to obtain a majority vote in favour of PKI in that particular village. On the other hand, if a rich and influential peasant was a *santri*, that is to say, a pious Muslim, this could induce his sharecroppers, as his following, to vote for the specific Islamic party represented by him. One might maintain that the absence of a pronounced class basis was one of the weaknesses which caused the catastrophic downfall of the PKI at the end of 1965.

A similar situation seems to exist in Kerala (south India), where communism also attracts many votes at elections. Kathleen Gough indicates that communist leaders at the village level prefer to tone down the class struggle which, from an ideological point of view, should be their main concern, in an effort to provide their party with some legal respectability and to achieve successes through compromises in the political arena. 'He is tempted to favor his own party members and special supporters at the expense of others, even of the propertyless classes.'[22]

It is important to be clear that the vertical type of political alignment is by no means restricted to organizations based on ideological affinity. In most of the new states, solidarity on a class basis is not yet well developed. Any type of cohesiveness or affinity may become the foundation of a political movement regardless of class composition. Ethnic affinities may equally function as rallying points.

We could relate this phenomenon to the issue of economic or political competition on a group basis. The ethnic trading minorities in many of the new states (Chinese in South-East Asia, Indians in Burma and East Africa and Syrians in West Africa) become the targets of group competition from a rising native trading class.[23] The idiom in which this type of ethnic alignment is expressed is often borrowed from the class struggle terminology. The political leaders claim to represent 'the people' who have to be protected from extortion and exploitation by 'foreign' capitalists.

However, the most vociferous leaders are usually not recruited from the class that could rightly complain of being exploited. It is not the poor peasantry that plays a primary role in this type of vertical organization, but those traders who are, economically and socially, not far removed from those they are opposing. They often get support from the bureaucracy and the military apparatus of the new states, and sometimes also from foreign powers. Their broad mass basis provides them with political strength; but what they actually aspire to is not emancipation for the masses. It is, basically, to occupy the places of their 'foreign' competitors, who derived their economic strength from the privilege of having been the first to develop their type of trade.

On the other hand, the ethnic minorities equally tend to follow a pattern of alignment according to ethnic affinity, regardless of class differences within their group.

vii Prospects for Revolution or Counter-Revolution under Populism

From the discussion so far, it should be possible to assess the potentials for revolution or counter-revolution inherent in the state of affairs already outlined.

Among the propertied classes within the country and capitalists and politicians abroad, populist regimes generally elicit serious misgivings. Attempts by the charismatic leaders to mobilize and dynamize the masses, not only through all kinds of political slogans but through the staging of huge demonstrations, are viewed as a potential threat to internal stability and to the privileged position of the gentry. The use of a near-Marxist terminology creates the impression that the populist leaders feel a strong affinity with communism. This impression is reinforced through a more or less consistent foreign policy attacking Western capitalism and imperialism, and through a tendency of most of the populist leaders to allow some elbow room to the communist movements within the country. The political manoeuvring of the populist leaders may easily be interpreted as attempts to prepare the ground for a communist take-over, although in fact both the policies and ideologies of such regimes are generally far removed from the aims pursued by the communist movements, and should rather be interpreted as intelligent attempts to take the wind out of the sails of the communists, or to use Donald Hindley's qualification of President Sukarno's policy: 'to domesticate the communists'.[24]

In fact, the chances of a successful communist revolution, under the conditions of a populist regime, seem to be minimal, to judge from historical experience. Much of the nationalist fervour, potentially present among the masses, is being capitalized on by the populist leaders. The way the communist movement is being incorporated within the frame of populist internal and external policies makes it difficult for the communist leadership to step down from a legal or semi-legal existence and from a policy of compromises with the official authorities, and to shift towards advocating an all-out class struggle. The vertical organization typical of societies where patronage-like relationships prevail hampers communist movements in adopting a pronounced class basis as a directive for political action.

Repression is, generally, moderate, and a certain observance of democratic rights and forms is mostly granted. Movements aiming at the emancipation of underprivileged groups are allowed within certain bounds to pursue their objectives, although there may be periods when strikes are forbidden and certain political activities seriously curtailed. Consequently, there is hardly any fertile ground for widespread revolutionary feeling, although the peasantry, who through lack of genuine economic development generally undergo impoverishment rather than experiencing economic progress, have enough to complain about. Despite attempts to exert a certain amount of thought control through an imposition of a fervently nationalist ideology, countervalues aspiring at greater social and economic equality are not systematically driven underground.

If the chances for revolution seem to be minimal under a populist regime, the chances for counter-revolution are considerable, and they increase with the continuation of such a regime. Foreign powers, in particular the United States, have generally viewed the anti-Western and seemingly anti-capitalist policies of these populist regimes with concern. They will attempt to promote a counter-revolutionary take-over by a military junta which will show a much greater lenience and consideration towards foreign capitalist interests, and consequently will no longer pursue a policy of independence with regard to Western powers.

There have been several instances of new states, that started their political life with a populist regime, undergoing a transition through a counter-revolution to the second type of regime, the true military dictatorship. Indonesia, Burma, Brazil, Cambodia and possibly Ghana, are cases in point. This repeated occurrence of a military take-over in a society after a period of populist rule must have a deeper cause. It is not enough to refer to the interest the United States government or other world powers might have in a more or less neutralist government being replaced by one more amenable to Western influence. In several of the cases I have in view, in addition to that factor, there is a clear connection between the overthrow of the regime and internal developments in the agrarian sphere.

Peter Worsley has pointed out the weakness of populist regimes. Their ideology is, as we have seen, founded on the erroneous assumption that the rural population is largely homogeneous, and not torn by class conflict. As long as the broad majority of the rural population still consists of petty landowning peasants or Marhaens, as defined by Sukarno, this ideology may hold and exert a more or less stabilizing influence. But as soon as involutionary trends, strengthened through continuous population growth and lack of economic development in a true sense, sharpen the class conflict between an impoverished peasantry, consisting of a high proportion of landless sharecroppers, and a thin rural upper layer of wealthy landowners and rural capitalists who accumulate lands at the expense of the indebted and impoverished poor peasants, the populist ideology starts to crumble.

Both in Indonesia and in Brazil the poor peasants, profiting from a measure of democratic freedom left to them under populist rule, started to organize themselves on a class basis – although patronage traits were not fully absent from the way the leftist peasant organizations functioned.[25] The populist regimes of Sukarno and Goulart had both enacted legislation that provided these peasant unions with some room to manoeuvre.

In Indonesia a land reform law and a regulation of sharecropping arrangements were adopted in 1960. There were complaints about the enactment of these laws being sabotaged by the regional authorities who largely belonged to the traditional bureaucratic elite, many of them with landed interests. As a consequence, the left-wing peasant union BTI, closely allied with the Indonesian Communist Party, started what they called a one-sided action in order to enforce a proper application of the law, and in the course of this action lands owned by wealthy landowners were occupied by force.

In fact, this was the beginning of a development that showed some aspects of a peasant revolution, which was, however, weakened by the fact that at the top level the communist leadership stuck to the legal principle of cooperation under Sukarno's populist Nasakom formula (involving a tripartite coalition between nationalists, religious groups and communists). It was also weakened by the fact that the PKI had not systematically selected its members in rural areas according to class criteria, which meant that there were, in different villages, some wealthy landowners among the PKI members. This situation could unfavourably affect its image among those poor peasants who belonged to the clientele of anti-communist (mostly orthodox Moslem) rich peasants. The absence of a solid class basis resulted in a cleavage within a village according to an *aliran* pattern rather than to a clear-cut class pattern, each *aliran* comprising a group of influential, and sometimes well-off party leaders with their following of sharecroppers and poor peasants.

In Brazil there were similar developments. Peasant unions undertook some successful legal actions, and in certain areas there were illegal invasions of landed estates by local peasants.[26] Here, again, there was an incipient peasant revolution, weakened by patronage-like relationships within the peasant unions.

In both countries the reaction of the landed gentry and of the high military authorities allied with them was similar. They were alarmed, and effected a military take-over, after having assured themselves of forthcoming foreign assistance. The mounting agrarian unrest, therefore, functioned as an accelerator for a counter-revolution, intended to stem the tide of peasant emancipation allowed or condoned under the populist regime.

In Indonesia and Brazil, the counter-revolutionary character of the military take-over soon became evident. The resulting regimes, despite certain attempts to retain some democratic forms and to make use of civilian personnel, are clearly under heavy military domination.

In both countries, all radical tendencies were crushed with bloody repression, the number of victims in the countryside of Java and Bali reaching at least several hundreds of thousands. The Western press rejoiced: the 'communist danger' had been averted from some large countries, vital for the 'defence of the free world'. As a matter of fact, the above description shows that, despite the optimism prevalent among some leftist leaders, the alleged danger of a communist revolution or take-over had probably never existed. However, it could be used as a convenient excuse for the action taken by those who had vested interests in the *status quo*.

The counter-revolutionary character also becomes evident from the fact that land reform has, to all intents and purposes, been shelved although a new agrarian statute adopted in 1965 by Brazil kept up a semblance of reform. In both countries, peasant unions were severely repressed or controlled. 'Foreign aid' flowed in and prospective foreign investors could try their fortune again, after getting the required guarantees from the military government.

viii. *Political Situation under Military Dictatorship*

Although I distinguish two main types of government in the Third World – the populist regime and the military dictatorship – I do not intend to suggest that these two rather extreme forms are the only possible ones. Social reality is not that simple and unambiguous. There will be several countries where the regime, to a certain extent, will embody a mixture of the two types, and where despite the strong position of the military and a general climate of political repression an attempt will still be made to manipulate the masses in a dynamic way through a nationalist appeal. There may be some other new states where neither of the two types of regime apply and where, for example, the leading politicians will experiment with a type of government modelled after a Western democratic system. This could occur in India for a lengthy period because of the numerical superiority of the Congress Party. In my argument the two types considered in detail are advanced as 'ideal types', in the Weberian sense.

Nor does my exposition of the way a populist regime may be transformed, through a counter-revolution, into a military dictatorship, imply that these two stages necessarily occur in the same sequence.

However, we must now examine the chances for revolutionary developments under a regime of the second type: the military dictatorship.

In contrast with populist regimes, which attempt to mobilize the popular masses in a dynamic way and leave some elbow room for social and political movements aiming at an emancipation of peasants and other underprivileged groups, the dictatorships are characterized by what Allan Holmberg has aptly called, though in a somewhat different context, a 'culture of repression'.[27] The general atmosphere is comparable to one prevailing under a system of slave plantations. The rural masses are being ordered about in a high-handed way and are driven to work through fear rather than through encouragement or material incentives. Typical of this was the conduct in parts of Java, with the cooperation of some foreign chemical companies, of the official 'Mass Guidance Rice Cultivation' campaign in 1969, intended to produce a Green Revolution. The peasants were admonished to buy fertilizer on credit and then to deliver their rice crop at a fixed price. The peasants soon discovered that it was hardly a paying proposition: fertilizer was sold at a high profit, whereas the fixed price for rice to be delivered to the authorities was low. However, lack of material incentive did not matter for the military local leaders: they simply arrested a score of peasants who were not willing to cooperate and told them that if they refused to buy fertilizer they would be considered as having been 'involved' in the Untung coup of 30 September 1965, and accordingly treated as pro-communist saboteurs of the Five Year Plan. That was, for the time being, enough to crush any resistance. It may partly explain, however, the rather poor rice crop in 1969.[28]

Another field where a 'culture of repression' prevails is in the vast *haciendas* of Latin America and the Philippines. It is in connection with the atmosphere in the Latin American *haciendas* that Holmberg has developed his concept by defining all the fears to which the labourers are subject. Under a populist regime a certain relaxation may have occurred, and labour unions may have functioned in their typical, patronage-like way. However, since under military dictatorship the labourers are no longer legally allowed to organize themselves under leaders of their own choice, the *hacendados* will apply force, or at least the threat of it, with greater success than under a populist regime. They either cooperate with the military and police force, or keep a private police corps in their own pay. They will try to prevent strangers from entering the *hacienda* area, in order to cut off the labourers from external political influences and from communication with potential troublemakers. Where a 'culture of repression' prevails, the agrarian labourers do not get chances to defend their rights in a lawsuit against the *hacendado*. The judges have to decide in conformity with the establishment.

The situation is little different in the plantations which previously under populist rule had been taken over by the government, and still remain under state management. According to reliable information, labourers in the plantations under official management in the northern part of Sumatra (Indonesia) are as defenceless against the management as they had been, during the colonial period, under a system of indentured labour. The officially recognized trade union of plantation labourers has practically become a tool for extreme repression and exploitation on the part of the state management, which is still largely in the hands of the military.

Under such conditions the patronage-like relationships, which still flourished under populist rule, also tend to crumble. The vertical organizations built up in order to muster a broad popular support, especially in view of elections, are no longer useful to a regime that largely relies on force. Since the rural masses are no longer courted, political leaders are no longer interested in mustering a broad following for whom they would try to obtain all kinds of favours. Patronage as an institution to provide protection for the weak no longer functions: there are too many of them, and they have to be kept in their place. The attitude of officials or *hacendados* is no longer paternalistic. They still need special protégés, but these are no longer ordinary peasants or labourers, but supervisors or special agents whom they try to win over with various favours in order to make them partners in the repressive system. To a certain extent, this was also the way aristocratic patronage functioned in Java under Dutch rule after the native chiefs (*priyayi*) had been made partners in the colonial system of exploitation.

However, in order to understand the functioning of these military dictatorships, we have also to view them in their relationship to foreign capitalist interests. These military regimes cannot be studied without any reference to their functions as political agents of the capitalist world powers – in particular, the United States. If political and economic dependence on foreign interests and powers is typical of the overall situation in the Third World since the end of the Second World War, this dependence is overwhelming as far as most of the military dictatorships are concerned.

The economic and political situation in the countries of the Third World, therefore, cannot be understood without due reference to the concept of neo-colonialism – which amounts to an attempt, by the industrialized countries of the West, to retain their economic and political power through the intermediary of a native officialdom that is only nominally independent and free.

In contrast with the authoritarian regimes of industrialized countries (like Nazi Germany or pre-war fascist Japan), the military regimes of the Third World, although they are allegedly ruled by 'strong men', are basically weak. They are rooted in an underdeveloped, agrarian economy and do not possess the means fundamentally to transform and modernize the economic system. Such a transformation would need enthusiastic cooperation on the part of the rural masses, and if there is one thing such regimes basing themselves upon repression are never able to muster, it is support among the poor peasantry. If any agrarian reforms or measures for community development are undertaken, they remain half-hearted and mostly ineffective in terms of a wholesale transformation of rural society, as I hope to show in the following chapter.

Because of all these negative factors, agrarian production generally suffers from stagnation or, at any rate, does not catch up with the rapid population increase. The only way to stay in power is to accept foreign aid – and in the next chapter we shall see what this usually amounts to. The basic weakness of these regimes becomes evident through this necessity to be bolstered up by foreign intervention. On the other hand, it is this foreign intervention, particularly in its military aspects, that sometimes grants these regimes, at least temporarily, a new lease of life. But this new lease of life does not mean a renewed vitality.

T–I

The most obvious example of the weakness just mentioned is the downfall of the Chiang Kai-shek regime in China. In 1927, Chiang Kai-shek had established a counter-revolutionary, military regime after having crushed the leftist groups who had been his allies during his march to the north. There are some indications that one of the primary reasons for his volte-face was the rural unrest in some southern provinces, which had seriously alarmed many young officers belonging to the landed gentry. As with General Suharto in Indonesia about forty years later, Chiang Kai-shek put an end to the coalition between the Kuomintang and communists which had been created by his predecessor, Sun Yat-sen. He immediately secured foreign aid and tried to crush the communists who had formed a rural base in Kiang-si province. In the long run (a struggle, with some interruptions, of over twenty years) his efforts to stem the tide were in vain.

Other historical examples of failing repression are Cuba under President Batista, and South Vietnam under the rule of successive generals who, despite all-out American assistance, have not been able to crush the National Liberation Front that has found its main support among the peasantry.

But there are many other countries of the Third World where military regimes are, for the moment, able to survive. One might ask whether their success in suppressing revolution is only temporary, and whether they are not, in the long run, doomed.

ix. *Prospects for Revolution under Military Dictatorship*

Harry Eckstein has cogently formulated the revolutionary potential inherent in a society dominated by repression: 'Repression may be both an obstacle to and a precipitant of internal war.'[29] Should we deduce from this statement that military dictatorships are in the long run bound to crumble under the blows of an imminent peasant revolution?

It is evident that social protest, although a strong mental factor in the societies under review, cannot be openly expressed in terms of a true emancipation movement in a 'culture of repression'. Such protest will either assume the form of disguised counterpoints, or express itself in illegal organization or guerrilla activity. However, the protest is bound to grow. Repression in itself fosters the counterforces that will, eventually, defeat its engineers. In the course of time, dissatisfaction mounts, and assumes a nationalist character that directs itself against the foreign interests which uphold the regime.*

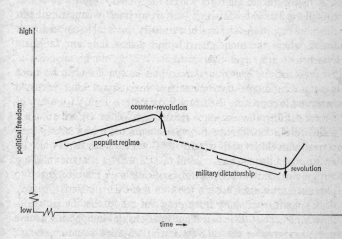

Graph 6. Relationship between amount of political freedom, counter-revolution and revolution.

It depends upon many factors whether a peasant revolution will materialize. In order to assess the strength of the revolutionary forces, we will have to discuss the position of several social layers. The peasant masses will, for the time being, be able to operate only underground. Since the patronage institution no longer works to their partial benefit, they will have to develop a new

---

* The general trend under a populist regime, and again under military dictatorship established after a counter-revolution, has been sketched in Graph 6.

strategy: they will have to learn how to organize largely on the basis of class solidarity. Since many of them lack the slight measure of protection they enjoyed under the system of patronage or quasi-patronage, they are thrown back upon their own resources. Guerrilla struggle may be an excellent school to learn the new type of solidarity and new organizational and ideological principles.

A few words on guerrilla warfare in general seem to be due at this place. The bases for such warfare are mostly concentrated in the more mountainous areas of a country, preferably covered with forest, where the main guerrilla forces may hide and build up reserves of arms and food provisions. It would be an error to assume that any guerrilla warfare can be considered to be allied with revolutionary developments of the peasant kind discussed here, and to constitute their preliminary stage. It may form part of a national liberation struggle that cannot yet be viewed as a true social revolution. Frantz Fanon's famous book was largely concerned with this type of guerrilla.[30] Guerrilla warfare may also be an isolated phenomenon, a kind of *jacquerie*, a peasant rebellion without any further ideological implications or ramifications into political unrest elsewhere in the country. Guerrilla activities may even present reactionary features, when they are led by rich landlords who exploit their patronage relationships in opposing a more or less progressive central administration. Such was to a certain extent the case with the Darul Islam movement in West Java which opposed Sukarno's populist regime, or is still the case with the Mafia-inspired unrest in Sicily.

One of the main criteria for assessing whether guerrilla warfare shows traits of a pre-revolutionary movement might be the support it gets from the poor peasant population in the surrounding districts. Moral and material support given to a guerrilla movement by an apparently settled rural population is a form of concealed rather than of open protest. The phenomenon is a sequel to another well-known aspect of peasant attitudes in the non-industrial countries: a deeply rooted distrust of officials and of anything emanating from the administration. Peasant distrust is a well-known attitude in many societies. In Asia, however, the negative attitude *vis-à-vis* government officials has been an in-grained attitude among peasants since early times.[31]

Despite all the professed intentions of the officialdom during the present century to introduce a welfare policy to replace the traditional exploitation of the peasantry, this new approach, either by colonial or by national governments, has done little to assuage the traditional distrust. On the contrary, the introduction of all kinds of welfare services has more often than not led to an increased burden, in taxes or services, and to a mounting opposition towards anybody representing official authority.

This negative attitude to officials may find its counterpart in a much more positive attitude towards political leaders who are in open opposition to those in power. Even though the peasants will be extremely cautious in expressing sympathy for the rebels operating near by, somewhere in the forests or the mountains, yet this may be the party with which their real sympathies lie.

The landed gentry will generally be the staunchest supporters of the regime. Among the urban bourgeoisie there will also be large groups more or less wedded to foreign interests and profiting from the opportunities created for scholarships, foreign travel and profitable appointments.

However, among the urban bourgeoisie, particularly the younger intelligentsia, and sometimes also among the lower clergy, there will be an increasing number of individuals disappointed with the many failures and unkept promises of the regime, who will reject the dependence on foreign powers and will in the end tend to shift their allegiance towards competing power centres. If there is also a class-conscious and numerically significant industrial labour class, a new-democratic alliance in the Maoist sense may become possible.

In a further stage, a progressive erosion of the official values with ensuing widespread corruption may ultimately cause a defection of the intellectuals and make them take sides with the revolutionary peasantry. Whereas, under a populist regime, intellectuals and other important groups still dream of attaining their aim, a better society, through legal action, the cold and bloody repression causes violent revolution to become the only available alternative to complete submission. In such cases, Mark Twain's comment on the moral justice of revolution as a reply to cold day-to-day repression[32] becomes convincing for those groups that would have wavered in a different situation. It is even not uncommon that, under these circumstances, groups among the intelligentsia assume leadership of the revolutionary movement.

It is a curious and often overlooked phenomenon that certain personalities of aristocratic origin remain aloof from the developments that involve the so-called urban elite in the capitalist exploitation of their country. Although a large majority of the old native aristocracy aligns with the conservative forces and profits from the privileges offered to the well-educated descendants of the old ruling class by foreign governments or interests, there are among this group, as a rule, a few individuals who remain apart and refuse to align themselves with the authorities representing a new bureaucratic bourgeoisie. Their aristocratic pride makes them abhor the money grabbing and corrupt practices typical of both the bureaucracy and the private entrepreneurs in the new states. This negative attitude towards those in power may drive them to the opposite role: an attempt to assume leadership of popular rebellion against the ruling cliques supported by foreign interests. Since they are mentally unable to align themselves with the bourgeois trends of the day, but are at the same time too intelligent to cling to chimeras of the past, they skip the bourgeois-capitalist phase and may become leaders of a true revolutionary movement involving the popular peasant masses. Their skill in handling poular masses through patronage relationships may transform them into suitable leaders of peasant movements.

Such red aristocrats or members of a gentry class have been found as leaders in several of the countries we are concerned with. One need only think of personalities such as Chou En-lai, Ho Chi-minh (Nguyen Tat Thanh) who was the son of a scholar, Prince Souphanouvong of Laos, Tan Thun of Burma, the Lava brothers in the Philippines, and many others.

In nineteenth-century Europe, the phenomenon of aristocrats opposing the capitalist trends of the day and assuming leadership of radical socialist movements was also apparent. Count de Saint-

Simon and Buonarrotti, Bakunin, Kropotkin and Leo Tolstoy, all represent this radical anti-capitalist trend under aristocratic leadership. Perhaps one should even mention, in this context, Karl Marx's aristocratic wife Jenny von Westphalen!

So we may deduce that patronage-like relationships may acquire, in a culture of repression, a positive function in respect of revolutionary developments. Whereas under populism patronage-like relationships within vertical organizations, broadly speaking, had a weakening function upon the revolutionary potential of leftist groups and therefore could be viewed as an obstacle to revolution, under conditions of extreme repression the situation may be reversed. Revolutionary leadership may make use of all kinds of traditional loyalties among sections of the peasant class, as for example kinship relationships or ethnic affinities, in order to enlist massive support. Provided that the leaders adopt a position which stresses the interests of the peasant class and does not manipulate the peasant movement simply in order to further their family interests as members of a gentry, their participation and leadership may immensely strengthen the revolutionary movement.

But we should not conclude that in any country of the Third World under military dictatorship a peasant revolution is imminent. The failure of peasant revolutions to materialize in Latin America cannot be easily dismissed as a short delay in what is inevitable. We do not know for sure whether revolutions are ever inevitable. Personal factors may be decisive, both for the occurrence and for the success of a revolution.

Are we, moreover, sure that a military dictatorship of the kind I have sketched will never be overthrown except through a peasant or new-democratic revolution? A counter-revolution can easily be dismissed as a possibility, since there is no gradual, legally admitted emancipation to be countered by force. A *coup d'état* bringing a different but similar type of military junta into power is a fairly frequent development. But there is also the possibility that a military dictatorship of the repressive type may have to yield, under popular pressure, to a populist regime also under military leadership: a regime of the Nasserite type which initiates significant land reforms and pursues a nationalist policy directed against foreign interests. The creation of such a populist regime may be provoked by a strong guerrilla activity. In such a case, it is possible that this will only be a first step towards a realization of a true new-democratic or peasant revolution. In that case, the transformation of the regime into a populist one might even be interpreted as a relaxation of the repression which could function as an accelerator for the revolutionary movement. However, the other possibility is that the peasants, satisfied with the land reform laws, will part with their guerrilla tactics. In that case, in the long run the fate of agrarian movements under populism may be repeated: a counter-revolution may occur, in the course of time.

One could ask oneself to what extent recent developments in Peru conform to the pattern just outlined. It is highly questionable whether the radical measures taken by the military junta, which assumed power during the summer of 1969, have really been stimulated by prevalent agrarian unrest. Moreover, populist measures such as nationalization of foreign interests and land reforms are, for the moment, still either restricted in scope or only extant on paper. An important aspect of the Peruvian case is that the reversal of policies occurred after the Americans had withdrawn their assistance, angered by steps taken against their oil interests.

This circumstance raises another query. Should we assume that even in a situation of extreme repression no peasant revolution will occur without an accelerator? If so, what type of accelerator could we think of, except a losing war or a relaxation of the repression? Could, for example, a withdrawal or retrenchment of foreign aid, for whatever reason, be viewed as an effective accelerator? We have as yet no answer to this question.

8

Prevention of Revolutions

When policy measures have been instituted specifically aimed at ameliorating conditions for the lower strata, they have either not been implemented and enforced or have been distorted so as to favor the not-so-poor and to discriminate against the masses.

GUNNAR MYRDAL

Revolution occurs because non-violent evolution is not occurring.

CHALMERS JOHNSON

i. *Introductory Remarks*

This chapter is concerned with the problem of whether it is possible to prevent revolutions by specific policies. I will pay particular attention to policies pursued or measures taken at a fairly early stage, intended to avert the danger of a revolutionary overthrow before the point of no return has been reached. The main problem of the present chapter will be to assess, on the basis of available historical evidence and of the extant literature, to what extent such policies might be deemed to be successful – and if so, whether they do more than provide a temporary delay.

There are, in principle, three ways open for those who aim to prevent revolution. The first approach tries to overcome an all-pervasive state of economic stagnation, or to counter involutionary tendencies leading towards a progressive deterioration of economic conditions. This method attempts to restore a normal process of evolution, in order to make any tendency towards radical transformation, i.e. revolution, superfluous. Such an approach is characteristic of those who propagate community development or other types of social reform as a means to promote steady, healthy development. Phillips Ruopp has made the anti-revolutionary philosophy behind this approach explicit in his credo:

The developmental differs radically from the cataclysmic, with the latter's delusive appeals to violent action. Development is gradual, but it is not a gradualness that lends itself as an excuse for inaction. It means growth, but it must be growth cultivated by unequivocal and constant witness to justice, liberty and compassion.[33]

The numerous frustrations and failures experienced in the course of such attempts to get the wheel of evolution turning again in South and South-East Asia are well described by Gunnar Myrdal in the *Asian Drama*; René Dumont has written a similar critical account, though rather of an impressionistic nature, about Africa south of the Sahara in *False Start in Africa*.[34]

A second approach, indicative of less self-confidence among those in authority, is a psychological one. In this case the leading politicians may have, explicitly or tacitly, arrived at the conclusion that attempts at promoting economic development are not likely to be successful. Instead, they try to substitute a certain measure of psychological satisfaction for a real satisfaction of material needs. Such a policy relies either upon slogans and propaganda or upon what Harry Eckstein has called 'diversions'.[35]

A third approach is still more negative. It is based on the belief that to curb the revolutionary upsurge is largely a matter of repression. In the last two chapters we have learnt to view repression as a major factor in the genesis of revolution rather than a remedy against it. Yet, there are many who rely on repression as the mainstay of a policy to contain revolutionary trends, and who consequently do not realize that repression, to use Eckstein's expression, 'is a two-edged sword'.

In actual practice the three approaches just mentioned are generally used in some kind of combination. But different types of regime may be distinguished according to the stress they put in their actual policy upon one of three approaches.

For example, one could characterize India as a country where stress is laid upon the first approach, the positive one. India's political system belongs, according to David Apter's distinction, to the type of 'reconciliation systems'. President Sukarno's regime in Indonesia put its main stress upon the psychological element, in truly populist style, and is identified by Apter as an example of what he calls a 'mobilization system';[36] whereas the present regime in Indonesia under General Suharto, though claiming to stress economic development, largely relies upon repression, as is evidenced by the huge numbers of political prisoners (assessed by Amnesty International in early 1973 at 55,000, as the lowest estimate. They add that 'the real figure may well be much greater').

I will try to analyse the three approaches in order.

ii. Welfare Measures or Panaceas?

It is logical enough that in different countries of the Third World strenuous attempts are made, both by populist and by counter-revolutionary regimes, to accelerate the rate of economic development through peaceful, that is to say non-revolutionary, means. Economic development is regarded as the best medicine to prevent revolutions. Everyone would agree that, if such steps could succeed, this would be the most preferable way to achieve emancipation and material progress. However, the tragedy of the present century – as a matter of fact, the central theme of the 'Asian Drama' – appears to be that no major country can now succeed in achieving an economic development rapid and general enough to transform an agrarian society into an industrial one without revolution.

In the first part of this book I mentioned the fact that 'late-comers' had much greater difficulties in bringing about 'modernization' than those countries that had made a start in the course of the nineteenth century. I referred to the observation made by authors such as Gerschenkron and Eisenstadt that late-comers have to modernize and industrialize according to a different sequence and at a different rate from the old-timers among the industrial nations.[37] I finally pointed out that the main reason for this is the strongly increased power of capitalist enterprise since the turn of the century, manifest in the creation of world-wide monopolistic or oligopolistic companies or trusts, which adversely affects the chances for newcomers to erect a competing industrial economy within the orbit of these capitalist foreign interests. To quote Elman Service:

This Western web of dominance is what has created an unprecedented environment for the new industrialization, and this is why the new technological evolution is best called revolution, for it must act *against* the dominance of the Euro-American system in the techno-economic sphere just as in political affairs.[38]

The last major country to industrialize without a full-fledged social revolution was Japan – and even there a thorough political overhaul of the kind of the Meiji 'revolution' was needed to make rapid industrial development possible.

It is against this background that we have to view the different measures attempted by the new states to initiate rapid economic development without resorting to a true social revolution. It is impossible for these governments, even though they profess a fiercely nationalistic, populist ideology, strongly denounce foreign capitalism the way Sukarno of Indonesia or Nkrumah of Ghana did, and strenuously attempt to follow a neutral and 'independent' course in foreign policy, actually to disengage themselves from the economic pressures of international capitalist enterprise. This dependence dooms all their attempts to failure.

The dependence upon foreign interests is enhanced through the numerous ties that are maintained between those interests and members of the new bureaucratic elite. The ideology of the new states, whether it is populist or more conservative, is opposed to a complete elimination of the traditional landed gentry, and their allies within the bureaucratic apparatus, from within their positions of power. The populist ideology, positing the basic homogeneity of 'the people', denies the necessity of a class strife against the landed gentry. Its lack of radicalism in internal affairs and disbelief in a true social revolution as a precondition for social and economic change, despite all the radical slogans it generally indulges in, causes a populist government, not to speak of a government adhering to a more conservative ideology, to become what Gunnar Myrdal has called 'a soft state'. A 'reconciliation system', to use

Apter's term, has still less possibility of squarely attacking the basic issue of vested landed interests opposing true rural development. Such regimes do not really touch the landed interests opposing radical social change; these interests are not slow in allying themselves, economically and politically, with foreign capitalist interests which are intent upon keeping a foothold in the underdeveloped economy.

It is this general state of affairs which seriously impairs any piecemeal attempt to counter the revolutionary 'danger' through measures aiming at more gradual economic development. In the following survey I shall discuss several of the most fervently propagated policies intended to prevent a development which, in the long run, would appear to make a revolutionary course inescapable. The policies can be summed up as follows: (a) community development or the creation of cooperatives; (b) agrarian reform; (c) birth control; (d) foreign aid; (e) improved varieties of food crops.

(a) Community Development or Cooperatives

Community development is an attempt to introduce radical innovations without overturning the existing social structure. It tries to make use of the traditional communal bonds in the village in order to introduce all kinds of technical improvements. In actual practice, it mostly amounts to an attempt to square the circle, and it is exactly this ambiguity that accounts for the numerous failures of community development programmes.

Preserving the existing social structure and attempting to revive the traditional village society which has been strongly impaired by the infringements of a money economy amounts in practice to an attempt to channel innovation through leaders who derive their position of strength and power from the existing social structure. And this is, precisely, what frustrates most attempts at innovation. Elsewhere I have tried to demonstrate that community development amounts to a 'betting on the strong' policy – a term I borrowed from Frank Lynch who was, at the time (1962), in favour of such an approach.[39] In order to overcome the severe impediments to innovation in the rural economy, many authorities tend to look for specific agents to introduce the innovations required. It is the more advanced farmers who are almost automatically selected. It is they who show a greater responsiveness to all kinds of innovations and technical improvements and who are much easier for government agencies or special services to approach. There is an implicit assumption that the advanced farmers will set an example to the poorer sections, who are expected to follow the model which they are able to observe close at hand. The innovation is intended to spread, like an oil stain, to other layers of rural society.

It is obvious that the underlying philosophy of this approach is an inherent belief in gradual evolution. It is assumed that the process of spreading knowledge and technical progress can only be a gradual one, and that the best agents for this evolutionary process have to be looked for among the most advanced individuals in rural society. In the village sphere this group generally consists of those well-to-do farmers who have enjoyed sufficient education or had enough contacts with urban elements to respond positively to all kinds of suggestions for the improvement of their production techniques. The philosophy behind this 'betting on the strong' approach is, therefore, that the progressive farmer, acting as an agent for the community development activities and receiving several privileges (fertilizers, improved seeds and insecticides at lowered prices), will function as the manager of a model farm within the village. Other villagers are expected to see for themselves the results that can be achieved by improved techniques, and, in due course, to follow the example set by the progressive farmer.

All this, however, presupposes the possession of a sizable plot of land and enough capital resources to finance technical innovations and to risk some losses if they fail. There are very few villagers who are able to fulfil these conditions in a rural society of the type dealt with here. In the densely populated rice-growing areas, in particular, where a rapid natural increase adds to the constant population pressure, the large majority of the peasantry can never afford to make a trial of the propagated innovations.

Where sharecropping prevails, and this is the case in a majority of the countries of the Third World, there is an additional obstacle. It is primarily the sharecropper who would be required to make the needed investments. But he would have to take into consideration the fact that a high proportion of the surplus product would accrue to the landowner. Similarly, the landowner shrinks from costly innovations because he does not want the sharecropper to get part of the resulting surplus production. And traditional sharecropping relationships and arrangements are generally not conducive to making experiments as a rational joint venture between landowner and sharecropper.

Therefore, the expected spread of the innovations to the rank and file of the villagers does not come about. The predicted oil-stain effect stops at the level of the wealthier landowners. If the new agricultural techniques have any effect on the poorer peasantry, it is rather by enabling the strong progressive farmers to buy additional land from indebted poorer peasants. Community development, if applied in the way described above, has a tendency to reinforce the existing social structure rather than to weaken it. For India it has been clearly shown[40] that the benefits of the programme largely accrue to the limited group of wealthy landowners. As a policy aimed at spreading better agricultural, and other, techniques among the peasant population, and at improving their lot in order to avert the danger of revolution, community development as generally applied must fail.

Similar objections may be raised against another panacea for the ills of underdeveloped economies: the creation of all kinds of rural cooperative. Again, these cooperatives are mostly based on the 'betting on the strong' principle.[41] Even if poor peasants are admitted as members, actual leadership of the cooperatives is generally in the hands of wealthier landowners. The activities of the cooperative will mostly benefit those who are already fairly prosperous. Moreover, introduction of cooperatives in a society where private farming, private trade, and private money-lending are not abolished, may produce a strange situation. A rich farmer, who is at the same time chairman of a cooperative, may channel the more profitable transactions to his private farm, leaving the less profitable ones to the cooperative. A private moneylender who is chairman of a cooperative may, in his latter capacity, extend loans to his insolvent debtors in order to let them repay.[42] Again, cooperatives function in a society with a distinct social structure. Their existence in itself is not enough to help change the structure and to surmount its inequalities. On the contrary, the new institution will be used by the existing power elite to further its aims, regardless of the egalitarian ideology professed by its propagandists.

(b) Agrarian Reform

Agrarian reform may be one of the primary targets of a social revolution. However, less radical land reforms are generally propagated, and sometimes attempted, by governments that are intent on preventing rather than fostering revolution. It is, none the less, the restricted nature of the reforms introduced that mostly prevents them from achieving their ultimate aim: to create suitable conditions for increased agricultural production. Again, the main difficulty is that if the existing social order is preserved, it is the powerful members of the gentry on the local or regional level who will ultimately decide upon the way the reforms are to be carried out. It is they who sit on the land tribunals; it is they who interpret the law, allow all kinds of circumventions and take care that the material interests of their peers will not be really affected. Even the best land reform legislation is bound to fail if the poor peasantry is not allowed to organize its strength in order to control the way the law is being carried out.

The manifold loopholes and occasions for law evasion in the Indian land reform legislation have been repeatedly pointed out.[43] A perceptive analysis of the effects of the Bombay State legislation on abolition of tenancy, 1956, has recently been published as a doctoral thesis at the University of Amsterdam.[44] It appears from Dr Baks's research that the professed aim of the law to grant 'land to the tiller' has been nearly completely frustrated by the way the new legislation has been carried out. His observations provide a clear picture of the way the social structure impinges upon all well-intended legislative measures and serves to preserve the interests of the power elite – in this case, the members of the local dominant castes.

Where the land was fertile, the landowners who had previously leased their lands to *adhivasi* (semi-tribal) tenants did all they could to prevent the latter from acquiring the ownership rights to which they were entitled, according to the new law. Consequently, before 'Tiller's Day' (1 April 1957), the day on which the Bombay Act XIII would be enacted, they took care to evict the tenants and to recover their lands for 'personal cultivation'. However, according to Dr Baks's findings, this personal cultivation did not amount to any more than appointing the former tenant as a 'manager', which meant that he had to do his work as usual, but without enjoying the security provided by the successive tenancy laws. In one village studied by Baks no *adhivasi* tenant had dared to sue the landowner before the land tribunal, where the landowning castes were strongly represented. A preservation of patronage relationships offered better security than a distant law administered by those of the same caste as the patrons.

Still more interesting is what happened in another village studied by Baks, where most of the lands worked by former *adhivasi* tenants were infertile. The landlord had not in general opposed the acquisition by the former tenants of landownership rights on the infertile plots worked by them before Tiller's Day. He had earlier taken care to retain the more fertile plots, through eviction of the tenants, and through using the formula of 'personal cultivation', although the actual supervision of the labourers was in the hands of an agent who lived in the village. The landlord had also divided the lands among his relatives in order to escape the ceiling regulations.

Since the plots acquired by the tenants were mostly uneconomic holdings they did not yield enough to enable the new owners to pay their annual instalments which would confirm their ownership rights. Consequently, they had to contract new debts – and there was nobody, not even the cooperative, offering easier conditions for loans than the former landlord.

Therefore the latter was able to retain, and even to reinforce, his economic power over the majority of the poor villagers. They had again to submit to the landlord-moneylender the decision as to the crops to be raised. Their freshly acquired ownership rights were nominal only; in their actual position there was no change for the better.

Similar experiences have been found with agrarian reforms in the Philippines. Instead of the traditional sharecropping (*kasama*) provision, mostly on a fifty-fifty basis for rice, in parts of the country which are declared to be Land Reform Areas the tenant can claim 'leasehold' rights on his plot if it forms part of a rice estate exceeding 115 hectares. According to the leasehold provisions he is entitled to 75 per cent of the harvest; but in that case he has to pay the full expenses for ploughing, seeds, fertilizer, etc., which were, under the traditional arrangements, borne equally by landowner and *kasama*.

According to recent information which I received from O. D. van den Muijzenberg, in a village in central Luzon where he has been doing research, the landlords flatly refused to provide loans to those *kasama* who had claimed leaseholdership rights according to the new law. Consequently, when in need of cash for the payment of hired labourers during the planting season, of fertilizer, etc. some of the latter came begging to restore the old *kasama* relationships on a fifty-fifty basis.

Such restricted agrarian reforms do not appear to be very helpful in stemming the tide of revolution. On the other hand, a peasant revolution necessarily carries radical land reforms in its wake, mostly without compensation to the former owners. In chapter ten, the basic significance of such land reforms for a wholesale social and economic transformation will be discussed.

(c) Birth Control

Birth control is also a policy frequently advocated in order to further economic development. In Kingsley Davis's *The Population of India and Pakistan*[45] the political implications of this policy compared with rapid industrialization are openly stated.

The truth is that any policy that rapidly industrialized Pakistan and India would be a far greater shock to the basic social institutions than would any policy that attacked fertility directly... The Russian example shows that fast industrialization is possible, but it also shows that the cost is heavy.

It is felt that slowing down of the natural increase would win time, and thus make gradual evolutionary solutions possible in societies where without a lowered birth rate only radical and revolutionary measures could bring about rapid industrial development.

The frustrations and failures experienced with birth control policies are of a somewhat different nature from those described in connection with community development and land reform. If birth control measures were really effective, they would certainly be of some help in furthering an accelerated rate of economic development – at least in combination with strenuous attempts to foster such a development.

Unfortunately, experience teaches that in agrarian countries of a significant size, suffering from an underdeveloped economy, birth control propaganda is ineffective. Even if a government sympathetic to the idea of birth control succeeds in influencing the birth rate among certain urban groups, it is completely unable to reach the large majority of the peasant population unless the latter has already achieved an economic level that makes it receptive to propaganda. Therefore, birth control policy in an underdeveloped country is caught in a vicious circle. It intends to improve the economic level of the population; but in order to achieve its aims, it needs a population that has already made several strides in the direction of economic development.[46]

There are a few underdeveloped countries where it is claimed that a lower birth rate has been achieved without previous significant economic development. Alfred Sauvy mentions Singapore, Malaysia, Taiwan and Hongkong.[47] All these countries have a relatively low total population size. A second characteristic is that economic development is distinctly faster than in the giant Asian countries (India, Pakistan, Indonesia) where the overpopulation problem is most pressing. Moreover, Hongkong and

Singapore are by no means predominantly agrarian countries. Industrialization had achieved a certain level prior to the introduction of birth control. Sauvy himself makes a comparison with India where birth control propaganda has been largely ineffective. His conclusion is that if economic development is not an indispensable precondition to a successful birth control campaign, the achievement of a certain cultural level which makes the people receptive to the campaign most certainly is.[48] But again, this higher cultural level presupposes a level of sophistication which is hardly to be expected in a traditional, predominantly agrarian, society.

It is, therefore, difficult to see how the introduction of birth control techniques as such could function as an antidote to revolution. It could perform an important supplementary function, but only in a society where economic development is already under way (which, in many agrarian societies, might depend upon the occurrence of a successful social revolution). Any attempt to promote economic development through birth control amounts to putting the cart before the horse.

(d) Foreign Aid

Foreign aid is another medicine prescribed by many doctors and frequently administered. As with community development and agrarian reforms, the difficulty is that foreign aid does not function in an economic and political vacuum. The type of aid offered and the way it is channelled into the underdeveloped economy is closely linked to the general pattern of economic relationships between the industrial and the non-industrial world.

The idea that foreign aid is extended on a purely altruistic basis, an injection of medicine into an ailing body, is very naïve indeed. In fact, it cannot be disengaged from the neo-colonialist pattern of trade relationships between the two types of economy. These are basically characterized by the declining trend in the prices of raw materials, which are the mainstay of most underdeveloped economies. To what extent altruism and idealism are really relevant for policies pursued by representatives of highly developed economies can best be demonstrated, as I pointed out earlier, by the cata-strophic failure of the three UNCTAD conferences. Any attempt at improving or stabilizing the prices for raw materials and com-mercial crops produced by underdeveloped countries met with fierce resistance from the representatives of the highly developed economies.

There is plenty of evidence to disprove the allegedly favourable effect of what has been presented as foreign aid. For the sake of simplicity I am restricting my argument to the most common type of foreign aid: the aid extended to the government of the recipient country. First of all, much of the aid is extended as inter-est-bearing loans. In due time both interest and loans will have to be repaid, and there is in most cases no prospect at all that the underdeveloped economies will have improved at such a rate that they will be able to bear the burden of the increasing debt.

The type of aid extended in the majority of cases is also charac-teristic of the general pattern of economic inter-relationships. Only seldom is it provided and used to promote overall industrial development in the economy. Industrial interests in the Western world are generally opposed to the idea of creating new serious competitors on the industrial market. If foreign aid is being used for industrial purposes, it is mostly directed towards consumer industries that are not those most essential for a sound economic development. Herbert Feldman has drawn attention to the erec-tion in Pakistan, out of funds extended as foreign aid, of factories for the production of soft drinks – decidedly not the most neces-sary items for the peasant population.[49] The same type of industry also occupies a significant place in the economy of the Philippines.[50]

Things are even worse when foreign assistance funds are used to promote the import of finished goods which the underdeveloped economy could just as well produce itself; frequently the govern-ment that receives aid is required to ship the goods with vessels owned by the country that extends it.

In cases where aid is extended in the form of grain deliveries, for example under the U.S. PL 480, it may, through its impact on the local grain prices, discourage food production within the country itself.

The most frustrating aspect of aid is that it tends to reinforce the position of the power elite in the new states. The official viewpoint is that aid will not be extended without a previous request from the recipient. It seems to be assumed, without question, that the official government of the recipient state can be identified with the people that are to receive assistance. But since these governments are often to a large extent dependent upon the much stronger powers that provide aid, there is no guarantee that the request will be based on the real needs of the population. And as the aid is channelled through the official administration of the recipient state, its actual utilization is determined by those in power and there is always the possibility that much of it will be misused or benefit corrupt officials rather than the people for whom it is professedly intended.

Even if foreign aid is not being extended as material assistance but in the form of know-how, its effect is not necessarily of benefit to the majority of the population. In a country where the ruling elite is socially far removed from the rural mass of the population, educational facilities may drain off better trained personnel from the countryside towards the towns, in which case the countryside will not profit from the improved facilities. Still less attractive is the prospect of a serious brain drain of the best trained experts to the industrialized countries.

It is hard to see how foreign aid can be considered an effective means of contributing to the improvement of underdeveloped countries along gradualist lines; if it does not, one cannot see how it can serve, in the long run, to prevent social revolutions.

(e) Green Revolution

There is one type of foreign aid that has been highly advertised, during the past few years, as a way of revitalizing the underdeveloped economies. The introduction of new strains of foodcrops ('miracle wheat', 'miracle rice') is supposed to suffice to get the evolutionist wheels of the ailing rural economies turning again.

The political implication of this propaganda becomes clear when certain authors speak about what they *hope* will happen (a rapid spread of the new varieties over large areas and a fast increase of the total grain production in countries like Pakistan, India and the Philippines) in terms of a 'green revolution', which evidently must serve to make a 'red revolution' superfluous.[51]

It is still too early to discuss the prospects for a realization of these plans on the basis of actual experiences. The way local and partial successes are being boosted in several publications, as harbingers of miracles in food production in the near future, should make us cautious as to the real reasons for this sudden optimism.

But there are more reasons for caution. There are many technical means for improving production levels in underdeveloped economies. The reasons why they are not utilized are mostly institutional and not technical. Underdeveloped economies do not usually provide the incentives needed to utilize all kinds of innovations that are technically possible and sometimes also available. To quote Ladejinsky:

It is relatively easy to use science to increase production, but only if the cultivator's relationship to the land and the state's treatment of him and of agriculture create incentives to invest, to improve the land and to raise productivity.[52]

It is difficult to see why the manifold factors resisting innovations should suddenly vanish on the introduction of new varieties of seed. Technical miracles are easier to perform than economic or sociological ones. If, at present, large irrigation works in India or Indonesia are only utilized to a limited percentage of their total capacity; if the introduction, by agricultural extension workers, of the Japanese method of planting rice meets with serious opposition on the part of the poorer peasantry,[53] why should one then expect the new varieties of seed to spread like wildfire? Higher yields may affect the grain prices. Rich landowners may be unwilling to urge their tenants to plant a variety that will obtain such high yields that the tenant might no longer be prepared to do additional work to raise a second crop on the landowner's field on the traditional basis. There may be manipulation of prices by traders. The officials delivering seeds and fertilizers may expect extra profit for themselves.

We have to take into consideration the fact that cultivation of the new varieties requires irrigated fields and the use of a substantial amount of chemical fertilizer.[54] This means that the new varieties will be suitable for limited areas only. Purely technical devices are not enough to surmount institutional obstacles to increased production, which are rooted in the prevalent economic, social and political structure, as was evidenced by the failure of the Mass Guidance Program introduced by the military regime in Indonesia. In fact, there is no basis for an attitude of undue optimism about the effectiveness of a 'green revolution'. At best one can assume an attitude of 'wait and see'.

Let us, however, assume for a moment that the introduction of new varieties will prove a success, though only a moderate one. Can we be sure that in that case the 'green revolution' will function as a remedy against a 'red' one?

This is by no means certain. The development would, in such a case, correspond to a reversed J-curve, that is to say, a long-term process of deterioration and involution, followed by a sudden rise in productivity and yields.

In our theoretical discussion of the genesis of revolutions in chapter six, we did not touch upon the possibility of a *reversed* J-curve as far as *economic* preconditions are concerned. If, however, a 'green revolution' achieved the miraculous results its advocates are aiming for, it is very possible that the sudden rise in yields would produce such a dislocation that it might promote a revolutionary development instead of preventing one. It has been repeatedly argued that the imbalances produced by economic growth might produce the opposite effect of what has been envisaged, that is to say, increased instability instead of increased stability.[55]

This possibility is reinforced by the fact that any improvements through foreign aid, including the introduction of new varieties, tend to accrue to those farmers whom we have earlier defined as strong. As in the case of community development or cooperatives the new development is likely to benefit primarily those farmers who possess enough irrigated land to be able to participate in the new programme. If they succeed in obtaining higher yields and in making a good business out of the new variety, their economic power within the village will increase accordingly. For the majority of the peasantry who are unable to follow suit or to apply the new variety on a profitable basis, such a development could result in increased dissatisfaction. If they see their neighbour prosper and become a true *kulak* and exploiter of their poverty, this may result in further polarization of the class tensions. The changes brought about through increased production and higher profits for a restricted group of larger landowners may also elicit new wants among the poorer peasantry, and consequently enhance social unrest instead of assuaging it. Far from preventing a 'red' revolution, measures such as community development or a 'green' revolution, through the strengthening of the existing power structure, might even, in the long run, promote it.

The true obstacles to an overall development are not removed through these isolated measures that keep the social and political structure intact. Even if a certain initial success is achieved in a purely technical and economic sense, it is likely to be of a temporary nature, and only to delay the ultimate failure which is bound to result from the institutional obstacles to a lasting change.

If we consider, once more, the different positive measures advocated, and in many cases applied, by those who want to forestall revolution, we find that they are all merely panaceas. Instead of tackling the central issue and waging a fight against the social structure with its concomitant stunting impact upon economic development, they attempt to promote the latter through isolated measures and a piecemeal approach. It is precisely the permanent influence of the social structure that frustrates all the one-sided attempts to counter the prevalent trends.

If, on the other hand, the governments of the new states were really willing to tackle the development problem as a whole, at least some of these policies would feature among the measures to be taken. The formation of cooperatives, technical innovation, propaganda for birth control and, first and foremost, land reform, would all form elements of the development plan. But such a plan would also have to attack the existing social order and the basis of the existing hierarchy in order to be really viable.

A plan such as this would, in fact, amount to a policy little short of revolution and, if really successful, it could hardly be counted among policies intended to *prevent* revolution. It remains highly questionable, however, whether such a 'revolution from above' can be expected in any major country under the existing general conditions.

iii. Practical or Psychological Approach?

Basically different from an approach which stresses welfare measures intended to promote rapid development is an approach which primarily aims at a psychological effect. Political scientists are used to making the distinction, first developed by Herbert Feith, between two types of politicians: 'administrators' and 'solidarity-makers'.[56] The former category is deemed to be practical-minded and to be primarily interested in stability and economic development. The latter category is allegedly more concerned with psychological factors and politics than with economics, and stresses a strategy directed at the stimulation of a spirit of national solidarity, as a precondition for a realization of further national tasks, including economic development. Within the context of Indonesian politics, ex-President Sukarno, the populist leader, was presented as the typical solidarity-maker, whereas his comrade-in-arms of the national struggle, the former Vice-President, Mohammad Hatta, was regarded as a true representative of the category of administrators.

Most Western writers show a distinct preference for the administrator type of politician. This preference is partly due to the greater familiarity in the West with the patterns of thinking peculiar to the administrators who are more Western in orientation and are expected to be exactly the type of hard-headed, practical leaders the underdeveloped countries need.[57] But this preference may be also partially attributed to the much greater willingness of the administrators to allow Western enterprise opportunities for investment and other kinds of business, whereas solidarity-makers are much more wary of Western capitalist interests and influences.

Populist regimes are typically led by solidarity-makers, whereas both reconciliation systems, patterned after a Western democratic model, and military dictatorships, are more likely to attempt the administrator-like approach.

Unfortunately, even the hard-headedness of the administrators proves completely inadequate in dealing with the almost insurmountable obstacles in the way of true economic development in the countries of the Third World under present circumstances. The belief in the effectiveness of a purely practical approach is rooted in a serious underestimation of the enormous *institutional* obstacles in the way of such a development throughout the Third World, and in a naïve assumption that patterns of development copied from the West are enough to perform the job. In the previous sections we have learnt to what extent the numerous practical measures advocated as panaceas are inadequate. Those applauded by Western commentators as cool-headed administrators generally lack imagination; that is to say, they have no idea of the magnitude of the task before them, which they claim to be able to solve with a few piecemeal measures, and they have no idea of the total social change that is required to get the wheels of human evolution turning again in the countries they profess to lead towards progress.

The failures of the positive approach tend, in the long run, to diminish the initial basic differences between the policies pursued by administrators and solidarity-makers. The administrators cannot refrain from using psychological devices in an effort to attain their ends. They will probably attempt to obtain a cooperative attitude from the poorer peasantry with respect to the specific measures advocated by them. If they are sincere, they may actually hope in so doing to succeed in spreading technical innovations to these people. Many of these administrators think in terms of inhibitions instead of obstacles and believe that if the psychological barriers to be found among the peasantry could be removed, their plans would work. They suppose, therefore, that the causes of the manifold failures are largely psychological. In their view, an important factor frustrating all their piecemeal policies is the peasant distrust of anything coming from official sources; a factor already mentioned earlier. The peasantry are often accused of showing lack of civic sense by responding negatively to all well-intended measures on the part of officials or other welfare workers.

However, one might argue that this peasant distrust is healthy in a society where what is being presented as welfare measures may, in fact, turn out to be a new form of exploitation. This very distrust might be regarded as a factor that could, under specific conditions, be transformed into something positive. As soon as the peasantry felt that a government or a popular movement took real interest in its basic needs and aspirations, an enormous fund of popular energy would become available. But in that case its support would go to a truly revolutionary cause. Such support is hardly to be expected in a situation where administrators operate in close alliance with the landed gentry.

This reference to a psychological approach on the part of the administrators is based on the supposition that the politicians concerned are sincere in their claim to promote popular welfare, in which case the basic reproach against them would be that their view is naïve and short-sighted. After so many postwar experiences they should have discovered that the panaceas do not work, and that all the bold new programmes advanced since President Harry S. Truman's Point Four seriously underestimate the huge institutional obstacles involved.

It is difficult, however, to go on believing in the good faith of those who advocate that a purely technical operation like the 'green revolution' could perform miracles within a few years, in the light of all the disappointing experiences caused by the institutional obstacles encountered throughout the past two decades.

Many advocates of an administrator's approach today should be well aware that they are 'betting on the strong'. They may not even be worried that the oil-stain effect is not forthcoming and is unlikely to be in the future. Some of them may simply be satisfied with the opportunities for foreign business firms and a restricted group of local officials and businessmen to profit from the facilities opened by the joint ventures allegedly intended to serve the popular masses.

iv. *Make-Believe*

It is, therefore, difficult to disengage the positive approach from a psychological one. Improved opportunities for the few may be combined with empty claims about improving the lot of 'the people' in general. Many of the gentry in Asia, when speaking about 'the people', are actually restricting this term to those who really count, in their view. Terms like community development and agrarian reform may contain a sizeable amount of hypocrisy. It is not always clear whom they intend to cheat: the poor peasants whom they would like to persuade into a more cooperative attitude, the foreign donors, or themselves.

The solidarity-makers have more imagination than the administrators in appreciating the extent of the psychological inhibitions to be surmounted. Their aim is to mobilize the masses but the basic weakness of their policies is the serious underestimation of the technical and organizational problems connected with economic development. Ex-President Sukarno, for one, dreamt of being able to solve the economic problems of his country by eliminating the impact of foreign capitalism and by welding the people together into one national unity. Sukarno certainly initiated a mobilization system – but neither he, himself, nor his assistants were clear about what they were mobilizing for.

Since populist regimes led by solidarity-makers of the Sukarno type also meet with serious failures, ultimately they must also resort to make-believe. For some time, official propaganda and indoctrination denying the true state of the economy may serve as a tranquillizer. But in the long run the remedy does not work, and the people are likely to become dissatisfied and restive. Preventive policies based on a purely psychological approach will eventually produce the contrary effect to what they originally intended to achieve. And the impossibility of achieving constructive policies through a purely political and psychological approach may make the ultimate aim – a better and more prosperous society – vanish more and more into the background. If this happens, and in the case of Sukarno it did happen, the make-believe becomes evident. As in the case of the administrators an excuse has to be found for the failures and a different psychological approach may be tried, that of diversions.

v. Religion as a Diversion

Diversions may, again, assume different forms. For many centuries, religion appeared to be the main method of keeping the people, especially in the countryside, satisfied and quiet. They could be restrained from expressions of dissatisfaction through a promise of heaven, or of a reincarnation as a being of a higher order if their behaviour was exemplary. There are still many today who consider religion to be the best antidote to 'atheist communism', and a highly efficient rostrum to gather strength against the danger of revolution.

How efficiently religion may be used as a rallying force against communists was demonstrated, some years ago, in Indonesia. The red-hunt was, to a large extent, engineered by orthodox Moslem groups, both in cities and in the countryside. The atheist character of communism was strongly stressed in the official army propaganda; Moslem students were some of the fiercest activists within the Kami student movement, although at that time many Catholics played an equally prominent role in the red-hunt. In the countryside, the cleavage between two powerful alirans, orthodox Islam and communism, coincided with the traditional opposition between orthodox Moslems (santri) and syncretists (abangan). The mass murders in East and Central Java were to a large extent due to the 'holy war' atmosphere provoked by Moslem leaders. In Hindu Bali, religion fulfilled a similar function as an effective weapon against communism.

In order to realize the immense power that Islam, in particular, has had up until now, as a kind of immunization against revolution, one needs only to take account of the fact that no predominantly Moslem country in Asia, despite apparently propitious social and economic conditions, has yet adopted communism as a leading ideology (if one excepts, of course, Moslems living within the orbit of the Soviet Union or the People's Republic of China).

But one cannot maintain that religion *as such* should be considered a lasting bulwark against social revolution, in the face of abundant historical evidence to the contrary. For example, in 1917 the Greek Orthodox Church was by no means an insurmountable obstacle to revolution in Russia. Nor was Roman Catholicism in Cuba sufficient to stem the tide of revolution.

As we have seen in an earlier chapter, religion in itself is not to be considered an ideology either favouring or opposing revolution. Although religion is currently being presented as a largely stabilizing factor in society, it may, as we have seen, contain countervalues embodying a protest against the existing hierarchical order. For a long time, religious sects were the only social protest groups of significance.

Since the second half of the eighteenth century movements of social protest, at least in the industrializing Western world, have increasingly stressed reason as opposed to religion. Religion, therefore, has become more and more associated with the establishment and with social conservatism, and become one of the pillars of the *status quo* in the world of Christianity.

In agrarian societies the situation was different, and more similar to conditions in medieval Europe. Although in pre-liberation China religion in the Confucianist form was associated with the establishment, there were many sects and currents that embodied an incipient protest against the prevalent order.[58]

Similarly, in Latin America today, Christianity increasingly assumes progressive, and sometimes even revolutionary, forms in order not to lose completely its moral appeal. Members of the Catholic and Protestant clergy in Latin America and some other countries, are gradually joining or even taking the lead in social protest movements. This is sometimes to retain a measure of influence upon the people but often out of genuine conviction; while at the same time some of the 'rationalist', atheist ideological currents are gradually becoming defenders of the prevalent social order. In a world where revolution is increasingly being incorporated into thinking of significant groups as a viable and possibly necessary road towards progress and emancipation, it is to be expected that revolutionary thoughts will also find expression within religious ideology; 'rational' atheism may easily become a part of the establishment in countries where an official rationalist ideology takes the role of a church, as in Eastern Europe.

How, then, can we explain the fact that Islam has, up till now, functioned as a real obstacle to revolutionary change? Perhaps this can partly be accounted for by the fact that in the countries of Asia and Africa, Islam, when confronted with Western Christian imperialism, became more or less identified with a progressive, nationalist trend opposing foreign political power. Therefore, the green banner of Islam could appeal to the masses as an ideology that did not appear to be tainted with the more extreme forms of imperialism and capitalism.

However, if orthodox Islam aligns itself, in the future, predominantly with conservative political and social forces, as it has done in Indonesia, and becomes or remains a staunch defender of landed interests, this will, in the long run, necessarily lead to a weakening of its appeal to the poorer sections of the peasantry.

There seems no reason to doubt that eventually the poor peasantry will revolt even in the Moslem countries of the Third World. What ideological form this revolt will take will depend upon the eventual ability of Islam to sever its connection with the establishment and to adapt itself to the revolutionary realities of tomorrow.

It does not seem that religion can lastingly perform its traditional function of a diversion, stemming the tide of 'red revolution.' On the contrary, it might be swallowed by the revolutionary upsurge and act as catalyst, in combination with non-religious ideologies.

vi. Other Diversions

There are other diversions attempted as an antidote to dissatisfaction. In the Roman Empire, bread and circuses were used to keep the melting-pot populations of the capital city quiet. Since the main shortage, in the present Third World, is food, some leaders are attempting to offer circuses alone. Eckstein writes with reason that 'no less than eschatological ideology, sport is the opiate of the masses in totalitarian countries, and not there alone'.[59]

In view of the ineffectiveness of the Roman emperors in stemming the tide of social unrest through bread *and* circuses, the new opiate is unlikely to work, even as a tranquillizer.

A popular type of diversion is the search for a scapegoat. This may be a foreign power. In Sukarno's case, confrontation with the Netherlands in order to recover West Irian could still be justified as a battle against colonial remnants, and as an excuse to attempt to crush the oppressive economic power of Dutch enterprise. But after the Irian affair had been settled in 1962, Sukarno started a new confrontation policy directed against the newly established state of Malaysia. Despite some very real reasons to oppose this new creation and the way it was called into life, this confrontation policy smacked decidedly of a diversion intended to relieve internal tensions. As we have seen, however, a war, especially a not too successful one, is more likely to produce what it was meant to prevent: a mounting dissatisfaction which spreads within the army and erupts either into revolution or into counter-revolution.

Another obvious target for diversion are minorities within a country. In particular the minorities of foreign descent specializing in trade, such as the Chinese in South-East Asia, the Indians in Burma and East Africa and Syrians in West Africa, are convenient scapegoats for a regime torn by internal tensions.

As in the case of external diversions, the scapegoat policy is not likely to delay the eruption of internal unrest for a long time. Soon the popular masses realize that the eviction or expulsion of trader groups of foreign or semi-foreign descent will not benefit them in the long run. No structural change will occur as far as the majority of the peasantry is concerned, and a restricted group of native traders will take over the former economic power position of the minority.[60] The diversion, therefore, may at best have a temporary effect only.

T–K

vii. *Repression: Right Hand and Left Hand*

If revolution cannot be prevented by positive welfare measures of the restricted piecemeal kind discussed above, and if a psychological approach is equally inoperative since it fails to satisfy material needs, there seems to remain only one medicine: repression.

However, in earlier chapters we have seen that repression is at best a 'two-edged sword'. Though it may delay revolution, in the long run it is likely to encourage it. To quote Eckstein once more:

Repression in societies with high internal war potential is little more than a narcotic intensifying the conditions it seeks to check and requiring ever larger doses to keep affairs in balance if other things are equal.[61]

However, whereas in earlier chapters we dealt only with pure repression, in the present one we are concerned with preventive policies of a more sophisticated nature. In practice, it seldom occurs that a regime relies on pure repression. There will always be attempts to combine repression either with some positive welfare measures or with psychological policies aimed at winning over at least part of the population to the side of the regime; still more probable are attempts to combine the three approaches.

Now we have to observe that all the positive or psychological policies discussed so far in practice go hand in hand with a certain modicum of repression. The amount of authoritarian rule in the countryside under a populist regime, even after democratic forms have been introduced at the central, regional, and local level, should not be underrated. Those who administer the laws on land reform, lead cooperatives, or try to introduce community development projects, are working in an atmosphere where the traditional submission to authoritarian rule is still in force. And foreign aid is generally extended to prop up the existing power structure and to safeguard the interests of both foreign investors and a landed gentry against popular discontent. The 'soft state' is often far from soft towards the poor peasantry, as soon as they attempt to take a stand and claim their most elementary rights. They are usually soft only in their dealings with the gentry who receive substantial indemnities for the land taken from them through reforms; they are also soft as far as the actual fulfilment of their paper plans is concerned.

On the other hand, even in those states where a semblance of democratic rule is no longer upheld and military dictatorship has taken its place, at least some lip service will be paid to the principles of community development and land reform, and steps will sometimes be taken to put these principles into effect. Campaigns for birth control will also be launched in such countries. And foreign aid to that type of government will, no doubt, be more readily available than to states where there is greater tolerance of popular movements (for example, the governments of Taiwan, South Korea and South Vietnam are much favoured recipients of American aid). A psychological approach will certainly be tried as being much less expensive than true welfare measures.

A most spectacular attempt to combine the three approaches was the Magsaysay policy in the Philippines during the fifties. After the 'mailed fist' policy of Manuel Roxas, relying on pure force, had miserably failed, Magsaysay, assisted by his American advisers, initiated a new approach. He tried to combine a 'right hand' policy with a 'left hand' one.[62]

The strategy would involve 'All-out Friendship or All-out Force', 'a combination of measures of military suppression and of political and economic reform'.[63]

There is agreement that Magsaysay's strategy, as far as the aim was to defeat the Huks, was, at the time, successful, though the extent of the successes and of the part played by some specific policies in securing a victory for the government may have been exaggerated.[64] The victory may not have been final. The Huks managed to accomplish a kind of resurrection, economic and social conditions have not basically changed, and repression is still much in evidence. Should we attribute this ultimate failure to President Magsaysay's premature death and to the much more conservative and less imaginative policies of his successor Carlos P. Garcia? It seems more appropriate to try to assess to what extent the 'right hand – left hand' strategy as such could be actually viewed as a promising alternative to social revolution.

It is claimed that President Magsaysay tried to introduce substantial innovations such as land reforms, community development, reclamation of new lands, and other positive measures intended to improve the economic situation in the countryside, especially in central Luzon. However, if one really considers the details of his approach, it appears that the programme, particularly the community development part of it, did not extend beyond the 'betting on the strong' approach. For a densely populated and seriously impoverished area like central Luzon such a policy cannot work. There are no indications that Magsaysay ever had in mind basically to change the prevalent power structure in the countryside or to attack the prerogatives of the rural gentry.

It is also striking that the publications hailing Magsaysay's clever strategy generally stress his 'psychological warfare', and his attempts to improve 'public relations'.[65] Most of his successful measures were in the realm of influencing the population psychologically, and in countering the Huk activity with the same type of counter-propaganda. Horlemann even observes that 'although all these measures did not bring about any modification in the existing economic evils, they certainly had a propagandistic effect, *even though it did not extend beyond the middle class*'.[66] However, unfortunately Horlemann does not produce any evidence to substantiate his statement. If this term 'middle class' is interpreted as the wealthier peasantry, this might be seen as a confirmation that Magsaysay's policy was based on the 'betting on the strong' principle, which also became evident in the community development programme he promoted. The Federation of Free Farmers equally showed the same orientation.

We are well enough informed about the right hand and we know it was heavily supported by the Americans whereas the Huks lacked any international support.[67] We are less clear about the left hand. Was it distributing real benefits to the mass of the people? Most probably these benefits were not distributed on a very significant scale, although some rather radical measures were taken, such as the establishment of a Complaints and Action Committee, the achievements of which were more than pure propaganda. On the whole, however, it could somewhat cynically be said that, along with the bombs and bullets scattered by the right hand, the left hand mostly offered pamphlets, and 'candies for the kids' whenever an army unit entered a village. And there is enough evidence to argue that, especially in central Luzon, Ramon Magsaysay did not succeed in winning over the majority of the poor peasantry.[68]

If, therefore, the situation in the Philippines is again haunted by the danger of revolution, as a superficial perusal of Manila newspapers makes abundantly clear, this is most probably due to the ineffectiveness of the Magsaysay strategy as a long-term approach.

Again, the preventive medicine may, at best, produce a delay. But authorities relying on repression against emancipation movements are doomed. Against a truly, and massively, rising peasantry, a 'whiff of grapeshot' will not ultimately work.

viii. *Conclusion*

If all known attempts to forestall revolution are, sooner or later, abortive; if it is impossible, in the larger countries of the Third World, to get the wheels of evolution turning again, without a social revolution – should we then conclude that a social revolution of the peasant type will be inevitable?

Since the most stringent problems are encountered in the large, densely populated countries of South and South-East Asia, most of whom suffer from involutionary processes, it is with the prospects for these countries that we are primarily concerned. Can we view China as a model for subsequent developments in these countries, or is it conceivable that they will remain in a situation where neither evolution nor revolution occurs, and that we could describe as a 'permanently transitional' society?[69]

In the first part of this book I have tried to demonstrate that human evolution does not take a course that can be summed up as a series of parallel developments. Both the sequence of stages and the final outcome may vary greatly. Social processes are never completely repeated, and the time factor remains an obstacle to any attempt to predict precisely on the basis of analogies.

Yet, we should not fall into the opposite trap of assuming that any country will follow its own course independently from what has happened elsewhere. This is, in my view, what Barrington Moore does when he argues that the Indian case proves that the Chinese model does not work for some types of Asian society.[70] According to Moore, China is a case where an agrarian revolution occurred, as a consequence of rural conditions typical for that country. On the other hand, in India, a country at least as poor as China, no revolution occurred and poverty remained. Evidently Moore considers what happened in India as final. He tries to demonstrate why the Indian peasants did not rebel on a massive scale, and finds a solution in several characteristics of Indian society: the fragmentation through a caste system, and a multilingual, decentralized state structure. It is, in particular, the caste system that produced a tendency to express dissatisfaction through the creation of a new caste or sub-caste, instead of seeking an alignment with other dissatisfied groups on a class basis. Moore also evidently views what I have called patronage as a social institution opposing rural rebellion through the measure of protection it provides to those who are economically weak. According to Moore, such a patron-like personal relationship between gentry and peasantry did not exist in China, but this point is open to argument.[71] Evidently Moore did not ask himself whether the difference between China and India could not be reduced, with all the necessary reservations, to a difference of phases. His study lacks an evolutionary perspective. Perhaps a peasant revolt has not yet occurred in India on a nation-wide scale because it has not yet reached the stage of cold repression. Moore himself correctly argues that, for the moment, 'a turn to the right' or, in our terminology, a counterrevolution, is more probable in India than a peasant revolution.[72] Although the rule of the postwar Congress party cannot be called populist in a true sense, there is still in India a measure of democratic freedom, and the military have, up till now, abstained from open intervention.

But the fact that the peasantry have not yet rebelled on a large scale does not at all mean that it will not do so in the future. However, before such a peasant revolution can be really successful the country may have to pass through the classical sequence of an agrarian revolution, already initiated by the Naxalite communist movement, followed by a military coup as a counter-class struggle on the part of the landed interests, accompanied by repression against the progressive forces, and then a rising tide of revolution.

Perhaps this attempt to apply the Chinese model is too crude – for example, the sequence might be seriously affected by regional separatism which might result in diverging developments in different parts of the country – but it seems more realistic than Moore's assumption that the rural population of India will never rise to claim its part in the general world movement of emancipation, which is the essence of human evolution.

Where an internal situation is permanently unstable it is unlikely that the human urge for 'safety', which is at the root of specific evolution culminating in stagnation and involution, will be able to stifle, for any length of time, the equally universal urge for a betterment of fate among the masses.

It does not seem very likely that any major country in the Third World will get stuck indefinitely in a post-traditional, yet transitional, situation and will never find its own way towards its own brand of modernity.

However, from the previous discussion it must have become clear that such modernization will never be achieved in a piecemeal manner, since modernization can only come about through a wholesale transformation of the old society.

9

Dissensions on Revolutionary Prospects and Strategy

Nothing to eat, nothing to wear,
But the enemy gives us food and clothes.
No guns in our hands, no bullets,
The enemy makes them for us to use.

We are the people who were born here,
And every inch of ground is ours.
If anyone wants to invade it,
We shall fight him to the death.

CHINESE GUERRILLA SONG

A. DIVERGENT PERSPECTIVES ON REVOLUTION

i. The Soviet 'New Look'

Chinese Marxists believe in agrarian revolution; Soviet Marxists do not. In this way one could sum up one of the basic aspects of the present Sino-Soviet rift which extends to the general attitude of the two leading communist powers towards the Third World.

However, even if this difference is accepted, one could still assume that both Soviet and Chinese Marxists are in favour of revolution as a precondition for the creation of a socialist society. Since the turn of the century communists have distinguished themselves from social democrats, whom they call 'reformists' or 'revisionists', by propagating revolution as the only road to a socialist victory, whereas the latter believed in a more gradualist, parliamentary road.

Since Stalin's death, however, it has become increasingly uncertain how far the Soviets still believe in revolution – leaving aside the question of whether it should be an agrarian, or a proletarian one – as a precondition for a socialist society as far as the Third World is concerned. In the early sixties they developed a kind of 'new look' version of Marxist theory according to which a peaceful transition towards socialism would become a real possibility, through the existence of a powerful Soviet bloc. There are two basic elements in the new Soviet theory: the concept of national democracy, held to be valid for some of the countries of the Third World and, in close connection with it, the concept of state capitalism which implies that in countries where this type of capitalism prevails both the actual situation and the potential for the future would be different from those in countries dominated by true capitalism.

It seems to me that it is the concept of state capitalism that forms the core of the new Soviet theory.

It will be hard to find one single issue where the Soviet and the Chinese views so widely diverge as in their evaluation of present trends and potential in the Third World. In view of the importance of the relationship between the Soviet Union and the People's Republic of China on the one hand and the non-aligned countries of South and South-East Asia such as India, Burma, and Indonesia, or the African countries, on the other, it seems relevant to take a closer look at the real sources of this divergence. It appears, then, that the crucial issue is the evaluation of what the Soviets, with a eulogistic overtone, call state capitalism, and the Chinese, with a derogatory connotation, bureaucratic capitalism.

The importance of this issue in the context of the Soviet view is clearly brought out in Levkovsky's study *Capitalism in India*:

At present there has emerged a large group of young states that have broken the fetters of colonialism, but have not joined the socialist camp. What is their position in the struggle between the two world systems? What will be the course of their further socio-economic and political development? Any attempt to answer these questions calls for an analysis of the new phenomena that are to be observed in the newly independent countries of the East. State capitalism ranks high in importance among these phenomena.[73]

Levkovsky's analysis coincides with a general trend in Soviet writings since about 1960. Following the declaration of 6 December 1960, issued by the Moscow meeting of representatives of communist and workers' parties,[74] Soviet publications started to develop the 'new look' of Marxist theory just described, in relation to the actual situation and future potential in the non-socialist countries of Asia, Africa and Latin America. This 'new look' was presented as an elaboration of Lenin's suggestion, made at the Second Congress of the Comintern, that a non-capitalist development towards socialism in the underdeveloped countries of Asia and Africa could be effected with the help of the proletariat of the Soviet country – a thesis that, to a certain extent, could be interpreted as a departure from the concept of a unilinear evolution which implied that the society would have to pass through the capitalist stage.

The main element of this 'new look', however, was an admission of a possibility of *peaceful*, evolutionary transition towards socialism, with the assistance of the socialist world, the Soviet Union in the first place – a possibility which Lenin never explicitly mentioned or considered. The political basis for such a peaceful, non-revolutionary, transition could be provided, according to the new Soviet theory, by the so-called 'national democracy', as a phase in which the national bourgeoisie plays an important role. According to another Soviet writer, V. I. Pavlov,

the people may enter the non-capitalist path of development only as a result of active struggle on the part of the working class and the toiling masses, of an alliance of all democratic and patriotic forces in a broad national front. National democracy is a form of government in which the unification of all the sound forces of a nation can be most successfully achieved. Reflecting as it does the interests not of any one particular class but of broad strata of people, a state of this type is called upon to consummate the objectives of the anti-imperialist, anti-feudal, democratic revolution.[75]

In a number of Soviet publications which have appeared since 1964,[76] the term 'democratic revolution' is further elaborated. The gist of the newer interpretation is that a number of countries, such as Syria and Burma, are presented as cases where such a revolutionary development has already taken place (actually as a revolution from above), and where a 'socialism' of a special type is being constructed. It is the *petite bourgeoisie* which has assumed the leadership in these 'revolutions'. But in point of fact such a 'revolution' by the *petite bourgeoisie* sometimes merely amounts to a military take-over, like that by General Ne Win in Burma in March 1962.

According to this 'newest look', which appears to have more or less overshadowed the concept of a 'national-democratic state' as developed in the early sixties, the true proletarian *social* revolution has, as it seems, completely receded into obscurity.

In advancing these innovations Lenin's name is being invoked.

But the reference to Lenin could hardly be upheld. In Lenin's opinion state capitalism appears as identical with state monopoly capitalism, whereas in his view a socialist society could be brought about only by socialist revolution. According to the Soviet re-interpretation of Marxist theory, the situation in the non-socialist developing countries of today is different. Socialism may be attained through a gradual, non-revolutionary path, or through a democratic revolution. State capitalism, which may convert a semi-colonial economy into a developed and independent national economy, is, in the Soviet view, the true potential lever for peaceful transition towards socialism, or for one effected through a democratic revolution, which may occur from above through a military take-over.

ii. *Soviet View of India and South-East Asia*

The Soviet view of Indian society, in particular, and of its prospects for the future, could be assessed as follows. There is a tendency to take a rather favourable view of Indian industrial development. Agrarian stagnation or semi-stagnation is acknowledged but not stressed as a decisive factor in India's future. Part of the industrial development and of other basic sectors of Indian business is in the hands of private capitalists. An important section of these, especially the larger businessmen, are closely tied to foreign monopolistic interests and are also striving for a monopolistic position. This negative aspect of Indian business is being labelled monopoly capitalism by Soviet authors. This private sector also attempts to encroach upon the state sector of capitalist enterprise and consequently the latter sector presents a dual character. Western imperialist influences, including those pretending to provide foreign aid, are said by these Soviet authors to aim at a strengthening of the monopolistic capitalist forces.

On the other hand, Soviet aid is largely directed towards strengthening the state sector. It is the aid from socialist countries which, according to this novel theory, could be of assistance in transforming the Indian economy in the long run into a socialist one without Indian society having to pass through all the stages of capitalist development.

When one studies such Soviet publications on the agrarian situation in India as Kotovsky's *Agrarian Reforms in India*, also published in English translation, one is struck by the sharp criticism of the agrarian reforms which are shown not to benefit the poor masses of the peasantry but only the richer farmers; and at the same time by a tendency to consider this transformation of a feudal rural society into one with strong capitalist elements as a process which should not be viewed as merely negative.[77]

Russian studies of South-East Asia in the early sixties generally conform to the same pattern. The Philippines are described as a country where monopolistic capitalism is dominant. In so far as a still weak but rising national bourgeoisie is increasingly opposing the largely American foreign interests, the Philippines present certain progressive traits. But in the Soviet literature on South-East Asia a marked distinction is made between countries such as the Philippines, Malaysia, Thailand and of course South Vietnam, where foreign or domestic monopolistic capital prevails and forces the government towards alignment with Western imperialism, and countries such as India, Burma and Indonesia (at least before the 1965 coup), where a national bourgeoisie, trying to control the state sector of the economy, plays a partly progressive role.

I. V. Vasiliev's study of *State Capitalism in Contemporary Burma* (published in 1961),[78] which has not been translated into English, expresses the generally accepted view among Soviet scholars at that time. However, even before the Untung coup in Indonesia, there was a tendency to consider the state sector of the national economy and the position of the national bourgeoisie in Burma and Indonesia to be weaker than in India, and consequently to be more likely to yield to the pressures of foreign and domestic monopolistic capital.[79]

Meanwhile, in more recent Soviet publications, Burma under General Ne Win has been promoted to a 'socialist' regime, or at least to a society taking the socialist road.[80]

iii. The Chinese Outlook

The view of the Chinese Communist Party, as far as the state sector of the economy is concerned, is diametrically opposed to that of the Soviets. In the English translations of their publications they consistently use a different term: bureaucratic capitalism. As far as I am aware there exists no elaborate theory of bureaucratic capitalism in Chinese Marxist literature comparable with the extensive treatment of state capitalism in recent Soviet literature. But the general trend of the Chinese view is quite clear: they associate this phenomenon mainly with the Kuomintang bureaucracy under Chiang Kai-shek during the thirties. The Chinese revolution was, in Mao Tse-tung's writings, consistently presented as one directed 'against imperialism, feudalism and bureaucrat-capitalism'. The national bourgeoisie is considered to be internally divided. 'The left-wingers among the national bourgeoisie who attach themselves to the working people' were considered as allies, whereas 'the few right-wingers among the national bourgeoisie who attach themselves to imperialism, feudalism and bureaucrat-capitalism' were viewed as enemies of the revolution.[81]

In the *Peking Review* of 25 December 1967 (no. 52) an article was published with the title ' "Public Sector" of Indian Economy is Scourge of the People'. The article is clearly directed against the Soviet attempt to attribute to the state capitalist sector a progressive nature, as well as against the tendency of the Indian leaders themselves who are claiming that this sector is a symbol of the socialist pattern of society. According to the Chinese view, there is no basic difference between state monopoly capitalism under bourgeois dictatorship and similar outgrowths in semi-colonial and semi-feudal countries. In such countries,

state monopoly capitalism is bound to integrate itself with foreign imperialism and the feudal landlord class at home to become bureaucrat-capitalism with comprador and feudal characteristics. This is exactly the case in India.

According to the *Peking Review* the public sector of the Indian economy, accounting for nearly half of the total capital of all Indian firms, has become 'a big mountain lying like a dead weight on the Indian people'.

In the same article, the writer attempts to refute the Soviet assertion that India could become a case of peaceful transition towards socialism. According to this article, bureaucratic monopoly capital and private monopoly capital in India are 'one and the same thing, both originating from the big compradors and big capitalists'. It is pointed out that the financial organs of the public sector provide credit for private monopoly capitalists, and supply them with cheap power and transport facilities, whereas they purchase their products at high prices. The state monopoly capital is also closely linked with feudal rajas and landlords.

The parallel with pre-liberation China under the Kuomintang regime is explicitly drawn: 'As in China before its liberation, comprador, feudal, state monopoly capitalism has become the economic foundation for the reactionary regime of the Indian Congress Party.'

Consequently, 'only by making a great revolution to overthrow the reactionary rule of the bureaucrat-comprador capitalist class and the landlord class and uprooting the regime's decadent economic base' can the Indian people attain real liberation.

Now it is evident that the harsh judgement on India is, to a certain extent, due to the political friction between that country and China. For Indonesia and Burma, the situation is hardly much different.[82] However, it is probable that, even as far as countries of the Third World are concerned having friendly relations with China at government level (as, for example, Pakistan), the appraisal would not be basically different; although in such cases the criticism would tend to be toned down in official publications, owing to foreign policy considerations. The difference with the Soviet Union might be that in the case of the Chinese such considerations would not seem seriously to affect Marxist analysis as applied to the internal dynamics within such a country. Friendly relations at the government level do not seem to preclude sympathy and perhaps even active support for revolutionary movements within such a society.

Symptomatic of the Chinese attitude is the friendly reception given to the new Japanese prime minister, Tanaka, upon his visit to China in September 1972, notwithstanding the fact that slogans were visible everywhere, denouncing the dangers of Japanese imperialism and militarism. Tanaka immediately reacted by warning that China should refrain from exporting revolution to Japan, whereupon Chou En-lai retorted that revolution was not for export, and that its occurrence was an internal affair.

iv. *Implications of Discussions on Revolutionary Prospects*

We should now assess the relevance of the divergences pointed out in relation to the central theme – revolution and evolution. The Soviet 'new look' Marxism of the early sixties implies that, after a national revolution has succeeded, a further development towards a socialist society can be brought about in an evolutionary way, if certain conditions are fulfilled: if there is a strong national bourgeoisie, opposed to foreign and domestic monopoly capital, which is building up a substantial state sector in the national economy, with a strong emphasis upon industrial development; if the mass of urban and rural workers (which means a strong Communist Party) provides effective political leadership during the transformation of society and manages to keep the contradictory tendencies inside the national bourgeoisie within bounds; and if, finally, the process of transformation is being supported by the countries within the socialist camp.

On the other hand, the Chinese stand is that nothing short of a true social revolution will accomplish the transition towards a socialist society.

What is the actual basis for the relative optimism among Soviet authors regarding the prospect for a peaceful transition in a country such as India? There does not appear to be much evidence in actual historical experience in favour of such expectations. Nearly every society which has entered the path leading towards what the Soviets call socialism, has achieved this either through revolutionary struggle or with the assistance of the Soviet army. The issue is being blurred by the newer version of the Soviet 'new look', according to which countries like Burma and Syria have already started off towards a socialist stage – but the claim that this could be effected simply by a democratic revolution enacted by the *petite bourgeoisie* testifies to a still more unwarranted optimism.

As the only exception of some significance, of how socialism could actually be achieved in a peaceful way, the Mongolian People's Republic might be cited. It is an example which frequently appears in the present-day Soviet publications, in addition to several peoples of Central Asia within the orbit of the Soviet Union.[83] It is perfectly clear that the possibilities in Mongolia, bordering on the Soviet Union and, since the end of the war, on People's China, and far removed from the impact of the United States, not to speak of peoples incorporated within the Soviet Union, could not be in any way compared to those in a country like India where American and British interests are still firmly rooted.[84] The way domestic military forces, often supported by the United States or other Western countries, have succeeded in the past few years in forestalling the introduction of even modest democratic or agrarian reforms in different countries of Asia, Africa and Latin America (one could think of Indonesia, Ghana and Brazil) appears rather to bear out the Chinese view that only through revolutionary action could the transition towards socialism be effected where capitalism is in power.

It is, on the other hand, very likely that, at least at the pinnacle of the cultural revolution, the Chinese Marxists have greatly overrated the immediate revolutionary potential in many countries outside the Western world. I would suggest that a deeper understanding of the psychological inhibitions and attitudes of submission due to the strength of traditional patronage relationships should make one more cautious in advocating armed peasant rebellion as an immediate step towards a final victory, even though in the long run it is the Chinese view that is decidedly the sounder and more realistic one. To expect, however, as the Soviets do, that a transition to socialism could be accomplished peacefully through a surrender by the progressive forces of the ultimate decisive power to the ruling bourgeoisie and their foreign allies, looks, in the light of what happened to China in the late twenties and in Indonesia, Ghana and Brazil in more recent times, like a fairy tale; even less likely is it to be achieved through a 'democratic' *petit-bourgeois* revolution from above.

But are the Soviets really that naïve? Might it not be that they are fully aware of the impossibility of either a peaceful transition or one through a revolution from above, but are only trying to retain cordial relationships with the present ruling class in India and other non-aligned countries, in particular countries like Burma and Syria, for reasons of foreign policy?[85]

The theory of the progressive state sector could also serve as a rationalization for the assistance extended by the Soviet Union to India precisely via that sector. It would be difficult to admit that all the assistance paid for by Soviet citizens is likely to be wasted as soon as the progressive tendencies have been repressed by an openly rightist regime. Another possibility is that, at the time when the 'new look' was advanced, the Soviets were so afraid of nuclear war with the United States that they were prepared to sacrifice truly leftist revolutionary possibilities in the Third World if this would avert the danger of American intervention with the inherent eventuality of escalation into nuclear war.

Still, it would be rash to attribute the Soviet 'new look' Marxist theory to sheer opportunism. The over-optimistic evaluation of present trends within Indian society might also damage the Soviet position *vis-à-vis* important sections of Indian society that increasingly oppose the present regime. The Soviet Union is a country where, in matters of major political significance, hardly any clear divergence is allowed between official policy and Marxist theory as expounded in universities and scholarly publications. Consequently, the apology provided by Soviet writers for present Soviet policy by stressing the national democracy prospects of peaceful transition or the democratic or socialist aspects of a regime like that of General Ne Win, may seriously impair the image of the Soviet Union as a protector of the underdog.

Therefore, I would suggest that the Soviet 'new look' is not simply a matter of expediency, but of actual belief in the new theory. It is remarkable how much attention Soviet authors pay to the industrial development of India, and how restricted their knowledge of the Indian countryside is. In my opinion, the absence of field research in its true sense in rural parts of South and South-East Asia on the part of Soviet scholars accounts for a defective knowledge of actual conditions there, despite the stereotype to the contrary popularized by *The Ugly American*.[86] The interpretation by Soviet scholars of the developments in the Indian countryside as a gradual transition towards capitalistic relationships, with a prospect of further evolutionary growth,[87] testifies to a lack of insight into the actual tendencies in many areas, most of all the densely populated ones.

A bureaucracy, closely cooperating with the rural gentry, cannot possibly fulfil the progressive role assigned to it by the Soviet theorists. The parallel with China under Chiang Kai-shek's rule is much more plausible. It becomes more and more questionable whether the Soviet Marxists can be called revolutionaries any more; this is why the Chinese label them 'modern revisionists'. Of course the 'new look' concerning the Third World is only one aspect of the more general tendency of the Soviet state to become part of the world establishment, and therefore to become ever less susceptible to true revolutionary thought.

The Chinese stand regarding revolutionary prospects seems at present somewhat ambiguous. At the time of the cultural revolution the Chinese stand was generally interpreted as an endorsement of revolutionary outbursts all over the world, strongly contrasting with the Soviet stand. Lin Piao's formula of a worldwide insurrection of the 'countryside' against the 'cities' was mostly taken as a support for any revolution in the Third World, regardless of the danger of American intervention. In his view it was precisely the spread of revolutionary outbursts all over the world which could seriously weaken American power and, thus, prevent a nuclear war through exposing the 'paper tiger'.

However, maybe in point of fact Lin Piao's strategy, endorsed by Mao in 1965, was from the outset primarily a symptom of restraint rather than of a rash, revolutionary strategy. It has been pointed out that China's endorsement of revolutionary struggles all over the world did, by no means, imply a direct military intervention on the part of China in the Vietnam war.[88] Their support was largely of a material and moral kind.

Except for a short period at the pinnacle of the cultural revolution (in 1967), in diplomatic practice the Chinese have shown a cautiousness which sometimes appeared to reduce the difference with the Soviet attitude to one only of degree.

It is not yet clear to what extent the elimination of Lin Piao and the present criticism in China of anything labelled 'ultra-leftist' should be interpreted as a reversal of Chinese international policy from a largely revolutionary one towards one in which considerations of Chinese national interest prevail. It seems clear enough, however, that China has become selective as regards the revolutionary movements it is prepared to support. Whereas revolutionary movements in Indo-China are still being firmly supported – although not to the point of provoking the danger of a direct military clash with the United States – other movements are being considered as 'ultra-leftist' and therefore not worthy of support; as for example in the case of Ceylon. However, it seems that the Chinese strategy towards revolutions in the Third World is also influenced by a tendency to view the Soviet Union as no less an external danger than the USA, to say the least. It seems clear that in China, in the long run, diplomacy may clash with the revolutionary principles accepted in theory.

B. DIVERGENT REVOLUTIONARY STRATEGIES

v. The Cuban and the Chinese Model

If the Chinese stand is to be interpreted as a prescription for everyone to follow the Chinese model – which I doubt – there are other true revolutionaries who warn against the easy assumption that a model which was successful at one time in one part of the world can simply be copied elsewhere. This caveat is the leading theme of Régis Debray's *Revolution in the Revolution*. What he means by this title is that the concept of revolution needs a continuous renewal, to adapt it to the specific surroundings where it is to take place and the tactical requirements dictated by the circumstances. Neither the Russian nor the Chinese model is suitable for the countries of Latin America where a completely different situation prevails. Yet, there is a tendency among revolutionaries to copy the last revolution. It is the same with generals who tend to copy the last war.[89]

The logical conclusion from Debray's argument would be that the guerrilla movement in each of the Latin American countries should develop its own tactical and strategic plan in accordance with the prevalent social, political, and military conditions. Unfortunately, this is the last thing Debray advocates. What he actually seems to recommend is ... blindly to follow the latest revolutionary model: Castro's. As if there were no basic differences between Cuba under Batista and other Latin American countries today; and as if what was possible in 1958 would still be viable ten years later, after the United States government had fully revised its policy towards revolutionary movements.

To quote Peter Worsley (in a lecture on 'Revolutionary Theory: Che Guevara and Régis Debray'):[90] 'It is clear that the enemy in 1968 is not the enemy that the twelve survivors of the Granma faced in Batista's Cuba in 1958, two days after they landed in the Sierra Maestra.' Worsley quotes Debray himself who has pointed out in another publication[91] that 'the revolution has revolutionized the counter-revolution. ... Cuba has raised the material and

ideological level of imperialist reaction *in less time than that of the
revolutionary vanguard.*'

Worsley also points towards other significant differences between Cuba yesterday and Latin America today:

The Cuban rebels even enjoyed at times a limited degree of support
from some other Latin American governments, initially. But today,
the President of Costa Rica no longer sends arms to guerillas as he
did to the 26th July Movement, nor does finance and military equipment come from Venezuela with official or quasi-official approval.
(Initially, too, British, French and some American journalists gave
Cuba a good press). Two years later, Cuba was fighting for its life
against an invasion launched from Nicaragua, and mild reforms in
the Dominican republic evoked instant invasion from American
Marines.[92]

However, the most basic difference is, of course, that the United
States government did not do much to support Batista; there was,
in the US, originally some sympathy with Castro; only after
Castro had introduced radical reforms and had proved that he was
not for sale did the US decide to treat Cuba as an enemy, which
resulted in driving Castro towards Marxism and, as a consequence,
towards cordial relations with, and assistance from, the big two of
the communist world. In these circumstances, it was highly unrealistic to expect that the Cuban miracle could be repeated in
1967, in a country like Bolivia. To quote Worsley once more:

The implications of these changes in the equation are clear. They
are not that revolution is impossible: an infinitely greater American
effort in Vietnam has been a signal failure. But it is going to be
infinitely more difficult than it ever was in Cuba. It is surely symbolic
that Guevara is dead, and that Debray has thirty years* in which to
reflect upon the accuracy of his theoretical model.[93]

There are several respects in which Debray's model, and Guevara's tactical approach, differ from the Chinese (and Vietnamese)
example, even though both models are built on the concept of a
strategic guerrilla basis in the interior of the country, from where
the revolution has to spread over ever larger areas in order to

*Debray has now been released from prison.

conquer, in the last phase, the urban centres. It is Worsley, again, who has clearly demonstrated the enormous difference between the two models:

It should be clearly noted though, that what the Chinese Communists did, though involving *guerilla* warfare proper on a great scale, was something rather different from what happened in Cuba. The Chinese strategy involved the establishment of a very large liberated area as a base from which the rest of the country could ultimately be won. Moreover, very large forces were involved, including whole military units up to the level of divisions, some of which had defected from the Kuomintang, others of which had been trained by the Communists before and after the Long March. They administered an enormous and populated territory no matter how marginal it was. [Here Worsley has the liberated territory around Yenan, in the northern Shensi province, in mind.W.] All this, then, is a far cry from the tiny, constantly moving groups of five to fifteen men which Guevara posits as the module for the Latin American guerilla band.

The possession of a liberated territory has profound implications. Isolation itself gives security. This security can be exploited to proselytise among the peasants to commence land and other social reforms, to train armies.[94]

vi. Focismo *or Party Leadership*

The difference between the two models appears in several distinctive features which will be discussed in subsequent sections. Debray's theoretical model, generalizing from the Cuban experience, posits *military* leadership and discipline as the organizational basis, instead of a communist party with a *civilian* leadership. Revolution has to spring from actual fighting experience, not from ideological concepts adopted by a party apparatus that may be far removed from actual fighting (it is this aspect which appears to be the central idea of what Castrists, and Debray in their wake, call *focismo* – the philosophy of *action*, concentrated in small fighting units, guerrilla *foci*, as the basic revolutionary element). On the other hand, the Chinese communists firmly cling to Mao's precept: 'The Party commands the gun and the gun must never be allowed to command the Party.' This adage stressing the supremacy of the party *vis-à-vis* the army has gained new strength in the wake of the latest developments culminating in the elimination of Lin Piao, whereas in the course of the cultural revolution the balance of power appeared to shift in favour of the military.

For several countries of Latin America to disengage revolutionary action from party leadership may be essential, especially as far as parties are concerned which are mainly based on trade unionist activities among urban workers, or which, through the precarious position of a party leadership situated semi-legally in an urban environment, may be too prone to concluding compromises with the authorities. How real this risk may be was proved in the Philippines in 1950. There the Huks, through convening a top committee meeting in Manila, allowed their leadership to be collectively caught and imprisoned by the authorities.[95] On the other hand, for the Chinese or Vietnamese type of party leadership, this disadvantage does not hold. They were well established in rural areas outside the actual authority and power of the counter-revolutionary forces.

Focismo as an ideology attaches much importance to revolutionary purity. It is opposed to policies of compromise and this is one of the reasons why both Guevara and Debray insist on political leadership by the supreme commander of the guerrilla, who will be able to let a strategic viewpoint prevail. This was one of the points where an attempt at an agreement between Guevara and the secretary of the Communist Party of Bolivia, Mario Monje, failed.[96]

vii. *Temporary Alliances*

Regular party leadership may furnish a revolutionary movement with much more room for tactical changes and manoeuvring. It has been one of the main strengths of Mao's policy that he was able at times to alternate his strategy of revolutionary struggle with one of compromise and temporary truce, if this could promote the ultimate aim. A combined struggle against a common enemy (the Japanese) could distinctly reinforce both the moral and the material position of his movement, if he took care not to lose the basis of his strategically strong position (his revolutionary army, and the liberated area as a territorial basis). In such circumstances even temporary deals with military leaders (for example, in 1936 with Chang Hsueh-liang, who allowed the kidnapping of Chiang Kai-shek in Sian) could be useful.

As with war, revolution is a real political instrument; 'a continuation of political transactions, an accomplishment of them by different means'[97] to vary Von Clausewitz's expression. This means that a rigid and dogmatic adherence to purity, and to an exclusively military point of view, would greatly weaken the revolutionary potential of a movement. If compromises are, under certain circumstances, justifiable, there must be cases in which coalitions with other groups and parties become practicable. But in Debray's model there is hardly any place for such coalitions. Hesitancy to enter coalitions is understandable. There are too many cases, in revolutionary history, where coalitions have led to treason and catastrophic defeat at the hands of the former coalition partners. Chiang Kai-shek's murderous attack on the communists who had earlier concluded an alliance with the Kuomintang under Sun Yat-sen is a case in point. So is the defeat of the Indonesian Communist Party at the hands of the army, supported by its former Nasakom partners in 1965. Aidit's contacts with a group of rebellious officers (the Untung group) in 1965 only endangered and worsened the position of the PKI because it had no military power of its own, since it lacked anything like a guerrilla basis.

We should now examine the reasons for such failures. In fact, the alliance of the Chinese Communist Party with the Kuomintang in the twenties had been concluded in accordance with the views of the Russian advisers of Sun Yat-sen. Under Stalin's influence the Comintern, at that time, advocated the so-called 'Bloc Within' strategy. This implied that the communist parties in the agrarian world of Asia, where there was no industrial proletariat strong enough to carry through a socialist revolution, had to ally themselves with bourgeois nationalist movements that were also revolutionary but did not aim at a complete overhaul of the social order. Individually the communists were, moreover, to enter and influence the large nationalist parties. Through these tactics they could attempt to help the bourgeois nationalists to victory and, at a later stage, to conquer the nationalist movement and to transform it into a socialist one. According to Stalin, the bourgeois nationalist movement was to be squeezed like a lemon and then thrown away.[98]

The basic assumption of this method of reasoning was that the agrarian countries of Asia should pass through a capitalist phase, which the bourgeois nationalists aimed at bringing about. A struggle for socialism had to be postponed until the bourgeois revolution had gained a victory and inaugurated a capitalist order.

Unfortunately for the Chinese communists, it was not they who outwitted the Kuomintang, but Chiang Kai-shek who outwitted them. He used them to carry him as a victorious commander-in-chief as far as Shanghai and Hankow. At the very moment when they started to claim their share in the victory, he turned against them and transformed the Chinese economic order not into a truly bourgeois capitalist but into a bureaucratic capitalist one which remained fully dependent upon the landed interests of the gentry which supported him, and upon foreign monopolies.

The Nasakom coalition of the Indonesian PKI was basically no different. Though the PKI was, at that time, considered to follow the Chinese line, the Nasakom coalition was, in fact, rather in conformity with the 'Bloc Within' formula advocated formerly by Stalin, and now reformulated by the Soviets as part of the 'national democracy' strategy. Here again the coalition was, in the long run, disastrous for the communists who did not possess arms and were consequently the weaker party within the coalition. Adherence to legality could only work as long as Sukarno's populist regime lasted. As soon as the PKI truly embarked upon a more revolutionary policy, in supporting peasant unrest, the former partners assisted by the army were able to crush them.

The defeat of the Chinese communists during the twenties was the reason why Mao Tse-tung developed a new theory of coalitions. According to his concept, a communist party is entitled to conclude coalitions, for example with parties representing the national bourgeoise; but on condition that the communist party will maintain the leadership of the movement and remain the stronger partner. This type of coalition has also been successfully applied by the communists within the National Liberation Front in Vietnam.

Mao's strategy is based on his view that although an immediate transition towards socialism is impossible, yet no capitalist phase needs to be allowed to precede a socialist revolution. The national bourgeoisie may play a positive role in bringing about a new democracy; but the communists have to maintain leadership in order to be able, immediately after the creation of a new democracy, to proceed on the revolutionary road towards socialism.[99]

It seems that the Chinese model of concluding coalitions does not present the same weaknesses as a 'Bloc Within' policy, and could not be simply discarded as a deviation from the revolutionary road.

Although the purism of Debray's model appears opposed to the idea of temporary alliances and compromises, yet it should be remembered that Castro also made openings to military people after he had already established a guerrilla basis, in order to speed up the decomposition of the army as an instrument of state power.[100]

viii. Guerrilla and Peasants

A third, and most basic distinction between the Chinese and the Cuban model, is, of course, a different approach toward the peasantry. For Mao it is a basic principle that 'the revolutionary is like the fish in the peasant sea: he is supported by the medium in which he lives'.

To quote Worsley again:

The guerilla Army not only establishes its own security by securing a liberated zone: it also provides it for the peasantry of that zone, who are no longer subject to landlord police, counter-insurgency forces, warlord armies, and all the varieties of repressive agents who intervene and make their land a battleground. Military security in turn produces that psychological assurance which political propaganda reinforces: then the peasant feels confident enough, in Mao's graphic phrase, to 'stand up'. Ideologically secure, and socially supported by Army, Party and society, he is prepared to place the revolution before everything.[101]

Further on in his article, Worsley contrasts Mao's prescriptions about the need to go to the masses, and try to help them solve their problems, with Debray's warning that guerrilleros have to 'avoid going to the villages'; that they have to observe 'constant vigilance, constant distrust, constant mobility', as the three golden rules; and that 'a given group of armed propagandists should abandon all hope of remaining unnoticed, "as fish in water" '.[102] Worsley admits that these prescriptions of Debray's are meant for the *first* phase of a guerrilla struggle. But he rightly remarks that 'it becomes increasingly difficult to see how the move from "absolute nomadism" to cleared autonomous zone is to be made today, and Debray has no theoretical answers.'[103]

Worse was that Guevara, fighting in Bolivia, had no practical answers. If one thing became clear from his diary it is that, although every time, in his monthly general short surveys, he deplored it, he saw no possibility at all of establishing any real contact with the peasant population.

Evidently, the aim of the guerrilla strategy, according to Debray and Guevara, was in the first place to show the weakness of the government apparatus and thus to shake the peasants' allegiance to official authority. This is why the revolutionary struggle should be fought primarily on the basis of military force.

Of course, as a general rule this cannot be enough. If we take account of the importance of patronage relationships in tempering the peasantry's revolutionary fervour, it is clear that a much more positive policy is needed than a show of force alone to win them over to the struggle. It is quite possible that in Cuba the general dissatisfaction with the Batista government was such that the peasantry were willing to follow any opponent of the government. Moreover, the government was, from a military point of view, very weak. But it would be highly unrealistic to assume that revolutionary guerrillas could ever hope to enlist significant support among the peasantry without first having come to know them and having tried, patiently and with political insight, to disengage them from patronage ties and to show them, through collective action, the prospects of a transfer of loyalty towards organizations based on a new solidarity on a class basis.

Does this mean that, instead of the Cuban, it is the Chinese model that should prevail? Again a caveat is needed. The situation in many Latin American countries is very different from that in China, as Debray repeatedly takes care to point out. Even many populous countries of Asia do not have the geographic possibilities for a development of vast, mountainous guerrilla territories like the one in Shensi province. The Indonesian communists who, after the abortive coup of 1965, have tried to apply the Chinese strategy in densely populated Java have experienced difficulty in following the Chinese model, under quite different geographical conditions.

Yet, although any revolutionary experiment should be adapted to the local conditions in a creative way, it should at the same time take cognizance of, and learn from, the experiences of past revolutions, both successful and unsuccessful. The Cuban model might appear inapplicable in Latin America today – but its lesson of what human devotion and courage can achieve is unique in world history. Che Guevara's failure in Bolivia will not be lost either, both for its example of human greatness and for the object lesson it provides on the weaknesses of *focismo*.

Perhaps the most important model for the Third World will be the successful revolutionary struggle in Vietnam, against a seemingly overwhelming foreign power. Yet, even here the rule will apply that revolutionaries should never repeat the last revolution.

Learning from the lessons of history is extremely difficult. Great revolutionaries have been successful in doing so. Marx and Engels studied the causes of the failing revolutions in 1848 and 1871; Lenin learned from the 1905 revolution; Mao from 1927; so should Latin American revolutionaries learn from the failure of Guevara in Bolivia.

If, however, as Debray seems to advocate, one single historical case is preferred as a model to be more or less slavishly copied for an entire continent, the example will not serve as a stimulant, but rather as an obstacle.

ix. *International Solidarity*

There is one final point in which Guevara's and Castro's concept shows a distinctive feature. They want the revolutionary movement to transcend national borders and to be based on international solidarity. Castro, in his preface to Guevara's *Bolivian Diary*, criticized the Communist Party leader Monje for having wished to let a national Bolivian standpoint prevail. Again, from a point of view of revolutionary purity, Guevara's view is only logical. In practice, his guerrilla band in Bolivia was international. The point of view that the interests of the people of the different countries of Latin America are similar and closely connected is also true.

Yet, it is questionable whether this international approach is the most promising one if the main aim is to enlist wider popular, and especially peasant, support. It is very doubtful that the people themselves are politically mature enough to understand an international type of movement. It is even possible that in order to convince the peasantry of a given region one should mainly employ local revolutionaries who speak the peasant's dialect and know his situation.

Since, moreover, the opposition of Latin Americans to the power of the US is largely a nationalist one, it is possible that a much larger movement could be enlisted by the guerrilla fighters if they based themselves primarily on a national liberation ideology.

Yet, international solidarity remains a highly important aspect in the process of world revolution. In view of the international character of counter-revolution, it is only too obvious that revolutionaries throughout the world cannot content themselves with the slogan that revolution is not an export article. However, a precondition for a realization of international solidarity is an attempt to study and understand other revolutionaries' views and approaches and to try to free oneself from the chauvinism inherent in advocating one's own approach and one's own experiences as the only road towards success.

10

Social Revolution and After

In a society like China's, revolution can be a fundamental and entirely natural fact of life, as hard to slow up as a pregnancy.

GRAHAM PECK

The most important thing is to prevent the emergency of revisionism during the period of socialism, in order to avoid a reversal of the revolution.

MAO TSE-TUNG

i. *Economic Achievements*

What happens after a successful revolution?

We are here particularly concerned with the effects of social revolutions of the type we are confronted with in the present non-industrial world. If we were to limit ourselves to agrarian revolutions in a more restricted sense, the only models we could use as a starting point for our discussion would be China and North Vietnam, and to a certain extent also Mexico in the more remote past, and Outer Mongolia, North Korea, and Cuba in more recent times. However, since Russia was also predominantly agrarian when the revolution of 1917 broke out and stretched far into Asia, it seems only logical to include the Soviet Union in our discussion; the more so since the after-effects of a communist revolution are still being largely judged, by many people, by what is known about the aftermath of the revolution in Russia. In view of their huge size and unique importance for the overall world situation my discussion will be largely centred on the two giants of communist power: the Soviet Union and China.

As far as the economic consequences of the Russian Revolution are concerned, there is no question any more of denying that the Soviet Union has entered, since that time, an era of rapid modernization and industrial development. We have seen in part one that there are still attempts, like Walt W. Rostow's,[101] to argue away a causal relationship between the revolution and the period of rapid economic progress following it; there have been attempts to minimize the Soviet economic successes on account of serious failures as far as agrarian production is concerned – a weakness that appeared to have been largely overcome in the past few years but made itself felt again in 1972. On the whole, however, one has to admit that communism as a political system is able to serve as an alternative path to industrial and technological progress, in itself not necessarily less effective than the Western one of liberal democracy. It could even be claimed that, since 1900, it has become the only practicable method for non-industrial countries.

As far as China is concerned, unanimity is less pronounced. The communist experiment in China is, up to now, of shorter duration. The difficulties that had to be surmounted in order to get economic development under way were, in view of the huge population densities in some parts of the country and the incredibly low level of *per capita* production in the whole countryside, tremendous even in comparison with those in Russia at the time of the revolution. Consequently, the general technological and industrial level of China is still far below one to be found in industrial countries; and China's achievements can only be fully appreciated if one views them against the background of her own, rather recent, past. Moreover, the relative isolation of China, and the reluctance of her authorities during the past decade to provide national production statistics (until Chou En-lai recently released some to Edgar Snow), and the American policy which prevented until very recently any American national from visiting the country, together with a host of anti-propaganda material from Washington, Taipei, Hongkong, and in recent years also from Moscow and Belgrade – all these factors have combined to contribute to a rather general picture of China according to which it is still a country of hunger and general misery. Only slowly is 'the curtain of ignorance'[105] being torn away.

Those who are more or less informed about China are fully aware that the achievements in this country in the fields of both agrarian and industrial production are nothing short of miraculous; against the background of China's own past and the trends of stagnation in neighbouring countries of South and South-East Asia, the Chinese successes in the economic and technological field are no less impressive than Russia's during the period between the two world wars.[106]

If one looks for a causal connection between revolutions and ensuing material successes and achievements, one could maintain that it is mainly to be looked for in the psychological sphere. As I already indicated in chapter six, when dealing with the effects of revolutions, a social revolution in which large masses of the population are involved releases huge resources of popular energy and directs them towards reconstruction and collective action. Unlike the purely psychological approach dealt with in chapter eight, which largely rests on make-believe, psychological devices are here used as concomitants of fundamental institutional change, as part of an overall strategy. The sentiment of being, at long last, acknowledged as human beings enjoying full equality and the many indications that the new, revolutionary authorities have embarked upon a policy to be pursued in favour of the poor masses, produce a positive attachment and an inclination to make an extra effort. One could use for this post-revolutionary approach the term 'mobilization system' coined by David Apter. The difference with the 'mobilization system' as applied by Sukarno and other populist leaders is that economic reconstruction and the fight against poverty and hunger receive high priority.

In China, this popular fervour was, to a large extent, due to radical agrarian reforms effected either in the course of the revolution or soon afterwards. In view of the serious fragmentation of land, a redistribution of landed property among former tenants or poor peasants could hardly be expected appreciably to increase agricultural production. Holdings remained marginal and uneconomic, and consequently there was little scope for introducing technological innovations and still less for introducing mechanical tools. Yet, the awareness of having become owners of the land they worked was enough incentive for an increased effort, resulting in higher productivity. The temporary gain in available food crops achieved through this production increase provided the new regime with the breathing space needed for developing other sectors of the economic system. It equally provided the communist leaders with the goodwill needed to introduce, in several phases, a collectivized rural economy which promised larger surface units, improved technology and, consequently, higher yields.

Despite the serious reverses during the bad years (1959–61) following the disequilibrium produced by the Great Leap Forward, the general trend of the Chinese economy has been steeply upward, in complete contrast with the trend in nearly all the countries of the Third World south of China, where the 'Asian Drama' has been unfolding.

Developments in China may be contrasted with those in Mexico, after the revolution of 1910. After a few years the peasant armies led by Zapata, 'the apostle of the peasants', succeeded in obtaining significant land reforms. Since, however, these were not accompanied by a wholesale overhaul of the economic structure and power relationships and the *hacienda* system was essentially left untouched, the revolution finally got stuck in a resurgence of social and economic inequalities in the countryside. Agrarian reforms which are not integrated in an ideology of overall social transformation may only produce an effect like the *jacqueries* in the Middle Ages or the peasant revolts in imperial China: a temporary relief from oppressive rule, without significant lasting results. The Mexican experience exemplifies the possibility that a peasant revolution aiming only at agrarian reforms as a final objective is bound to end up in a Thermidor-like restoration. In other Latin American countries like Bolivia where substantial land reforms have been attempted, a similar development could to a certain extent be observed.[107]

ii. *The Issue of Freedom in the Soviet Union*

If, however, we have to admit that a radical social revolution exceeding the limited aim of agrarian reforms may produce remarkable results in the material and economic field, does this imply that the successes achieved by the revolution will outlast the first years of euphoria and enthusiasm?

Here we have to remember how Hannah Arendt stressed that in the idea of revolution the struggle for greater freedom is more essential than an effort for economic and technological progress. She rightly observed that, both in the United States and in the Soviet Union, there is a tendency to forget that the two revolutions which were the foundation of the present political system in each country were aimed not only at material progress, but at greater freedom for the people. In her view this forgetfulness is symptomatic of the present state of mind, both among certain Marxists and among those Americans who pretend to be democrats, but do not like to be reminded of the Bill of Rights.[108]

The concept of evolution elaborated in the present work makes this issue still more fundamental. I advanced, in the first part of this book, the view that the basic criterion for evolution is *emancipation*, that is: liberation. If revolution is considered to be an accelerated process of evolution, its outcome should necessarily also be emancipation, that is to say, liberation. How can this be reconciled with the strong element of oppression inherent in any regime born out of communist revolution, an element which is openly acknowledged in the term: dictatorship of the proletariat?

For Barrington Moore, a communist revolution does not engender greater freedom, even though it may create a modern industrial society. The end of his book does not present any true perspective for the future. He asks whether the final result of modernization is not bound to be lack of freedom. The only difference, in his view,[109] is that whereas liberal democracy ends up in oppression of other peoples, the communist road towards modernity ends up in oppression of their own people.

Now, a tendency towards renewed bondage is certainly present, and under communist regimes even strong. The question as to what extent the two great communist revolutions have brought about emancipation is legitimate enough. It is, in particular, the extreme harshness of Stalinist rule that impels us to ask searching and fundamental questions. Still, even for Russia one could claim that acording to the emancipation criterion the harvest of revolution was, on the balance, positive rather than negative. We have to consider that revolutions of the type discussed in this part of the book always occur in societies under a harsh, authoritarian regime. In such societies the mass of the population suffers under heavy oppression. Revolution can only succeed because there are broad layers of the population for whom conditions are unbearable. Freedom, a certain amount of material well-being, and educational facilities exceeding the most elementary level, are only available to a thin layer of the population.

It is against this background that the issue of emancipation has to be considered. We have at least to admit that, if lack of freedom according to our criteria in several actual cases is a characteristic of the post-revolutionary situation, it has also been a characteristic of pre-revolutionary society. The worst we could say is that the revolution did *not* bring about the type and amount of freedom considered essential by those living in certain parts of the industrial world.

The ideology of the dictatorship of the proletariat insists that, whereas in the pre-revolutionary situation a small minority oppressed a large majority, after the revolution it is the small minority of former oppressors that is being oppressed by the large majority. Of course, this rationalization does not fit the facts. If we review especially the course of events in Russia, we may conclude that, after a rather short period of enlarged democratic freedoms, the dictatorship gradually assumed forms, especially under Stalin's rule, which resulted in the oppression of several groups that could by no means be identified as former oppressors themselves.

But this does not yet imply that, as far as emancipation is concerned, the Russian revolution had completely missed its target. The irregular, discontinuous course of the emancipation process which is the essence of human evolution has been discussed in part one. Even apart from the fact that emancipation is never an unambiguous process, and that new freedoms necessarily imply new liabilities and new restrictions (for example obligations towards landlords being replaced by those towards collectivities, or society as a whole), it is clear that for large groups of Russian society traditional disabilities were removed by the revolutionary upsurge. The first years brought serious dislocation and food shortages which were, to a significant extent, imputable to the First World War, succeeded by foreign intervention. Then followed a period of rapid development in the field of urban industry which, in connection with the role attributed to the working class under socialism, appreciably strengthened the position of industrial labour, both morally and materially. For them there was, undeniably, a significant degree of emancipation from previous disabilities, even though trade unions in the Western sense were not forthcoming.

Another important aspect of emancipation was the rapid spread of educational facilities. Under Tsarism and the domination of the Greek Orthodox church, education had remained restricted to a minority. In the countryside, in particular, illiteracy prevailed. The rapid spread of education in accordance with the revolutionary ideology of popular enlightenment has done more than any other single measure to free the mass of the people from bondages keeping them shackled under Tsarism. It may be true that from a Western, liberal point of view, an education which is strongly connected with a distinct party ideology could not be reconciled with the principle of freedom of thought and expression considered basic in many industrial countries. Yet, the ability to read in itself, and the concomitant broadening of interest and perspective through acquaintance with Marxist ideas, together with a highly increased level of technical knowledge and ability, were certainly conducive to a state of mind that would not indefinitely remain satisfied with ready-made answers imposed by a powerful party machine and enforced by an omnipotent secret police. The spread of education since the revolution has led to many more people in the Soviet Union asking searching questions about all kinds of problems; they are no longer satisfied with the crude replies that dogmatic Marxists imposed during Stalin's era. Here, again, emancipation has clearly been on the advance, though not without temporary reverses and relapses, since the Tsarist pre-revolutionary regime with a secret police, the *ochrana*, providing a model for the terror of the GPU during the Stalinist era.

One could ask whether it was really the 1917 revolution that contributed to the fitful and uneven course of emancipation in post-revolutionary Russia. It could also be argued that the same type of emancipation would have occurred with less friction if, instead of being shaken by a socialist revolution, the country had embarked upon the journey towards modernization and industrial development along the lines of Western democracy; that is to say if the bourgeois revolution of February 1917 had not been followed by the socialist October revolution.

Although any attempt at establishing causal relationships amounts to a comparison between what really happened with what could have happened if one factor had been missing from the course of events ('if' in history, in Sidney Hook's terminology),[110] it is very doubtful whether this type of question could be rightly asked in connection with the occurrence of a social revolution. My argument suggests that the type of social revolution dealt with in this part of my study only occurs under definite, rather narrowly circumscribed, conditions. It is severe repression in a predominantly agrarian, traditional society that is typical of countries where this type of social revolution can occur, all other roads towards evolution being blocked. It is not by mere chance that attempts to introduce purely democratic reforms fail. Moreover, foreign capitalist interests, mainly concentrated in the raw materials sector exploited for the benefit of the industrial countries, are opposed to a gradual process of industrial development. This is why dictatorial measures, restricting the power of both foreign interests and a landed gentry, are a precondition, in countries of this type, for real modernization. Therefore a comparison with other types of modernization, suitable for different societies under different conditions, is not very relevant.

The final judgement as to what extent the Russian revolution has really furthered emancipation will rest on criteria which undeniably contain a subjective element. It is difficult to balance against each other, in quantitative terms, the groups that are enjoying greater freedoms and those that feel oppressed by communist dictatorship. It is equally impossible to draw up a balance between, for example, the enlargement of interests and vistas due to rapidly spreading popular enlightenment, and the suffering caused by the terrorism of the secret police and other organs of suppression. We should, for that matter, be careful before assuming that this terror was experienced by the whole population of the Soviet Union, before and after the Second World War. It is possible that the persecution threatened restricted social groups only, particularly urban ones. The terror, in the early thirties, against the *kulaks* (strong peasants) could not be viewed as a terror directed against the peasantry as a whole.

We have not yet specifically touched upon the problem of emancipation in connection with the rural population of the Soviet Union. As we have seen earlier, Moore advances an extreme view, though not especially in connection with the Soviet Union: he states that a communist revolution, although carried out with appreciable assistance on the part of the peasant population, would result in an ultimate destruction of the peasantry as a class.[111] He evidently views the elimination of the peasantry as an inevitable result of industrial development under whatever conditions.[112] Furthermore he particularly mentions the harshness towards the broad masses with which the process of modernization was carried out in the Soviet Union under Stalin. Elsewhere he even speaks of 'a dying class'. I find that there is some lack of clarity in Moore's remark. Certainly a peasantry transformed into salaried workers on collective farms cannot be called 'a dying class'. What he apparently means is that the peasantry under communism suffer from discrimination on the part of the authorities and are subject to all kinds of repression. But it seems to me that if this is what he implies his assessment is very one-sided, even for the Soviet Union. Since the balance for the peasantry, in connection with the emancipation issue, is of the greatest importance for an evaluation of the success of the Russian revolution, and since at the time of the revolution the peasantry constituted a large majority, as in China and the Third World today, I would like to dwell upon this theme for a while.

It seems undeniable that for the majority of the rural population the balance of the revolution has been positive. It is true that collectivization, during the thirties, met with fierce resistance from important sections of the rural population, which negatively affected both grain harvests and cattle herds. It is also true that during the persecution of the *kulaks* many suffered who could not be called wealthy landowners and exploiters in any reasonable sense. It is finally true that Soviet agriculture has suffered in the past from many deficiencies, which have been mostly attributed, by foreign observers, to the forced collectivization and the ensuing lack of incentive for individual agriculturists. There is also no doubt that resistance to collectivization has remained rather strong, and that an attitude among *kolkhoz* members of stressing the private plot and private selling on the market has been regularly reported and criticized in the Soviet press.

Yet, it is hardly to be doubted that since the start of the collectivization programme rural technology, the standard of living, and the cultural levels have enormously improved. If one were to assert that in the Soviet Union the peasants as a class have disappeared, this would be correct only in the sense that a well-paid worker in a collective farm can hardly be called a peasant any more. Even if it is true that total grain production in the Soviet Union suffered stagnation for many years, it cannot be denied that these yields were produced by a much smaller working force, which indicates an appreciably higher level of *per capita* production. The primary effect of collective farming was that industrial development in urban centres requiring a rapid absorption of many workers from the countryside could be stepped up without jeopardizing the level of agrarian production. Collective farming and state farming were conducive to a much faster rate of mechanization than private farming by small peasants would have allowed. Although a too rapid introduction of mechanized agriculture often led to bad management and a bad state of repair, because of lack of experience among the *kolkhoz* workers, in the course of time the favourable effects of mechanization made themselves felt.

As far as I can understand, the deficiencies of Soviet agriculture, which have led to a certain stagnation, are to be attributed to its traditional orientation towards extensive farming owing to the vastness of the territory rather than to collective farming as a system. Mechanized farming is more suited to increasing *per capita* production than production per surface area. Only in recent years have the Soviet authorities become aware of the necessity and profitability of more intensive agriculture including an increased use of fertilizer.[113]

Therefore my conclusion is that Moore's statement regarding the repression and elimination of a peasantry under communism should be qualified. The emancipation of the peasants by no means ceased with collectivization.

iii. The Issue of Freedom in China

Still less could one maintain that the urge for freedom manifesting itself in the Chinese revolution was subsequently quelled after the revolution had achieved its material aims. Terror and repression have been much less in evidence in the People's Republic of China than in the Soviet Union. After a short period of organized violence against those who were considered to have been the worst exploiters and oppressors in the Chinese countryside, there has been a serious and lasting attempt to dispense with sheer force and to resort to education and persuasion. Although this persuasion, in the view of Western liberals, might often take forms which, in Western terminology, would be called 'brainwashing', this appeal to human reason and avoidance of physical force has made Chinese communist rule fundamentally different from the 'reign of terror' that had been typical not only of Chiang Kai-shek's regime, but also of the way many imperial rulers, regional governors, and local landlords exerted power over the rural population in earlier centuries.[114]

For the broad masses of the Chinese, the revolution of the late forties has undoubtedly brought about an abolition of many disabilities, and both material and cultural improvements, of such a magnitude that they can be viewed as great strides on the way towards emancipation. Of course new duties towards the collectivities and towards society at large, and new restrictions arise as a consequence of fundamental social changes; but to label them as nothing but a new type of bondage would be a serious distortion of realities, both in the present and in the past.

Moore's assessment of communist rule as a harbinger of renewed oppression, if debatable for the Soviet Union under Stalinist rule, is quite untenable as far as China after the revolution is concerned.[115] Mao Tse-tung's leadership has throughout been marked by traits of humanity and a rejection of violence, much in contrast with the ruthlessness characteristic of Stalin's rule.

Moore's misinterpretation of China becomes still more glaring when he refers to the position of the Chinese peasantry, although here he expresses himself more cautiously.[116] By any standard, China's peasantry is not 'a dying class'. Not only does it still form a large majority of the population, but it is acknowledged by the Chinese leaders as one of the main pillars of society. Agriculture is still considered the basis of the Chinese economy, and industry has been, since the reassessment of mistakes made during the Great Leap Forward, largely geared to the needs of agriculture.

If private agriculture has been nearly eliminated, the Chinese rural population is still a true peasantry, although technologically much better trained and equipped than previously and much more adapted to modern concepts of production and social life. It does not lose the character of a peasantry because it has been brought together in collective bodies (teams, brigades, and people's communes). The difference with the peasantry in Asia south of China is not that the peasantry in China has ceased to exist, but that, on the contrary, it is only since the revolution that it has begun to develop its full life and constructive vigour.

We might conclude, unlike Moore, that in the large communist countries ideals of revolutionary freedom proved to be much more than mere slogans used by shrewd politicians. These ideals expressing a desire for greater freedom retain their vigour, even after a revolution has attained an initial success and considerable achievements in the material field, as permanent sources for inspiration, despite manifold reverses and relapses. A revolution is, moreover, never satisfied with emulating the achievements of the old-timers. In material respects, the aim is always to improve on the old-timers. And in its spiritual aspirations, any revolutionary movement always attempts to formulate an ideal that reaches beyond that which previous attempts have actually achieved. This revolutionary aspiration will remain a potent factor, even though it appears, for some time, to be quelled by forces aiming at restoration and stabilization.

iv. The Thermidor Issue in the Soviet Union: Embourgeoisement

This takes us to a second important issue of post-revolutionary developments: the problem as to what extent a revolution is automatically condemned to finish up in a Thermidor and an ultimate restoration. Again, the course of events in the Soviet Union and China provide illuminating insights.

Whereas, under Stalin's rule, serious infractions upon the ideal of freedom presented the most glaring departure from the original revolutionary ideal, in the post-Stalin era the revolutionary ideals as such are losing much of their initial impact and motivating power. Along with a distinctly improved level of material welfare, and more intensive contacts with people and ideas from the Western world, there is a rapidly growing desire to enjoy the amenities of the good life without bothering too much about revolutionary ideals or Marxist principles. Although certain aspects of a Thermidorian reaction and a tendency towards stabilization were already apparent under Stalin's rule, it is only since the dictator's demise that true Thermidorian trends are getting the upper hand in many circles of Soviet society. Perhaps Stalin's isolationist policy as expressed, *inter alia*, in the Zhdanov doctrine, and his harshness and ruthlessness towards intellectuals, after the end of the Second World War, should be viewed as a last attempt to contain the increasing urge among this group for a more Western style of life, stimulated by a measure of elbow room afforded them in wartime.

There are many symptoms of this tendency towards an increasingly bourgeois style which, still more than the previously described conciliatory attitudes of the Soviets towards several regimes in the Third World, has earned them the term, coined by their Chinese colleagues, of 'modern revisionists'.

Even under Stalin there had been several compromises with the requirements of practical life, which had in fact been departures from the Marxist principles that had originally inspired the revolution led by Lenin. For example, the 'dictatorship of the proletariat' which had been anticipated by classic Marxists as a rather short episode needed to enforce the victory of socialism, but soon to be followed by a more democratic and decentralized type of government, had developed under Stalin into a rigid bureaucratic structure of a lasting character and with a tight police control. The permanency of dictatorship was justified by the isolation of the socialist state and its encirclement by enemies.

Another Marxist principle, the building of a socialist economy, had to yield in the late twenties to a system of differential wages as a practical means of creating incentives for higher production. There was, at the time, a strong opposition to the widening wage differential which was considered irreconcilable with the Marxist principle of 'to each according to his effort', that should be valid for a 'socialist society'. Wide wage differentials have now become permanent features of the Soviet economic system. The Marxist dream of an ultimate era of 'communism', when the old formula would be replaced by a new formula: 'to each according to his needs', is receding into a very remote future.

What characterizes the post-Stalin period is that what should have been a temporary compromise is increasingly being accepted as a lasting characteristic of Soviet society. Although the terror and arbitrariness imposed under Stalin have somewhat subsided and given way to a still largely monolithic but less authoritarian type of government, the total structure of society is dominated by bureaucratic forms which stifle any attempt at a fundamental renewal. Franz Kafka's well-known sally: 'Every revolution evaporates and leaves behind only the slimes of a new bureaucracy', is at last coming true in Russia. The injustices of bureaucracy are well described in novels like Dudincev's *Not by Bread Alone*, or Solzhenitsyn's *Cancer Ward*, which is not allowed to be published in the Soviet Union.[117]

An increasing importance is being attached to social status, and with a rising standard of general welfare Soviet society becomes, in several respects, ever more similar to industrial societies in the West. Marxism-Leninism remains the leading ideology. But with a party monopoly to authoritatively interpret the Marxist bible, those elements in the catechism that are contrary to the prevalent trends may be kept in the background. And many among the younger generation, especially, look with envy and admiration – partly due to ignorance – at the Western world with its 'freedoms'. More is heard, in our press, about protests on the part of Soviet students who criticize the Soviets for not yet being bourgeois enough than about opposition on the part of those who feel that the original revolutionary and egalitarian ideals are being betrayed.

v. The Thermidor Issue in China: Cultural Revolution

It is against the background of these Thermidorian tendencies in the Soviet Union that we have to view the so-called 'Great Proletarian Cultural Revolution' in China. Of course, there were also in China, in the years after the revolution, along with the distinct improvement in material welfare, certain tendencies towards self-contentment, bureaucratic rigidity, a loss of faith in the original revolutionary ideals and an inclination to seek compromises with the realities of life and with the frailties of human nature.

In the course of those years, the communist leadership repeatedly launched campaigns to counter such retrograde tendencies. In the early fifties, the *San Fan* (three-anti) campaign was directed at all kinds of malpractices in the newly built state apparatus, such as corruption, waste, and bureaucratic conduct. In 1957 it was the party that, in a 'rectification' campaign, was called upon to purify itself from all kinds of relapses into bourgeois tendencies and bureaucratic attitudes. During the ensuing 'hundred flowers' period, students and intellectuals started seriously to criticize the Communist Party as such, but the criticism was soon suppressed and turned into a campaign for 'counter-criticism'. After a certain relaxation during the years of bad harvests (1959–61), a purification campaign was again started among local party cadres, as part of a broader campaign for 'socialist education'.

We could, therefore, characterize the period preceding the Cultural Revolution as one where two contrasting tendencies within the Communist Party were contending in a dialectical way. Sometimes the Thermidorian trend temporarily got the upper hand, whereas in other periods Mao's leadership made an effort to keep the revolutionary principles aloft, in a strenuous attempt to prevent a relapse into attitudes of complacency and bureaucratic rigidity which threatened to dissolve the revolution from within.

The Cultural Revolution may be viewed as the culminating point of Mao's efforts to keep his revolutionary powder dry. Through this campaign, Mao Tse-tung and his followers in the party leadership made a heroic attempt to revive the fervour of the guerrilla fighters of the first hour. The reason why the Soviets failed fully to transform society was, according to the Chinese leaders, because they had neglected thoroughly to educate the people in socialist thought and behaviour as an essential precondition for such a fundamental change. Starting from Marx's somewhat deterministic thesis that the consciousness of men, belonging to the superstructure of society, is ultimately dependent upon their 'social being' as determined by the technological basis of society and the prevalent economic system, the Soviet leaders assumed that a transformation of the economic basis, that is to say, a transfer of the means of production from private persons to the state, would be enough to give birth to a new Soviet man, a truly socialist being, as a product of the new society.

The Chinese innovators hold, on the basis of experiences in the Soviet Union and elsewhere, that what we might call a structural revolution, in the sense of a remoulding of the prevalent economic system, is not enough. No new man will automatically emerge from a transformation of economic and political relationships. If we do not take care to re-educate human beings and to imbue them with revolutionary ideals, the gains of the revolution will get lost in human selfishness and attachment to personal gain.[118]

Mao Tse-tung and his followers decided to use youth as shock troops against those powers that stood for the interests of a new establishment. Through the 'Great Proletarian Cultural Revolution', which stressed a thorough re-education of everyone in true revolutionary ideas, through the process of a continuous struggle and discussion, all the institutions that had grown into a kind of new establishment were assailed: schools and universities, the party and significant sectors of the bureaucracy. The army had been reorganized in an early period, under Lin Piao, according to revolutionary, more or less democratic, principles, and could now serve as a model and an ally. Attitudes of self-sacrifice, in the service of society, were propagated. One could say that Marx's 'dialectical materialism' was, in Mao's exegetics, transformed into a 'dialectical moralism'. The stress laid upon the educability of everyone, which is also one of the leading principles in Mao's humanitarian policy towards delinquents both political and criminal, may have deeper roots in the old Confucian ideal that man can be improved through education.

The stress laid by Mao and his followers upon both moral elements and mental factors, as opposed to material external conditions, is in conformity with the stress laid throughout this book upon mental factors as determinants of evolutionary and revolutionary processes. The determinist preoccupation of many Marxists with material conditions and technological factors led to a general neglect of the autonomous forces of spiritual motivations as decisive factors throughout the history of mankind. Just as mental factors are decisive for the evolutionary process in terms of an urge for emancipation, in opposing the tendencies towards adaptation and stabilization, and just as the origin of revolutions can be found in the earliest mental protests in terms of counterpoints against the more or less stabilized institutional set-up, so in the same vein the contradiction between Thermidorian tendencies and those aiming at a continuing revolutionary development may be conceived in terms of a fierce struggle between two mental attitudes: one of them standing for stabilization and adaptation to the outside world, the other one concerned with a preservation of the revolutionary tradition in order not to forsake the initial gains of the revolution in the field of human emancipation.

Stress was particularly laid, in the course of the Cultural Revolution, upon egalitarian principles. Egotism and the desire for personal gain were made targets of criticism. More egalitarian forms of remuneration were introduced, both in factories and people's communes.[119] Various kinds of privileges, enjoyed by the cadres, qualified workers, or experts, were taken away and they were forced to take part in the work of the rank and file.

Another important principle of the Cultural Revolution was a trend towards greater freedom and democracy. In mobilizing the people, the 'mass line', which involves a steady movement in any decision-making 'from the masses and towards the masses', was much accentuated. The Red Guards, later on the Revolutionary Rebels in the factories, were allowed and urged to 'bombard the headquarters', to criticize everybody, including the highest party bosses – except one: the leader Mao Tse-tung, who was accorded, in the course of the Cultural Revolution, the status and attributes of a near-deity. Wall posters were most open in criticizing those in power, both within schools, factories, or offices, and those in high government or party positions. Whereas many cultural expressions and institutions, borrowed from the West, were criticized for their 'bourgeois' content, the Paris Commune was made a model of democratic decision-making.[120]

Finally, the Cultural Revolution stressed the principle of an ongoing class struggle, much in contrast with the Soviet view that, since a 'socialist society' is established, no further class struggle is needed.

It was said that the Cultural Revolution resulted in an overall victory, in the autumn of 1968, since everywhere in the country new administrative organs called revolutionary committees had been formed. It is clear, however, that in the course of the Cultural Revolution highly significant changes have occurred in its form and content.

Whereas the movement had started in mid 1966 in the schools and universities, with the conspicuous and much-publicized activities of the Red Guards, after a while it shifted towards the urban factories and government offices where the Revolutionary Rebels came forward as challengers of established authority. In 1967 the movement also spread to the People's Communes in the countryside, but it seems that there the Cultural Revolution developed more slowly.

There was also a gradual shift as far as the immediate objectives of the Cultural Revolution were concerned. Although the Red

Guards had started with a movement aiming at a wholesale trans-formation of the educational system, it soon became clear that revised programmes and revised curricula were not forthcoming for the time being. Universities and schools were closed, and all the attention was directed at radical changes in the political system, including government administration at the lower levels and actual party leadership. As far as changes were introduced, for example in the way a factory was run, these were considered to be temporary only. All final decisions had to be postponed until the bodies to be entrusted with decision-making and the procedures to be followed had been figured out, in line with the principles laid down in the course of the Cultural Revolution. Only after the new political system had received its final form through the establish-ment of tripartite revolutionary committees at all levels and through a thorough reorganization of the Communist Party, could experiments start as far as the further objectives of the Cul-tural Revolution were concerned. Schools and universities were re-opened, new fully revised curricula and instruction methods were launched, at first on a tentative basis. Experimentation in this educational field is still in full swing. A bold innovation is in-volvement of industrial workers and poor peasants, not only in the running of schools but in actual teaching as well.

In other fields experimentation is equally under way. 'Learn from Taching' and 'learn from Tachai' campaigns serve to develop all kinds of new initiatives, and in particular to attempt more egalitarian systems of remuneration in the fields of industry, mining, and agriculture. In this respect the Cultural Revolution seems far from finished. The stress, however, has shifted from the political to other fields of action. As far as agricultural production is concerned, the greater awareness of collective interests among the peasantry has already yielded impressive results.

Another type of change the Cultural Revolution has undergone since its start in mid 1966 is the methods used for waging the renewed class struggle. Throughout the autumn of 1966 it was largely conducted through mass discussions, big wall-posters, and mass demonstrations exposing not only all kinds of abuses of power in the field of politics and government administration, but also the bourgeois style of life and capitalist way of thinking of private individuals, who were clinging to the 'four olds' (old traditions, ideas, culture, and habits). Some violence occurred, although it was strongly rejected as a method for imposing the views of a majority upon a minority.[121]

During the winter, activities spread from the schools and the streets towards the countryside where the Red Guards started to wander in small bands, as well as towards the factories and government offices. Groups of labourers, stimulated by the Red Guards, started actions as Revolutionary Rebels and attempted to conquer power within their plants or offices. There was, in the first months of 1967, a serious threat to disrupt economic life, the more so since in many places different groups of rebels started to fight among themselves, each of them claiming to represent the thoughts of Chairman Mao in their purest form. Sometimes, one of the 'rebel' factions was in fact a tool in the hands of the party cadres who, in this way, attempted to defend their positions.[122] So-called 'royalists', evidently, had attempted to infiltrate the rebel movements. Forms of 'comprehensive democracy', propagated by Lin Piao, led to an attempt to establish a 'Shanghai Commune'.[123]

However, soon it became clear that the Chinese leaders were growing aware of the danger of chaos and disruption. Several measures were taken to counter this danger and to ward off tendencies towards anarchy. Prime Minister Chou En-lai seems to have secured a regular functioning of the government administration at the central level, through protecting several of his ministers who had been attacked in wall posters.[124] Warnings were spread that the Paris Commune had been defeated partly as a result of excessive democracy, which therefore should be restrained by more disciplined behaviour. Perhaps the most important shift in policy, however, was a strong appeal to rebel groups to form revolutionary alliances. Soon it became clear that, henceforth, the leaders of the Cultural Revolution would stress the 'three-in-one' type of body as a model for the direction of any administrative unit. In practice this meant that 'revolutionary committees' were to be formed everywhere, on a tripartite basis, in which the Revolutionary Rebels were to be supplemented by old cadres and army or militia people. What had been announced as a Shanghai Commune became one of the first revolutionary committees formed on the newly propagated 'three-in-one' basis.[125]

An important aspect of this retrenchment of policy was the reinstalment of old cadres as a significant element within the total structure. The Red Guards and Revolutionary Rebels had tended to view most of the cadres as representing the 'four olds' that had to be overthrown. However, the 8 August 1966 resolution had already stated that 'the good cadres and the relatively good ones are in the majority'.[126] Mao Tse-tung kept maintaining this throughout the Cultural Revolution. In the eyes of the rebel activists, however, the resurrection of many old cadres in positions of power must have looked like a defeat, and it took a long time, in many places, until the rebels were prepared to accept the new three-in-one principle. Perhaps still more significant, from a point of view of retrenchment of policies, was the appeal made to the army as a mediating force. But the appeal was not made to the army as an organization, still less as a power centre, but rather to the most advanced and experienced element within Chinese society as far as revolutionary thinking was concerned. Yet the prominent role attributed to the army could also be interpreted as an attempt to keep the more radical elements in check, and there are indications that this is what actually happened.[127]

The further advance of the Cultural Revolution shows contradictory tendencies, at some moments the more radical elements appearing to get the upper hand, whereas at other moments more moderate elements appeared to be in the ascendancy.[128] But in the course of 1968 stabilization seems to have become the main trend. During the summer Mao Tse-tung allegedly chided the Red Guards in Hsin-hua university for having been unable to solve their dissensions and form a 'Great Alliance'. He sanctioned, through the well-known gift of mangoes, the instalment of a propaganda team of workers, in which army people also participated, to solve the problems that had arisen.[129] In August 1968 Chiang Ching, Mao's wife, until then one of the most enthusiastic supporters of the Red Guards, admonished them to stop opposing the reinstalment of many of the old cadres in their functions, against whom they had directed their fierce verbal attacks; they should keep in mind that, in Mao's words, the great majority of the cadres were essentially good and had only needed some re-education.

The reconstruction of the Party at its 9th Congress (April 1969) could be viewed as a final step towards stabilization.

At the end of 1970 a start was made with a resurrection of party committees at all levels. There are rumours that these committees are, to a certain extent, gradually taking over functions which were thus far fulfilled by the revolutionary committees. In the Western press this shift is sometimes interpreted as a re-trenchment of the excessive power acquired during the Cultural Revolution by the army, in view of the crucial role the latter plays within the revolutionary committees. There seems to be a general trend to reduce the power of the army, in the wake of the dramatic and still rather mysterious Lin Piao incident in September 1971. On the other hand, it seems that within all kinds of party committees and other party organs army people still keep a prominent place.

A more convincing symptom of the general trend toward stabilization can be found in the drive against 'ultra-leftists' which started officially about the same time. Although the elimination of the 'ultra-left' group headed by Wang Li, formerly a prominent leader in the Cutural Revolution, occurred as early as 1967 yet, as an officially endorsed drive, the criticism of ultra-leftist tendencies gained momentum about the time when it became clear that leaders such as Lin Piao and Chen Po-ta had been removed from their top positions.

There are, at the same time, signs that there is a cutback in the excessive freedom of discussion and criticism enjoyed in the first phase of the Cultural Revolution, and that the party discipline is being reconfirmed, although the general atmosphere in factories and people's communes still makes a distinctly democratic impression.

It is not yet clear to what extent the drive against 'ultra-leftists' is connected with the recent shift in Chinese foreign policy, culminating in the visit of President Nixon and the admission of Peking to the United Nations. It would not be the first time in world history that a Thermidor is initiated in the realm of foreign policy.

Should all such symptoms be taken as evidence that the Cultural Revolution itself could be viewed as a movement that finally got stuck in a kind of Thermidor, and that consequently the fight of Mao and his allies against a Thermidor was a last stand, a losing battle? Are the laws of human nature reasserting themselves, and has a process started that will, inevitably, lead to an ultimate stabilization and restoration, as in the Soviet Union after Stalin's abortive last attempt to stem the tide?

One should consider, however, whether it is reasonable to assume that Mao Tse-tung has attempted to attain his targets at one stroke. This would be very much against the usual pattern of Chinese communist tactics. In contrast with Soviet policies, especially under Stalin, that were often characterized by a tendency to pursue a policy, once decided upon, to extremes, the Chinese method may rather be described in terms of two steps forwards, one step backwards.

The second of the sixteen points (8 August resolution) has expressed this tactical approach most clearly in stating that the revolutionary way is always a zigzag one and cannot be smooth and even in view of the manifold resistances.

There are still enough signs of a lasting revolutionary spirit and of bold experiments in line with Mao Tse-tung's thought. Highly important are the strenuous attempts to eliminate from the education system anything that remains of the traditional mandarin attitudes.

Typical is a vow, made collectively by a group of newly registered students at the two universities of Peking after a symbolic four days' march from Tien-tsin:

We, students, workers, peasants and soldiers, do not attach any particular importance to the 'engineer's visiting-card' ...We will never allow ourselves to be corrupted, either by our self-interest or by a desire to acquire personal fame. Our decision has been taken: though we take up a new post, our revolutionary awareness remains as it was. Though our environment is different, our position of workers born of the people will remain unchanged. Called upon to fulfil a new task, we will continue to wage our struggle in the same manner . . .[130]

A highly important institution intended to counteract elitist tendencies among cadres is the '7 May Cadre School' erected in large numbers all over China, after Mao's instruction at the end of 1968. The main aim is to bring all the cadres, working either in the party or in the administration, nearer to the people and to eradicate any tendencies towards bureaucratic or mandarin attitudes.

It is therefore quite possible that the successive advances and retreats in the course of the Cultural Revolution and afterwards should simply be viewed as applications of the tactical principle of two steps forward, one step backwards.

Granqvist quotes in his enlightening book, *The Red Guard*, a leading member of the Shanghai authors' society, who said to him: 'The class war moves forward like waves in the sea.' The Swedish journalist goes on to ask himself 'whether it is the troughs or the crests of the waves that must be considered fundamental'.[131]

I would not hesitate to reply that, in China of the past seven years, the crests were decisive for the whole movement. What we do not know, however, is whether the crests really advance. Or do they crash upon the sands of old society or, as appears still more likely, upon the rocks of human nature? Should we conclude, from the tendency to retrench the tide of revolution in several significant aspects, that the waves are bound to break upon the basic unchangeability of human nature?

vi. Long-Term Results of the Cultural Revolution

It is much too early for us to attempt anything like an assessment of the ultimate outcome of the Cultural Revolution. One of the main objectives of the Cultural Revolution has been to educate the people towards a higher political consciousness, and to elicit a greater self-reliance among them. The fourth point of the 16-point resolution encourages reliance on the masses and advocates letting them educate themselves during the campaign so that they learn to differentiate between what is right and what is wrong. The masses have been made to realize that any authority may be challenged and required to account for its actions towards them. The Communist Party, now reestablished, should never become an elite party again. It is required to follow the mass line, and to draw its strength from the masses. There are strong indications that, for the moment, one of the more lasting results of the campaign has been to introduce a much more democratic and egalitarian atmosphere into the factories and the People's Communes.

But can such an experiment in human emancipation and true democratic attitudes and practices have any chance of being successful in the long run? The question as to what extent the Maoist experiment has a chance of succeeding has been raised in an article by the Dutch sociologist Jacques van Doorn, who has drawn attention to the relevance of Robert Michels's 'iron law of oligarchy' for an assessment of the prospects of Mao's policy.[132]

Michels's thesis maintains that it is impossible for a left-wing radical movement to realize its aims without building up a rigid bureaucratic organization. The cadres who started with highly idealistic intentions are gradually impelled to dominate the popular masses that brought them to power. Therefore, any human organization, however radical and democratic its ideology, is bound to develop into a tool through which those chosen as representatives of the people or of distinct sections of the people are gradually constituting themselves as an oligarchy dominating those who brought them to power.

Van Doorn has grasped that what Mao has attempted through his bold experiment is to ward off the danger of bureaucratization and of tendencies towards oligarchic rule. Essentially, these tendencies more or less coincide with what we have learnt to discern as basic elements of a Thermidorian reaction. Van Doorn admits that what Maoism has in view is to avoid the type of Stalinist rigidity which was, at the time, a confirmation of Michels's 'iron law'.

Van Doorn contrasts both views in relation to the expected

effects of a 'mobilization of the masses'. Whereas Michels argues that such a mobilization implies that the masses are put out of play as an independent force, Mao, on the contrary, regards such a mobilization as a dynamic force. Through a very elaborate mechanism of social control Mao attempts to minimize rigidity in the functioning of political organizations. The essential difference is that whereas Michels's approach is deterministic, Mao's outlook is rather voluntarist and utopian: the sky is the limit. Although Van Doorn appreciates the intelligence and boldness of Mao's reply to Michels's 'iron law', in his final sentences he expresses disbelief in Mao's attempt. He seems to regard the ultimate failure of Mao's attempt as all but inevitable.[133]

In order to understand the enormous significance of Mao's experiment we must now turn to another element in his revolutionary strategy: the appeal to altruism and to collective values.

The most exciting aspect of the Cultural Revolution is the strenuous attempt made to substitute moral impulses for egotistical motives, as incentives for increased production. Blumer[134] wrongly holds that Lin Piao's admonition in his 1 October 1967 speech to 'fight self-interest' should be viewed as a kind of termination of the Cultural Revolution, since the struggle which thus far had been directed at others was now to be turned inward. But in my view, the attempt to introduce a new moral attitude could be viewed as the most basic element of the Cultural Revolution. In contrast with the leaders of the Soviet Union, the Chinese ones are not oblivious of Marx's utopian view of an ultimate 'communist society', where distribution of material goods will be 'to each according to his needs'. Whereas in the Soviet Union wage differentials tend to widen, in China attempts are made to bridge them. The new tentative method of allotting working points in the People's Communes, not only according to individual production, but also according to the level of socialist devotion,[135] seems a significant step from the 'socialist' towards the 'communist' principle. My own experience during a short visit to China (around New Year of 1971) was that such a transformation of incentives is being implanted in a cautious, tentative way. The ultimate success of the new method entirely depends on the question of whether it will prove possible to keep production at a reasonable, and constantly rising, level on the basis of devotion to a social group or to a cause, rather than to the interest of the individual and his traditional larger ego, his family. Similarly, one could ask oneself whether it is possible to live up to the requirements of modern technology if one trains technicians who are not 'red and expert', to use Liu Shao-chi's dualistic terminology, but who rather 'put politics in command', and are therefore expected to be primarily 'red'. I was strongly impressed, during my visit, by the general stress laid on the idea that modern science and technology were not to be viewed as a preserve of highly trained and specialized 'experts', but as a field where experimenting and active participation by ordinary workers and peasants was to be strongly encouraged.

What happened in China since 1949 is already a 'miracle' in terms of any predictions that could have been made at that time.[136] Social scientists will simply have to adjust to the changing realities – changing because of the self-confidence of a group of men who did not allow themselves to be held back by all the Cassandras shouting: *Impossible*! Mao and his comrades are attempting something that is seemingly unfeasible, according to any known standard. But if they succeed, the social scientists will have to admit that they have been wrong – and will have to readjust their ideas. It is, in the last resort, man who makes history.

If, for example, we keep in mind that a division of labour, in terms of extreme specialization, is not in accordance with prevalent trends in the electronic age, the search for a whole man adaptable to many highly divergent functions, far from being a mark of backwardness, may prove a highly progressive idea consonant with further technological progress.

There is one additional point which makes Mao's fight against selfishness particularly interesting. In contrast to the Soviet brand of communism, Mao does not aspire to a high standard of living for the people. There is, within the philosophy of the Cultural Revolution, an appeal to observe great sobriety in living habits and tastes. Contrary to what was generally claimed by Marxists, that the formula 'to each according to his needs' could only be the product of a high level of welfare, Mao attempts to introduce a new principle of distribution in a society where both production and consumption *per capita* will necessarily remain low according to any Western standard for a considerable time to come.

His appeal to sobriety has, first and foremost, a moral tinge, as an element in the education of man as a social being, prepared for self-restraint and self-sacrifice. But, at the same time, the appeal may be forthcoming from strong utilitarian motives, connected with the present phase of economic development. If China wants to make giant strides towards an industrial society, it has to encourage investment and to discourage any excessive consumption. Strategic considerations, such as the forming of a bumper stock, may also play an important role. At any rate, for several years the commune members have been urged not to consume what they produce in excess of their basic needs, but to sell to the state in excess of the quota fixed in advance.

Of course the risk remains that the attempt to develop popular moral and political consciousness will fail. In that case, if the individual peasant feels that he will not sufficiently profit from an increase in production, the policy may in the long run function as a disincentive.

One might also suggest that the stress on sobriety is a temporary policy only, in order to speed up industrial development. The implication, then, would be that as soon as China has technically caught up with the strong industrial nations, it will no longer be able to withstand the lure of higher living standards with all Thermidorian aspects that such a shift in attitude will bring about. Again, the answer to this question can only be given by the Chinese people themselves. But we have to admit that, on the whole, the odds seem to be against Mao's courageous and ambitious experiment.

However, it is clear that the emancipation movement in China proceeds, but not without shifts and temporary reverses. Even if, under all kinds of pressures, some of the basic principles of the Cultural Revolution, such as the fight against material incentives and the ultimate power of the party bureaucracy, will have to be given up, it does not yet mean that China will definitely have found its Thermidor. The concluding sentences of Granqvist's book are very much to the point:

But Mao's final goal is still the creation of a society in which it is impossible for a certain group of people – be they experts, intellectuals, or Party members – to regard themselves as superior to the masses. We see here the principle of equality pushed to its utmost limits. It is the most extreme experiment in utopianism ever attempted, one based on the assumption that man can be re-educated to learn both self-discipline and unselfishness. The testing of this assumption is of decisive importance to the future of Maoism. Do we as yet know enough about man to be able to say whether it is false?

It is quite possible that Mao's main objective, in starting this brave experiment and breathtaking upheaval at the end of his life, was to remind the young, once and for all, of the true, ultimate principles of the Chinese revolution. In so doing, he has tried to prepare the people to fight for their freedoms and for a better society, if new authoritarian and bureaucratic forms should ever again be imposed in the future.

Perhaps it is the first time in history that a ruler has given an object lesson to the people on how to make revolution; the only weakness seems to be that he himself was exempted from criticism and that any struggle had to be fought in *his* name. But even this could be explained as the only way, in the circumstances, to provide the revolutionary movement with a fixed point, an ideology, from which to start the struggle and to move the world.

And what if the Chinese revolution, despite all efforts, ends up in a Thermidor? In that case one can predict without any risk that there will be other societies, in Asia, in Latin America, in Africa, to take up the torch where the Chinese have left it behind.

vii. *Towards a More Egalitarian Society: Beyond Yankee City*

A final point we have to discuss in this chapter is the inspiration other movements, especially in the industrial part of the world, may derive from the Chinese Cultural Revolution.

In the first place one is inclined to think of the student unrest in

France during spring 1968. The term 'cultural revolution' was often used for these events, and both the bourgeois press and the Peking press spread a real 'Chinese myth' during the 'May revolt'.[137] Robert Guillain has pointed out several similarities between the Chinese Cultural Revolution and what happened in France.[138] There are several elements in the Cultural Revolution that might attract young people in an industrial society.

First, there is the protest of a young generation that has been excluded from any active participation in decision-making matters of the greatest interest to themselves: the field of higher education. The problem had become increasingly acute because of the traditionalism and pedantic classicism characteristic of French universities, in view of the steadily increasing numbers of students from less privileged strata of society who experience the criteria applied in examinations as discriminatory. Essentially, the problem is similar to its counterpart in Chinese universities. The demand is for much greater co-responsibility and democratic influence within their own educational sphere. It was forwarded with the same tinge of anarchy characteristic of the Red Guard movement.

But beyond the immediate interests of the students, their protests also touch upon the broader problems of society. The French students wanted an education better adapted to the social realities of today, and especially of tomorrow. Their attempt to find companions-in-arms among the industrial workers was an important indication that their outlook was not purely parochial.

But one has to be careful in attempting to trace Chinese influences in what happened, and is happening, in Europe. The *direct* inspiration drawn by the French student movement from what had occurred in the Chinese universities seems to have been minimal, and to have been largely restricted to the activities of comparatively small Maoist groups.[139] Other sources of inspiration such as André Gorz, Herbert Marcuse, Fidel Castro and Che Guevara appear to have been at least as important.

Nevertheless, one should not underestimate the influence of the Chinese Cultural Revolution and of the rapid spread of the little red book among European youth in general. In an article, published on 16 May 1968, Paul Blanquart summed up the various spiritual influences operative during that period in France, and among these influences he mentioned the Chinese Cultural Revolution: 'A great revolution touching man in his most profound self, transforming the moral face of the whole society, according priority to audacity, mobilizing the masses without reservation, respecting their spirit of initiative, etc.'[140] If Maoism can succeed, even partially, in transforming China into a society where a trend towards egalitarianism will become a permanent trait, the impact of the Chinese inspiration might, in the longer run, grow.

As a social protest, the student movement was directed against the authoritarian structure of Western society and against the injustices of the establishment. Here one of the main inspirations was Herbert Marcuse, who for some time has been the mouthpiece of those who are dissatisfied with the type of society created in the industrial world, and with the cold conformism imposed by the prevalent structure. Marcuse could also be cited as a philosopher who stresses the importance of freedom and opposes the pursuit of material goods in present industrial society, while challenging the whole concept of a welfare state as interpreted in the West, and appealing for a more sober style of life. However, his teachings remain largely theoretical, whereas European youth could point towards Chinese society as one where a real attempt had been made to take egalitarianism seriously.

Although one can readily assume that in this desire to return to a more sober way of life there is an element of romanticism, comparable with the eighteenth-century sentimental yearning for a Paradise Lost and for the primitive life led by the noble savage – yet the dissatisfaction with the welfare state is real enough; it is important that a rebellion like the one in Paris could still happen in the late twentieth centry, in an industrial country like France. It might be a symptom that revolutionary thinking has not completely vanished in industrial society.

The interesting thing about the May events in France is that they show that the American model of industrial society is not being universally accepted as a *non plus ultra*. In Lloyd Warner's picture of a stratified society, inequality of status and economic power are inbuilt, and the American creed of equality only functions as a sedative to make inequality more palatable.[141]

The heroic attempt of the Chinese Cultural Revolution to create a new type of society in which inequality is not accepted as normal, and where no privileges at all are derived from the status and position of the parents, means an attempt to transcend the ideological border of Western democracy, and to put into practice a way of life that has remained a dream both in America and in the Soviet Union. Melvin Tumin's criticism of Warner is relevant here:

Historically, the evidence seems to be that every time power and property are distributed unequally, no matter what the cultural definition, prestige and esteem differentiations have tended to result as well. Historically, however, no systematic effort has ever been made, under propitious circumstances, to develop the tradition that each man is as socially worthy as all other men so long as he performs his appropriate tasks conscientiously. While such a tradition seems utterly utopian, no known facts in psychological or social science have yet demonstrated its impossibility or its dysfunctionality for the continuity of a society. The achievement of a full institutionalization of such a tradition seems far too remote to contemplate. Some successive approximations at such a tradition, however, are not out of the range of prospective social innovation.[142]

The fact that backward China was the first country to attempt to take the egalitarian ideology seriously could be interpreted as a new example of the phenomenon I call the 'dialectics of progress'. On the other hand, the inspiration immediately drawn from this bold attempt in some advanced countries testifies to the vitality of the new model, and to the vigour of contrapuntal forces in industrial society that may, in the future, challenge the established order based on the Yankee City type of social hierarchy.

Again, there is an indication that, even in industrial society, revolution may remain a more permanent phenomenon than was assumed until recently. The other, more sobering, possibility is that the students should simply be considered as an underprivileged group within modern industrial society, who in a large majority will be satisfied if their claim for greater responsibilities and influence within the structure of higher education is met. This idea has been outlined by Alain Touraine in his article in *Le Monde*.[143] Touraine's analysis basically coincides with that of Warner and Low,[144] who have argued that labour unrest would subside if industrial workers, who up till then have not sufficiently profited from economic growth, were granted a more secure and rewarding role within industrial society as it is. Both Touraine and Warner seem to consider the groups they were concerned with as a kind of 'proletarian rearguard',[145] not yet well adjusted to industrial society, and therefore sometimes a source of social unrest, but in the long run to be satisfied, and at the same time tamed, by modern industrial society, without being able to change its structure and outlook.

Which of the two alternatives – a development towards new revolutions, or an increasing absorption into the established social order – will prevail in the future is still in the hands of human beings who can, within certain bounds, mould their own future. This future is not yet fixed, owing to the creativity and originality of man. The bold Chinese experiment of attempting to create a new man, utopian as it looks, might prove, in the long run, to be decisive for the fate of humanity.

Epilogue: Repetition and Uniqueness in an Open-ended Universe

i. The Concept of Causality

Deinde philosophari – philosophy comes next – is a phrase always used in combination with the adage *primum vivere:* live first!

In this book philosophy comes next for another reason: this epilogue is meant to provide a deeper methodological foundation, as well as a kind of vindication for the thinking behind the theorizing in the earlier chapters. It may, at the same time, serve to iron out some apparent inconsistencies.

For example, the reader will have noticed that some thoughts were based on what one could call a kind of 'voluntarism', in contrast to theories which are, in nineteenth-century fashion, based rather on a deterministic way of thinking. Yet, it has also been assumed that revolutionary developments can, to a certain extent, be predicted. One might argue that the two concepts are contradictory, in the sense that if the future is open-ended and dependent on the human will, future human behaviour cannot at the same time be analysed in terms of general patterns and repetitive sequences, and hence be predictable.

It seems, therefore, that I am under an obligation to explain how I think the relationship between the repetitive and the unique aspects of human behaviour can be combined into one more or less consistent concept of continuity and change. I shall try to point out that the combination of fixed patterns with creativity is by no means restricted to the realm of human behaviour. These two faces of nature are part and parcel of any process belonging to the endless chain of events that make up the history of our planet, of which natural evolution is one of the most fundamental aspects.

Because of the short-term view of the great majority of

scientists, the repetitive aspect has up till now received disproportionate attention and the aspects of novelty and uniqueness have been mostly overlooked. I shall try to demonstrate that postulating something like human 'free will', far from being a naïve assumption contradicting the scientifically established laws of nature, should be considered as fully consistent with scientific thinking. We only need some searching re-thinking on the concept of causality and on the limits of the applicability of mechanistic concepts that try to reduce what will happen to what is known from the past. We also need to bridge the gap between natural science and evolutionary thinking by demonstrating that an attempt to comprehend better the essence of novelty and uniqueness, far from belonging to a mode of thinking associated, as a kind of relic, with a pre-scientific past, may on the contrary add a new quality of perspicacity to the natural sciences without in any way impairing the tremendous value of scientific and technological achievements in the last hundred years or so.

What I hope to demonstrate is that social scientists and other students of man and society have been wrong in trying to imitate physical scientific models as closely as possible. They should realize that they could have a specific approach no less scientific than that prevalent in natural sciences; and that if they could succeed in tackling the problems of novelty and uniqueness, which are the essence of historical thinking, in a way that could be called truly scientific, this might encourage natural scientists to add a new dimension to their research: the historical one.[1]

What is the essence of a causal nexus between two events? Definitely not a relationship implying that one would produce the other by some inherent force of nature. This would amount to an anthropomorphic interpretation, lending a kind of magic aspect to nature and supposing the functioning of certain mysterious forces within nature; one could call it a more sophisticated and complicated version of the spirits and gods who dominate the universe, according to the world view of 'primitive' peoples. The *causa agens* concept is part of a pre-scientific image of the world.

Yet, according to any definition of causality, the specific nexus between the two events carries the characteristic of a certain *necessity.* We do not speak of causality if the coincidence of two events is, in our opinion, purely fortuitous. Even if there is a regular sequence to be observed (for example, the rise of the sun after the cock's crow) this does not constitute a causal nexus: the sun would still rise without the cock's crow. The whole secret of scientific and technological progress has been, as far as possible, to detect and eliminate the element of chance in all our calculations and constructions. Science attempts to make events predictable and, hence, manageable. Causality, as a relationship between two events characterized by an element of necessity, forms the core of the scientific method.

The essence of this concept of necessity as a basic aspect of any causal nexus is the element of repetition. When we say that one occurrence is the *cause* of another one, we mean by it, not only that the latter followed in time upon the former, but that if at any time the former events reoccurred the latter would follow *as a matter of course.*

The *general law of causality* holds[2] that natural processes are governed by repetition (in the following we will have to qualify this 'law'). Specific causal laws establish a definite repetitive sequence between two units of a natural process, implying that *if* A occurs, B will inescapably follow.

Now, in point of fact the nexus is more complicated. In a certain sense, one could call the whole complex situation, *including* the one factor one wishes to establish as the initial agent, the cause of the *new* complex situation that is being assessed as an effect.[3] We should, however, exclude from the initial situation, as elements of the cause, all those factors that, according to our knowledge, are *not* relevant to the process and that are not necessary to obtain the effect.

On the other hand, there are cases where a certain group of factors has contributed to the occurrence of the effect but according to our knowledge and experience the effect would have materialized even without the presence of these factors, as a corollary of a combination of conditions that could be discovered at an earlier stage; although perhaps then the whole chain of events would have been somewhat different. In that case we would tend to call the original combination of conditions the cause, whereas the group of immediate factors that could as well be omitted in the sequence should rather be defined as the impulse or precipitant, but not the fundamental cause.[4]

Any assessment of a causal nexus, therefore, amounts to a comparison between what actually happened and what would have happened *if* ... As causes we can only acknowledge those conditions or elements in the initial situation that could *not* be left out without affecting the further course of events up to the final result. If, according to our experience, a certain element or group of elements could have been omitted without disrupting the chain of events, they could not be considered as causes. Both the real and the imagined chain of events are conceived in terms of repetition and reproducibility.

Summarizing the foregoing, we arrive at the conclusion that an analysis of chains of events in terms of causality does not reveal any forces functioning in nature, nor any mysterious connection between certain occurrences; it only establishes a repetitive process detected through our experience or, if we have attempted to isolate certain factors, through experimentation. Kant's thesis that establishing causal relationships is part of our innate intelligence and should be viewed as independent from actual experience cannot be upheld. It was Hume, attacked by Kant, who was essentially right.[5]

ii. *Uniqueness and Repetition*

This argument is not marred by the fact that, in modern physics, many laws are not expressed in causal terms in a strict sense, but as statistical probabilities. Statistical laws, as a matter of fact, cannot be disengaged from the concept of causality as I have just developed it. A statistical formulation of probabilities is nothing but a specific application of the principle of causality. Any statistical correlation presupposes that processes of nature are governed by repetition and that if at a certain time a definite correlation can be observed in a given percentage of cases, it is to be expected that the percentage itself can be reduced to a number of repetitive factors, and hence is likely to remain constant. Therefore, I cannot agree with David Bohm's view[6] that statistical laws are fundamentally different from causal ones, and should be reduced to contingency, chance, or randomness as opposed to the principle of necessity inherent in repetitive processes.

If, therefore, repetition is at the root of any causal relationship, we should reject Heinrich Rickert's claim that history, as an individualizing discipline in contrast with the generalizing natural sciences, is characterized by a specific type of causality, namely individual causality.[7] In this conception, the cause-to-effect nexus receives precisely the magic tinge of a process produced by some intrinsic force deemed to be inherent in the unique, non-repetitive, socio-historical course of events. In my view, we should on the contrary reject any use of the concept of causality in cases where repetition is being ruled out.

However, in regarding uniqueness as a characteristic of historical processes, Rickert's view does have a positive value for our argument. Bohm also admits 'that the process of becoming will necessarily have, at each moment, certain aspects that are concrete and unique'.[8]

Causality, as we have seen, is typical of all repetitive processes. However, if we ask whether all natural or historical processes are governed by repetition, we arrive at a different picture. The general law of causality, stating that natural processes are dominated by repetition, should be qualified. The law can only be applied where initial conditions are identical. Whether they are so, in any given situation, remains an open question to be looked at carefully. Identity in the realm of matter is not as universal as some scientists in the past have tended to assume. The radical Dutch philosopher and founder of the science of semantics, G. Mannoury, has commented: 'Two sequential processes in nature are as much alike as two drops of water, that is to say: quite strikingly so, provided that one does not look too sharply.'[9]

The natural sciences were originally built upon one general axiom: the saying from Ecclesiastes that 'there is no new thing under the Sun'. The Golden Rule established that the amount of energy available remains constant; so does the available mass of matter. The laws of nature established, once and for all, how the myriads of particles would interact. If there was an element of uncertainty in the microcosmos of the small particles, statistical laws re-established the predictability within larger structures and organisms, allowing technology to make calculations of the greatest precision.

The general pattern of scientific thinking, not long ago, started from the premise that any process should be explained from the situation *prior* to the process, and in accordance with laws of a generic and universal nature.

In this model, time appears as a factor not fundamentally different from the spatial dimensions. In principle, all natural processes are reversible – at least on the microscopical level. The adage 'nothing new can ever be created' is reinforced by a physical model that excludes the uni-dimensional and uni-directional flow of time as a significant additional datum.

One of the few aspects where this uni-directional time appears in classical physics is in the second law of thermodynamics: physical processes would be characterized by increasing entropy, which would amount to an increasing amount of molecular disorder and randomness, that is to say: lack of structure and organization.

Contrasting with this dominant physical model is the world of living organisms of which we form a part. If there is one striking characteristic of the 'living' world, it is the continuous creation of new things 'under the Sun'. Physicists and chemists admit that actual processes in the field of biology as we observe them, and some even in the realm of organic chemistry below the level of living matter, move away from a state of equilibrium. But these processes involving a diminishing, instead of an increasing, entropy and consequently a trend towards greater structural organization instead of growing molecular disorder are not allowed by physicists to disturb the sacrosanct second law of thermodynamics.[10] These irreversible processes are relegated to a localized, exceptional area of natural laws, due to a constant flow of energy from the biosphere, derived from the sun. As a general pattern of natural processes, however, increasing entropy is maintained as a universal trend, dominating the world of nature.

As already stated, the basic reversibility of processes is being upheld at the microscopical level. However, natural sciences derive their enormous complexity from the coexistence of many different levels within the realm of nature. David Bohm attempts to give an impression of this complexity, of 'the inexhaustible *depth* in the properties and qualities of matter'. In his view, current physics were too exclusively preoccupied with 'the simple procedure of just going through level after level of smaller and smaller particles', in an effort to explain at each level 'the substructure of the entities above it in size'.[11] Bohm wants, instead, to introduce the concept of a 'qualitative infinity of nature', in which at each level specific background conditions may significantly alter the structure of natural laws as derived from the substructure at lower levels.

Similarly, in the realm of biology different levels may be distinguished. Haldane[12] distinguishes 'the processes which concern biologists as molecular, physiological, ontogenetical, historical, and evolutionary'. With each level a specific time scale is connected. 'Molecular processes are completed in times which may be as short as a hundred thousandth of a second though they may be as long as a second.' The time scale of physiological processes 'is of the order of a hundredth of a second to an hour'. Ontogenetic processes 'often occur only once in a lifetime', historical ones last 'through a number of lifetimes' and involve 'thousands or millions of individuals', whereas evolutionary changes 'vaster than empires and more slow', generally take much longer.

At the molecular and physiological levels, the reversible concept of time still seems fully adequate to describe biological processes. Causal laws, formulated in terms of repetitive processes, may cover both fields of biological research.

However, at the ontological level the situation is different. Here, the flow of time is definitely uni-directional. Yet, as far as one looks at the daily biological processes of birth, growth, and decay, the model of a world of nature where there is 'no new thing under the Sun' can still, to a certain extent, be maintained. Ontological processes are cyclical. The elements of living matter are steadily being dissolved and recombined into new structures. But the unchangeable laws of nature remain inexorable and bear out that other biblical saying: 'Dust thou art – to dust returnest.'

However, if we proceed to still higher levels and consider what happens in organic life over much longer lapses of time, it becomes much more difficult to ignore the uni-directional flow towards ever more complex structures as an independent variable. These long-term irreversible processes become truly manifest in the realm of natural evolution. And here one clearly observes that science, in its present state, encounters great difficulties in coping with this 'disturbing' factor in modern science. The continuous tendency of large numbers of scientists to 'explain away' any sign that new things are constantly appearing on the horizon makes a pedantic and artificial impression.

Of course the usual argument is that nothing can happen that is contrary to the laws of nature, and that the new formations appearing in the course of time on the earth's crust or in the depths of the sea are only new combinations of the same basic elements that had always been operative – rather like the changes in a kaleidoscope. Moreover, the new formations are in no way exempt from the general natural laws based on principles of causality. Any formation of a new structure, or a new species, is in principle reproducible wherever the initial conditions repeat themselves, and therefore lacks uniqueness. Certainly, all this is true.

The attempt, by some leading scientists, to reproduce the physical conditions under which organic life appeared for the first time on the earth[13] may, no doubt, at some time prove successful. But does this in any way detract from the fact that, when life appeared for the first time, it *was* brand new (at least on our planet) and as such without any precedent in nature? Are physical or chemical laws, formulated in terms of constant repetition, in any way suitable to 'explain' the historical course producing ever more complicated structures, and thus belying the imaginary trend towards ever-increasing entropy?

If causality can only be conceived in terms of repetition, one should ponder over the futility of an attempt to explain all that is new away *only* by claiming – what in itself is certainly true – that any new formation can be repeated *if* identical preconditions are reproduced. But what *should* be explained, and never can be in terms of science as it stands, is *how* it is that time and again in the history of our planet new, unprecedented conditions arise that disprove the assumption of identity as the basis of the general law of causality.

What has, until now, saved science as it stands from the necessity of adjusting its tenets and its models to the realities of the history of living nature is probably the fact that the great majority of scientists have thus far avoided facing long-term developments and formulating long-term laws. I am sure – without being in any way an expert in the natural sciences – that science could, without any loss to the enormous precision achieved as far as short-term processes and technology are concerned, try to complete its model with a set of insights allowing for elements of novelty supplementing the repetitive patterns that have been the substance of science as it stands.

I would suggest that in order to understand the processes of nature we should drop the axiom, inherent in the general law of causality, that nature is dominated by identity. We should, on the contrary, try to understand that any natural process shows aspects of identity combined with aspects of uniqueness.

This becomes apparent in the structure of physical matter. Structure as such is, essentially, in contradiction to the supposition of an all-pervading identity. Any structure had its origin in a previous differentiation and variation. One could assert that any physical particle shows, in its composition and arrangement, the *history* of its creation. Long before organic life made its appearance, either on the earth or somewhere else in the universe, molecules were already becoming ever more complex and diversified. Why should this history of physical matter be excluded from the field of science? And why not admit that any first change in the structure of matter, though in principle always reproducible, could be welcomed as a new phenomenon in the line of irreversible processes away from the entropical death?[14]

A continuous interplay between repetition and novelty; a steady but comparatively slow creation of new forms, time and again offering a pattern that is there to be repeated and recreated in full accordance with all laws based on causality – that is how one could conceive the eternal process of nature.

iii. *The Delusions of Mechanistic and Deterministic Explanations*

Why is there a stubborn reluctance among so many scientists to recognize novelty as an autonomous factor in nature? We could relate this rejection to the distinct bias in favour of so-called determinism, as a general outlook among most scientists, and of mechanistic explanations of all natural phenomena.[15]

Science has won its great victories in the face of strong resistance on the part of various social forces that were opposed to admitting a rational scientific outlook on the world of nature. There was a tendency to associate determinism with rationality, and voluntarism in its manifold forms with a belief in irrational forces and tendencies contrary to the inflexible laws of nature.

Mechanistic explanations were much in favour in that they had been able, in so many cases, to disprove claims by people who did not believe in science that certain events could be attributed to supernatural forces. Reducing all processes to previous causes that fully determined what would happen next, and what would happen under any similar conditions, appeared to be the appropriate, and at the same time the only correct, way to further science and technological progress and to build a rational and consistent composite of scientific truths.

This deterministic and mechanistic bias is, for example, apparent in the definite refusal, by the great majority of scientists, to accept finalistic interpretations of natural processes.

Finalistic explanations attempt to view processes not primarily as a function of previous conditions, but of the eventual stage they are leading to. According to this type of interpretation, processes are, in a certain sense, determined not so much by the preceding conditions but by the final outcome. Sometimes in this connection the Aristotelian term, *causa finalis*, is used.

This type of interpretation was, for a time, rather popular among some biologists. For example, about the turn of the century it appeared that living matter had a tendency, regardless of manipulations with the original embryo, to reproduce a complete organism.[16] This was, at that time, considered by some biologists as proof that natural processes are taking a definite direction, and that this direction is partly determined by the ultimate shape of an organism.

The discussion between mechanical and finalistic interpretations was especially heated as far as the process of evolution as such was concerned. Whereas determinists with a mechanistic outlook stuck to the Darwinian interpretation of random variations and natural selection through better adaptation to the environment, finalists claimed that the relatively rapid and consistent process of evolution – slow as it was in terms of time-measuring as applied by mankind – could hardly be explained by randomnesss combined with natural selection alone, and that a definite direction of the processes must be supposed to account for the apparent consistency of the cumulative evolutionary process.

The tendency of many finalists to appeal to certain unobservable properties of matter, as for example Bergson's assumption of a 'vital force' inherent in living matter, made this type of interpretation unacceptable to the great majority of scientists, including biologists. Moreover, finalistic positions were often assumed by religious groups or individuals who interpreted them as a justification, or even rehabilitation, for views conceiving natural processes as directed by divine powers. This association of finalism with irrational and rather vague philosophies has doomed this school of thinking in the eyes of official science.

Biologists and biochemists still generally tend to reject any explanation of phenomena in the realm of living matter in finalistic terms. Recently this rejection has been expressed most strongly by Jacques Monod, who went to the point of equating this rejection, without any further argument, with the quest for scientific objectivity: 'The postulate of the objectivity of nature is the cornerstone of the scientific method. That is to say, a systematic refusal to consider any interpretation of phenomena in terms of final causes, of a "project", as conducive to "true" knowledge.'[17]

Monod admits that living beings are characterized by what he calls a teleonomic structure. But he is convinced that it should be possible fully to reduce the seemingly spontaneous emergence of new forms to processes at a microscopic level.

Crucial in his analysis is the demonstrated capacity of certain molecules and cellular particles to select the counterparts with which they form combinations. Biochemists are accustomed to define this specific propensity to select as *information*. It seems possible, for biochemists, to recognize the specific code of cellular particles determining the future growth and reproduction of living organisms. As a convenient manner to explain phenomena like those discovered by Driesch, this term, information, seems quite appropriate. But one sometimes gets the impression that the terminology also serves to explain away any finalistic element in the biological process.

In Monod's book this purpose becomes obvious where he attempts to argue that *because* the information was already there in the constituent particles, though not yet explicit, the formation of the ensuing epigenetic structure is not a creation, but a revelation.[18]

Here the mechanistic overtones are, again, evident: the natural process is fully determined by what was already present from the outset. The question remains of whether or not biochemists of the type of Monod are deceiving themselves. Is information any more than an image? Certainly these scientists do not assume that the living particles have actually received the information of the ultimate shape they will have to assume and the direction in which they will have to develop, as a child being told of its future life in a fairy tale.

In fact, the whole information imagery only serves to conceal that it is the ultimate shape of the organism that is determining the natural process as such. What is significant, however, for the experimenting scientist who wants to influence the natural process and to predict its outcome is that he may 'read' the future process and the ultimate shape from some physical characteristics of the original molecule. It is the scientist, not the particle, who has acquired the information.

If we want to detach ourselves from any imagery, we have to

admit that, strictly speaking, the whole concept of determinism is pure imagery. A natural process is no more determined by its previous conditions and causes than by magic forces. We cannot discover anything in the world, from God to a law of nature, that might determine what will happen next. The only thing we can do is to observe repetition. This observation, if done several times under conditions that exclude disturbing factors outside the causal nexus, leads us to the conclusion that *if* A, *then* B will 'necessarily' follow. Only in *that* restricted sense is the process determined; that is to say, not by any force, but ... by our own observation of the repetition as valid. It is only the sequence or correlation that matters. Any attempt to reduce a process to previous causes adds nothing to our comprehension and even impairs our understanding of what is really going on.

Therefore, mechanistic explanations are no more scientific than finalistic ones. Both are nothing but attempts to help our understanding by introducing a more or less anthropocentric concept. In the former case it is man as an agent of change who is being introduced as a model for nature; in the latter case it is man as a planner and a prescient being. But *both* types of interpretation exceed the limits of our experience and are, to a certain extent, *meta*physical.

If we disengage ourselves from all historically understandable preconceptions against finalistic explanations, we will have to postulate that what matters is the most convenient and comprehensible formulation of all kinds of repetitive natural processes, some of them highly complicated. Could we not admit that in some cases a formulation of the process in terms of where it starts from, and in others a formulation in terms of where it leads to, would be most convenient?

However, it can be left to the biologists and chemists to decide whether the foregoing argument is acceptable to them. What matters to us, at this point, is that the whole bogey of determinism crumbles, if looked at in this way. For what appears to be determined by causal laws are only those processes where identity of initial conditions can be demonstrated. The unique occurrences – unique but for the probability that they will immediately be followed by a chain of identical, and therefore causal, processes – escape in the first instance the fate of being determined. In nature, in its irreversible aspects, there is always one event that is the first of its kind. Can it be said, in any scientific sense, to be determined? The identical processes that may soon follow, no doubt are. But what about new creations that are, the moment they first appear, unique? Can they, in any scientific sense, be reduced to laws governing simpler structures? Or have we simply to admit that the certainties acquired by mechanistic explanations were, in fact, turning a blind eye towards an important element in reality?

iv. Randomness and Novelty

In my argument thus far I may have conveyed the impression that scientists have completely ignored the non-repetitive aspects of natural processes. This is certainly not the case. It is not only in recent studies by biologists that one encounters statements to the effect that it is impossible to reduce all natural processes to repetitive sequences of events.[19] In physics there is also a tendency to recognize novelty and uniqueness as fundamental aspects of many natural processes. For example, Bohm states that in some situations a given combination of events may 'result in some irreversible change or in some qualitatively new line of development'.[20]

In situations like the one where, according to Oparin, a billion years ago or more life may have originated in the atmosphere of the earth,[21] 'the system is irrevocably launched on its new path'.

Bohm even assumes that changing conditions may 'eventually lead to a stage of the universe in which new kinds of entities satisfying new kinds of laws will come into being'.[22] 'Irrevocable qualitative changes do take place, which could not even in principle be reversed.' 'The laws that apply cannot be completely separated from the historical processes in which these systems come to obtain their characteristic properties,' particularly when one studies processes over longer periods of time.[23]

Unfortunately, Bohm attempts to reduce all such new developments to one basic principle: the randomness of chance fluctuations:

One of the most characteristic features of chance fluctuation is that *in a long enough time* or *in a large enough aggregate*, every possible combination of events or objects will eventually occur, even combinations which would at first sight seem very unlikely to be produced.[24]

In Bohm's view, it is precisely the notion of *chance contingencies* that supplements the notion of causality to encompass the totality of natural processes. He writes:

The tendency for contingencies lying outside a given context to fluctuate approximately independently of happenings inside that context has demonstrated itself to be so widespread that one may enunciate it as a principle; namely the principle of randomness.[25]

Causal laws are inadequate to explain natural processes in their totality:

Actual experience shows that the necessity of causal relationship is always limited and conditioned by contingencies arising outside the context in which the laws in question operate. These contingencies satisfy certain characteristic laws of their own: viz. the laws of chance, an approximate mathematical expression of which is given by the theory of probability.

Bohm connects these contingencies with the diversity of levels in nature:

Of course, by broadening the context, we may see that what were chance contingencies in the narrower context present the aspect of being the results of necessary causal connections in the broader context. But, then, these necessary causal connections are subject to still newer contingencies, coming from still broader contexts. Thus, we never really can eliminate contingencies. Rather, the categories of necessary causal connection and chance contingencies are seen to represent two sides of all processes.[26]

It is this 'two-sided character of necessity and contingency' which, according to David Bohm, accounts for the 'richness and structure' of natural processes. He, therefore, extends the notion of natural law beyond the operation of causality as a concept expressing exclusively the repetitive side of nature. It is the chance phenomenon that lends nature its 'qualitative infinity' and ultimately produces 'novelty' and irreversibility.[27]

Although Bohm, therefore, has made a serious attempt to leave room, within his philosophy, for the undeniable phenomena of novelty and irreversibility, the method he uses to explain these phenomena away through reducing them to chance and randomness looks highly artificial. Even if we could agree that chance may play, within certain natural processes, an independent role in such a way that it cannot be reduced to some deeper underlying repetitive causal nexus, it does not follow at all that *any* non-repetitive process should be attributed to the operation of the mathematical laws of chance.[28] We could only derive such knowledge from a very broad range of experience, and in view of the comparatively long-term character of most irreversible processes it is not at all easy to put the above hypothesis to an experimental test.

In the absence of such experimental proof I would tend to view Bohm's artificial attempt to explain away novelty through reducing it to randomness and chance as being basically a relic from a mechanistic way of thinking. In fact, one could sum up this way of thinking in the following manner: 'If it is not a specific "cause" that has produced a certain phenomenon, it *must* be due to pure chance – else I should believe in miracles.' Assuming 'novelty' and 'uniqueness' as independent variables smacks too much of irrationality. Evidently, it did not occur to Dr Bohm that it is much more irrational to assume that, by pure chance, throughout the history of our earth all contingencies would have moved, in a broader context, in one general direction – that of natural evolution.

For the same reason I consider the Darwinian concept of natural selection to be basically mechanistic. It pretends to explain away non-causal factors through reducing the evolutionary process to pure chance, combined with the tautological assumption that what survives proves to be more fit than what succumbs or is extinguished in the course of time. But, again, the assumption of randomness is not the result of serious research based on experience or experiment, but an axiom derived from an aversion to admitting the possibility that there may be some method in the madness of biological long-term change.

It appears to me much more rational and scientific simply to admit that we do not know whether evolutionary change is due to randomness or to the operation of some principle of direction. But it could well be that, if there is some system in the process of long-term change and novelty which is not simply a play of random factors, we could, in the long run, discover some regularities in the way uniqueness and novelty occur, which might even provide a clue to comprehend this continuous process of creation in repetitive, and therefore causal, terms.

One more issue remains to be discussed: are new things predictable? Or is prediction always based on former experience, and thus on repetition? It is comparison that enables us to predict future processes. We have seen that identity is far from omnipresent in nature. Where there is no complete identity, is prediction possible?

Biology shows that it is. In macrobiology – including medicine – precise prediction is quite often impossible. But analogous, not *exactly* similar, processes observed in the past may provide a practical basis for prediction, in terms not of certainties but of high probabilities. One could, perhaps, put forward the hypothesis that the greater the similarity of initial conditions, the higher the probability of analogous processes. However, this again should not be an axiom but a hypothesis that could be tested by experiment. At any rate, one could not exclude beforehand the possibility of predicting seemingly unique events by way of analogy.

However, is prediction also possible in the case of processes that are new, not because of the complexity of organisms but because they belong to the category of unique occurrences in the evolutionary line of irreversible processes? Let us take a concrete example: are mutations in biology predictable?

According to the prevalent view among geneticists, the occurrence of mutations is fully dominated by chance. It is not even possible to induce premeditated and directed mutations by physical or chemical manipulations. The occurrence of mutations is basically a random process, and induced genetic change may only produce a desired result in the sense that the process of creation of mutations is accelerated; however, they retain their character of randomness, and the only way to obtain successful new mutations is through a selection of those chance mutations that correspond with the desired properties.[29]

This situation looks like a confirmation of the mechanistic view that evolution progresses through a process of natural selection. However, even if we accept this view, it does not necessarily follow that the course of evolution is unpredictable. In many cases where the process of biological evolution could be reconstructed, sequences of successful mutations followed upon each other according to a distinct pattern. Long-term evolutionary processes sometimes follow an analogous course. For example, certain types of eyes were developed among very different animal species, which rather points towards a certain parallelism in evolutionary processes. Therefore, prediction by way of analogy may, again, come within the realm of scientific possibilities.

v. Determinism and Voluntarism in the Science of Man

The foregoing insights may help us to a more confident approach to the problem of human, and particularly social, evolution.

First of all, we can start by dismissing the heated discussion between determinists and voluntarists as totally irrelevant. What do the determinists claim? That, although he acts under the illusion of having a free will, man is actually unfree, since all he does is fully determined by the forces of nature governing the universe of which man forms an integral part. Since no living being is exempted from the general law of causality, and the human race cannot form an exception according to any scientific standard, the determinists claim that any talk of a free will must have anti-scientific, irrational roots and be associated with attributing to God, or some other supernatural force, a specific divine purpose in creating mankind. According to the determinists, it is only the utter complexity of nature that prevents science from actually predicting, in Laplace's sense, the future course of events, including the myriads of human actions as an ultimate product of the strictly mechanical operation of brain-cells. However, as we have seen, Laplacean determinism has, for a long time, lost its authority among natural scientists. If social scientists were to adhere to such a philosophy, they would simply be following an outworn model borrowed from nineteenth-century physics.

If our analysis can be upheld it should make clear that accepting some scope for free decision-making by living organisms is fully reconcilable with scientific thinking based on the general law of causality. The latter law finds its limit inasmuch as it is only valid where full identity of initial conditions can be demonstrated, and where, consequently, repetition as a universal principle holds. However, what is typical of living organisms of a higher order is their great complexity, which implies an increasing range of traits or situations that can be assessed as unique, not having been encountered in earlier experience. Even though actions and reactions in new situations will, in all probability, show a very strong analogy with patterns fixed in terms of full identity and repetition, in acknowledging this element of uniqueness as part and parcel of organic life an amount of freedom of action is implicitly postulated.

On the other hand, it is this semi-autonomous activity by living beings, first and foremost man, that is increasingly determining the course of nature on earth, and very recently even outside our planet. Man as an engineer, man as an agriculturist, man as a breeder of animals, man as a destroyer of forests, man as a warrior, or as an entrepreneur, polluting the air and contaminating the earth, has become a dominant factor in directing causal sequences in the nature of our planet. For determinists it has always been extremely difficult to explain away human action by impersonal mechanical forces that are accountable even for the most complicated human thoughts and artistic expressions. Even if any single human act were to be attributed to outside forces one had to admit that the most compulsive motive forces originated from actions or words of other human beings, who again had been motivated by other people – which, as any *probatio diabolica*, led the whole argument *ad absurdum*.

Our foregoing reductions of causality to the realm of identity, and the specific place attributed by us to the concept of uniqueness, liberates us from a host of artificialities and inconsistencies in our way of thinking. In order to affirm our scientific outlook we need no longer keep up the pretence of discussing free will as an illusion, and of building up the sciences of man in accordance with a model borrowed from those natural scientists who have never yet felt really compelled to integrate the concepts of uniqueness and evolution towards greater complexity within their outlook.

On the other hand, our awareness that man *is* able, to a large extent, to determine the course of nature, by influencing both our physical environment and living organisms, *including* the activities of other human beings, presupposes that identity and causality are dominating the course of nature in such a way that an enormous number of processes are predictable and therefore amenable to human manipulation (even though not all the consequences of human intrusion were premeditated and planned!). Determining the course of nature by man presupposes that this course can be accounted for in terms of repetition of causes and effects. In the case of *man* as an agent, a mechanistic, and even a finalistic (as far as there is premeditation) interpretation, of course, remains valid and logical. For practical purposes, at a macro-physical or chemical level, the calculability of processes initiated by human interference may sometimes appear near-absolute, which seems to provide some encouragement for the view that nature is fully dominated by causality and by inescapable laws. However, as soon as human interference touches upon the world of living matter the power of mankind appears less absolute, which we may now attribute to the much increased impact of the element of uniqueness in the field of biology, if compared with physics or chemistry. And as soon as human interference affects other human beings, the causal nexus has to be applied with still more reservations, and still more scope has to be left to a certain amount of human autonomy, originating in the element of uniqueness and individual variation.

vi. *The Limits of Causality in the Science of Man*

This does not mean that causality is absent from the realm of human interaction, and from social life in particular. There are two types of uniformity in human behaviour within a society. First, there are the uniformities that can be attributed to the regularities to be observed in the biological world. Many of the peculiarities of human behaviour are, in some way, correlated with the properties of living organisms, and differentiated according to such natural phenomena as heredity, age, sex and physical environment. This much accounts at least for some of the uniformity and predictability of human behaviour.

On top of these natural regularities, man himself has imposed a whole set of regularities of his own making, at least within the confines of his actual power. One of the primary concerns of man living in community with other human beings is how to make life calculable. Many of the institutions created by mankind serve precisely this purpose. Among such institutions are culture as a whole, calling into being a tremendous amount of uniformity in human behaviour, as far as the culture extends. Education and socialization of children is the primary mechanism through which such uniformities in thought and behaviour are being brought about. Law as a means of social control for influencing human behaviour is another source of uniformity. Law fulfils its function as a means for social control largely through a complicated system of punishments and rewards, thus restraining most people from certain actions and inducing them to certain other activities.[30] It is of less importance whether, for example, penal law exerts its psychological influence mainly through a direct impact of the threat of punishment, as Jeremy Bentham posited, or through a general attitude of obedience and conformity fostered by the moral impact of a sanctioning through penal law, as Anders V. Lundstedt maintained.[31] What matters most is that the social functions of law are to be looked for in the realm of expectations stimulated by law or by stereotyped legal decisions, rather than in the direct effect of decisions taken by legal agents in individual cases, as most jurists still hold. It is the expectation of definite sanctions or rewards that, generally, bring about a certain conformity in the behaviour of the citizen.

Language could equally be mentioned as an agent of uniformity, and so is fashion. Whereas in the past uniformities were largely transmitted through oral or visual tradition, they are in more recent times increasingly transmitted through written texts or still more modern means of communication.

It is the whole set of regularities, produced by both physical properties and human institutions, that makes a good deal of human behaviour calculable, and hence predictable. Much of social life can very well be conceived in terms of causality, or of statistical laws based on observed degrees of probability.

But, despite the huge influence of causal nexuses due to all these uniformities, there is no reason at all to consider human society to be fully determined by causal relationships, and on this account to deny the possibility of a certain scope for invention and creative activity due to elements of uniqueness and originality. It is mainly *these* elements of creativity that account for the ongoing process of human evolution – or revolution, for that matter.

vii. *Prediction of Revolutions*

To what extent is human action predictable, inasmuch as it *escapes* the boundaries of uniform behaviour? To be more precise, if we consider revolution as a breakthrough disrupting the regularities of an established social order, how can we then expect revolutions to be, more or less, predictable?

In classical Marxism, revolutions are part and parcel of a process that is essentially determined by laws governing the course of human history. Although this course is not unilinear but subject to a dialectical process of thesis–antithesis–synthesis and so forth, Marxism considers the process to be essentially fixed by the economic and technological basis and the prevalent contradictions within the class relationships. The actual course of revolutions may be influenced by individual decisions of leaders and rulers, but in the determinist outlook of classical Marxists revolution as such cannot be averted if the basic conditions are there. Since the

Marxists assumed that a development towards class struggle was present in any society, a situation would necessarily develop and mature where revolution would become inevitable. This assumption was at the basis of the expectation that, in the long run, a world revolution would arise.

This deterministic view created a somewhat paradoxical position as to the necessity of revolutionary action. If revolution was going to happen anyway, why do anything about it? Moreover, if revolutionary action was, in its turn, determined by existing conditions, would not such an assumption easily foster an atmosphere of fatalism and inactivity, since for everyone who defaulted there would always be many others to pursue a course that was, anyway, inevitable?

Actually, this was not the prevalent mood among the rising industrial proletariat. Their rather weak position in the first period of growth of the labour movement made them view a theory that claimed their ultimate victory to be inevitable as a very strong stimulus for their struggle.

Marx himself would not have adopted a quietistic interpretation of his determinist view. It has been repeatedly demonstrated[32] that he did not endorse the extreme determinist position that was, later on, taken by some of his epigones. He certainly believed in creative action as a catalyst of the opposing forces. And Lenin, the first Marxist to lead a successful proletarian revolution, was certainly not hampered in his actions by determinist considerations.

Quietistic interpretations of Marxist determinism were rather to be found among the so-called revisionists who assumed that a socialist society would automatically arise from the existing contradictions, even without any revolutionary activity on the part of the labour movement. And after developments in Germany in the early twenties and elsewhere in Europe had belied the expectation that world revolution was imminent, this determinism may have contributed to an atmosphere of, 'What can we do about an ultimate victory of socialism, anyway?' It became, then, the voluntarist and activist Nazis who, for some time, determined the course of world history.

The Marxist belief that the course of world history is determined is being challenged, at present, by several sociologists. Recently, a new concept has been introduced: that of possibilism.[33] Its implication is that history is open-ended, and that there are many alternative possibilities.

Although open-endedness as a concept appeals to me, I could not endorse possibilism if it claims that all solutions have equal chances of materializing. I maintain that a good deal of future actions and developments are, within certain boundaries, predictable. Surely they are predictable, inasmuch as uniformity is prevalent, and patterns known from the past can be expected to repeat themselves. There are some future developments that are much more *probable* than other ones, certainly in the short run.

For example, there is reason enough to expect that the struggle of the underprivileged groups and peoples for emancipation will continue. Our concept of social evolution implies that certain trends, known from the past, are very likely to reproduce themselves in the future, even though in modified form.

Therefore, instead of possibilism I would put forward probabilism as a substitute for an outlived determinism.

There remains the problem which we also encountered in a field like biology, to what extent one could predict developments that can be considered as essentially unique. Among these, we should possibly include the phenomenon of revolution.

I would suggest that here, again, the unique is new only in its specific shape. It does provide a new pattern or model for repetitive processes. But at the same time, even revolutions show many analogies with previous, more or less comparable, occurrences. This is where prediction, again, appears as a real possibility. Uniqueness and uniformity of identity are so interwoven into the fabric of history that no miraculous divination is needed to predict in general terms what is essentially unpredictable in its specificity.

Our difference with the Marxist view is not that it claims that historical processes are dialectical. Human evolution has not been proceeding, in the past, in a rectilinear way. There have been many paradoxes and contradictions in its development during the past millennium. Nor was emancipation, the driving force of evolution, a steady and uninterrupted process. There have been many reverses and reactions, and many gains in freedom had to be bought with the sacrifice of other freedoms or other values. The assessment of a certain achievement as a step towards emancipation always implies a value judgement. But then value-freedom, as a requirement of the social sciences, is an antiquated point of view.[34]

It is, therefore, to be expected that evolution in the future will, again, be a process fraught with contradicitions, conflicts, and inconsistencies.[35]

Perhaps Marx and his followers have overrated the significance and omnipresence of class struggle. Kropotkin may have been right when, as a reaction, he strongly stressed the element of co-operation as at least as essential in human beings as the element of strife.[36] And, although Mao Tse-tung decidedly calls himself a follower of Marx, one gets sometimes the impression that Kropotkin's stress on the human ability for cooperation, his plea for comparatively small units where community life can take place, and finally his belief in freedom of expression and action for the individual, are nearer to Mao's views than some of the strictly Marxist tenets.[37]

This basic belief in human beings, which Marx and Engels essentially shared, *may* presage a happier world in the future. But, for the time being, we are living in a world where strife and struggle are uppermost.

There is a *probability* of continuing evolution. However, there is no certainty: we have to remain aware of the *possibility* that mankind will prefer self-destruction to further emancipation. There have been animal species in the past that have faced complete destruction. How can we be sure that mankind will escape such a fate?

I hope, however, to have convinced some of my readers, that mankind, and each member of the human race for his part, have the fate of humanity within their own hands. Nineteenth-century man would not have accepted as an excuse that it was God's will to destroy mankind. Nor should twentieth-century man accept as an excuse that destruction of mankind was predetermined by the laws of nature. Our experience of a free will is no illusion. If we really believe in a free will we can move the world.

Notes

FOREWORD

1. A specimen of this approach can be found in Chalmers Johnson, *Revolution and the Social System*, 1964.

PART ONE

1. Berthold Laufer, in a review of R. H. Lowie, 'Culture and Ethnology', in *The American Anthropologist*, Vol. 20, 1918, p. 90.
2. Marshall D. Sahlins and Elman R. Service (eds.), *Evolution and Culture*, 1960, p. 1.
3. H. R. Barringer *et al.* (eds.), *Social Change in Developing Areas*, 1965, p. 19.
4. ibid., p. 1.
5. See, for example, Edward B. Tylor, *Primitive Culture*, Vol. 1, 1920, p. 53.
6. Claude Lévi-Strauss, *Race and History*, 1952, pp. 26ff.; Michel Leiris, *Race and Culture*, 1951, pp. 35ff.; for a refutation of this view see Raymond Aron, *Trois essais sur l'âge industriel*, 1966, pp. 117ff.
7. Barringer *et al.* (eds.), op. cit., p. 21.
8. Lewis H. Morgan, *Ancient Society or Researches in the Lines of Human Progress from Savagery through Barbarism to Civilization*, 1963; Friedrich Engels, *The Origin of the Family, Private Property and the State*, 1902.
9. See, for example, G. Elliot Smith, *Human History*, 1930.
10. See, for example, F. Graebner, *Methode der Ethnologie*, 1911, pp. 132ff.
11. Max Weber, *Wirtschaft und Gesellschaft*, 1925, pp. 725–6.
12. Otto B. van der Sprenkel, 'Max Weber on China', *History and Theory*, Vol. 3, 1964, pp. 348–70.

13. R. Coulborn (ed.), *Feudalism in History*, 1965.

14. See, for example, Karl A. Wittfogel, *Oriental Despotism: A Comparative Study of Total Power*, 1957, p. 410.

15. Karl Marx, *Grundrisse der Kritik der politischen Ökonomie*, completed in 1858, but published for the first time in Moscow in 1939.

16. Leo Trotzki, *Geschichte der Russischen Revolution*, Vol. 2, 1933, pp. 674–707.

17. *Premières sociétés des classes et mode de production asiatique*, special issue of *Recherches Internationales*, 1967, pp. 62ff.

18. *Obščee i osobennoe w istoričeskom razwitii stran wostoka* ('The Generic and the Specific in the Historical Development of Eastern Countries'; discussion papers on the Asiatic mode of production), 1966. See also *Premières sociétés etc.*, op. cit.

19. Leslie A. White, *The Evolution of Culture: The Development of Civilization to the Fall of Rome*, 1959; V. Gordon Childe, *Social Evolution*, 1951.

20. Julian H. Steward, *Theory of Culture Change: The Methodology of Multilinear Evolution*, 1955. On p. 17 he formulates his strictures as to classic evolutionism in the following terms: '... the postulated cultural sequences are so general that they are neither very arguable nor very useful'.

21. Wittfogel, op. cit., pp. 438ff. on 'Asiatic Restoration' and in particular p. 446 on 'Retrogressive Societal Development'.

22. ibid., pp. 366–7, 447.

23. ibid., p. 429.

24. For a more general and more basic criticism of Wittfogel's views see S. N. Eisenstadt, 'The Study of Oriental Despotisms as Systems of Total Power', *Journal of Asian Studies*, Vol. 17, 1958, pp. 436–46. On China see E. G. Pulleyblank, *Journal of the Economic and Social History of the Orient*, Vol. 1, Part 3, 1958, pp. 351–3; Joseph Needham, *Science and Society*, Vol. 23, 1959, pp. 58–65; Needham, 'Du passé culturel, social et philosophique chinois et de ses rapports avec la Chine contemporaine', *Comprendre*, Vol. 21–2, pp. 261–81; *Comprendre*, Vol. 23–4, pp. 113–28; Otto B. van der Sprenkel, 'Max Weber on China', *History and Theory*, Vol. 3, 1964, pp. 248–370. For Ceylon see E. R. Leach, 'Hydraulic Society in Ceylon', *Past and Present*, Vol. 15, 1959, pp. 2–26.

25. A certain amount of autonomy granted, within a 'hydraulic society', to bodies such as 'villages, guilds, and secondary religious organizations', is considered by Wittfogel to be 'politi-

cally irrelevant' (op. cit., pp. 124ff.). 'At best they established a kind of Beggars' Democracy.' How irrelevant Wittfogel deems those counterforces is made clear by his comparison of these 'freedoms' with those within the confines of a modern 'concentration camp'!

26. Van der Sprenkel, op. cit.

27. Joseph Needham, op. cit.

28. The use of modern industry for extending 'total political power' far beyond the limits of traditional 'hydraulic society' is the only element of 'modernity' Wittfogel is prepared to admit (op. cit., p. 440).

29. Karl Marx, Das Kapital, Vol. 1, ch. 12.4. See also note 61 of Das Kapital, where Marx refers to Th. Stamford Raffles's The History of Java.

30. C. van Vollenhoven, an authority on Indonesian customary law, demonstrated this in the early decades of this century. See, for example, his polemical pamphlet 'De Indonesiër en zijn grond' ('The Indonesian and his Land'), 1919, p. 52, where he sharply refutes Raffles's view.

31. Daniel Thorner, 'Marx on India and the Asiatic Mode of Production', Contributions to Indian Sociology, Vol. 9, 1966, pp. 33–66; see in particular p. 57: 'The descriptions of Indian villages sent home by military men and administrators in the 18th and 19th centuries provide little evidence for Marx's picture of land-holdings by the entire village and even less for tilling in common.' On Ceylon see Ralph Pieris, 'Title to Land in Kandyan Law', Essays Presented to Sir Paul Pieris, 1955.

32. See, for example, F. Tökei, Sur le mode de production asiatique, 1966; Maurice Godelier, La notion de 'mode de production asiatique' et les schémas marxistes d'évolution des sociétés 1965; a more adequate analysis is provided in some articles in the successive volumes of La Pensée, in the French volume Premières sociétés etc. mentioned in note 17, and in the Soviet symposium quoted in note 18; for a short survey of the discussion see P. Vidal-Naquet, 'Histoire et idéologie: Karl Wittfogel et le concept de "Mode de production asiatique" ', Annales: Economies Sociétés Civilisations, Vol. 19.

33. Barringer et al. (eds.), op. cit.

34. Daniel Lerner, The Passing of Traditional Society: Modernizing the Middle East, 1958.

35. Walt W. Rostow, The Stages of Economic Growth, 1960, pp.

93–7. A similar view is taken by Wittfogel (op. cit., pp. 427–9) who follows S. O. Zagorsky in this respect.

36. See, for example, G. A. Almond and J. S. Coleman (eds.), *The Politics of Developing Areas*, 1960, pp. 17–19, 532ff.; Lucian W. Pye and Sidney Verba (eds.), *Political Culture and Political Development*, 1965, pp. 4–5.

37. Lerner, op. cit., p. 10.

38. Barringer *et al.* (eds.), op. cit., p. 277.

39. Harry Hoetink, *Het nieuwe evolutionisme*, 1965; also published in Spanish as 'El nuevo evolucionismo', *America Latina*, Vol. 8, 1965, pp. 26ff. A highly sophisticated approach to the issue of modernization is also taken by R. P. Dore, *City Life in Japan: A Study of a Tokyo Ward*, 1958.

40. See, for example, S. M. Lipset in S. M. Lipset and A. Solari (eds.), *Elites in Latin America*, 1967, pp. 42ff.

41. Barringer *et al.* (eds.), op. cit., p. 101.

42. Lewis H. Morgan, *Ancient Society or Researches in the Lines of Human Progress from Savagery through Barbarism to Civilization*, 1963, pp. 17–18; see also the third chapter, 'Ratio of Human Progress'; Edward B. Tylor, *Primitive Culture*, Vol. 1, p. 61.

43. Tylor in *Encyclopedia Britannica*, 9th ed., 1878, subtitled 'Anthropology', Vol. 2, p. 121; quoted from Barringer *et al.* (eds.), op. cit., p. 77, where Morris T. Opler accuses Tylor of 'a certain smugness and paternalism concerning native peoples'.

44. Rostow, op. cit., pp. 8–9.

45. See, however, the attempt by Morgan to analyse the 'ratio of human progress' (op. cit., pp. 19ff.). See also, for the time factor, Jan Romein, 'The Significance of the Comparative Approach in Asian Historiography', in Soedjatmoko *et al.* (eds.), *An Introduction to Indonesian Historiography*, 1965, pp. 380–94.

46. Barringer *et al.* (eds.), op. cit., p. 101.

47. Lévi-Strauss, op. cit., pp. 26–7.

48. Barringer *et al.* (eds.), op. cit., p. 54.

49. ibid., p. 104.

50. Leslie A. White, *The Evolution of Culture: The Development of Civilization to the Fall of Rome*, 1959, ch. 2, in particular p. 56. He calls technology 'the basis and determinant of cultural systems' (p. 18). Social organization, in Professor White's view, is not an independent variable, but 'is determined by the factors of

subsistence, offense-defense, and reproduction and is to be explained in these terms' (p. 67).

51. Sahlins and Service (eds.), *Evolution and Culture*, p. 35.

52. Morgan, op. cit., ch. 2.

53. Herbert Spencer, *The Principles of Sociology*, Vol. 1, 1876, pp. 470ff., 481ff.

54. See also Sahlins and Service (eds.), op. cit., pp. 21, 36, mentioning as criteria for progress 'greater organization', 'geometric increase in the division of labor', 'better integration'.

55. ibid., p. 14.

56. ibid., p. 16.

57. Clifford Geertz, *Agricultural Involution: The Processes of Ecological Change in Indonesia*, 1963.

58. Barringer *et al.* (eds.), op. cit., p. 45.

59. ibid., p. 104.

60. Raoul Naroll, 'A Preliminary Index of Social Development', *American Anthropologist*, Vol. 58, 1956, p. 695.

61. Barringer *et al.* (eds.), op. cit., p. 17.

62. ibid., p. 9.

63. ibid., p. 105.

64. See Peter M. Worsley in his review of Sahlins and Service (eds.), *Evolution and Culture*, in *Science and Society*, Vol. 26, 1962, pp. 366–7, where he criticizes the criterion of 'higher levels of integration'. 'Can we use this criterion meaningfully to decide whether Stalin's centralized Russia is "higher" or "lower" than China which combined similar features with decentralized communes which perform many functions of government "normally" provided for by special local and centralized bureaucratic structures?'

65. J. D. Bernal, *Science in History*, 1954, pp. 26–7.

66. For a recent research project see F. van Heek *et al.* (eds.), *Het verborgen talent: milieu, schoolkeuze en schoolgeschiktheid (The Hidden Talent; Environment, School Choice and Fitness for School)*, 1968.

67. Engels, op. cit., ch. 9.

68. Robert H. Lowie, *Primitive Society*, 1920, p. 191, argues 'that a genuine matriarchate is nowhere to be found, though in a few places feminine prerogatives have evolved to a marked degree in certain directions'.

69. Margaret Mead, *Sex and Temperament in Three Primitive So-

cieties, 1935. According to her interpretation, among the Mundugumor both males and females were expected to behave in a way associated in our society with the masculine role. Among the Arapesh both males and females fulfilled 'feminine' roles, whereas among the Tchambuli our sex roles were essentially reversed.

70. Even E. E. Evans-Pritchard in *The Position of Women in Primitive Societies and Other Essays in Social Anthropology*, 1965, still clings to some outworn stereotypes, such as 'deep biological and psychological factors' accountable for the unequal status of men and women. 'Men are always in the ascendancy, and this is perhaps the more evident the higher the civilization', p. 54. He claims that his opinion 'has in any case a certain *a priori* validity'. I would suggest that the same '*a priori* validity' could be claimed by anyone who argues that races or social classes differ as to innate abilities.

71. In this connection it is important to note that Lowie, although not endorsing an evolutionist perspective, also admits a correlation, and a probable causal nexus, between cattle raising or plough culture on the one hand and female inferiority on the other (op. cit., pp. 193–4): 'Among stock-raising populations the status of woman is almost uniformly one of decided and absolute inferiority;' '. . . it is not merely domestication but also plough-culture that is linked with masculine effort in the history of civilization'. 'We see why the economically dependent women of China, of Central Asia and India should be on an unequivocally lower plane than man.'

72. Jan Romein, 'The Common Human Pattern: Origin and Scope of Historical Theories', *Journal of World History*, Vol. 4, 1958, pp. 449ff.

73. Engels, op. cit.: 'Liberation of woman has become possible. . .only through industry', ch. 9.

74. A statistical comparative survey is provided by Leo W. Simmons, *The Role of the Aged in Primitive Society*, 1945.

75. Barringer *et al.* (eds.), op. cit., p. 63.

76. See for example Margaret Mead (ed.), *Cooperation and Competition among Primitive Peoples*, 1957.

77. William H. Whyte, *The Organization Man*, 1956.

78. Barringer *et al.* (eds.), op. cit., p. 58.

79. ibid., p. 57.

80. Sahlins and Service (eds.), op. cit., p. 38.

81. Talcott Parsons, *Societies: Evolutionary and Comparative Perspectives*, 1966, pp. 21–2.

82. Barringer *et al.* (eds.), op. cit., p. 16.

83. A. Goldenweiser, 'Loose Ends of a Theory on the Individual Pattern and Involution in Primitive Society', in R. H. Lowie (ed.), *Essays in Anthropology Presented to A. L. Kroeber*, 1936, pp. 99–104.

84. Geertz, op. cit., p. 82.

85. ibid., p. 82.

86. Barringer *et al.* (eds.), op. cit., p. 16.

87. ibid., pp. 16, 29ff.

88. ibid., pp. 14, 31. He evidently views rational problem-solving as a substitute for the trial-and-error process.

89. ibid., p. 13.

90. Morris E. Opler in Barringer *et al.* (eds.), op. cit., pp. 82ff.

91. Sahlins and Service (eds.), op. cit., pp. 69ff. on 'The Law of Cultural Dominance'.

92. The significance of cultural borrowing has been seriously overrated by the diffusionist school which was another reaction against evolutionism. Some diffusionists, such as G. Elliot Smith (see for example *Elephants and Ethnologists*, 1924, p. 105), excluded, to all intents and purposes, the possibility of independent invention. Others, like Fritz Graebner, in theory admitted the sporadic occurrence of invention. But in their view the whole matter was too speculative. Ethnologists should rather restrict themselves to what was near at hand, which was cultural borrowing (see Graebner, op. cit., p. 107). See also Lowie, op. cit., pp. 434–5. However, it should be pointed out that Lowie could not be justly labelled as a 'diffusionist' pure and simple. For example, in his treatment of the clan he leaves full scope for independent invention.

93. Jan Romein, *Aera van Europa: De Europese geschiedenis als afwijking van het Algemeen Menselijk Patroon* (Era of Europe: European History as a Deviation from the 'Common Human Pattern'), 1954. Romein's generalization as far as agrarian societies are concerned has rightly been criticized by A. J. F. Köbben, 'Het A(lgemeen) M(enselijk) P(atroon) en de volkenkundige' ('The Common Human Pattern and the Cultural Anthropologist'), *Mens en Maatschappij*, Vol. 32, 1957, pp. 193ff.

94. David Kaplan, in Sahlins and Service (eds.), op. cit., p. 89.

95. Kaplan, op. cit., p. 88.

96. ibid., p. 89.

97. ibid., p. 91.

98. Morgan, op. cit., ch. 3 ('Ratio of Human Progress').

99. Jan Romein, 'De dialektiek van de vooruitgang: bijdrage tot het ontwikkelingsbegrip in de geschiedenis' (The Dialectics of Progress: a Contribution to our Understanding of Evolution within History), *Forum*, Vol. 4, Part 2, 1935, pp. 732–77 and 828–55; reprinted in extended form in Romein, *Het onvoltooid verleden; cultuur-historische studies* (The Imperfect Past; Studies in Cultural History), 1948.

100. See, for example, Jos. Kulischer, *Allgemeine Wirtschaftsgeschichte des Mittelalters und der Neuzeit*, Vol. 2, 1928, pp. 192–3.

101. K. Horner (pseud. of A. Pannekoek), 'De Derde Internationale en de Wereldrevolutie' 'The Third International and World Revolution', *De Nieuwe Tijd*, Vol. 25, 1920, p. 267.

102. Engels, op. cit., p. 189.

103. They invoked the well-known Marxism formulas: 'No social formation ever disappears before all the productive forces are developed for which it has room', and: 'Centralization of the means of production and socialization of labour at last reach a point where they become incompatible with their capitalist integument. This integument is burst asunder. The knell of capitalist private property sounds. The expropriators are expropriated.'

104. It is ironical that Engels in his *Grundsätze des Kommunismus*, written in 1847, prophesied that a communist revolution would occur much earlier and easier in advanced England than in backward Germany! *Marx/Engels Gesamt Ausgabe*, Vol. 6, 1932, p. 516 (sub. question 19).

105. V. I. Lenin, *Imperialism: The Highest Stage of Capitalism*, 1944, p. 110. He quotes from Hilferding's *Finanzkapital*: 'This movement for independence threatens European capital precisely in its most valuable and most promising fields of exploitation . . .'

106. *Pravda*, 18 May 1913, reproduced in V. I. Lenin, *O nacional'nom i nacional'no-kolonial'nom voprose*, 1956, pp. 79–80; also quoted by Jean Chesneaux, *L'Asie orientale aux XIXme et XXme siècles*, 1966, p. 333, dealing with Romein's 'law of the retarding lead' as applied to Asia.

107. Leo Trotzki, op. cit., Vol. 1, 1931, p. 21.

108. Sahlins and Service (eds.), op. cit., pp. 99–100. They also mention Thorstein Veblen who commented upon the backwardness of

England's industrial development in comparison with Germany's in terms of 'the penalty of taking the lead'.

109. Leo Trotzki, op. cit., Vol. 1, pp. 17ff., 25, 60.

110. Leo Trotzki, op. cit., Vol. 2, 1933, pp. 674–707.

111. ibid.

112. Barringer *et al.* (eds.), op. cit., p. 8

113. Quoted from ibid., p. 71.

114. Translations: *nil natura per saltum*: nothing occurs in nature by leaps. *Nil natura nisi per saltum*: everything occurs in nature by leaps. *Nil humanum nisi per saltum*: everything human occurs by leaps.

115. As far as I am aware, Romein's theory has been summarized for the first time in English in W. F. Wertheim, 'The Better Earth', *Comprendre*, Vol. 19, 1958, pp. 103–9.

116. Sahlins and Service (eds.), op. cit., p. 98.

117. ibid., p. 97.

118. ibid., p. 104.

119. ibid., pp. 30–33.

120. ibid., pp. 109ff.

121. ibid., p. 119.

122. ibid., p. 115.

123. It seems to me that in the foregoing I have done full justice to the brilliant booklet *Evolution and Culture*. In the same way as its authors had overlooked Romein's and my previous publications, I was not aware of their publications when I summarized Romein's 'Dialectics of Progress' in my book *East-West Parallels: Sociological Approaches to Modern Asia*, published in 1964. As soon as I had acquainted myself with Sahlins's and Service's study, I restored the omission in a lecture read in Dutch before the section of non-Western sociology of the Nederlandse Sociologische Vereniging, published in *De Nieuwe Stem*, with the title 'Maatschappelijke evolutie' ('Social Evolution'), Vol. 21, 1966, pp. 216–33. The present discussion of 'evolution' is a much extended elaboration of the contents of that lecture.

124. The point was made by the Dutch Marxist A. S. de Leeuw in a critical review of Romein's work, 'De onvoltooide theorie van Jan Romein' ('The Incomplete Theory of Jan Romein'), *Politiek en Cultuur*, 1937, pp. 608–11, where he refers to Lenin's criticism of Bukharin's views in the early twenties. Capitalist power had not started to crumble in the weakest economic and political structures, as Bukharin had argued, but in an economic structure of

'intermediate weakness'. 'Without having attained a certain level of capitalism we could not have succeeded,' said Lenin. The source to which De Leeuw refers (*Leninski Sbornik*, Vol. 11, pp. 397ff.) was not available in the Netherlands.

125. Sahlins and Service (eds.), op. cit., p. 97.
126. S. N. Eisenstadt, *Modernization: Protest and Change*, 1966.
127. ibid., pp. 46–7; A. Gerschenkron, *Economic Backwardness in Historical Perspective*, 1962, pp. 353–4.
128. 'The take-off towards economic growth that Rostow and Gerschenkron hope to find in the history of every capitalist country, occurred for the last time in Japan' (Witold Kula, 'Les débuts du capitalisme en Pologne dans la perspective de l'histoire comparée', lecture read at the Library of the Polish Academy in Rome, 1960, p. 24).
129. Kula, op. cit., for a critical appraisal.
130. Ch. Wagley, 'The Brazilian Revolution: Social Change since 1930', in R. N. Adams *et al.* (eds.), *Social Change in Latin America Today: Its Implications for United States Policy*, 1960, p 221. See also Hoetink, op. cit.; Wertheim, op. cit., pp. 142ff.
131. Eisenstadt, op. cit., p. 147.
132. Kula, op. cit.
133. Eisenstadt, op. cit., p. 100.
134. Seymour M. Lipset, *The First New Nation: The United States in Historical and Comparative Perspective*, 1963, p. 59.
135. Jean-Jacques Servan-Schreiber, *The American Challenge*, 1967.
136. Eisenstadt, op. cit., pp. 38ff.
137. ibid., p. 40.
138. Kula, op. cit., p. 24; Ragnar Nurkse, *Problems of Capital Formation in Underdeveloped Countries*, 1955, p. 10.
139. Kenneth E. Boulding, 'Where are we Going if Anywhere? A Look at Postcivilization', *Human Organization*, Vol. 21, 1962, pp. 162ff.
140. A. Stärcke, 'Het geweten' ('The Conscience'), *Nederlands Maandschrift voor Geneeskunde*, Vol. 16, 1930, p. 58.
141. Alain Touraine in *Le Monde*, 7 and 8 March 1968.
142. Bartlett H. Stoodley (ed.), *Society and Self: A Reader in Social Psychology*, 1962, p. 2.
143. Talcott Parsons, *Societies: Evolutionary and Comparative Perspectives*, 1966, p. 10.
144. Parsons, op. cit., p. 11.
145. ibid., p. 35.

146. *International Encyclopedia of the Social Sciences*, Vol. 16, *sub voce* 'Verstehen', p. 311.

147. Émile Durkheim, *Les règles de la méthode sociologique*, 1919, p. 35.

148. Durkheim, *De la division du travail social*, 1893, pp. 189ff.

149. A. R. Radcliffe-Brown, *Method in Social Anthropology*, ed. M. N. Srinivas, 1958, pp. 168–9.

150. S. F. Nadel, *The Foundations of Social Anthropology*, 1963, p. 107. He also quotes several other sociologists and social anthropologists who consider institutions to be really existing entities.

151. Ralph Linton, *The Study of Man: An Introduction*, 1936, ch. 8; Robert K. Merton endorses Linton's view in *Social Theory and Social Structure*, 1957, pp. 368ff.

152. Max Weber, *Gesammelte Aufsätze zur Wissenschaftslehre*, 1922, p. 515. 'Reification' of social concepts has recently been criticized by Norbert Elias, *Was ist Soziologie?*, 1970.

153. *International Encyclopedia of the Social Sciences*, Vol. 15, *sub voce* 'Stratification, Social', p. 303; Vol. 16, *sub voce* 'Weber, Max', p. 495; however, the author of the latter article, Reinhard Bendix, timely remembers that 'one consequence of Weber's primary concern with action and its meaning was his conceptualization of collectivities in terms of social behaviour rather than of structures' (Vol. 16, p. 498).

154. Weber, op. cit., pp. 444–5.

155. Weber, op. cit., p. 446; 'The chance of agreement as an empirically valid datum can here, too, on the average and *ceteris paribus* be deemed to increase to the extent that one may take for granted that those who obey are doing so for the reason that they experience dominance, also subjectively, as binding for themselves. Insomuch as this is, on the average and approximately, the case, to that extent "dominance" rests on an acceptance of legitimacy'.

156. Max Weber, op. cit., p. 514.

157. Max Weber, *Wirtschaft und Gesellschaft*, 1925, p. 13; see also p. 26.

158. Marianne Weber, *Max Weber: Ein Lebensbild*, 1926, p. 216.

159. ibid., pp. 324–5.

160. Bendix, op. cit., p. 495.

161. Marianne Weber, op. cit., pp. 325–8. She gives the following reason why Weber introduced the 'ideal type': 'Historical perception remains necessarily in a constant flow. Therefore, its final incorporation in a closed system of concepts from which one could deduce reality, is senseless.'

162. ibid., pp. 689–94.

163. Bendix, op. cit., p. 495.

164. Bendix has also realized that at the background of Weber's rejection of social structures as realities was a more dynamic view of social processes: 'The view of society as a balance between opposing forces is the reason why Weber quite explicitly rejected the attempt to interpret social structures as wholes' (Reinhard Bendix, *Max Weber: An Intellectual Portrait*, 1960, pp. 269ff.).

165. Robert S. Lynd and Helen M. Lynd, *Middletown*, 1929, contented themselves with a very rough division of the people into two groups: the business people and the working-men. In their follow-up study *Middletown in Transition: A Study in Cultural Conflicts*, 1937, the treatment of social classes was somewhat more elaborated (pp. 444–65); but it was not by far the central issue it became in the study by Warner *et al.*

166. W. Lloyd Warner and Paul S. Lunt, *The Social Life of a Modern Community*, Vol. 1 of the Yankee City Series, 1941, pp. 10–11.

167. Dietrich Herzog, *Klassengesellschaft ohne Klassenkonflikt: Eine Studie über William Lloyd Warner und die Entwicklung der neuen amerikanischen Stratifikationsforschung*, 1965.

168. Warner and Lunt, op. cit., p. 14.

169. Lynd, op. cit., pp. 444ff.

170. Warner and Lunt, op. cit., pp. 4–5.

171. St. Clair Drake and Horace R. Cayton, *Black Metropolis: A Study of Negro Life in a Northern City*, 1945. In a 'methodological note' Warner explains that the selection of 'a metropolitan area with great social complexity and rapid social change' was made on purpose (pp. 776ff.).

172. W. L. Warner, M. Meeker and K. Eells, *Social Class in America: A Manual of Procedure for the Measurement of Social Status*, 1949, p. 5.

173. Lewis A. Coser, *The Functions of Social Conflict*, 1956, p. 137. See also Max Gluckman, *Custom and Conflict in Africa*, 1955, pp. 47–8.

174. See, for example, Bronislaw Malinowski, *The Dynamics of Culture Change: An Inquiry into Race Relations in Africa*, ed. Phyllis M. Kaberry, 1945, pp. 15,17.

175. Oliver C. Cox, *Caste, Class, and Race: A Study in Social Dynamics*, 1959, pp. 305ff.

176. Elizabeth Bott, *Family and Social Network: Roles, Norms and External Relationships in Ordinary Urban Families*, 1964, p. 175.

177. ibid., p. 191.
178. H. J. Friedericy, *De standen by de Boeginezen en Makassaren* (Social Classes with the Buginese and the Macassarese), 1933; see, for example, pp. 68ff.
179. H. Th. Chabot, *Verwantschap, stand en sexe in Zuid-Celebes* (Kinship, Social Class, and Sex in South Celebes), 1950; see, for example, p. 5.
180. ibid., p. 79 where he explicitly characterizes the stratification principles as drawn up by Friedericy as representing the aristocracy's image of society. See also Chabot's contribution to Koentjaraningrat (ed.), *Villages in Indonesia*, 1967, p. 197.
181. Selosoemardjan, *Social Changes in Jogjakarta*, 1962, p. 22.
182. H. J. van Mook, 'Kuta Gede', in W. F. Wertheim *et al.* (eds.), *The Indonesian Town: Studies in Urban Sociology*, 1958, pp. 287–8.
183. Allison Davis, Burleigh B. Gardner and Mary R. Gardner, *Deep South: A Sociological Study of Caste and Class*, 1965, p. 65.
184. See Chabot, in Koentjaraningrat (ed.), op. cit., pp. 191, 209.
185. Warner and Lunt, op. cit., p. 169; Warner and Lunt, *The Status System of a Modern Community*, Vol. 2 of the Yankee City Series, 1942, pp. 48–9.
186. Warner and Lunt, *The Social Life of a Modern Community*, pp. 174–5.
187. ibid., p. 175.
188. ibid., pp. 180ff.
189. Ralf Dahrendorf, *Class and Class Conflict in Industrial Society*, 1959, p. 159. See also John Rex, *Key Problems of Sociological Theory*, 1961.
190. Warner and Lunt, op. cit., p. 49.
191. See, for example, W. F. Wertheim, *East-West Parallels: Sociological Approaches to Modern Asia*, 1964, pp. 23ff.
192. See, for example, Eugene L. Horowitz in O. Klineberg (ed.), *Characteristics of the American Negro*, 1944, p. 247, where he speaks about attitudes of the members of minorities: 'Members of minority groups partake in the general culture of which they are a part, including the pattern of preferences with respect to "racial" background. They tend to maintain the same pattern as those who belong to other segments of the population, with one exception: if they are members of minorities which are discriminated against, they may move their own group from its usually low position in the list and put it at the top. This, however, is only a surface phenomenon, for they have been exposed

to the prevailing attitude toward their own group and tend to accept it along with all the rest of the pattern. However, they cannot consciously accept this unfavorable description of themselves and *they reject it by repression*.' (italics are mine. W.).

193. The basic study was F. J. Roethlisberger and William J. Dickson, *Management and the Worker: An Account of a Research Program Conducted by the Western Electric Company, Hawthorne, Chicago*, 1939, pp. 525–48.

194. See, for example, J. A. A. van Doorn and C. J. Lammers, *Moderne sociologie: systematiek en analyse* (*Modern Sociology: Systematics and Analysis*), 1959, p. 202.

195. Margaret Mead, *New Lives for Old: Cultural Transformation – Manus 1928–1953*, 1956, p. 114.

196. ibid., p. 158.

197. Percy S. Cohen, *Modern Social Theory*, 1968, p. 169.

198. Max Gluckman, *Custom and Conflict in Africa*, *passim*.

199. J. F. Glastra van Loon and E. W. Vercruijsse, 'De sociale functie van het recht' ('The Social Function of Law'), *Mens en Maatschappij*, Vol. 37, 1962, p. 9. In a later publication, *Mens en Maatschappij*, Vol. 38, 1963, pp. 341ff., the authors have admitted that legal norms are not the only determinants.

PART TWO

1. Hannah Arendt, *On Revolution*, 1963, p. 41.

2. ibid., p. 41.

3. Barrington Moore Jr, *Social Origins of Dictatorship and Democracy: Lord and Peasant in the Making of the Modern World*, 1966, pp. 201–2.

4. A. N. Condorcet, 'Sur le sens du mot révolutionnaire', in *Oeuvres*, Vol. 12, 1847, p. 615.

5. Arendt, op. cit., pp. 36, 291 n., 25.

6. ibid., pp. 37ff.

7. Honoré, Count of Mirabeau, opened his *Aux Bataves sur le Stathoudérat* with the words: 'C'est un jour de deuil pour l'Europe que celui où l'invasion prussienne a déconcerté vos nobles projects, infortunés Bataves!' ('It was a day of mourning for Europe when the Prussian invasion disrupted your noble plans, unfortunate Batavians!') Interestingly, he calls the 'restoration' a 'revolution' in this pamphlet, 1831, p. 81. So did several of his Dutch contemporaries.

8. I refer to the definition attempted by Herbert Aptheker, *The Nature of Democracy, Freedom and Revolution*, 1967, p. 76.

9. Arendt, op. cit., p. 9.

10. Giovanni Blumer, *Die chinesische Kulturrevolution 1965/67*, 1968, pp. 60, 161.

11. Joan Robinson, *The Cultural Revolution in China*, 1969, p. 24.

12. Jawaharlal Nehru, *An Autobiography*, 1955, p. 283.

13. Edward A. Ross, *Principles of Sociology*, 1920, p. 153.

14. See, for example, Stokely Carmichael and Charles V. Hamilton, *Black Power: The Politics of Liberation in America*, 1967, p. 53: 'Those of us who advocate Black Power are quite clear in our minds that a "non-violent" approach to civil rights is an approach black people cannot afford and a luxury white people do not deserve.'

15. Lyford P. Edwards, *The Natural History of Revolution*, 1965, p. 24.

16. George Modelski in James N. Rosenau (ed.), *International Aspects of Civil Strife*, 1964, p. 16.

17. See, for example, V. I. Lenin, *Collected Works*, Vol. 9, p. 236–7: 'For from the democratic revolution we shall at once and precisely in accordance with the measure of our strength, the strength of the class-conscious and organized proletariat begin to pass to the socialist revolution'. Leon Trotsky, *Itogi i perspektivy russkoj revoljucii*, 1906; reprinted in Leon Trotsky, *Permanent Revolution, and Results and Prospects*, 1962.

18. See, for example, Lin Piao, in his famous article 'Long Live the Victory of the People's War', *Peking Review*, Vol. 8, No. 36, September 1965; Mao Tse-tung, 'On New Democracy', in *Selected Works of Mao Tse-tung*, Vol. 3, 1954, especially p. 118.

19. Crane Brinton, *The Anatomy of Revolution*, 1965, pp. 59–60.

20. Franz Marek, *Philosophie der Weltrevolution*, 1966, p. 68.

21. See, for example, the preface to the Russian edition of the *Communist Manifesto*, published in 1882.

22. In a lecture read for the Verbond van Wetenschappelijke Onderzoekers (Dutch Association of Scientific Researchers), March 1968, published in *Wetenschap en Samenleving*, Vol. 22, 1968, pp. 62ff.

23. Marek, op. cit., pp. 92ff.

24. The Second Havana Declaration, 4 February 1962.

25. Marek, op. cit., p. 80.

26. N. A. Simonija, *Ob osobennostjach nacional'no-osvoboditel'nych revoljucij*, 1969, p. 49.

27. Barrington Moore, op. cit.

28. ibid., p. 433.

29. ibid., p. 77.

30. ibid., p. 467.

31. ibid., p. 227.

32. ibid., pp. 227, 467, 486.

33. In a paper published in September 1850 (*Werke*, Vol. 9, 1957, p. 232) Marx had already used the term 'uninterrupted revolution'.

34. See, for example, J. V. Stalin, *Foundations of Leninism*, 1924.

35. The concept of 'uninterrupted revolution' in its original Marxian and Leninist sense is also accepted by the Chinese communist leaders as appears from Lin Piao's article quoted above. It means, in their view, that the 'new-democratic' revolution can, without much delay, develop into a 'socialist' one.

36. For the foregoing exposition I am indebted to the chapter on world revolution in G. Harmsen, *Marx contra de marxistische ideologie* (*Marx against Marxist Ideology*), 1968, and to Marek, op. cit. See also Thomas P. Thornton, 'The Emergence of Communist Revolutionary Doctrine', in Cyril E. Black and Thomas P. Thornton (eds.), *Communism and Revolution: The Strategic Uses of Political Violence*, 1964, pp. 43ff.

37. See, for a discussion of this theory, Kurt Steinhaus, *Zur Theorie des internationalen Klassenkampfes*, 1967.

38. James N. Rosenau (ed.), *International Aspects of Civil Strife*, 1964, p. 41. See also Karl W. Deutsch, in Harry Eckstein (ed.), *Internal War: Problems and Approaches*, 1964, p. 102: 'In most internal wars, elements of domestic strife and of external intervention are intermingled in varying proportions.'

39. Jan Romein, *Carillon der tijden: studies en toespraken op cultuurhistorisch terrein* (*Carillon of the Times: Studies and Lectures in the Field of Cultural History*), 1953, p. 59.

40. J. Presser, *Amerika: Van kolonie tot wereldmacht* (*America: From Colony to World Power*), 1949, p. 131.

41. Deutsch, op. cit., p. 105.

42. J. Suys, *Politiek en vrede: rekenschap van een antithese* (*Politics and Peace: Account of an Antithesis*), 1955, p. 34.

43. ibid., p. 34.

44. Deutsch, op. cit., p. 101.

45. I. Deutscher, *Stalin: A Political Biography*, 1949, p. 554.
46. Harmsen, op. cit. See also Modelski, op. cit., p. 43. For the Soviet attitude towards the Chinese revolution after the Second World War see Charles B. McLane, *Soviet Strategies in Southeast Asia: An Explanation of Eastern Policy under Lenin and Stalin*, 1966, pp. 251, 369–70.
47. See, for example, Emanuel Sarkisyanz, *Russland und der Messianismus des Orients: Sendungsbewusstsein und politischer Chiliasmus des Ostens*, 1955.
48. See, for example, Lin Piao in his earlier quoted article.
49. Manfred Halpern in Rosenau (ed.), op. cit., p. 279.
50. V. I. Lenin, *O nacional'nom i nacional'no-osvoboditel' nom voprose*, 1956, pp. 44–5.
51. See, for example, Lawrence Stone, 'Theories of Revolution', *World Politics*, Vol. 18, 1965, p. 159, quoting George S. Pettee, *The Process of Revolution*, 1938, as having used that expression. Crane Brinton, op. cit., also restricts his treatment of the revolutionary phenomenon to four 'great' revolutions.
52. See, for example, G. B. Sansom, *The Western World and Japan*, 1950, p. 351.
53. A curious comparison since, as we have seen, 'the Glorious Revolution' was anything but a true revolution! Perhaps it should be called a 'palace revolution'.
54. Sansom, op. cit., p. 355.
55. ibid., p. 351.
56. Moore, op. cit., p. 112.
57. ibid., p. 149.
58. ibid., p. 146.
59. A similar conclusion can be found in Aptheker, op. cit., pp. 84 ff., on 'The Slaveholders' Counter-Revolution'.
60. For a detailed discussion of several types of millenarian movements I refer to A. J. F. Köbben, 'Prophetic Movements as an Expression of Social Protest', *International Archives of Ethnography*, Vol. XLIX, No. 1, 1960.
61. R. R. Palmer, *The Age of the Democratic Revolution: A Political History of Europe and America, 1760–1800*, Vol. 2 (The Struggle), 1964, p. 128.
62. Brinton, op. cit. For a highly critical appraisal of Brinton's work see Harry Eckstein, 'On the Etiology of Internal Wars', *History and Theory*, Vol. 4, 1965, pp. 134ff.
63. Brinton, op. cit., pp. 16ff.

64. ibid., p. 18.
65. ibid., pp. 226ff.
66. ibid., p. 15.
67. The scantiness of the extant literature on revolutions in general and on their process in particular is brought to light in Lawrence Stone's excellent article, op. cit., pp. 159ff. Besides Brinton's study, one could mention Rex D. Hopper, 'The Revolutionary Process: A Frame of Reference for the Study of Revolutionary Movements', *Social Forces*, Vol. 28, 1950, pp. 270ff., on the distinctive phases of revolutions. Much more superficial is Lyford P. Edwards, *The National History of Revolution*, published for the first time in 1927.
68. Barrington Moore, *Social Origins of Dictatorship and Democracy: Lord and Peasant in the Making of the Modern World*, 1966, pp. 485–6.
69. ibid., p. 505.
70. ibid., pp. 505–6.
71. Mark Twain, *A Yankee at the Court of King Arthur*, Vol. 1, 1890, p. 132.
72. Stone, op. cit., p. 164.
73. Chalmers Johnson, *Revolution and the Social System*, 1964. See also, from the same author, *Revolutionary Change*, 1968.
74. Eckstein, op. cit.
75. Eric Hobsbawm, *The Age of Revolution: Europe 1789–1848*, 1962, p. 57, asserts the same for the peasantry in France.
76. Erich Kuttner, *Het hongerjaar 1566 (The Hunger Year 1566)*, 1949.
77. Stone, op. cit., p. 106.
78. ibid., p. 169.
79. Alexis de Tocqueville, *The Old Régime and the French Revolution*, 1955.
80. Brinton, op. cit., pp. 34–6
81. James C. Davies, 'Toward a Theory of Revolution', *American Sociological Review*, Vol. 27, 1962, pp. 5ff.
82. Stone, op. cit., p. 171.
83. ibid., p. 173.
84. Brinton, op. cit., p. 31.
85. See, for example, Moore, op. cit., pp. 13ff.
86. Brinton, op. cit., p. 30.
87. Hobsbawm, op. cit., pp. 60–61.
88. Palmer, op. cit., Vol. 1 (The Challenge), 1959, pp. 482ff. Similarly

C. E. Labrousse, *La crise de l'économie française à la fin de l'ancien régime et au début de la Révolution*, Vol. 1, 1943, pp. 32ff.

89. R. H. Tawney, *Land and Labour in China*, 1937, p. 72. See also Lucien Blanco, *Les origines de la révolution chinoise*, 1967, pp. 148ff.

90. Tawney, op. cit., p. 73.

91. Brinton, op. cit., p. 250.

92. Davies, op. cit., p. 7. See also Eric Wolf, *Peasant Wars of the Twentieth Century*, 1969, viewing middle peasants as the core of peasant revolutionary movements (pp. 290ff.).

93. As far as China is concerned I do not think Wolf has convincingly proved his point. From William Hinton, *Fanshen: A Documentary of Revolution in a Chinese Village*, 1966, one gets a different impression, at least for the period after 1945.

94. Brinton, op. cit., p. 32.

95. Davies, op. cit., p. 12.

96. Moore, op. cit., p. 220.

97. Davies, in his article quoted above, tries to explain why it did not occur in the United States.

98. A. J. Piekaar, *Atjeh en de oorlog met Japan* (Acheh and the War against Japan), 1949, pp. 298ff.

99. Clifford Geertz, *The Social History of an Indonesian Town*, 1965.

100. W. F. Wertheim, *Indonesian Society in Transition: A Study of Social Change*, 1959, pp. 110ff.

101. B.C.C.M.M. van Suchtelen, *Nederlands nieuwe eereschuld aan Indië* (Netherland's New Debt of Honour to the Indies), 1939.

102. Wertheim, *East-West Parallels: Approaches to Modern Asia*, 1964, pp. 211ff.; J. H. Boeke, 'Objective and Personal Elements in Colonial Welfare Policy' in W. F. Wertheim *et al.* (eds.), *Indonesian Economics: The Concept of Dualism in Theory and Policy*, 1961, pp. 265ff.

103. Chalmers Johnson, *Revolution and the Social System*, 1964, pp. 5 ff.

104. Eckstein, op. cit., p. 154.

105. Stone, op. cit., p. 166.

106. Eckstein, op. cit., pp. 140ff.

107. The concept of 'accelerator' and the significance of lost wars in this respect has been extensively dealt with in Johnson, *Revolutionary Change*, 1968, pp. 99ff.

108. See, for example, Hinton, op. cit., pp. 73ff.
109. Crane Brinton, *The Anatomy of Revolution*, 1965, pp. 36ff., 252.
110. Johnson, op. cit., pp. 153.
111. Johnson, *Revolution and the Social System*, p. 12.
112. Brinton, op. cit., pp. 67ff.
113. ibid., pp. 39ff.
114. Lawrence Stone, 'Theories of Revolution', *World Politics*, Vol. 18, 1965, p. 165.
115. Rex D. Hopper, 'The Revolutionary Process: A Frame of Reference for the Study of Revolutionary Movements', *Social Forces*, Vol. 28, 1950, p. 273.
116. Not only Crane Brinton extends this sequence unto a general pattern; it is also endorsed by Hopper, op. cit., p. 276.
117. Brinton, op. cit., pp. 122–3.
118. ibid., p. 123.
119. ibid., p. 90.
120. ibid., p. 161.
121. ibid., p. 241.
122. ibid., pp. 207, 222ff.
123. Moore, op. cit., p. 506.

PART THREE

1. Clifford Geertz, *Agricultural Involution: The Process of Ecological Change in Indonesia*, 1963, p. 78.
2. Gunnar Myrdal, *Asian Drama: An Inquiry into the Poverty of Nations*, Vol. 1, 1967, p. 569.
3. ibid., p. 569.
4. See, for example, J. K. Campbell, *Honour, Family, and Patronage: A Study of Institutions and Moral Values in a Greek Mountain Community*, 1964.
5. The debate on the *jajmani* system has been summed up by H. A. Gould, 'The Hindu Jajmani System: A Case of Economic Particularism', *Southwestern Journal of Anthropology*, Vol. 14, 1958, pp. 428ff.; Pauline M. Kolenda, 'Toward a Model of the Hindu Jajmani System', *Human Organization*, Vol. 22, 1962, pp. 11ff.
6. William H. Wiser, *The Hindu Jajmani System: a Socio-Economic System Interrelating Members of a Hindu Village Community in Services*, 1936.

7. Th. O. Beidelman, A Comparative Analysis of the Jajmani System, 1959.

8. J. C. Breman, Meesters en knechten: veranderingen in de relaties tussen land heren en landarbeiders in Zuid-Gujerat, India (Masters and Servants: Changing Relationships between Landlords and Agricultural Labourers in South Gujerat, India), 1970.

9. Oscar Lewis, Village Life in Northern India: Studies in an Indian Village, 1958; Baljit Singh, Next Step in Village India, 1961, pp. 1–15.

10. H. ten Dam in W. F. Wertheim et al. (eds.), Indonesian Economics: The Concept of Dualism in Theory and Policy, 1961, p. 366.

11. L. K. Mahapatra, Structural Implications of Ritual Kinship in Peasant Societies, unpublished mimeographed paper.

12. Eric R. Wolf, Peasants, 1966, pp. 88–9.

13. Clifford Geertz, op. cit., p. 90; Hildred Geertz, in Ruth T. McVey (ed.), Indonesia, 1963, pp. 41ff.

14. See, for example, M. Srinivas, Caste in Modern India and Other Essays, 1962; I. P. Desai, Some Aspects of Family in Mahuva: A Sociological Study of Jointness in a Small Town, 1964.

15. See, for example, E. R. Leach (ed.), Aspects of Caste in South India, Ceylon and North-West Pakistan, 1962, pp. 6ff.; Lloyd T. Rudolph and Susanne Hoeber Rudolph, 'The Political Role of India's Caste Associations', Pacific Affairs, Vol. 33, 1960, pp. 5ff.

16. See, for example, V. H. Joshi, Economic Development and Social Change in a South Gujerat Village, 1966.

17. See, for example, T. Scarlett Epstein, Economic Development and Social Change in South India, 1962, pp. 37ff.

18. W. F. Wertheim, East-West Parallels: Sociological Approaches to Modern Asia, 1964, pp. 125ff.

19. Peter M. Worsley, The Third World, 1967, pp. 127ff., 164ff.; the same author in Ghita Ionescu and Ernest Gellner (eds.), Populism, 1969, pp. 212–51.

20. Clifford Geertz, The Social History of an Indonesian Town, 1965, pp. 127ff.

21. See, for example, Robert R. Jay, Religion and Politics in Rural Central Java, 1963, pp. 90ff.

22. Kathleen Gough, 'Communist Rural Councillors in Kerala', Journal of Asian and African Studies, Vol. 3, 1968, p. 200.

23. Wertheim, op. cit., pp. 76ff.

24. Donald Hindley, *The Communist Party of Indonesia 1951–1963*, 1964, p. 286.

25. W. F. Wertheim, 'From Aliran towards Class Struggle in the Countryside of Java', *Pacific Viewpoint*, Vol. 10, 1969, pp. 1ff.; and the discussion between Benno Galjart and Gerrit Huizer in *America Latina*, Vol. 7, 1964 and Vol. 8, 1965.

26. Galjart and Huizer, op. cit.

27. Allan R. Holmberg, 'Algunas relaciones entre la privación psico-biologica y el cambio cultural en los Andes', *America Indigena*, Vol. 27, 1967, pp. 3ff.

28. Ernst Utrecht, *Indonesië's nieuwe orde: Ontbinding en neo-kolonisatie* (*Indonesia's New Order: Dissolution and the Rise of Neo-Colonialism*), 1970, pp. 130ff.; J. M. D. Lagendijk, *Gegesik Wetan: een rijstdorp in de noord-javaanse kustvlakte* (*A Rice Village in the Coastal Plain of Northern Java*), 1971, p. 71. See also Gary Hansen, 'Episodes in Rural Modernization: Problems in the Bimas Program', *Indonesia*, No. 11, 1971, p. 65.

29. Harry Eckstein, 'On the Etiology of Internal War', *History and Theory*, Vol. 4, 1965, p. 143.

30. Frantz Fanon, *The Wretched of the Earth*, 1967.

31. J. H. Boeke, *The Interests of the Voiceless Far East*, 1948, p. 7.

32. Quoted above in chapter six, pp. 178–9.

33. Phillips Ruopp (ed.), *Approaches to Community Development: A Symposium Introductory to Problems and Methods of Village Welfare in Underdeveloped Areas*, 1953, p. 18.

34. René Dumont, *False Start in Africa*, 1966.

35. Eckstein, op. cit., p. 156.

36. David E. Apter, in Clifford Geertz (ed.), *Old Societies and New States*, 1963, p. 93.

37. Refer to chapter three of the present volume.

38. Elman R. Service, *History, Evolution and Revolution*, unpublished mimeographed paper, p. 4.

39. W. F. Wertheim, *East-West Parallels: Sociological Approaches to Modern Asia*, 1964, pp. 259ff.

40. S. C. Dube, *India's Changing Villages: Human Factors in Community Development*, 1958, pp. 82ff.

41. The issue is being evaded in studies like Mohammad Hatta, *The Cooperative Movement in Indonesia*, Ithaca, 1957. H. ten Dam, however, has pointed out the inefficiency of Indonesian cooperatives for improving the plight of the poorer sections of the peasantry, owing to the preponderant role of the wealthier land-

owners within these cooperatives: Wertheim *et al.* (eds.), *Indonesian Economics: The Concept of Dualism in Theory and Policy*, 1961, pp. 368ff. For India see René Dumont, *Terres vivantes: Voyages d'un agronome autour du monde*, 1961, pp. 179-83.

42. Dumont, op. cit., p. 131.

43. Daniel Thorner, *The Agrarian Prospect in India: Five Lectures on Land Reform*, 1955; Grigory Kotovsky, *Agrarian Reforms in India*, 1964.

44. C. Baks, *Afschaffing van pacht: Een onderzoek naar de sociale gevolgen van de afschaffing van pacht in twee dorpen van Zuid-Gujerat, India* (Abolition of Tenancy: An Inquiry into its Social Effects in Two Villages of South Gujerat, India), 1969.

45. Kingsley Davis, *The Population of India and Pakistan*, 1951, p. 229.

46. See, for example, Gunnar Myrdal, *Asian Drama: An Inquiry into the Poverty of Nations*, Vol. 2, pp. 1513ff.

47. Alfred Sauvy, *Malthus et les deux Marx: le problème de la faim et de la guerre dans le monde*, 1963, pp. 237ff.

48. ibid.

49. Herbert Feldman, 'Aid as Imperialism?', *International Affairs*, Vol. 43, 1967, p. 229.

50. See John J. Carroll, *Changing Patterns of Social Structure in the Philippines, 1869-1963*, 1968, p. 83: 'food and beverages' provide the largest number of industrial plants: 35 per cent of the total number of establishments in 1959.

51. M. A. Hussein Mullick, 'Pakistans Wirtschaftentwicklung: Bilanz nach 21 Jahren', *Zeitschrift für Kulturaustausch*, Vol. 18, 1968, Heft 2/3.

52. W. A. Ladejinsky, *Foreign Affairs*, Vol. 42, 1964, p. 446.

53. T. Scarlett Epstein, *Economic Development and Social Change in South India*, 1962, pp. 63ff.

54. P. N. Radhakrishnan, 'Management of HYVP', *Economic and Political Weekly*, Vol. 4, 1969, pp. 249-50. I further refer to Gunnar Myrdal, *The Challenge of World Poverty: A World Anti-Poverty Programme in Outline*, 1970, pp. 123ff.; Clifton R. Wharton, 'The Green Revolution: Cornucopia or Pandora's Box?', *Foreign Affairs*, Vol. 47, 1969, pp. 468ff.

55. See, for example, I. and R. Feierabend, 'Aggressive Behaviors within Politics, 1948-1962: A Cross-National Study', *Journal of Conflict Resolution*, Vol. 10, 1966, pp. 249ff.

56. Herbert Feith, *The Decline of Constitutional Democracy in Indonesia*, 1962, pp. 113ff.; J. D. Legge, *Indonesia*, 1964, pp. 161ff.

57. For a critical view on this preference refer to Harry J. Benda, in his review of Feith's book, *Journal of Asian Studies*, Vol. 24, 1964, pp. 305ff.

58. C. K. Yang, *Religion in Chinese Society: A Study of Contemporary Social Functions of Religion and Some of Their Historical Factors*, 1967, chapters nine and ten.

59. Eckstein, op. cit., p. 156.

60. Wertheim, op. cit., p. 81.

61. Eckstein, op. cit., p. 154.

62. Jürgen Horlemann, *Modelle der Kolonialen Konter-revolution: Beschreibung und Dokumente*, 1968, pp. 122ff., refers in this connection to Boyd T. Bashore, 'Two Rail Strategy in Limited War', *Military Review*, May 1960.

63. William J. Pomeroy, *Guerilla and Counter Guerilla Warfare: Liberation and Suppression in the Present Period*, 1964, pp. 65–6; Napoleon D. Valeriano and Charles T. R. Bohannan, *Counter-Guerilla Operations: The Philippine Experience*, 1962, pp. 29, 103.

64. This is, particularly, Pomeroy's opinion; he largely ascribes the misfortunes of the Huks to their own tactical mistakes (op. cit., pp. 66ff.). Horlemann supports Pomeroy's view to a certain extent only, but he also refutes, largely on the basis of the experience in Vietnam, the claim of American military experts that the Philippine counter-revolutionary strategy could basically be applied everywhere (op. cit., pp. 105ff., 144ff.).

65. See, for example, Valeriano and Bohannan, op. cit., pp. 105ff., 200ff.; see also the other documents reproduced in abstract in Horlemann, op. cit., pp. 110ff.

66. Horlemann, op. cit., p. 103.

67. Pomeroy, op. cit., pp. 66, 69–70; Horlemann, op. cit., pp. 100ff., 107; Carl H. Landé, *Leaders, Factions and Parties: The Structure of Philippine Politics*, 1965, p. 93.

68. Ansil Ramsay, 'Ramon Magsaysay and the Philippine Peasantry', *Philippine Social Sciences and Humanities Review*, Vol. 30, 1965, p. 75.

69. Clifford Geertz, *The Social History of an Indonesian Town*, 1965, p. 152.

70. Barrington Moore, *Social Origins of Dictatorship and Democracy: Lord and Peasant in the Making of the Modern World*, 1966, pp. 482–3.

71. ibid., pp. 202ff., 213, 334ff.; however, in *Fabric of Chinese Society: A Study of the Social Life of a Chinese County Seat*, Morton Fried treats the so-called *kan-ch'ing* institution which also shows some patronage-like characteristics outside the operation of clan relationships, 1956, pp. 103ff., *passim*.

72. Moore, op. cit., p. 482.

73. A. I. Levkovsky, *Capitalism in India: Basic Trends in its Development*, 1966, p. 510.

74. *Kommunist*, Vol. 37, No. 17, 1960, p. 20.

75. V. I. Pavlov, *India: Economic Freedom versus Imperialism*, 1964, p. 236. The basic ideas of the thesis of 'regimes of national democracy' have been reproduced in *Ost-Probleme*, Vol. 14, No. 2, 1962, pp. 34ff. A crucial publication is B. N. Ponomarëv, 'O gosudarstve nacional'noi demokratii', *Kommunist*, Vol. 38, No. 8, 1961. See also William T. Shinn Jr, 'The National Democratic State: A Communist Program for Less-Developed Areas', *World Politics*, Vol. 15, 1962–3, pp. 377ff.

76. N. A. Simonija, *Ob osobennostjach nacional'no-osvoboditel'nych revoljucij*, 1968; H. Carrère d'Encausse and S. R. Schram, *l'U.R.S.S. et la Chine devant les révolutions dans les sociétés pré-industrielles*, 1970, pp. 83ff.; B. G. Gafurov et al. (eds.), *Asia in Soviet Studies*, 1969, in particular the articles by R. A. Ulyanovsky and K. N. Brutents. See also Y. Zhukov et al., *The Third World: Problems and Prospects*, 1970, in particular chapters six and seven by A. Iskenderov.

77. Grigory Kotovsky, *Agrarian Reforms in India*, 1964, pp. 163ff.

78. I. V. Vasiljev, *Gosudarstvenny kapitalizm v sovremennoj Birme*, 1961.

79. See, for example, G. A. Martysheva, *Jugo-vostočnaja Azija posle vtoroj mirovoj vojny*, 1960, pp. 271ff.

80. The claim that Burma is building socialism has been qualified in Y. Zhukov et al., op. cit., pp. 216ff.

81. See *Selected Writings of Mao Tse-tung*, Vol. 4, 1961, pp. 207ff.

82. See, for Burma, the text quoted in Carrère d'Encausse et al., op. cit., p. 82.

83. See J. Zedenbal, 'Vom Feudalismus zum Sozialismus – Was die Erfahrungen der nicht-kapitalistischen Entwicklungen der Mongolei lehren', in *Probleme des Friedens und des Sozialismus*, No. 3, 1961.

84. This is increasingly realized by Soviet scholars. See Y. Zhukov et al., op. cit., p. 185n.

85. Apparently this is Shinn's interpretation of the Soviet 'new look'. He views the programme based on the concept of 'national democracy' as a tactical move meant to promote, in the long run, 'ultimate communist revolution in the developing countries', op. cit., p. 378.

86. William J. Lederer and Eugene Burdick, *The Ugly American*, 1958, pp. 276ff.

87. See, for example, N. R. Guseva *et al.* (eds.), *Narody Južnoj Azii*, 1963, pp. 226ff., in particular p. 236.

88. Uri Ra'anan, 'Peking's Foreign Policy "Debate"', in Tang Tsou (ed.), *China in Crisis*, Vol. 2 (*China's Policies in Asia and American Alternatives*), 1968, pp. 23ff.

89. Régis Debray, *Revolution in the Revolution: Armed Struggle and Political Struggle in Latin America*, 1967, p. 23: 'All decisive revolutionary processes must begin and have begun with certain missteps ... because the existing points of departure are those left by the preceding historical period, and they are used, even if unconsciously.'

90. P. M. Worsley, *Revolutionary Theory: Che Guevara and Régis Debray*, mimeographed text, p. 8. The paper has been published in Leo Huberman and Paul H. Sweezy (eds.), *Régis Debray and the Latin American Revolution*, 1969, pp. 119ff.

91. Régis Debray, 'Problems of Revolution and Strategy in Latin America', *New Left Review*, Vol. 45, September–October 1967, pp. 13–41.

92. Worsley, op. cit., p. 9.

93. ibid., pp. 4–5.

94. ibid., pp. 4–5.

95. Pomeroy, op. cit., p. 68.

96. *The Diary of Che Guevara, Bolivia: November 7, 1966 – October 7, 1967*, 1968, pp. 13, 43ff.

97. Worsley, op. cit., p. 7.

98. Ruth T. McVey, *The Rise of Indonesian Communism*, 1965, pp. 82–3.

99. For the concept of new-democratic revolution refer to chapter five.

100. Debray, op. cit., pp. 84ff.

101. Worsley, op. cit., p. 5.

102. ibid., p. 12.

103. ibid., p. 13.

104. Walt W. Rostow, *The Stages of Economic Growth: A Non-Communist Manifesto*, 1963, pp. 65ff.

105. Felix Greene, A Curtain of Ignorance, 1965.
106. See, for example, René Dumont, La Chine surpeupléet, Tiers Monde affamé, 1965; Keith Buchanan, The Transformation of the Chinese Earth, 1970; W. F. Wertheim, 'La Chine est-elle sous-peuplée? Production agricole et main-d'oeuvre rurale', Population, Vol. 20, 1965, pp. 477ff.; Max Biehl, Die Landwirtschaft in China und Indien: Vergleich zweier Entwicklungswege, 1966.
107. See, for example, Gerrit J. Huizer, Peasant Unrest in Latin America: Its Origins, Forms of Expression and Potential, 1971, pp. 111ff.
108. Hannah Arendt, On Revolution, 1963, pp. 217ff. See also chapter six of the present volume.
109. Moore, op. cit., p. 508.
110. See the Epilogue of the present volume. See also Sidney Hook, The Hero in History: A Study in Limitation and Possibility, 1943, where a chapter carries the title: ' "If" in History'; J. C. Squire (ed.), If or History Rewritten, 1931.
111. Moore, op. cit., p. 227: 'The peasantry would cease to exist.'
112. ibid., p. 505: 'The dying wail of a class over whom the wave of progress is about to roll.'
113. See, for example, René Dumont, Sovkhoz, kolkhoz, ou le problématique communisme, 1964, pp. 215ff.
114. Karl A. Wittfogel has undoubtedly exaggerated this feature in his Oriental Despotism: A Comparative Study of Total Power, 1957.
115. Moore, op. cit., p. 227, where he uses the words 'relentless terror'.
116. ibid., p. 506-7.
117. V. D. Dudintsev, Not by Bread Alone, 1968; A. Solzhenitsyn, Cancer Ward, 1968.
118. The same idea is also expressed in Cancer Ward.
119. See Ione Kramer, 'Life on East Wind Road', Eastern Horizon, Vol. 6, No. 8, 1967, pp. 21ff.; S. A. Christiansen, 'A Further Letter from a Foreign Student', Eastern Horizon, Vol. 7, No. 4, 1968, p. 48; Rewi Alley, 'Shaoshing over Two Years', Eastern Horizon, Vol. 7, No. 6, 1968, pp. 17ff.; Rewi Alley, 'Cultural Revolution Comes to Communes on the Pohai Bay', Eastern Horizon, Vol. 8, No. 1, 1969, pp. 24–32.
120. Point nine of the sixteen-point resolution, 8 August 1966.
121. Point six of the sixteen-point resolution.

122. Giovanni Blumer, *Die chinesische Kulturrevolution 1965–1967*, 1968, p. 250.

123. ibid., pp. 276ff.

124. Hans Granqvist, *The Red Guard: A Report on Mao's Revolution*, 1967, p. 154.

125. Blumer, op. cit., pp. 284–5.

126. Point eight of the sixteen-point resolution.

127. For a more detailed discussion of the troubles in several provinces, especially in 1967, see *The Cultural Revolution in the Provinces*, 1971.

128. The most perspicacious survey of the developments until the end of 1967 can be found in Blumer's study mentioned in note 122; also Jean Daubier, *Histore de la révolution culturelle prolétarienne en China (1965–1969)*, 1970; Jan Myrdal and Gun Kessle, *China: The Revolution Continued*, 1970; *The Cultural Revolution in the Provinces*, 1971.

129. Gerald Tannenbaum, 'The Cultural Revolution – IV', *Eastern Horizon*, Vol. 8, No. 2, 1969, p. 7.

130. I. Vandermeersch, 'La reforme des universités en Chine', in *La Nouvelle Chine*, No. 1, 1971, p. 30.

131. Granqvist, op. cit., p. 40.

132. J. A. A. van Doorn, 'De voortgezette revolutie: China en de ijzeren wet der oligarchisering' ('The Continued Revolution: China and the Iron Law of "Oligarchization" '), *Sociologische Gids*, Vol. 16, 1969, pp. 155ff.; Robert Michels, *Zur Soziologie des Parteiwesens in der modernen Demokratie: Untersuchungen über die oligarchischen Tendenzen des Gruppenlebens*, 1925.

133. Van Doorn, op. cit., pp. 175–6.

134. Blumer, op. cit., pp. 361ff.

135. I refer again to the articles in *Eastern Horizon* quoted in note 119. I also refer to Ian Davies, 'The Chinese Communes – An Australian Student's View', *Eastern Horizon*, Vol. 8, No. 1, 1969, pp. 39–40.

136. See, for example, J. H. Boeke, 'Agrarian Reforms in the Far East', *The American Journal of Sociology*, Vol. 57, 1951–2, p. 324: 'In Russia only the kolkhoz has made an end to his [the *kulak's* or exploiting landlord's] existence, and the kolkhoz organization is quite unsuited to the densely populated Eastern countries. For these reasons the struggle against large landownership is no effectual means of restoring and assuring the welfare of the peasantry.'

137. Alain Schnapp and Pierre Vidal-Naquet (eds.), *Journal de la Commune Étudiante: Textes et documents, novembre 67–juin 68*, 1969, p. 346.

138. Robert Guillain, 'La Révolution Culturelle chinoise a préfiguré sur certaines points les évènements français', *Le Monde*, 6 June 1968.

139. Schnapp and Vidal-Naquet (eds.), op. cit., pp. 346ff.

140. ibid., p. 562.

141. See, for example, W. L. Warner *et al.*, *Democracy in Jonesville: A Study in Equality and Inequality*, 1929, p. 297.

142. Melvin M. Tumin, 'Some Principles of Stratification: A Critical Analysis', in Reinhard Bendix and Seymour Martin Lipset (eds.), *Class, Status and Power*, 1966, p. 57.

143. Alain Touraine, 'Naissance d'un mouvement étudiant', II, *Le Monde*, 8 March 1968, comparing the student revolt with millenarian movements caused by the impact of industrial growth upon traditional structure.

144. W. Lloyd Warner and J. O. Low, *The Social System of the Modern Factory. The Strike: A Social Analysis*, Vol. 4 of the Yankee City Series, 1947.

145. J. A. A. van Doorn, *De proletarische achterhoede; Een sociologische critiek (The Proletarian Rearguard: A Sociological Criticism)*, 1954.

EPILOGUE

1. Rushton Coulborn, *Feudalism in History*, 1956, pp. 392–4: 'History is the fundamental knowledge in every world of existence, and the physical scientist is at last being forced to recognize this.' See also C. F. von Weizsäcker, *The History of Nature*, 1949.

2. See Philipp Frank, *Das Kausalgesetz und seine Grenzen*, 1932, pp. 228ff., on the difficulties one meets if one wants to formulate the law in a way that is not tautological.

3. David Bohm, *Causality and Chance in Modern Physics*, 1957, p. 9, distinguishes between 'conditions' which he calls 'background causes' that remain relatively constant, and 'immediate causes' which are themselves part of the process of change.

4. See also the discussion by Bohm, op. cit., pp. 16ff., of 'one-to-many and many-to-one causal relationships'.

5. David Hume, *A Treatise of Human Nature*, Vol. 1, 1739, pp. 148ff.

and in particular p. 160: 'The idea of cause and effect is derived from *experience*.'

6. Bohm, op. cit., pp. 22ff.

7. Heinrich Rickert, *Die Grenzen der naturwissenschaftlicher Begriffsbildung: Eine logische Einleitung in die historischen Wissenschaften*, 1929, pp. 376ff.; the same concept can be found in Max Weber, *Gesammelte Aufsätze zur Wissenschaftslehre*, 1922, p. 172.

8. Bohm, op. cit., p. 158.

9. G. Mannoury, *Mathesis en Mystiek: een signifiese studie van kommunisties standpunt (Mathematics and Mysticism: A Study in Semantics from a Communist Standpoint)*, p. 70.

10. For S. R. de Groot and P. Mazure, *Non-Equilibrium Thermodynamics*, 1962, the tendency towards increased entropy is the only type of process they are studying under the heading of 'irreversible' non-equilibrium processes. However, the second law of thermodynamics is also still basically upheld in H. J. Morowitz, *Energy Flow in Biology*, 1968, although he convincingly shows that the biological processes to be encountered on our planet are rather to be conceived in terms of increasing negentropy, p. 79.

11. Bohm, op. cit., pp. 138–9.

12. J. B. S. Haldane, 'Time in Biology', *Scientific World*, Vol. 9, No. 4, 1965, pp. 4ff.

13. See, for example, A. I. Oparin, *The Origin of Life*, 1955; J. D. Bernal, *The Origin of Life*, 1967.

14. It should be noted, however, that the extreme prediction, formerly derived from the second law of thermodynamics, of an eventual 'heat death' of the universe does not seem to be adhered to any longer by well-known physicists. See Bohm, op. cit., p. 163.

15. For a thorough criticism of 'the philosophy of mechanism' and of 'Laplacean determinism' I refer to Bohm, op. cit., chapter five.

16. I refer to the well-known experiments with embryos of sea-urchins. See Hans Driesch, 'Die Lokalisation morphogenetischer Vorgänge: Ein Beweis vitalistisches Geschehens', *Archiv für Entwicklungsmechanik*, Vol. 8, 1899, pp. 35–112.

17. Jacques Monod, *Le hasard et la nécessité: Essai sur la philosophie naturelle de la biologie moderne*, 1970, p. 32.

18. J. Monod, op. cit., p. 102.

19. For newer biological models of evolution, and concepts like

'evolutionary feedback', and 'effects' becoming 'the cause of cause in a self-regulatory system', see for example Herbert Barringer *et al.* (eds.), *Social Change in Developing Areas*, 1965, pp. 14–15. Professor Alfred E. Emerson claims, on the same page, that 'biological evolution is not rigidly deterministic', and that 'considerable uniqueness exists'.

20. Bohm, op. cit., p. 24.

21. According to more recent discoveries, however, life may have originated outside the earth.

22. Bohm, op. cit., p. 162.

23. ibid., pp. 162–3.

24. ibid., p. 24.

25. ibid., p. 22.

26. ibid., p. 29.

27. ibid., p. 162.

28. A similar argument, reducing any creation of novel structures to chance contingency, can be found in Jacques Monod, op. cit., p. 127: 'Le hasard *seul* est à la source de toute nouveauté, de toute création dans la biosphère.' He has been criticized, on this point, by Madeleine Barthélemy–Madaule, *L'idéologie du hasard et de la nécessité*, 1972.

29. See, for example, François Jacob, *La logique du vivant: Une histoire de l'hérédité*, 1970, p. 309.

30. Such a view has been basically expressed by Jeremy Bentham; see, for example, *The Rationale of Reward*, 1825.

31. Jeremy Bentham, *The Rationale of Punishment*, 1830; A. V. Lundstedt, *Superstition or Rationality in Action for Peace? A Criticism of Jurisprudence*, 1925; Lundstedt, *Legal Thinking Revised: My Views on Law*, 1956.

32. See, for example, G. J. Harmsen, *Marx contra de marxistische ideologen: historisch-wijsgerige beschouwingen* (*Marx against the Marxist Ideologues: Historico-Philosophical Reflections*), 1968, pp. 61ff., 74ff. He quotes Marx's words: 'Tout ce que je sais, c'est que je ne suis pas marxiste.' ('All I know is that I am not a Marxist').

33. G. W. Locher, 'The Future and the Past: Wertheim's Interpretation of Indonesia's Social Change', *Bijdragen voor de Taal-, Land– en Volkenkunde*, Vol. 117, 1961, p. 79. In a later publication Locher has expressed agreement with my proposal to substitute 'probabilism' for 'possibilism'. See *Bijdragen*, Vol. 127, 1971, pp. 158–9.

34. Alvin W. Gouldner, 'Anti-Minotaur: The Myth of a Value-Free Sociology', *Social Problems*, Vol. 9, 1962, pp. 199ff.
35. The basic weakness of Pierre Teilhard de Chardin's otherwise stimulating view of natural and human evolution is that the process towards progress, in his opinion, develops in a non-dialectical way. Humanity, in his view, gradually grows towards an increasing degree of cooperation and consciousness of the need for greater unity. From some of his pages, especially in *Le phénomène humain*, 1955, one could get the impression that this type of human evolution proceeds practically without friction, contradictions and inner conflicts, although in his concluding remarks the author attempts to refute this criticism of his having been too naïve and too optimistic (pp. 345ff.).
36. P. Kropotkin, *Mutual Aid: A Factor of Evolution*, 1904, pp. 283ff.
37. In his novel *Cancer Ward* Solzhenitsyn also remembers Kropotkin's pioneering attempt to develop a humanized kind of socialism where moral principles prevail over material incentives.

Index